THE WEED WHISPERER

Recent Collections

Virtual Doonesbury
Planet Doonesbury
Buck Wild Doonesbury
Duke 2000: Whatever It Takes
The Revolt of the English Majors
Peace Out, Dawg!
Got War?
Talk to the Hand
Heckuva Job, Bushie!
Welcome to the Nerd Farm!
Tee Time in Berzerkistan
Red Rascal's War
Squared Away

Anthologies

The Doonesbury Chronicles
Doonesbury's Greatest Hits
The People's Doonesbury
Doonesbury Dossier: The Reagan Years
Doonesbury Deluxe: Selected Glances Askance
Recycled Doonesbury: Second Thoughts on a Gilded Age
The Portable Doonesbury
The Bundled Doonesbury
40: A Doonesbury Retrospective

Special Collections

Action Figure!: The Life and Times of Doonesbury's Uncle Duke
Dude: The Big Book of Zonker
Flashbacks: Twenty-Five Years of Doonesbury
The Sandbox: Dispatches from Troops in Iraq and Afghanistan
The War in Quotes
"My Shorts R Bunching. Thoughts?": The Tweets of Roland Hedley

Wounded Warrior Series

The Long Road Home: One Step at a Time
The War Within: One More Step at a Time
Signature Wound: Rocking TBI
Mel's Story: Surviving Military Sexual Assault

Z&Z
BUD
Artisanal Cannabis

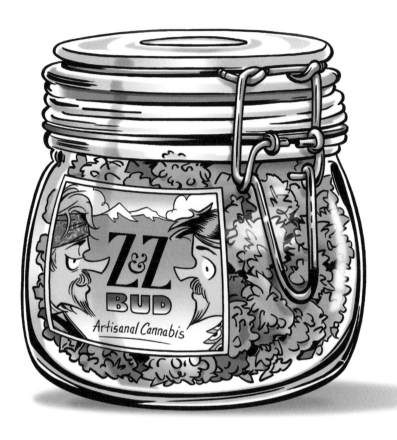

THE WEED WHISPERER

A DOONESBURY BOOK

by G. B. TRUDEAU

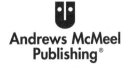

Andrews McMeel
Publishing®
Kansas City • Sydney • London

Andrews McMeel Publishing, LLC
an Andrews McMeel Universal company
1130 Walnut Street, Kansas City, Missouri 64106

www.andrewsmcmeel.com

15 16 17 18 19 TEN 10 9 8 7 6 5 4 3 2 1

ISBN: 978-1-4494-7224-5

Library of Congress Control Number: 2015943416

DOONESBURY may be viewed on the Internet at
www.doonesbury.com and www.GoComics.com.

ATTENTION: SCHOOLS AND BUSINESSES

Andrews McMeel books are available at quantity discounts with bulk purchase for educational, business, or sales promotional use. For information, please e-mail the Andrews McMeel Publishing Special Sales Department: specialsales@amuniversal.com.

"Of *course* I know how to roll a joint."
—Martha Stewart

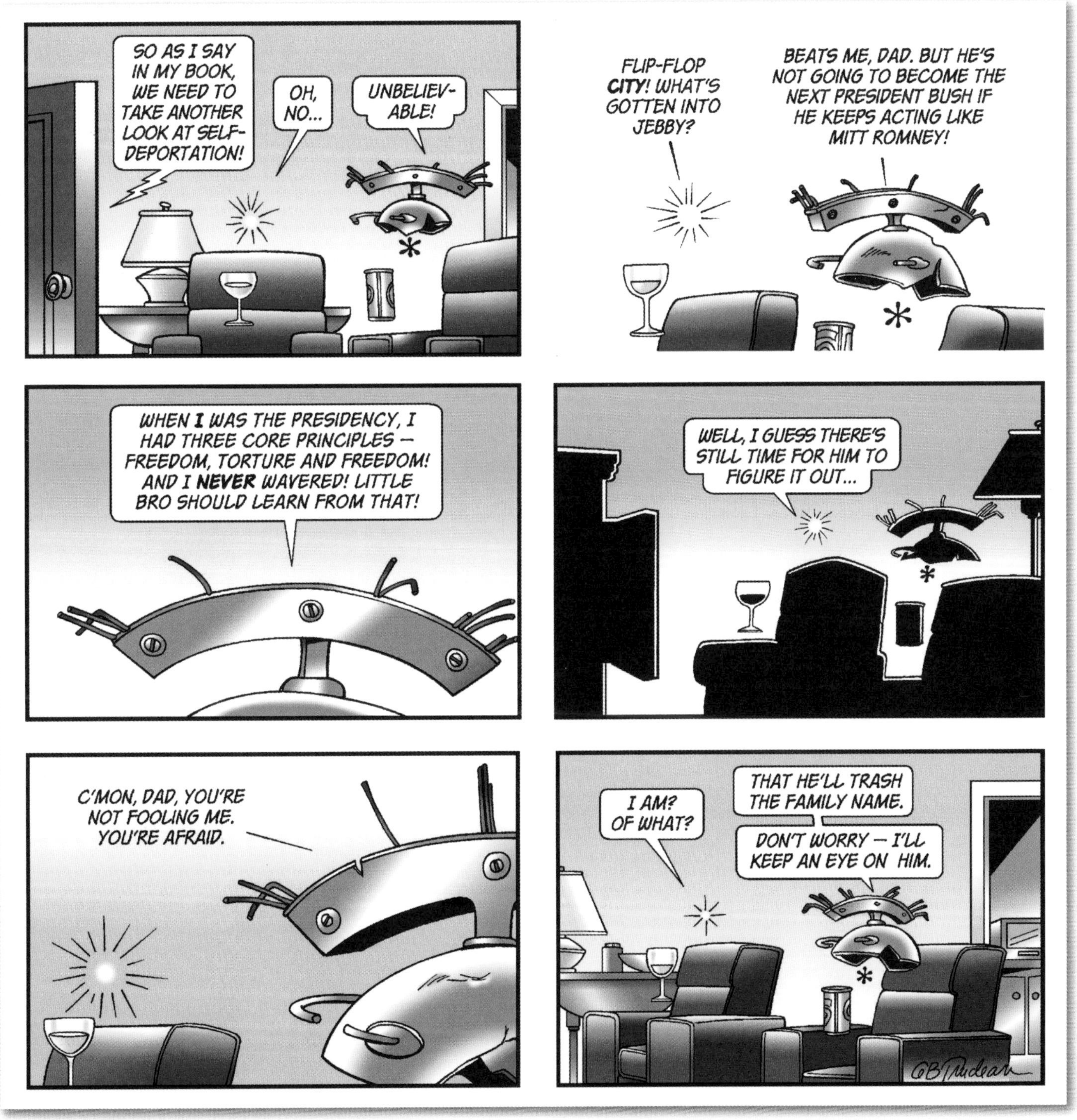
SO AS I SAY IN MY BOOK, WE NEED TO TAKE ANOTHER LOOK AT SELF-DEPORTATION!
OH, NO...
UNBELIEV-ABLE!
FLIP-FLOP CITY! WHAT'S GOTTEN INTO JEBBY?
BEATS ME, DAD. BUT HE'S NOT GOING TO BECOME THE NEXT PRESIDENT BUSH IF HE KEEPS ACTING LIKE MITT ROMNEY!
WHEN I WAS THE PRESIDENCY, I HAD THREE CORE PRINCIPLES — FREEDOM, TORTURE AND FREEDOM! AND I NEVER WAVERED! LITTLE BRO SHOULD LEARN FROM THAT!
WELL, I GUESS THERE'S STILL TIME FOR HIM TO FIGURE IT OUT...
C'MON, DAD, YOU'RE NOT FOOLING ME. YOU'RE AFRAID.
I AM? OF WHAT?
THAT HE'LL TRASH THE FAMILY NAME.
DON'T WORRY — I'LL KEEP AN EYE ON HIM.
GBTrudeau

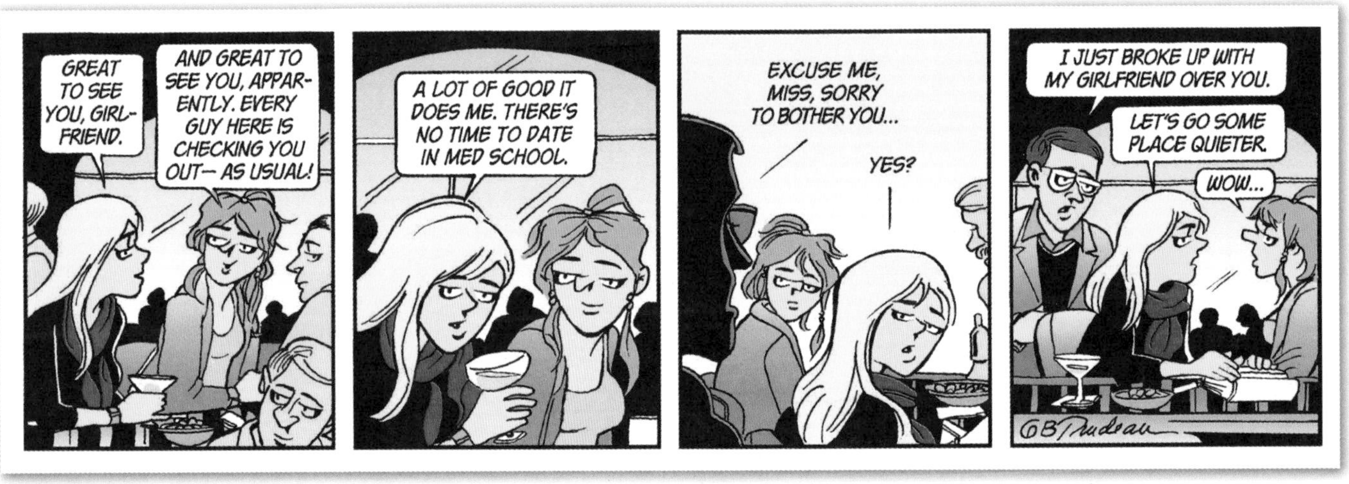
GREAT TO SEE YOU, GIRL-FRIEND.
AND GREAT TO SEE YOU, APPAR-ENTLY. EVERY GUY HERE IS CHECKING YOU OUT— AS USUAL!
A LOT OF GOOD IT DOES ME. THERE'S NO TIME TO DATE IN MED SCHOOL.
EXCUSE ME, MISS, SORRY TO BOTHER YOU...
YES?
I JUST BROKE UP WITH MY GIRLFRIEND OVER YOU.
LET'S GO SOME PLACE QUIETER.
WOW...

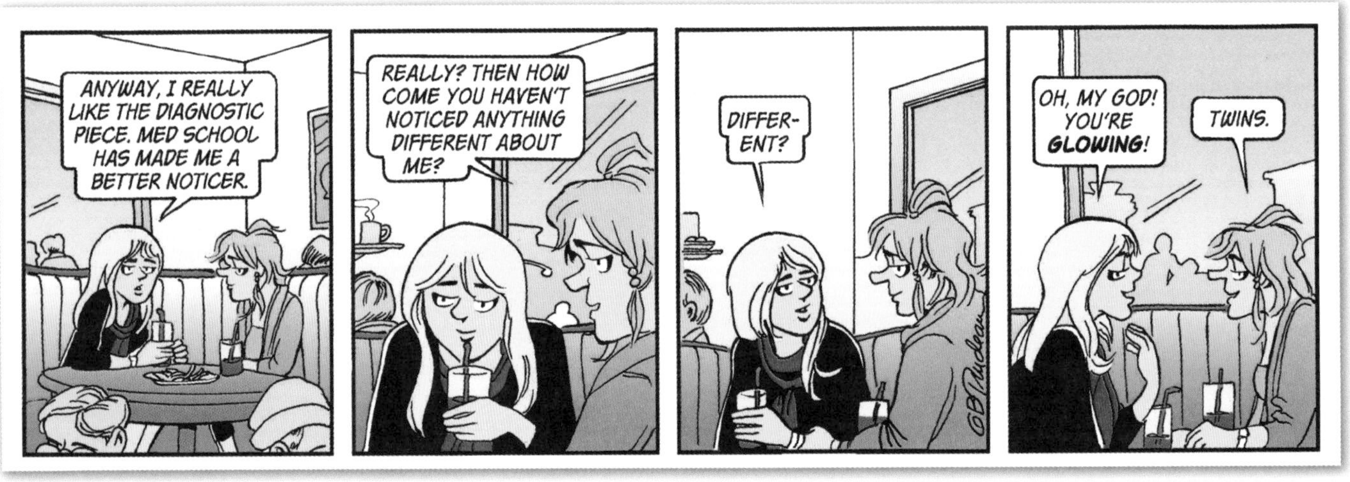
ANYWAY, I REALLY LIKE THE DIAGNOSTIC PIECE. MED SCHOOL HAS MADE ME A BETTER NOTICER.
REALLY? THEN HOW COME YOU HAVEN'T NOTICED ANYTHING DIFFERENT ABOUT ME?
DIFFER-ENT?
OH, MY GOD! YOU'RE **GLOWING**!
TWINS.

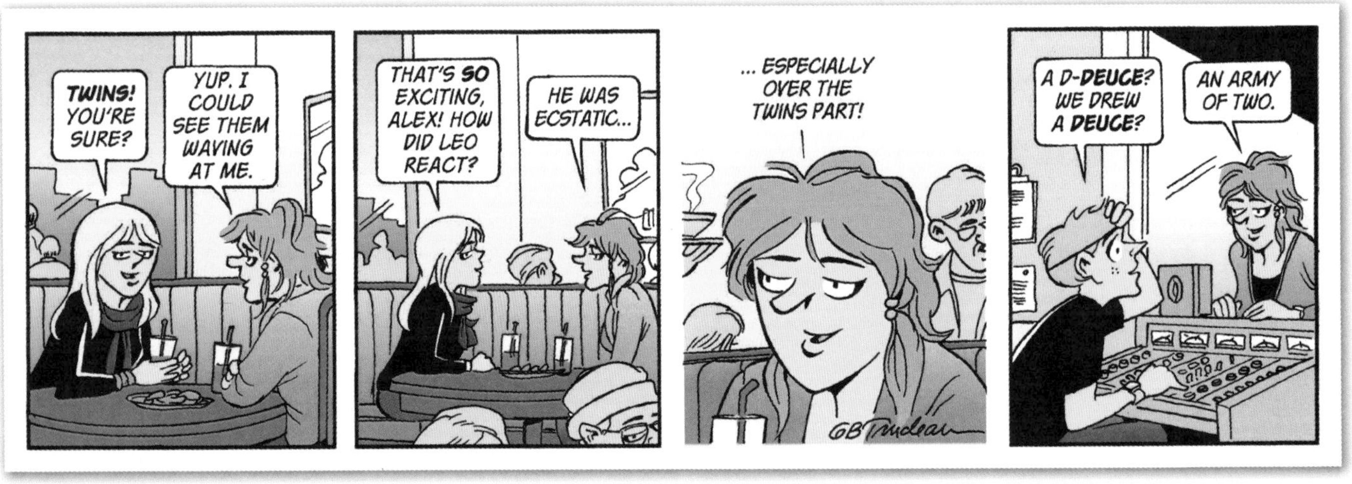
TWINS! YOU'RE SURE?
YUP. I COULD SEE THEM WAVING AT ME.
THAT'S **SO** EXCITING, ALEX! HOW DID LEO REACT?
HE WAS ECSTATIC...
... ESPECIALLY OVER THE TWINS PART!
A D-**DEUCE**? WE DREW A **DEUCE**?
AN ARMY OF TWO.

YOU... COULD S-SEE THEM?

YUP. TWO LITTLE PEANUTS.

WOW... L-L-LIFE DIFFERENT NOW...

REAL DIFFERENT.

BUT SU... SU... PERSTITIOUS! CAN'T... TELL ANYONE 'TIL S-S-SECOND TRI... TRI!

AGREED.

WHEN WAS THIS?

YESTERDAY.

SO WHEN'S THE DUE DATE, ALEX?

JUNE 17!

JUNE 17? SO YOU'RE HAVING TWIN BABIES JUST AS YOU'RE BOTH GRADUATING AND LOOKING FOR WORK?

RIGHT!

AND YOU SAY THIS WAS A PLANNED PREGNANCY?

DID I? I DON'T REMEMBER SAYING THAT.

FUNNY HOW THINGS CAN TURN OUT. YOU ALWAYS THOUGHT I WAS THE DUDE MAGNET...

BUT YOU'RE THE ONE WHO'S MARRIED WITH TWINS ON THE WAY...

... WHILE I'M STILL SORTING THROUGH CHAT REQUESTS ON MATCH.COM!

UH-HUH. HOW MANY?

WELL, HUNDREDS. BUT I'M SURE IT'S MOSTLY LOSERS.

YEAH, SOUNDS AWFUL.

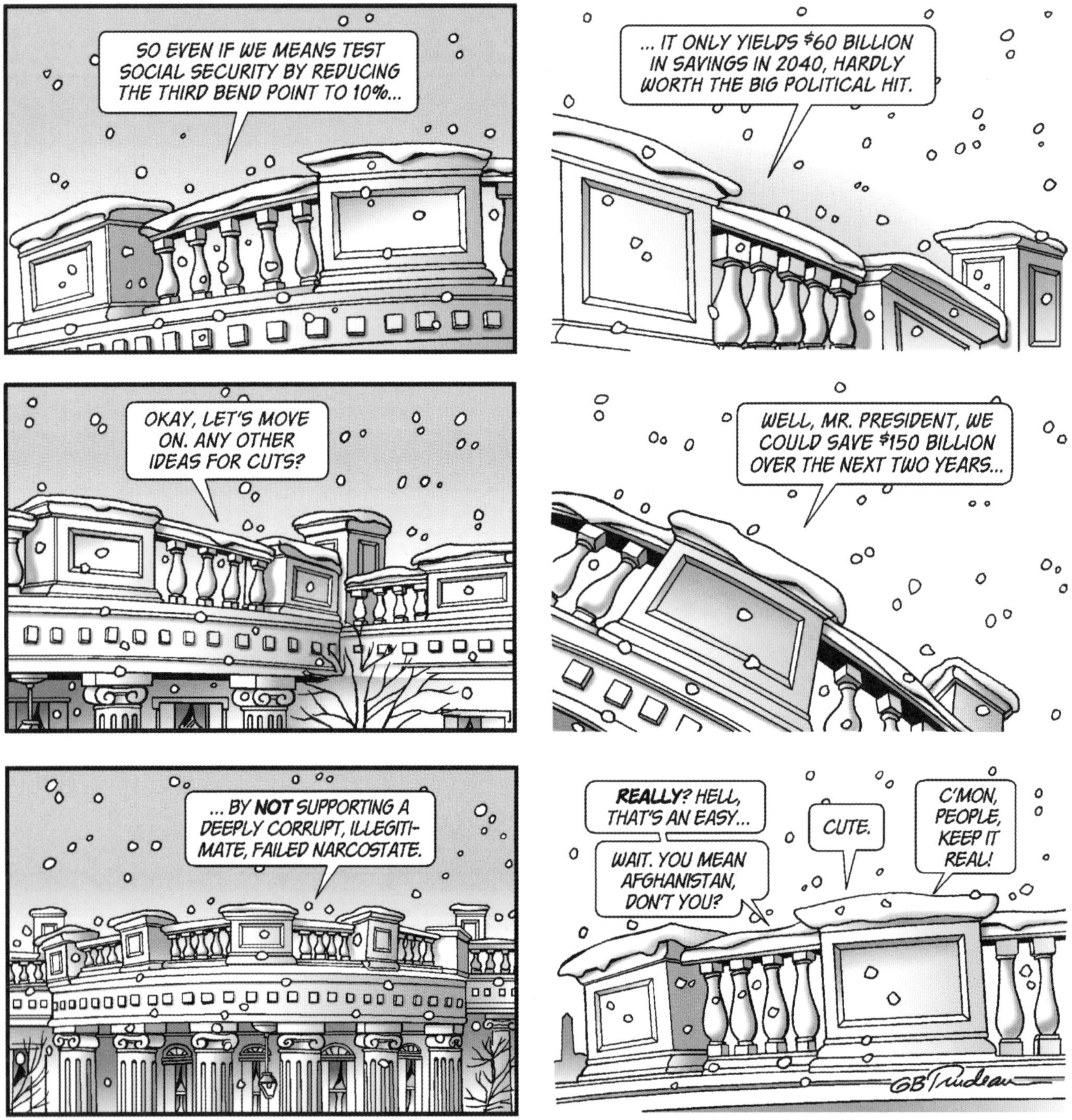
SO EVEN IF WE MEANS TEST SOCIAL SECURITY BY REDUCING THE THIRD BEND POINT TO 10%...
... IT ONLY YIELDS $60 BILLION IN SAVINGS IN 2040, HARDLY WORTH THE BIG POLITICAL HIT.
OKAY, LET'S MOVE ON. ANY OTHER IDEAS FOR CUTS?
WELL, MR. PRESIDENT, WE COULD SAVE $150 BILLION OVER THE NEXT TWO YEARS...
... BY NOT SUPPORTING A DEEPLY CORRUPT, ILLEGITIMATE, FAILED NARCOSTATE.
REALLY? HELL, THAT'S AN EASY...
WAIT. YOU MEAN AFGHANISTAN, DON'T YOU?
CUTE.
C'MON, PEOPLE, KEEP IT REAL!
GBTrudeau

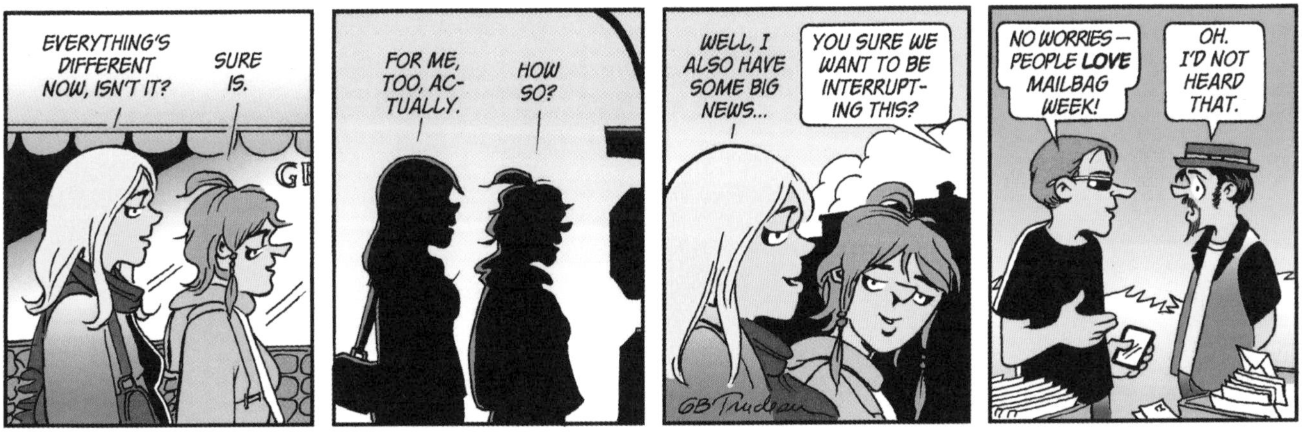
EVERYTHING'S DIFFERENT NOW, ISN'T IT?
SURE IS.
FOR ME, TOO, AC-TUALLY.
HOW SO?
WELL, I ALSO HAVE SOME BIG NEWS...
YOU SURE WE WANT TO BE INTERRUPT-ING THIS?
NO WORRIES — PEOPLE **LOVE** MAILBAG WEEK!
OH. I'D NOT HEARD THAT.

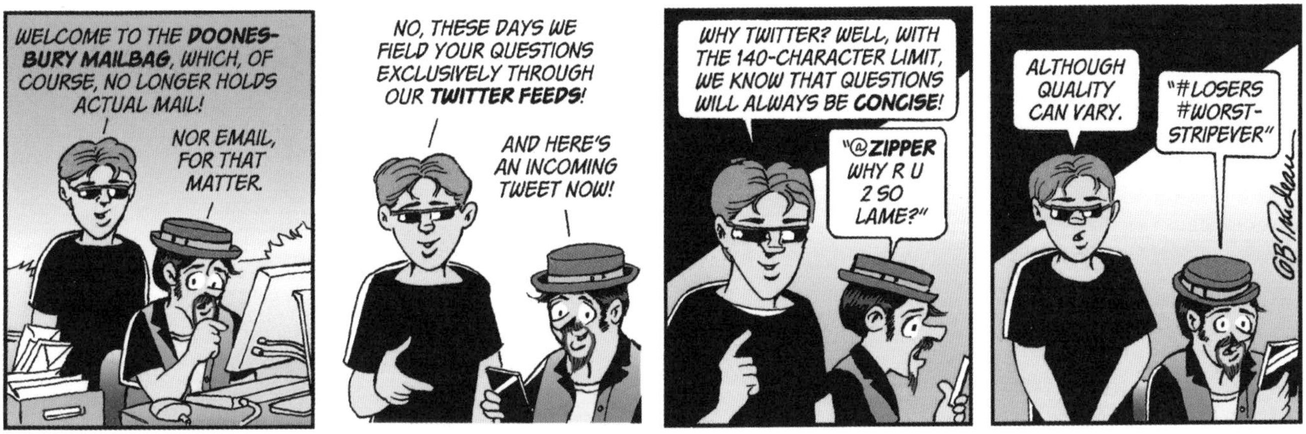
WELCOME TO THE **DOONES-BURY MAILBAG**, WHICH, OF COURSE, NO LONGER HOLDS ACTUAL MAIL!
NOR EMAIL, FOR THAT MATTER.
NO, THESE DAYS WE FIELD YOUR QUESTIONS EXCLUSIVELY THROUGH OUR **TWITTER FEEDS**!
AND HERE'S AN INCOMING TWEET NOW!
WHY TWITTER? WELL, WITH THE 140-CHARACTER LIMIT, WE KNOW THAT QUESTIONS WILL ALWAYS BE **CONCISE**!
"@**ZIPPER** WHY R U 2 SO LAME?"
ALTHOUGH QUALITY CAN VARY.
"#LOSERS #WORST-STRIPEVER"

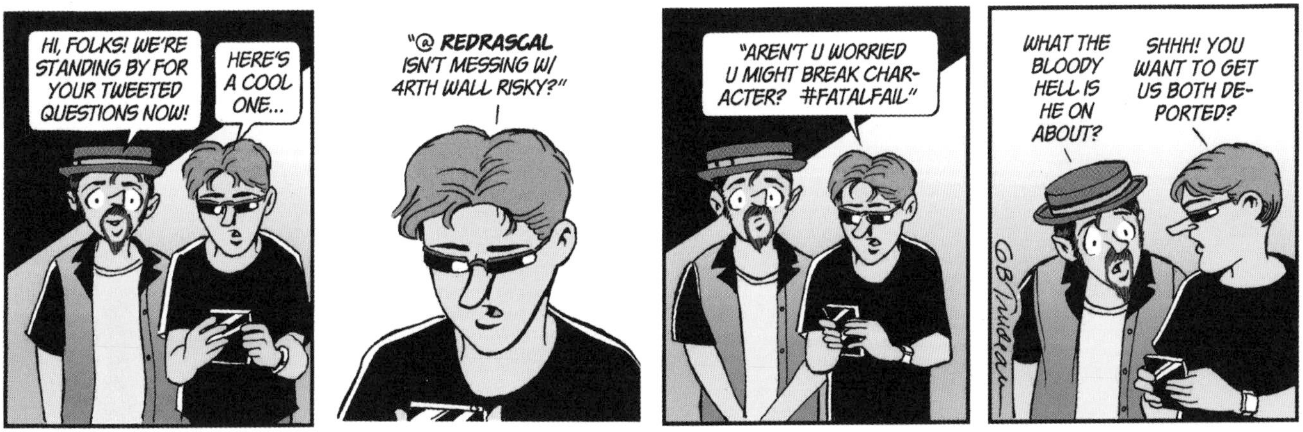
HI, FOLKS! WE'RE STANDING BY FOR YOUR TWEETED QUESTIONS NOW!
HERE'S A COOL ONE...
"@ **REDRASCAL** ISN'T MESSING W/ 4RTH WALL RISKY?"
"AREN'T U WORRIED U MIGHT BREAK CHAR-ACTER? #FATALFAIL"
WHAT THE BLOODY HELL IS HE ON ABOUT?
SHHH! YOU WANT TO GET US BOTH DE-PORTED?

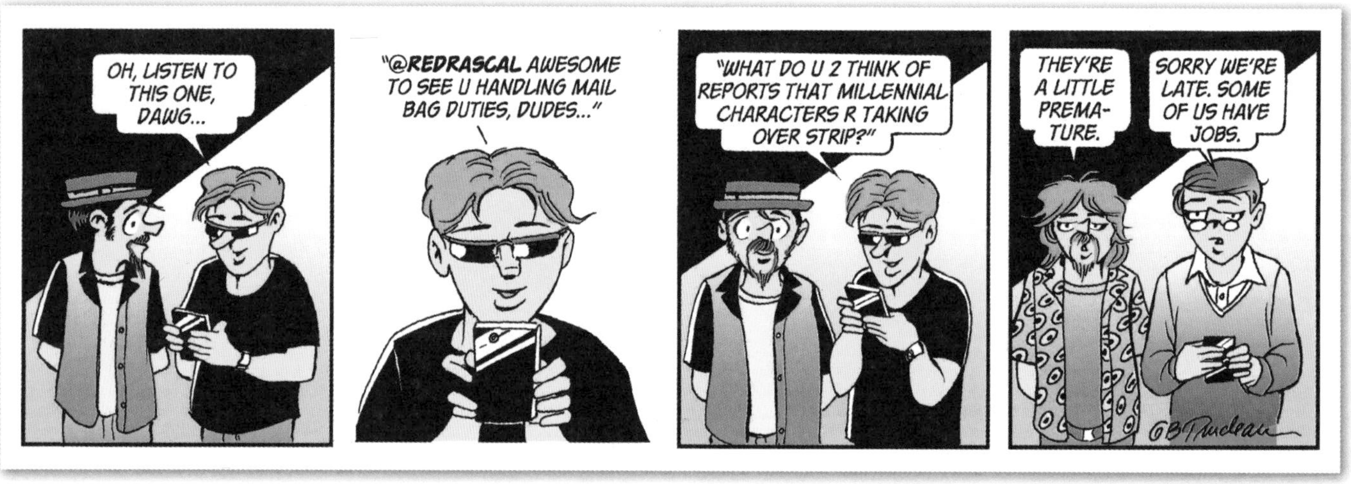
OH, LISTEN TO THIS ONE, DAWG...
"@REDRASCAL AWESOME TO SEE U HANDLING MAIL BAG DUTIES, DUDES..."
"WHAT DO U 2 THINK OF REPORTS THAT MILLENNIAL CHARACTERS R TAKING OVER STRIP?"
THEY'RE A LITTLE PREMA-TURE.
SORRY WE'RE LATE. SOME OF US HAVE JOBS.
©B Trudeau

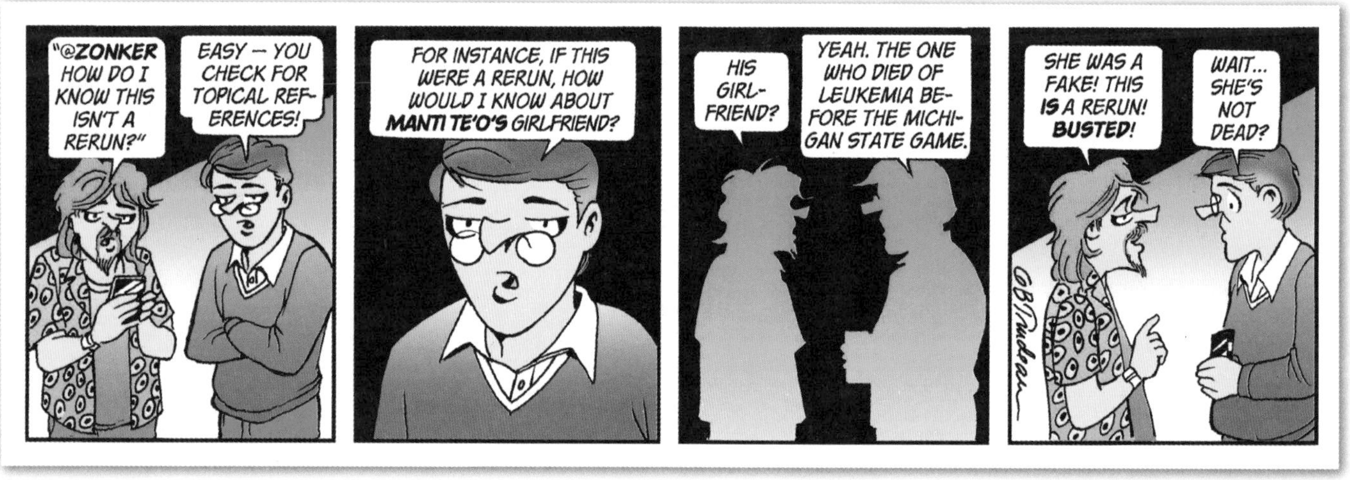
"@ZONKER HOW DO I KNOW THIS ISN'T A RERUN?"
EASY — YOU CHECK FOR TOPICAL REF-ERENCES!
FOR INSTANCE, IF THIS WERE A RERUN, HOW WOULD I KNOW ABOUT MANTI TE'O'S GIRLFRIEND?
HIS GIRL-FRIEND?
YEAH. THE ONE WHO DIED OF LEUKEMIA BE-FORE THE MICHI-GAN STATE GAME.
SHE WAS A FAKE! THIS IS A RERUN! BUSTED!
WAIT... SHE'S NOT DEAD?
©B Trudeau

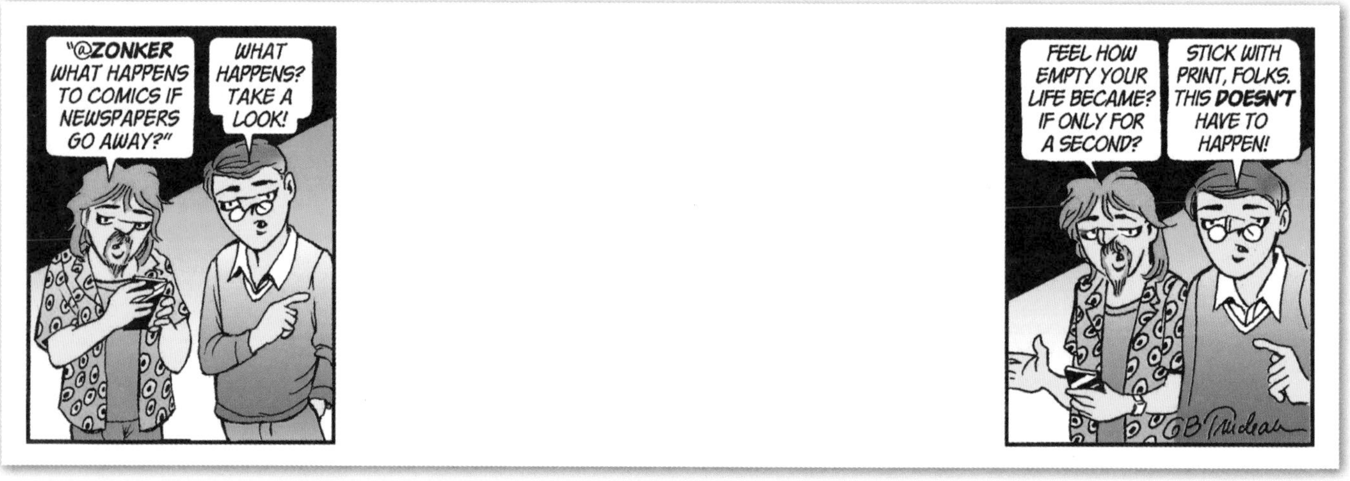
"@ZONKER WHAT HAPPENS TO COMICS IF NEWSPAPERS GO AWAY?"
WHAT HAPPENS? TAKE A LOOK!
FEEL HOW EMPTY YOUR LIFE BECAME? IF ONLY FOR A SECOND?
STICK WITH PRINT, FOLKS. THIS DOESN'T HAVE TO HAPPEN!
©B Trudeau

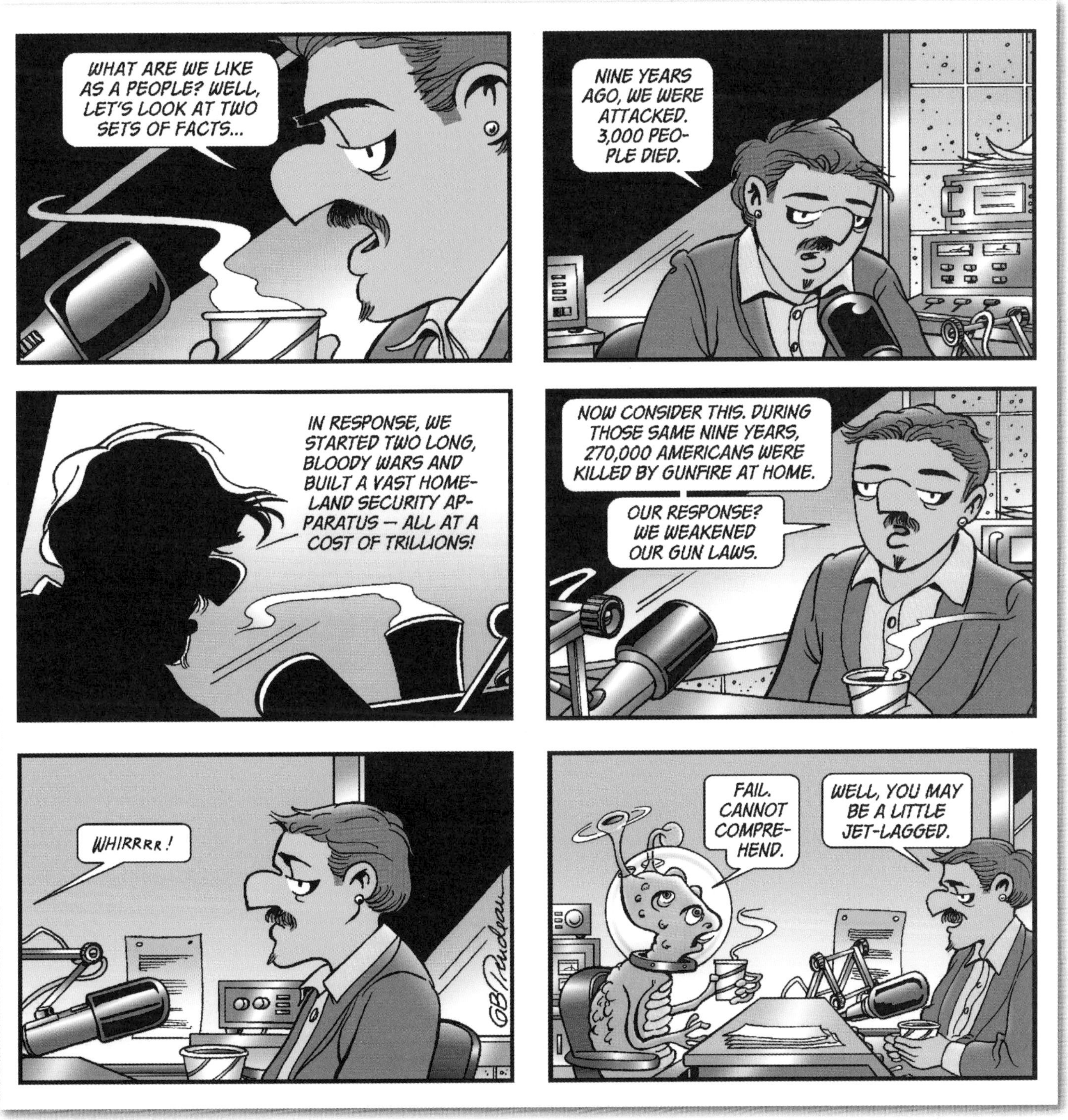
WHAT ARE WE LIKE AS A PEOPLE? WELL, LET'S LOOK AT TWO SETS OF FACTS...
NINE YEARS AGO, WE WERE ATTACKED. 3,000 PEOPLE DIED.
IN RESPONSE, WE STARTED TWO LONG, BLOODY WARS AND BUILT A VAST HOMELAND SECURITY APPARATUS — ALL AT A COST OF TRILLIONS!
NOW CONSIDER THIS. DURING THOSE SAME NINE YEARS, 270,000 AMERICANS WERE KILLED BY GUNFIRE AT HOME.
OUR RESPONSE? WE WEAKENED OUR GUN LAWS.
WHIRRRR!
FAIL. CANNOT COMPREHEND.
WELL, YOU MAY BE A LITTLE JET-LAGGED.
GB Trudeau

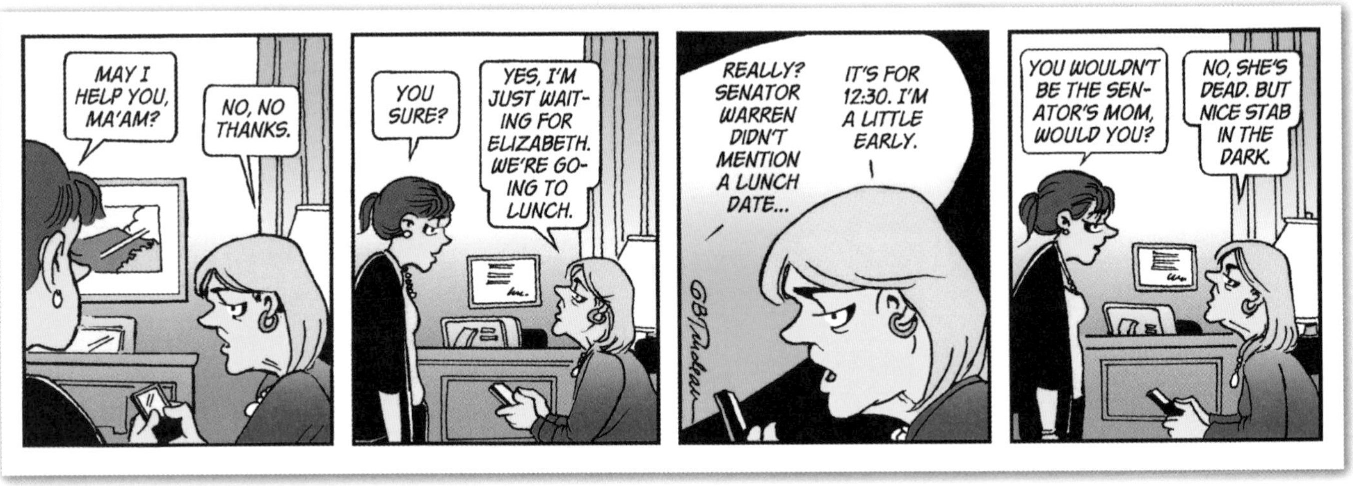
MAY I HELP YOU, MA'AM?
NO, NO THANKS.
YOU SURE?
YES, I'M JUST WAITING FOR ELIZABETH. WE'RE GOING TO LUNCH.
REALLY? SENATOR WARREN DIDN'T MENTION A LUNCH DATE...
IT'S FOR 12:30. I'M A LITTLE EARLY.
YOU WOULDN'T BE THE SENATOR'S MOM, WOULD YOU?
NO, SHE'S DEAD. BUT NICE STAB IN THE DARK.

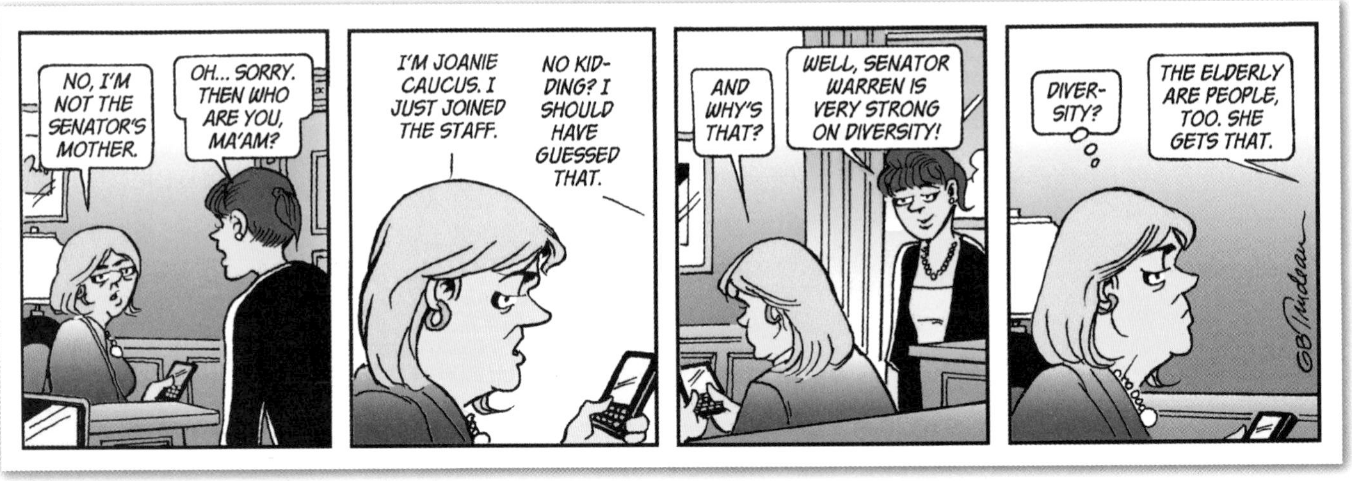
NO, I'M NOT THE SENATOR'S MOTHER.
OH... SORRY. THEN WHO ARE YOU, MA'AM?
I'M JOANIE CAUCUS. I JUST JOINED THE STAFF.
NO KIDDING? I SHOULD HAVE GUESSED THAT.
AND WHY'S THAT?
WELL, SENATOR WARREN IS VERY STRONG ON DIVERSITY!
DIVERSITY?
THE ELDERLY ARE PEOPLE, TOO. SHE GETS THAT.

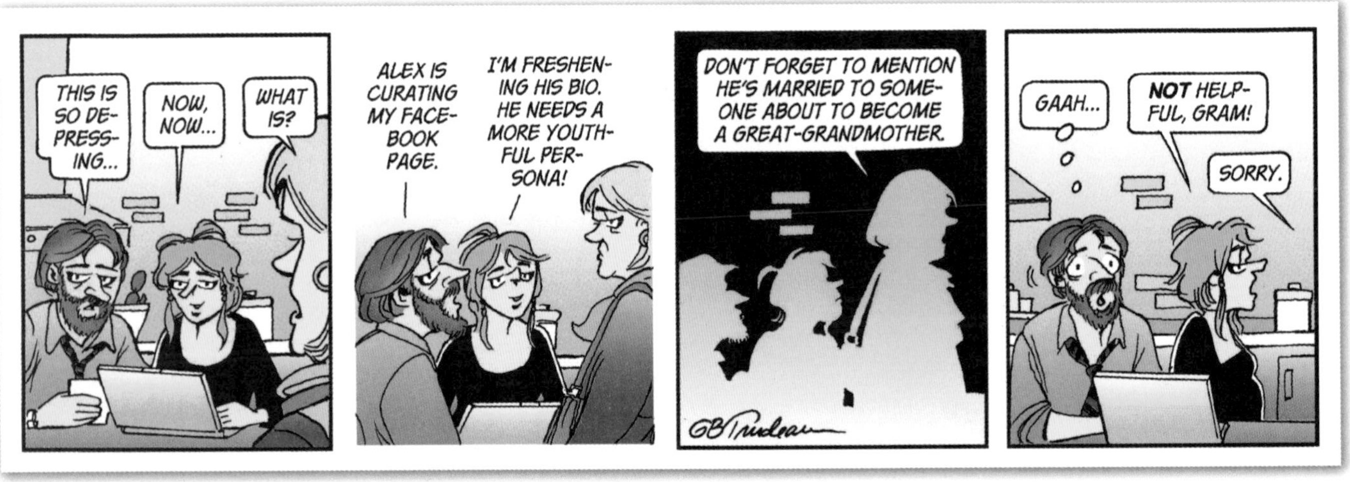
THIS IS SO DEPRESSING...
NOW, NOW...
WHAT IS?
ALEX IS CURATING MY FACEBOOK PAGE.
I'M FRESHENING HIS BIO. HE NEEDS A MORE YOUTHFUL PERSONA!
DON'T FORGET TO MENTION HE'S MARRIED TO SOMEONE ABOUT TO BECOME A GREAT-GRANDMOTHER.
GAAH...
NOT HELPFUL, GRAM!
SORRY.

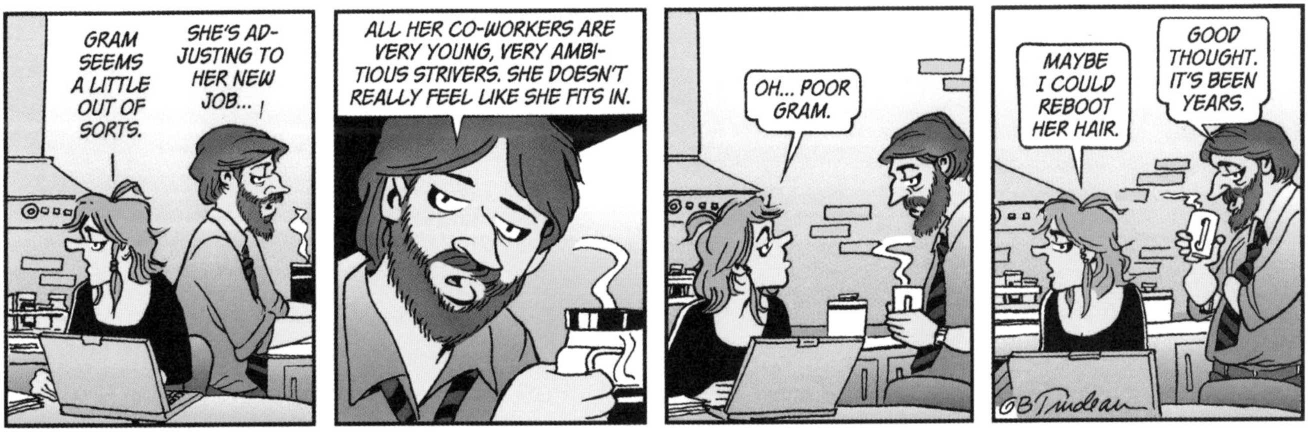
GRAM SEEMS A LITTLE OUT OF SORTS.
SHE'S AD-JUSTING TO HER NEW JOB...
ALL HER CO-WORKERS ARE VERY YOUNG, VERY AMBI-TIOUS STRIVERS. SHE DOESN'T REALLY FEEL LIKE SHE FITS IN.
OH... POOR GRAM.
MAYBE I COULD REBOOT HER HAIR.
GOOD THOUGHT. IT'S BEEN YEARS.
GB Trudeau

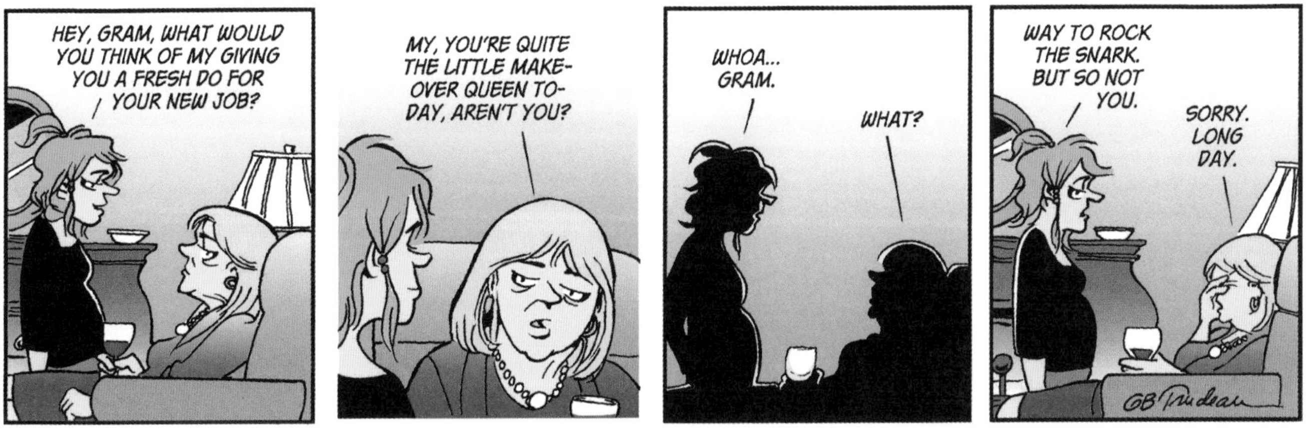
HEY, GRAM, WHAT WOULD YOU THINK OF MY GIVING YOU A FRESH DO FOR YOUR NEW JOB?
MY, YOU'RE QUITE THE LITTLE MAKE-OVER QUEEN TO-DAY, AREN'T YOU?
WHOA... GRAM.
WHAT?
WAY TO ROCK THE SNARK. BUT SO NOT YOU.
SORRY. LONG DAY.
GB Trudeau

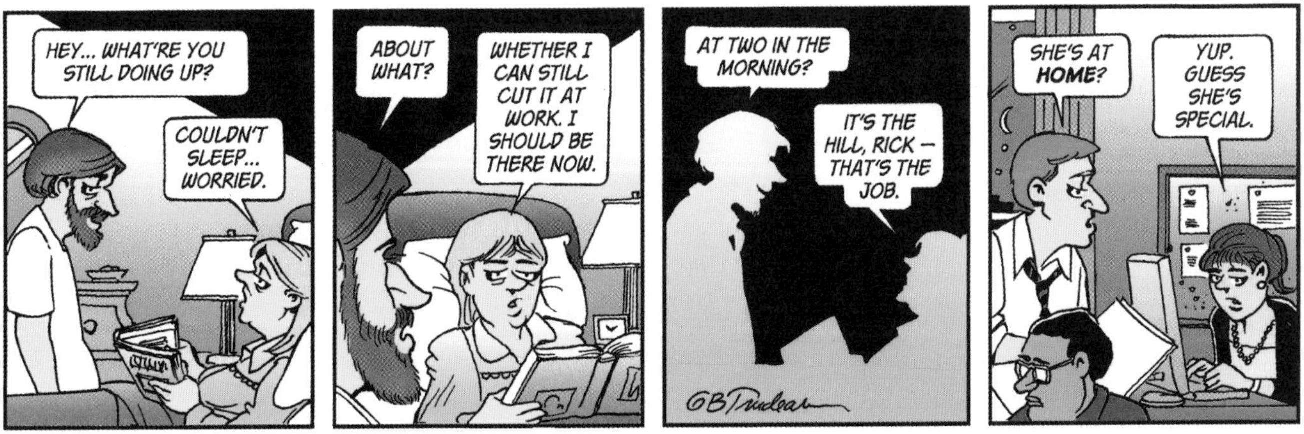
HEY... WHAT'RE YOU STILL DOING UP?
COULDN'T SLEEP... WORRIED.
ABOUT WHAT?
WHETHER I CAN STILL CUT IT AT WORK. I SHOULD BE THERE NOW.
AT TWO IN THE MORNING?
IT'S THE HILL, RICK — THAT'S THE JOB.
GB Trudeau
SHE'S AT **HOME**?
YUP. GUESS SHE'S SPECIAL.

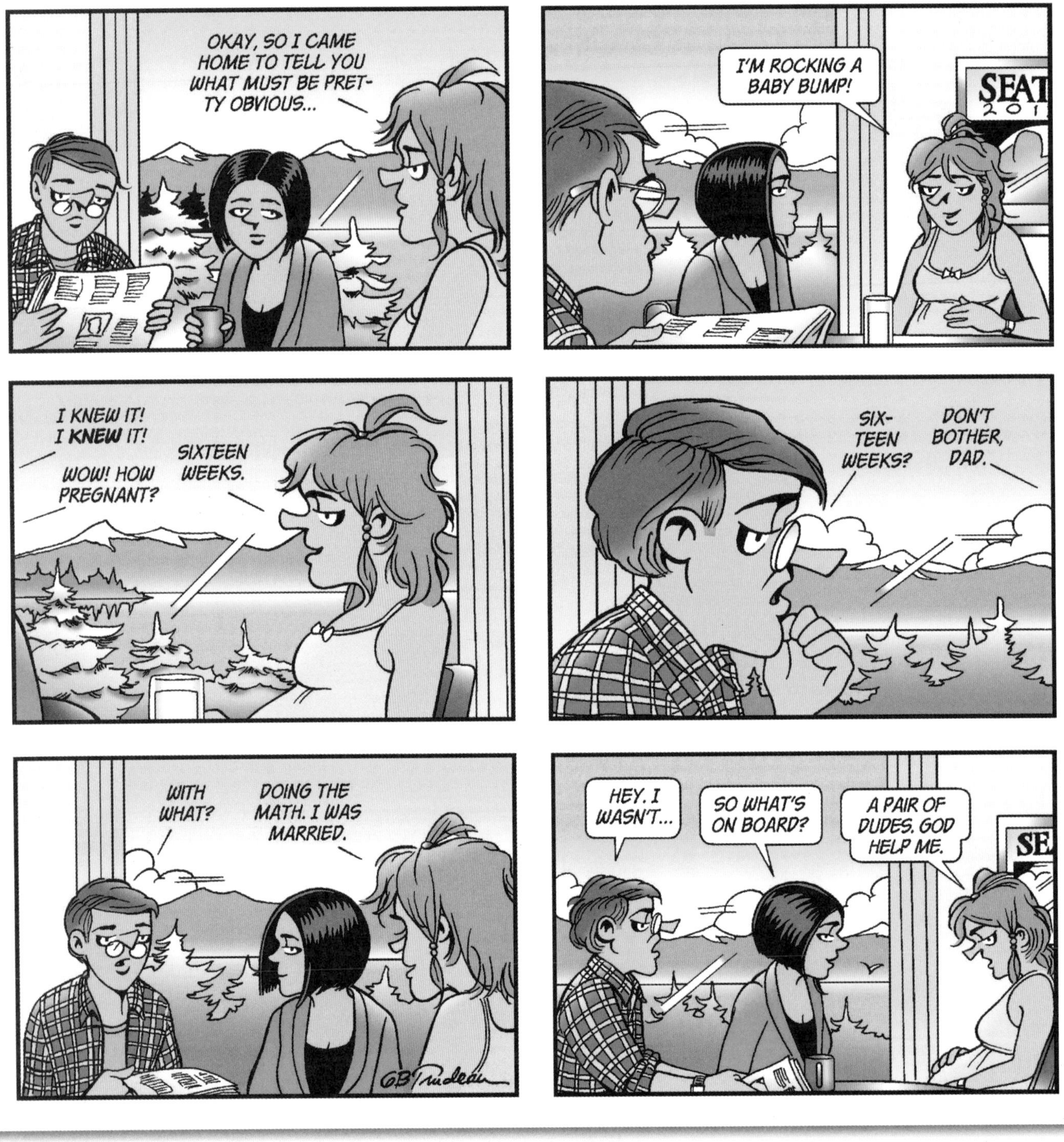
OKAY, SO I CAME HOME TO TELL YOU WHAT MUST BE PRET-TY OBVIOUS...
I'M ROCKING A BABY BUMP!
SEAT
201
I KNEW IT! I **KNEW** IT!
WOW! HOW PREGNANT?
SIXTEEN WEEKS.
SIX-TEEN WEEKS?
DON'T BOTHER, DAD.
WITH WHAT?
DOING THE MATH. I WAS MARRIED.
HEY. I WASN'T...
SO WHAT'S ON BOARD?
A PAIR OF DUDES. GOD HELP ME.
SE

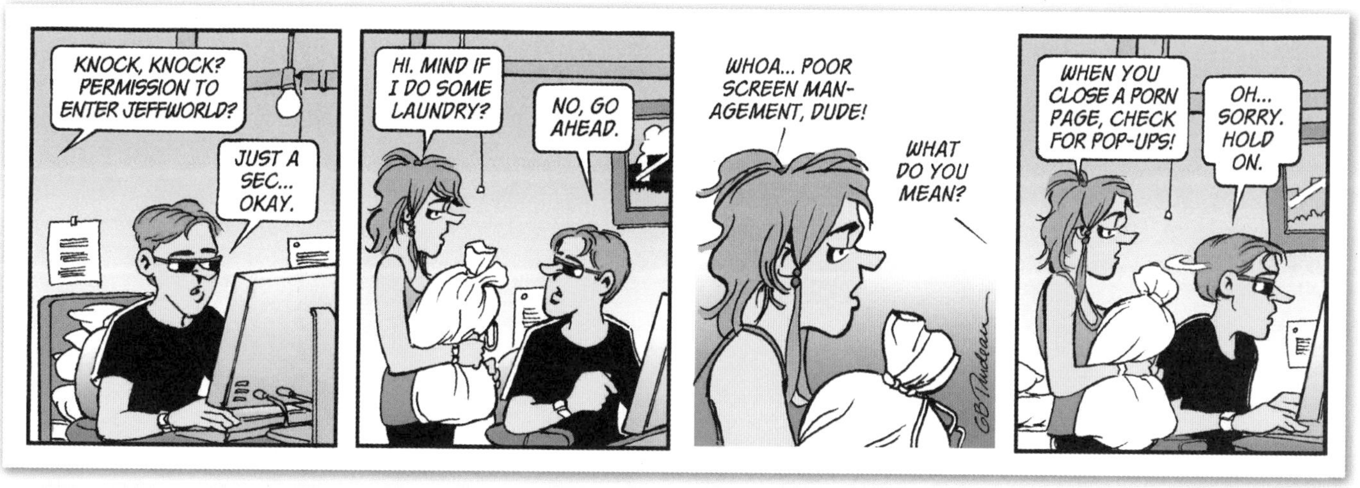
KNOCK, KNOCK? PERMISSION TO ENTER JEFFWORLD?
JUST A SEC... OKAY.
HI. MIND IF I DO SOME LAUNDRY?
NO, GO AHEAD.
WHOA... POOR SCREEN MAN-AGEMENT, DUDE!
WHAT DO YOU MEAN?
WHEN YOU CLOSE A PORN PAGE, CHECK FOR POP-UPS!
OH... SORRY. HOLD ON.

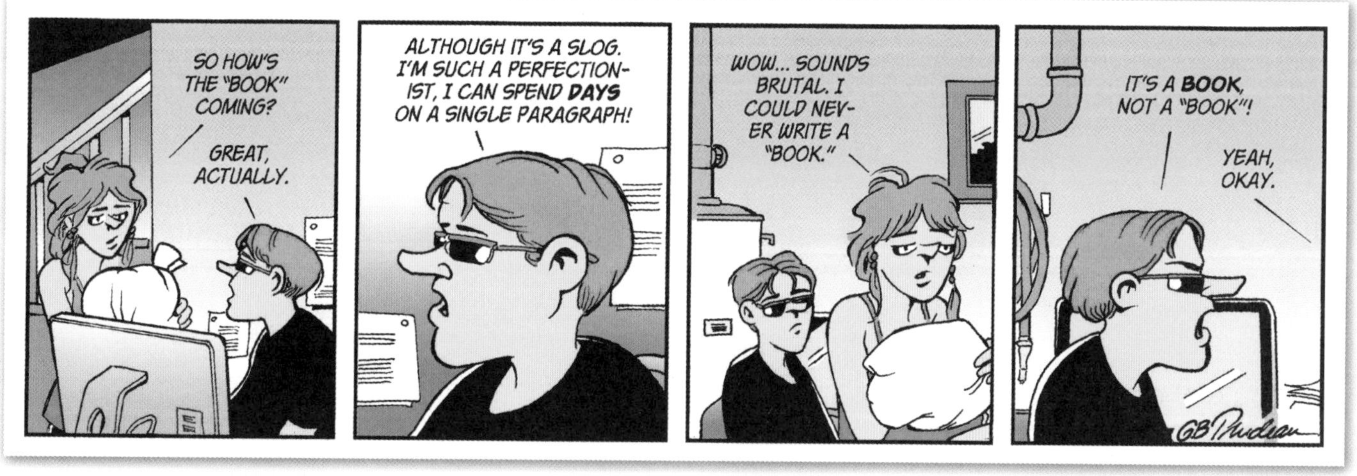
SO HOW'S THE "BOOK" COMING?
GREAT, ACTUALLY.
ALTHOUGH IT'S A SLOG. I'M SUCH A PERFECTION-IST, I CAN SPEND **DAYS** ON A SINGLE PARAGRAPH!
WOW... SOUNDS BRUTAL. I COULD NEV-ER WRITE A "BOOK."
IT'S A **BOOK**, NOT A "BOOK"!
YEAH, OKAY.

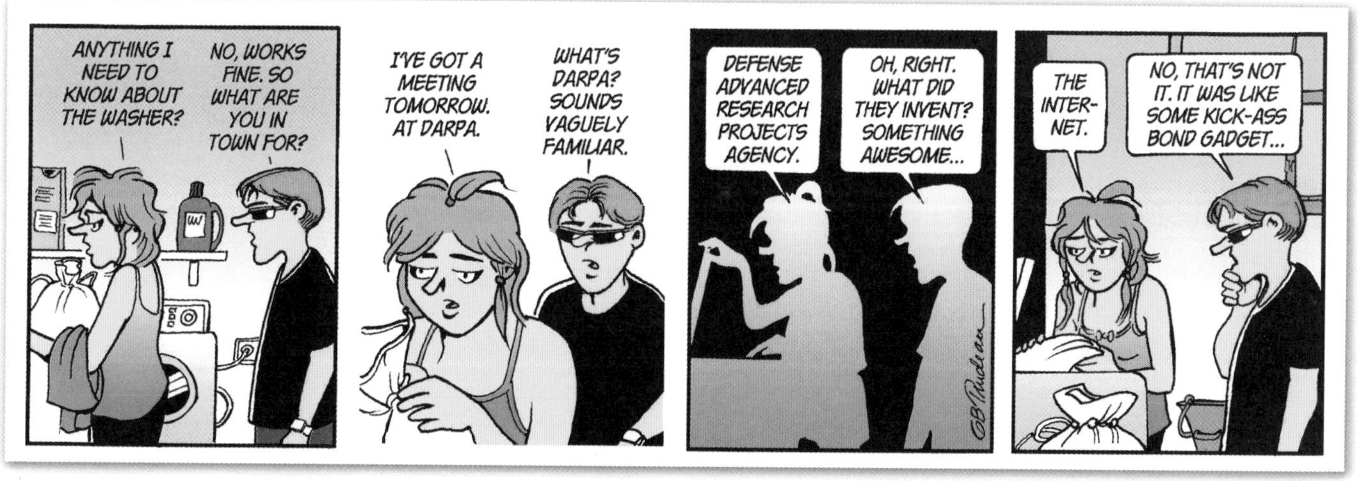
ANYTHING I NEED TO KNOW ABOUT THE WASHER?
NO, WORKS FINE. SO WHAT ARE YOU IN TOWN FOR?
I'VE GOT A MEETING TOMORROW. AT DARPA.
WHAT'S DARPA? SOUNDS VAGUELY FAMILIAR.
DEFENSE ADVANCED RESEARCH PROJECTS AGENCY.
OH, RIGHT. WHAT DID THEY INVENT? SOMETHING AWESOME...
THE INTER-NET.
NO, THAT'S NOT IT. IT WAS LIKE SOME KICK-ASS BOND GADGET...

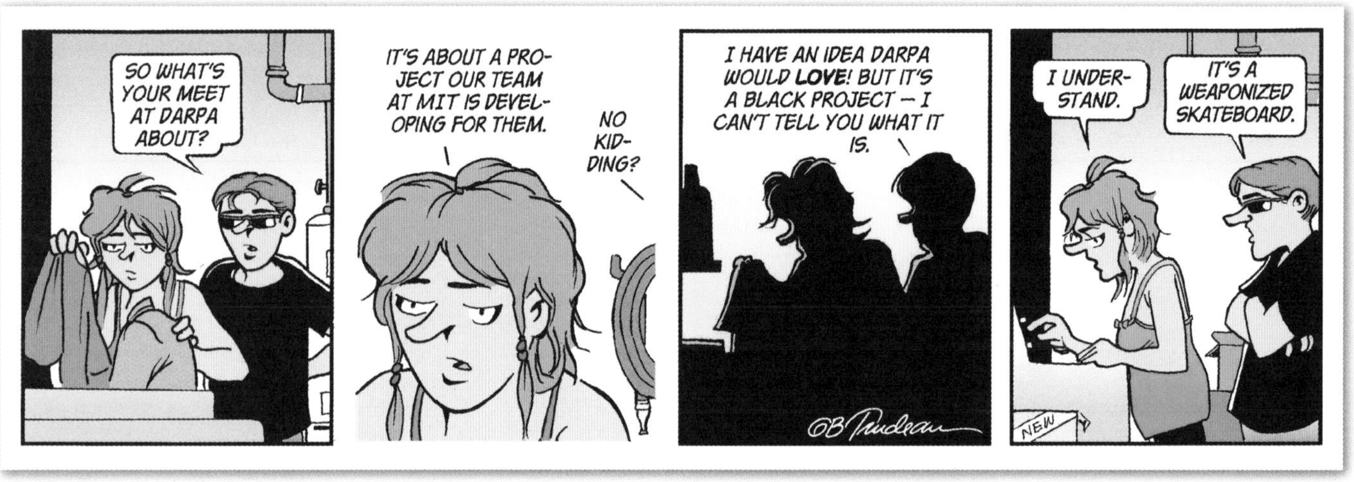
SO WHAT'S YOUR MEET AT DARPA ABOUT?
IT'S ABOUT A PROJECT OUR TEAM AT MIT IS DEVELOPING FOR THEM.
NO KIDDING?
I HAVE AN IDEA DARPA WOULD **LOVE**! BUT IT'S A BLACK PROJECT — I CAN'T TELL YOU WHAT IT IS.
I UNDERSTAND.
IT'S A WEAPONIZED SKATEBOARD.
NEW

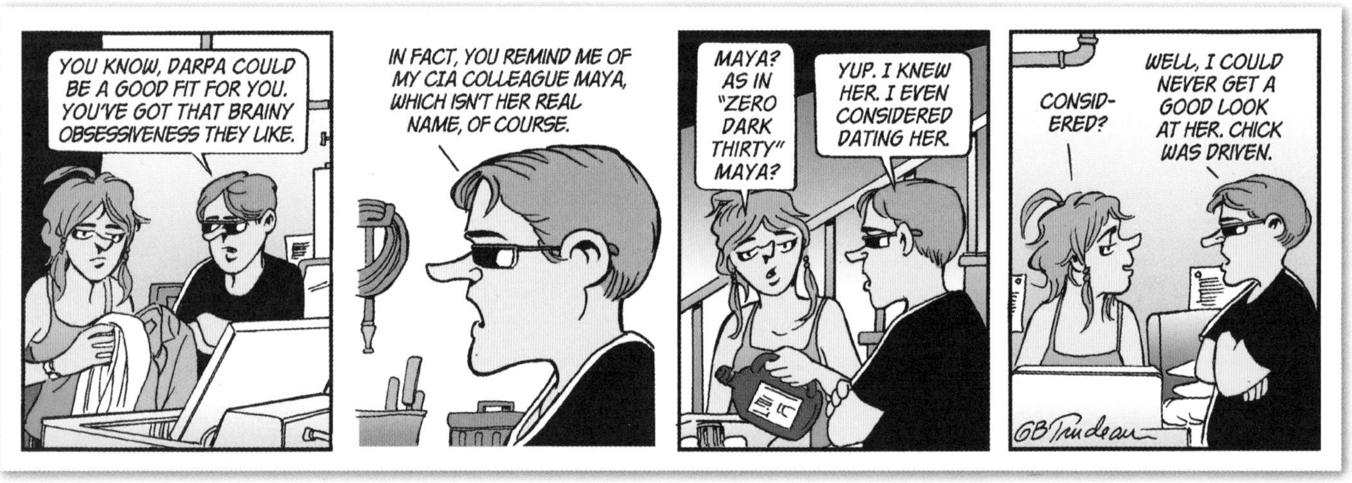
YOU KNOW, DARPA COULD BE A GOOD FIT FOR YOU. YOU'VE GOT THAT BRAINY OBSESSIVENESS THEY LIKE.
IN FACT, YOU REMIND ME OF MY CIA COLLEAGUE MAYA, WHICH ISN'T HER REAL NAME, OF COURSE.
MAYA? AS IN "ZERO DARK THIRTY" MAYA?
YUP. I KNEW HER. I EVEN CONSIDERED DATING HER.
CONSIDERED?
WELL, I COULD NEVER GET A GOOD LOOK AT HER. CHICK WAS DRIVEN.

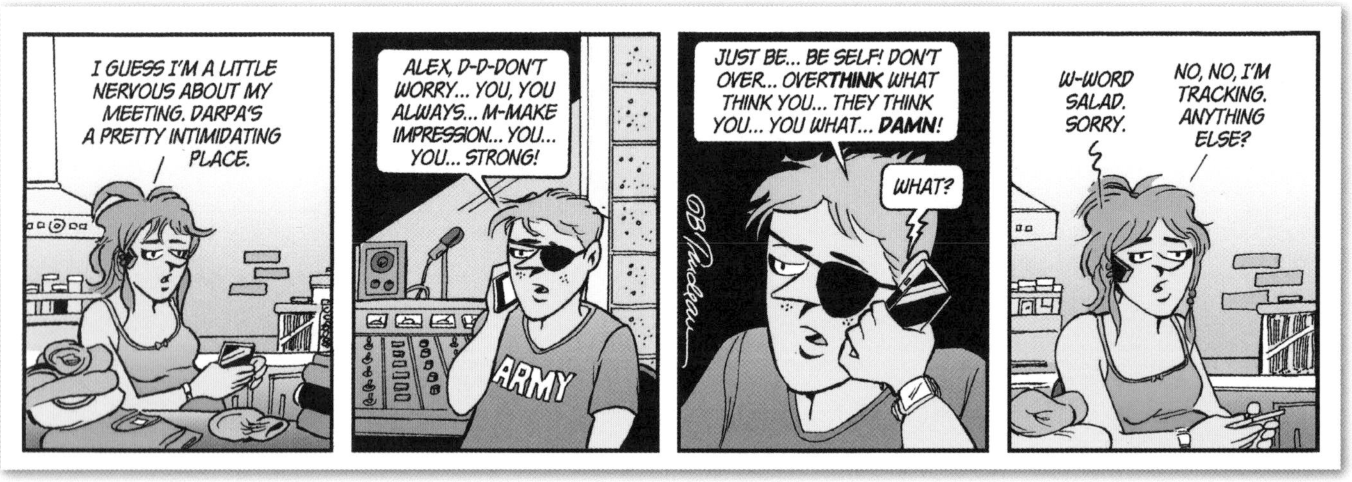
I GUESS I'M A LITTLE NERVOUS ABOUT MY MEETING. DARPA'S A PRETTY INTIMIDATING PLACE.
ALEX, D-D-DON'T WORRY... YOU, YOU ALWAYS... M-MAKE IMPRESSION... YOU... YOU... STRONG!
ARMY
JUST BE... BE SELF! DON'T OVER... OVER**THINK** WHAT THINK YOU... THEY THINK YOU... YOU WHAT... **DAMN**!
WHAT?
W-WORD SALAD. SORRY.
NO, NO, I'M TRACKING. ANYTHING ELSE?

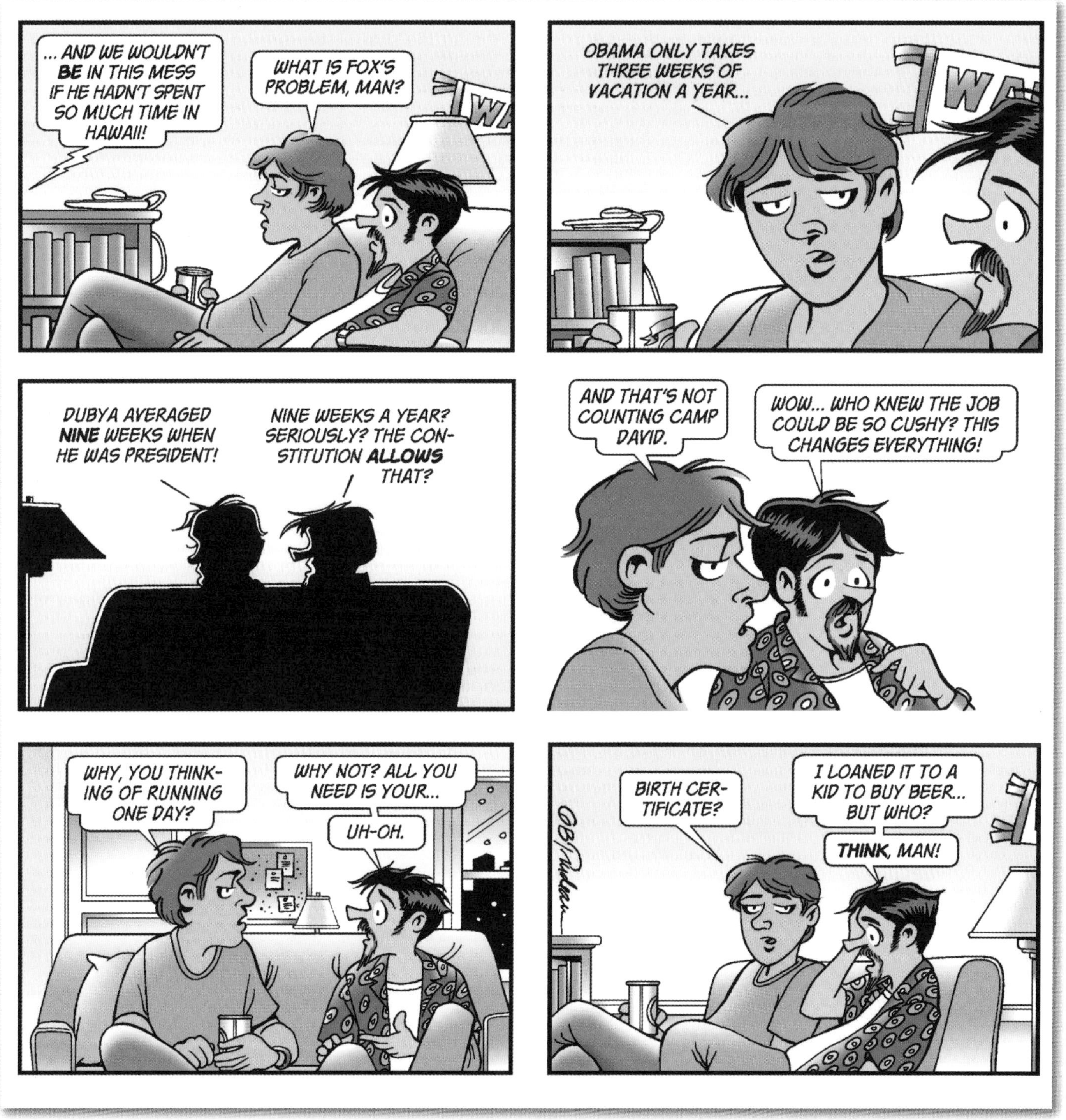
... AND WE WOULDN'T BE IN THIS MESS IF HE HADN'T SPENT SO MUCH TIME IN HAWAII!
WHAT IS FOX'S PROBLEM, MAN?
WA
OBAMA ONLY TAKES THREE WEEKS OF VACATION A YEAR...
DUBYA AVERAGED NINE WEEKS WHEN HE WAS PRESIDENT!
NINE WEEKS A YEAR? SERIOUSLY? THE CON-STITUTION ALLOWS THAT?
AND THAT'S NOT COUNTING CAMP DAVID.
WOW... WHO KNEW THE JOB COULD BE SO CUSHY? THIS CHANGES EVERYTHING!
WHY, YOU THINK-ING OF RUNNING ONE DAY?
WHY NOT? ALL YOU NEED IS YOUR...
UH-OH.
BIRTH CER-TIFICATE?
I LOANED IT TO A KID TO BUY BEER... BUT WHO?
THINK, MAN!

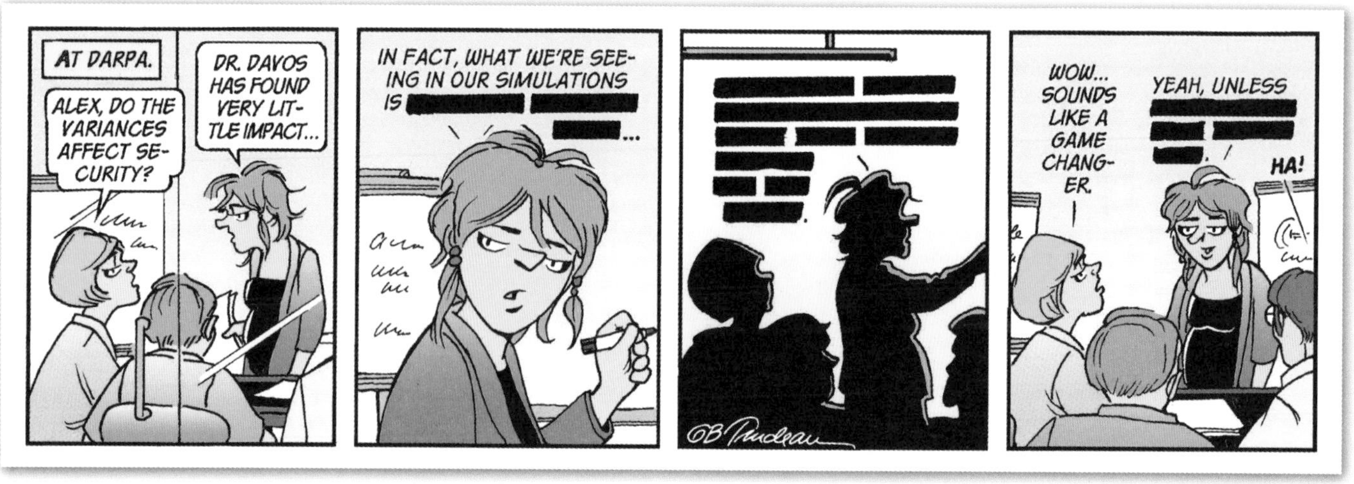
AT DARPA.
ALEX, DO THE VARIANCES AFFECT SE-CURITY?
DR. DAVOS HAS FOUND VERY LIT-TLE IMPACT...
IN FACT, WHAT WE'RE SEE-ING IN OUR SIMULATIONS IS [redacted]...
[redacted]
WOW... SOUNDS LIKE A GAME CHANG-ER.
YEAH, UNLESS [redacted].
HA!

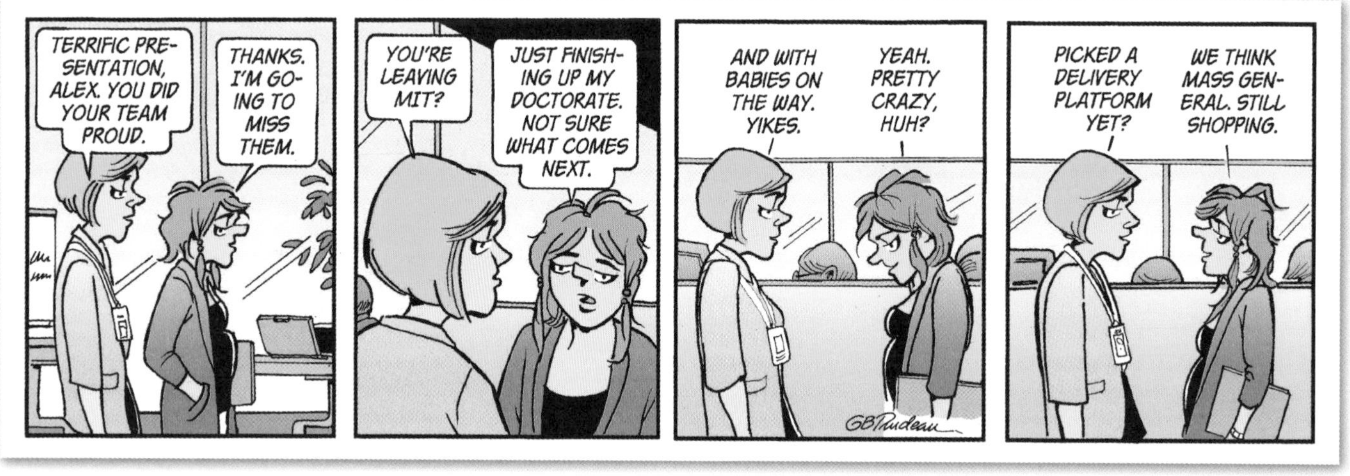
TERRIFIC PRE-SENTATION, ALEX. YOU DID YOUR TEAM PROUD.
THANKS. I'M GO-ING TO MISS THEM.
YOU'RE LEAVING MIT?
JUST FINISH-ING UP MY DOCTORATE. NOT SURE WHAT COMES NEXT.
AND WITH BABIES ON THE WAY. YIKES.
YEAH. PRETTY CRAZY, HUH?
PICKED A DELIVERY PLATFORM YET?
WE THINK MASS GEN-ERAL. STILL SHOPPING.

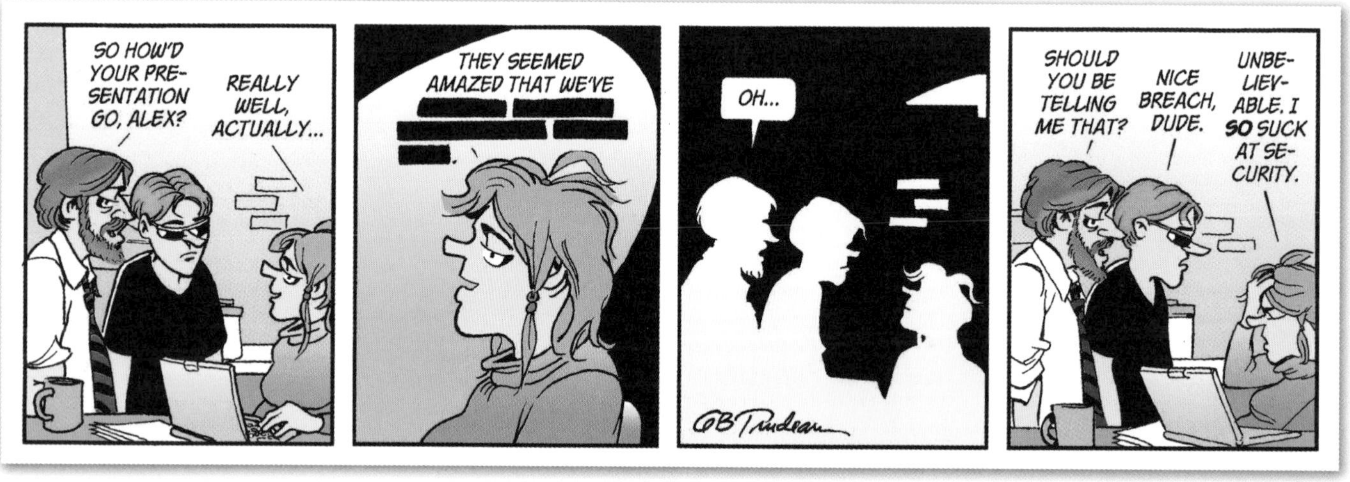
SO HOW'D YOUR PRE-SENTATION GO, ALEX?
REALLY WELL, ACTUALLY...
THEY SEEMED AMAZED THAT WE'VE [redacted].
OH...
SHOULD YOU BE TELLING ME THAT?
NICE BREACH, DUDE.
UNBE-LIEV-ABLE. I SO SUCK AT SE-CURITY.

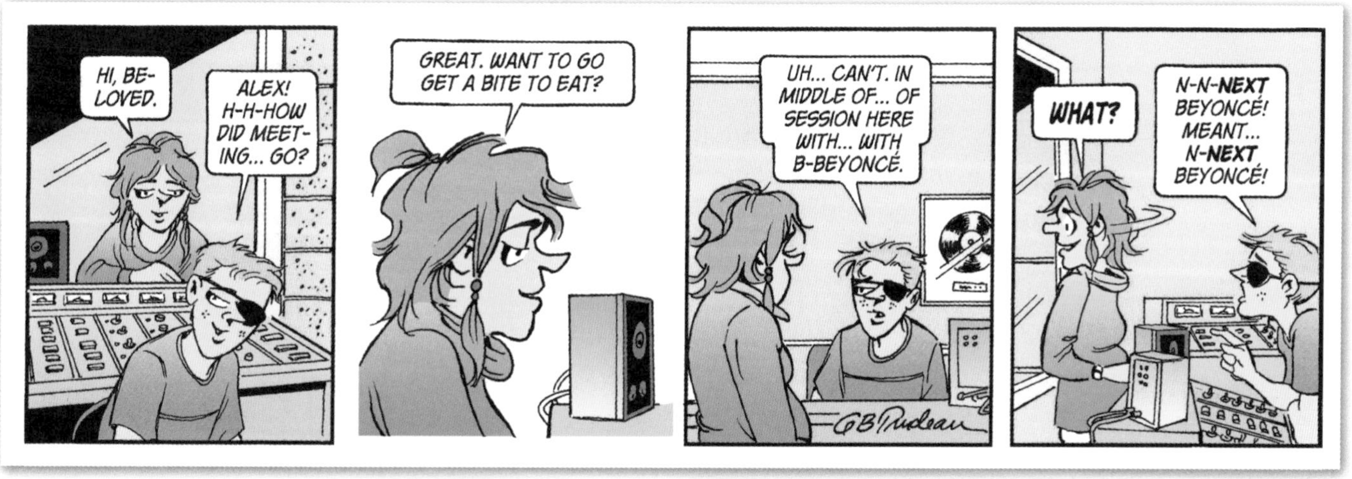
HI, BE-LOVED.
ALEX! H-H-HOW DID MEET-ING... GO?
GREAT. WANT TO GO GET A BITE TO EAT?
UH... CAN'T. IN MIDDLE OF... OF SESSION HERE WITH... WITH B-BEYONCÉ.
WHAT?
N-N-**NEXT** BEYONCÉ! MEANT... N-**NEXT** BEYONCÉ!

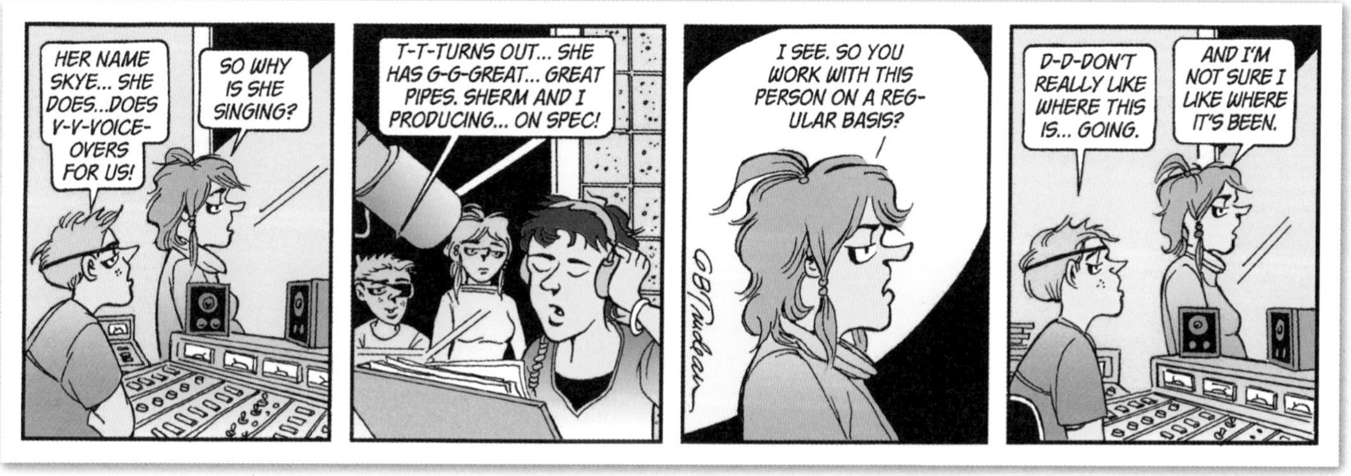
HER NAME SKYE... SHE DOES...DOES V-V-VOICE-OVERS FOR US!
SO WHY IS SHE SINGING?
T-T-TURNS OUT... SHE HAS G-G-GREAT... GREAT PIPES. SHERM AND I PRODUCING... ON SPEC!
I SEE. SO YOU WORK WITH THIS PERSON ON A REG-ULAR BASIS?
D-D-DON'T REALLY LIKE WHERE THIS IS... GOING.
AND I'M NOT SURE I LIKE WHERE IT'S BEEN.

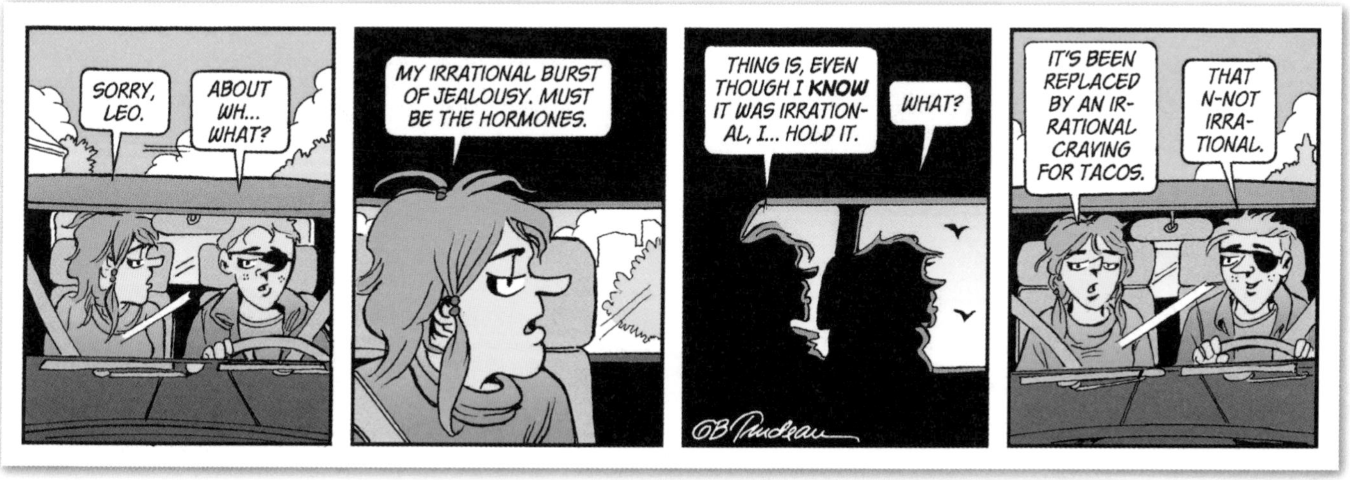
SORRY, LEO.
ABOUT WH... WHAT?
MY IRRATIONAL BURST OF JEALOUSY. MUST BE THE HORMONES.
THING IS, EVEN THOUGH I **KNOW** IT WAS IRRATION-AL, I... HOLD IT.
WHAT?
IT'S BEEN REPLACED BY AN IR-RATIONAL CRAVING FOR TACOS.
THAT N-NOT IRRA-TIONAL.

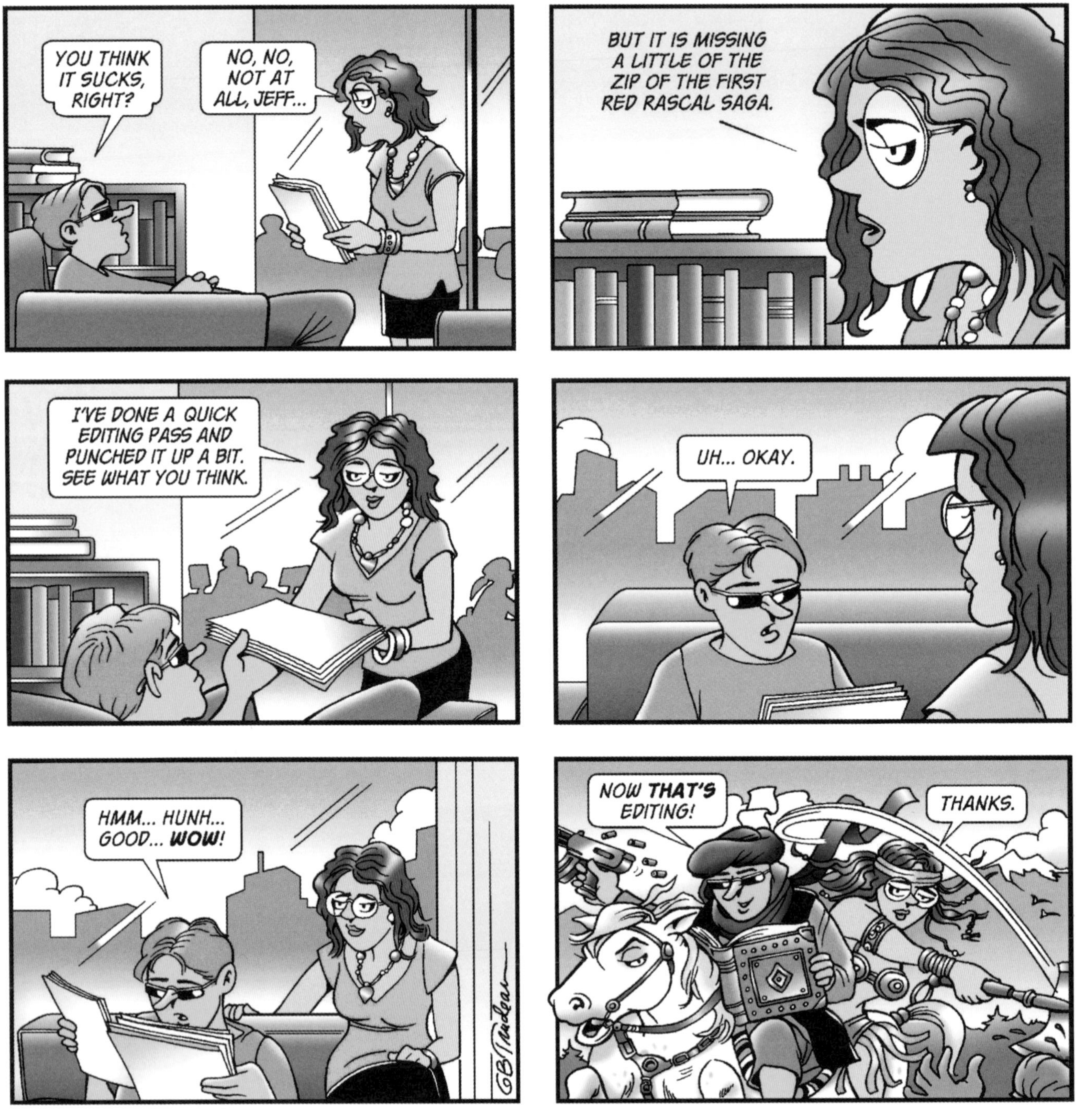
YOU THINK IT SUCKS, RIGHT?
NO, NO, NOT AT ALL, JEFF...
BUT IT IS MISSING A LITTLE OF THE ZIP OF THE FIRST RED RASCAL SAGA.
I'VE DONE A QUICK EDITING PASS AND PUNCHED IT UP A BIT. SEE WHAT YOU THINK.
UH... OKAY.
HMM... HUNH... GOOD... **WOW**!
NOW **THAT'S** EDITING!
THANKS.

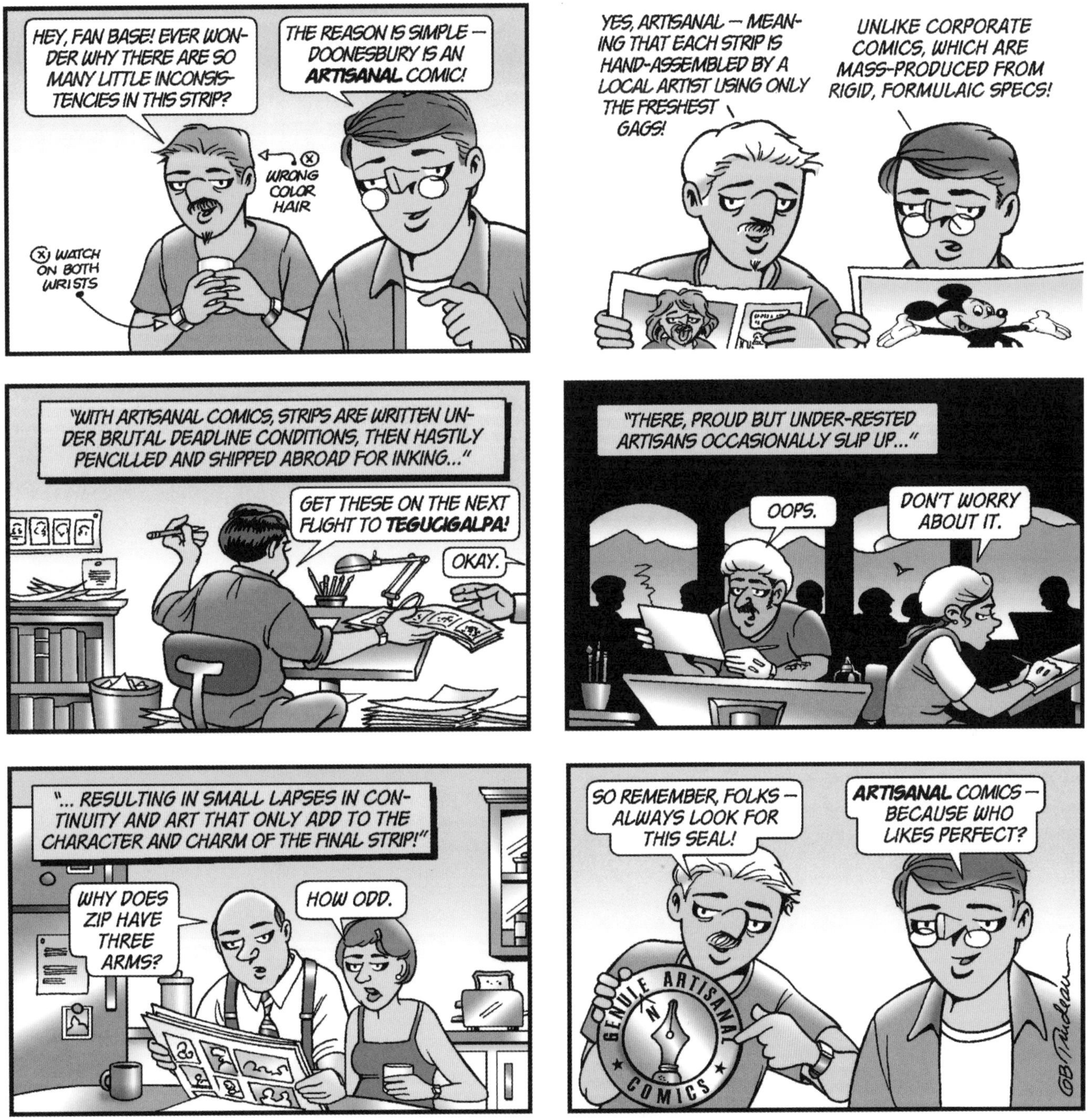
HEY, FAN BASE! EVER WONDER WHY THERE ARE SO MANY LITTLE INCONSISTENCIES IN THIS STRIP?
THE REASON IS SIMPLE — DOONESBURY IS AN **ARTISANAL** COMIC!
WRONG COLOR HAIR
WATCH ON BOTH WRISTS
YES, ARTISANAL — MEANING THAT EACH STRIP IS HAND-ASSEMBLED BY A LOCAL ARTIST USING ONLY THE FRESHEST GAGS!
UNLIKE CORPORATE COMICS, WHICH ARE MASS-PRODUCED FROM RIGID, FORMULAIC SPECS!
"WITH ARTISANAL COMICS, STRIPS ARE WRITTEN UNDER BRUTAL DEADLINE CONDITIONS, THEN HASTILY PENCILLED AND SHIPPED ABROAD FOR INKING..."
GET THESE ON THE NEXT FLIGHT TO **TEGUCIGALPA!**
OKAY.
"THERE, PROUD BUT UNDER-RESTED ARTISANS OCCASIONALLY SLIP UP..."
OOPS.
DON'T WORRY ABOUT IT.
"... RESULTING IN SMALL LAPSES IN CONTINUITY AND ART THAT ONLY ADD TO THE CHARACTER AND CHARM OF THE FINAL STRIP!"
WHY DOES ZIP HAVE THREE ARMS?
HOW ODD.
SO REMEMBER, FOLKS — ALWAYS LOOK FOR THIS SEAL!
GENUINE ARTISANAL COMICS
ARTISANAL COMICS — BECAUSE WHO LIKES PERFECT?
GBTrudeau

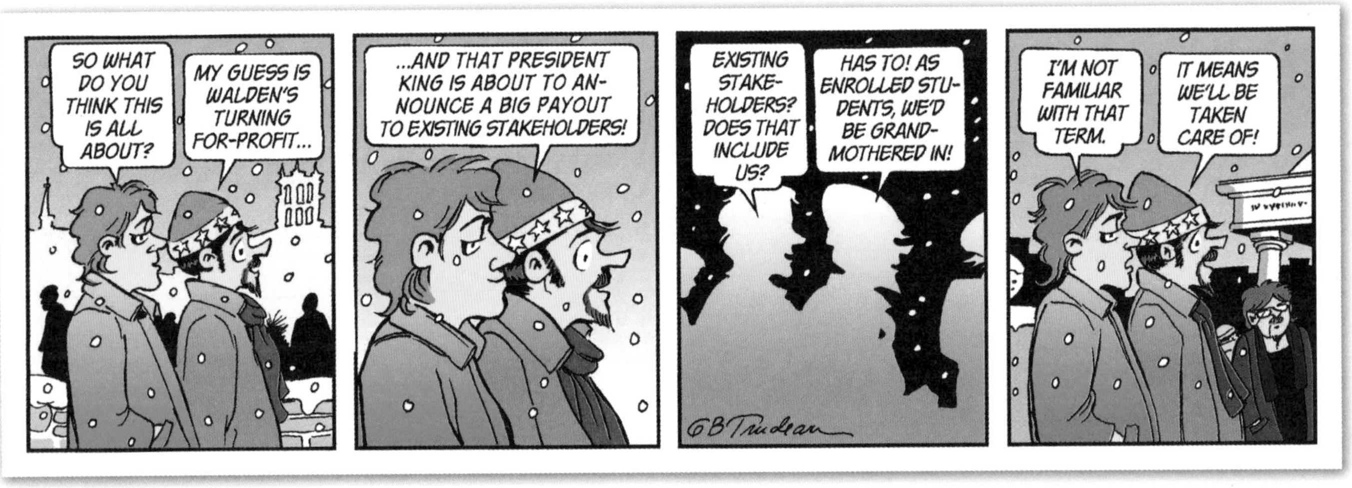
SO WHAT DO YOU THINK THIS IS ALL ABOUT?
MY GUESS IS WALDEN'S TURNING FOR-PROFIT...
...AND THAT PRESIDENT KING IS ABOUT TO ANNOUNCE A BIG PAYOUT TO EXISTING STAKEHOLDERS!
EXISTING STAKEHOLDERS? DOES THAT INCLUDE US?
HAS TO! AS ENROLLED STUDENTS, WE'D BE GRANDMOTHERED IN!
I'M NOT FAMILIAR WITH THAT TERM.
IT MEANS WE'LL BE TAKEN CARE OF!

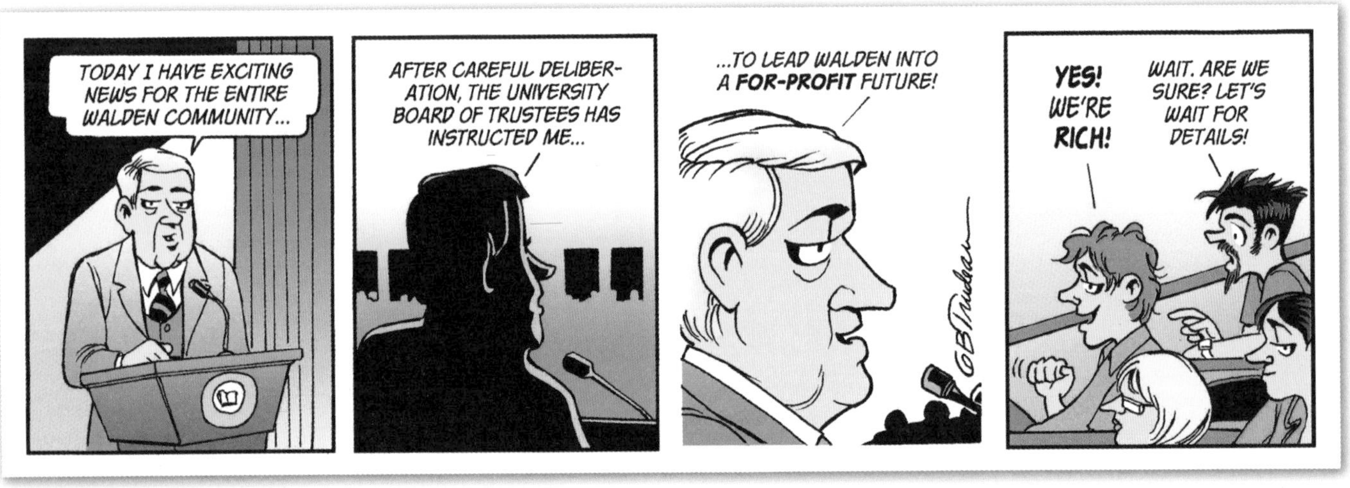
TODAY I HAVE EXCITING NEWS FOR THE ENTIRE WALDEN COMMUNITY...
AFTER CAREFUL DELIBERATION, THE UNIVERSITY BOARD OF TRUSTEES HAS INSTRUCTED ME...
...TO LEAD WALDEN INTO A **FOR-PROFIT** FUTURE!
YES! WE'RE RICH!
WAIT. ARE WE SURE? LET'S WAIT FOR DETAILS!

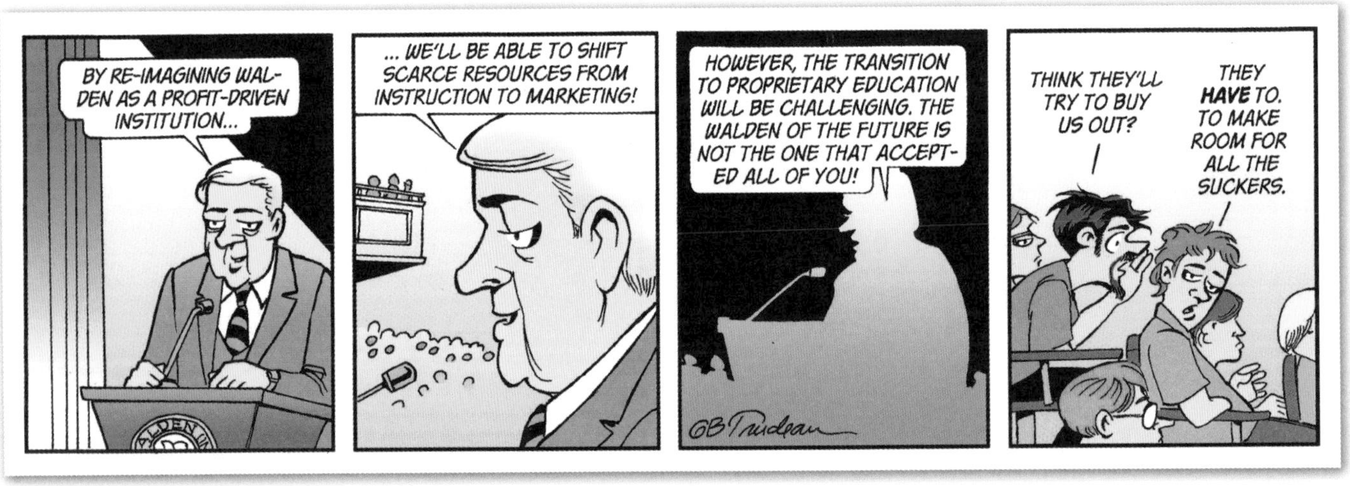
BY RE-IMAGINING WALDEN AS A PROFIT-DRIVEN INSTITUTION...
... WE'LL BE ABLE TO SHIFT SCARCE RESOURCES FROM INSTRUCTION TO MARKETING!
HOWEVER, THE TRANSITION TO PROPRIETARY EDUCATION WILL BE CHALLENGING. THE WALDEN OF THE FUTURE IS NOT THE ONE THAT ACCEPTED ALL OF YOU!
THINK THEY'LL TRY TO BUY US OUT?
THEY **HAVE** TO. TO MAKE ROOM FOR ALL THE SUCKERS.

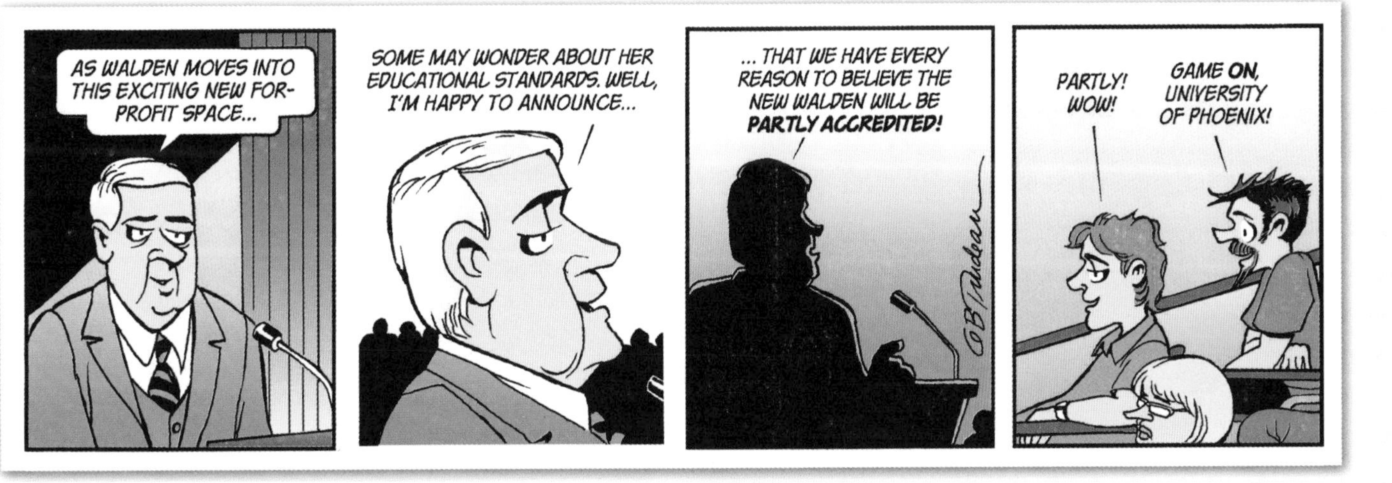
AS WALDEN MOVES INTO THIS EXCITING NEW FOR-PROFIT SPACE...
SOME MAY WONDER ABOUT HER EDUCATIONAL STANDARDS. WELL, I'M HAPPY TO ANNOUNCE...
... THAT WE HAVE EVERY REASON TO BELIEVE THE NEW WALDEN WILL BE **PARTLY ACCREDITED!**
PARTLY! WOW!
GAME **ON**, UNIVERSITY OF PHOENIX!

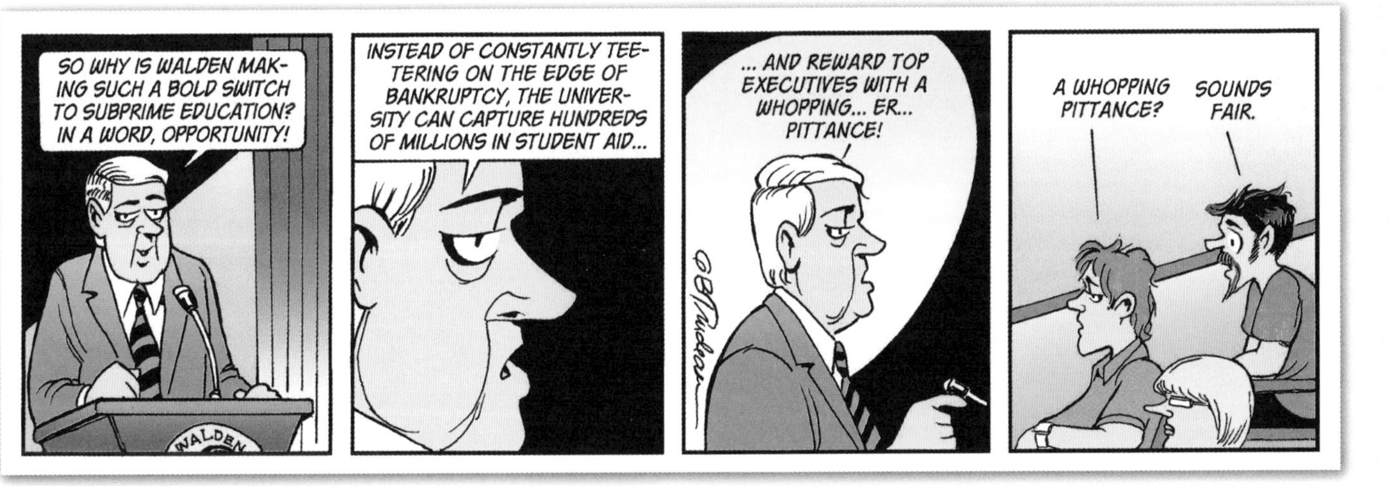
SO WHY IS WALDEN MAKING SUCH A BOLD SWITCH TO SUBPRIME EDUCATION? IN A WORD, OPPORTUNITY!
INSTEAD OF CONSTANTLY TEETERING ON THE EDGE OF BANKRUPTCY, THE UNIVERSITY CAN CAPTURE HUNDREDS OF MILLIONS IN STUDENT AID...
... AND REWARD TOP EXECUTIVES WITH A WHOPPING... ER... PITTANCE!
A WHOPPING PITTANCE?
SOUNDS FAIR.
WALDEN

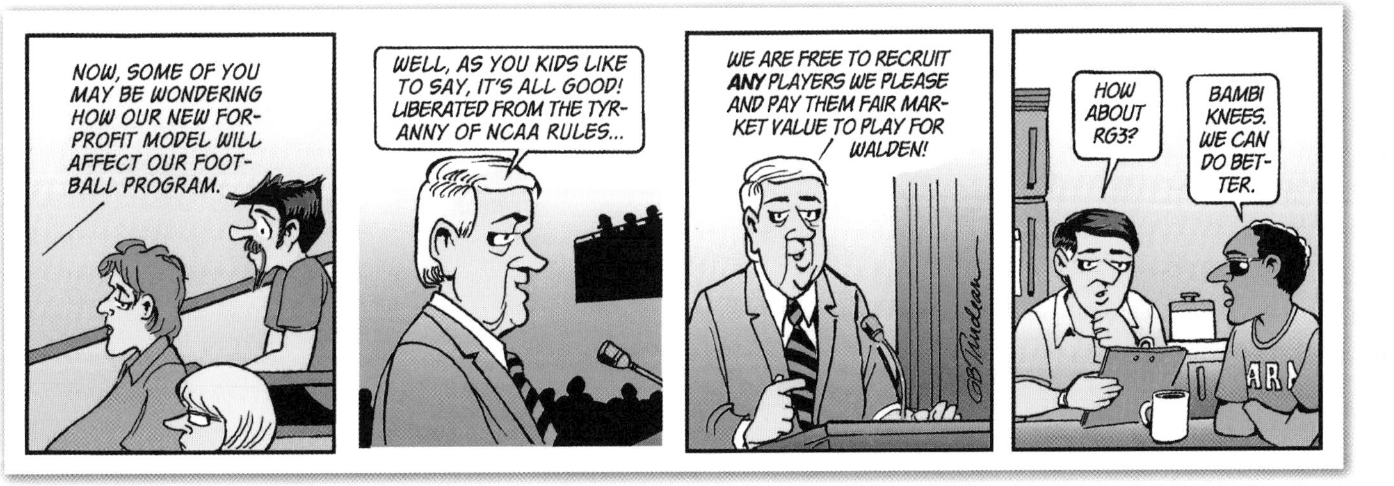
NOW, SOME OF YOU MAY BE WONDERING HOW OUR NEW FOR-PROFIT MODEL WILL AFFECT OUR FOOTBALL PROGRAM.
WELL, AS YOU KIDS LIKE TO SAY, IT'S ALL GOOD! LIBERATED FROM THE TYRANNY OF NCAA RULES...
WE ARE FREE TO RECRUIT **ANY** PLAYERS WE PLEASE AND PAY THEM FAIR MARKET VALUE TO PLAY FOR WALDEN!
HOW ABOUT RG3?
BAMBI KNEES. WE CAN DO BETTER.

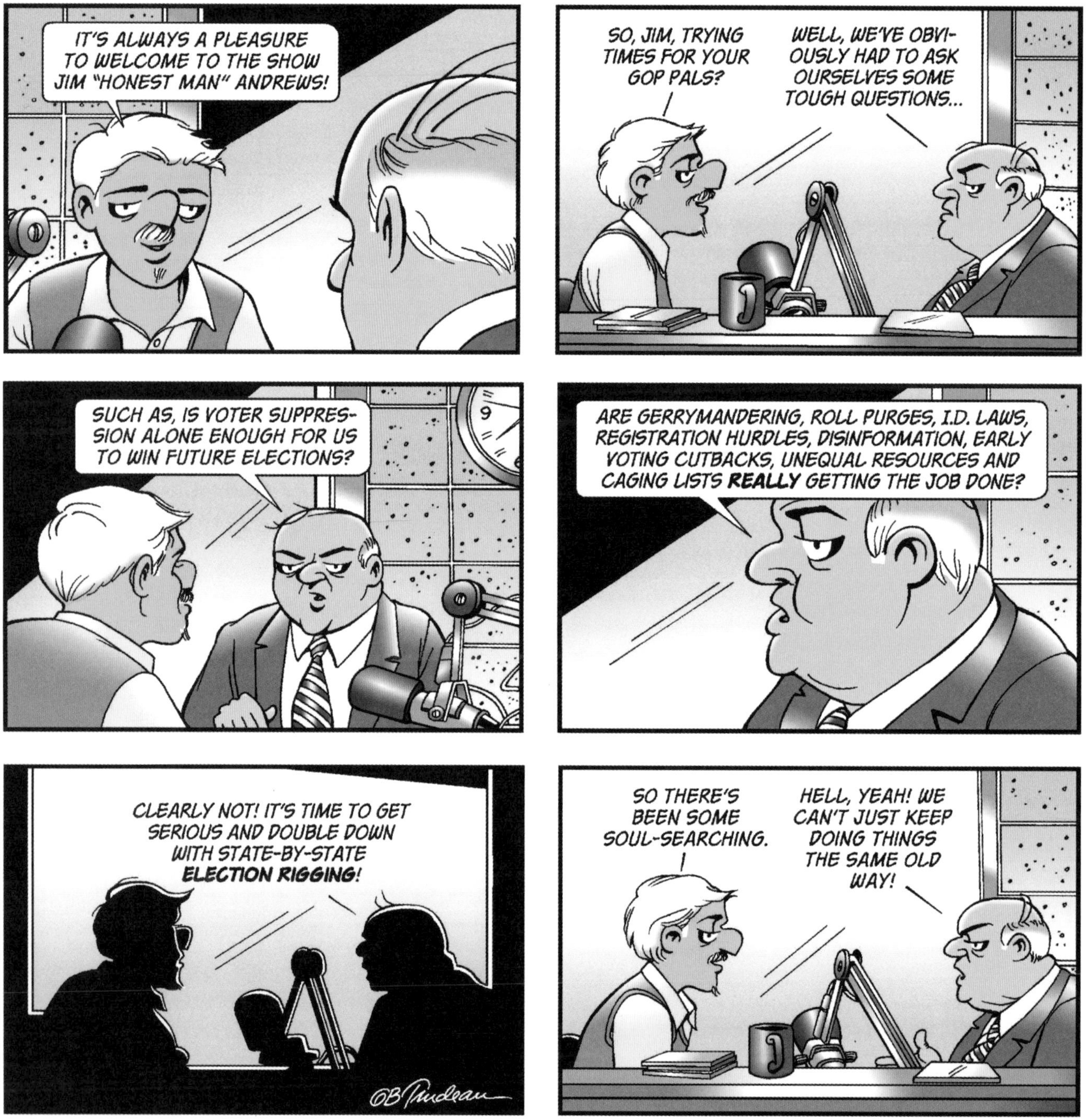
IT'S ALWAYS A PLEASURE TO WELCOME TO THE SHOW JIM "HONEST MAN" ANDREWS!
SO, JIM, TRYING TIMES FOR YOUR GOP PALS?
WELL, WE'VE OBVI-OUSLY HAD TO ASK OURSELVES SOME TOUGH QUESTIONS...
SUCH AS, IS VOTER SUPPRES-SION ALONE ENOUGH FOR US TO WIN FUTURE ELECTIONS?
ARE GERRYMANDERING, ROLL PURGES, I.D. LAWS, REGISTRATION HURDLES, DISINFORMATION, EARLY VOTING CUTBACKS, UNEQUAL RESOURCES AND CAGING LISTS **REALLY** GETTING THE JOB DONE?
CLEARLY NOT! IT'S TIME TO GET SERIOUS AND DOUBLE DOWN WITH STATE-BY-STATE **ELECTION RIGGING**!
SO THERE'S BEEN SOME SOUL-SEARCHING.
HELL, YEAH! WE CAN'T JUST KEEP DOING THINGS THE SAME OLD WAY!
GB Trudeau

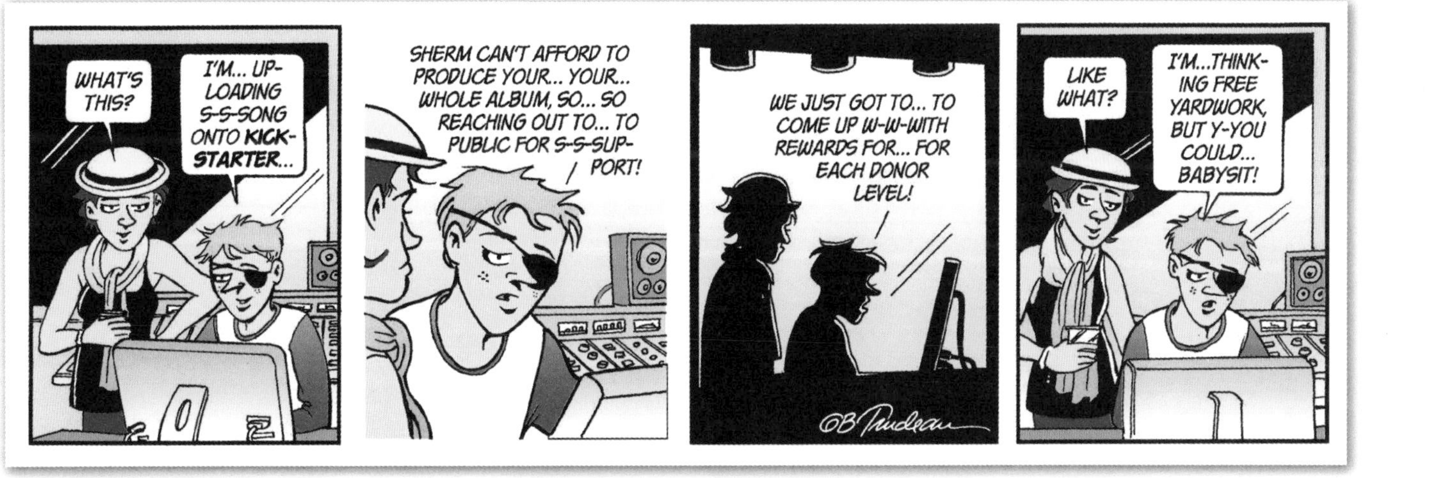
WHAT'S THIS?
I'M... UP-LOADING S-S-SONG ONTO KICK-STARTER...
SHERM CAN'T AFFORD TO PRODUCE YOUR... YOUR... WHOLE ALBUM, SO... SO REACHING OUT TO... TO PUBLIC FOR S-S-SUP-PORT!
WE JUST GOT TO... TO COME UP W-W-WITH REWARDS FOR... FOR EACH DONOR LEVEL!
LIKE WHAT?
I'M...THINK-ING FREE YARDWORK, BUT Y-YOU COULD... BABYSIT!

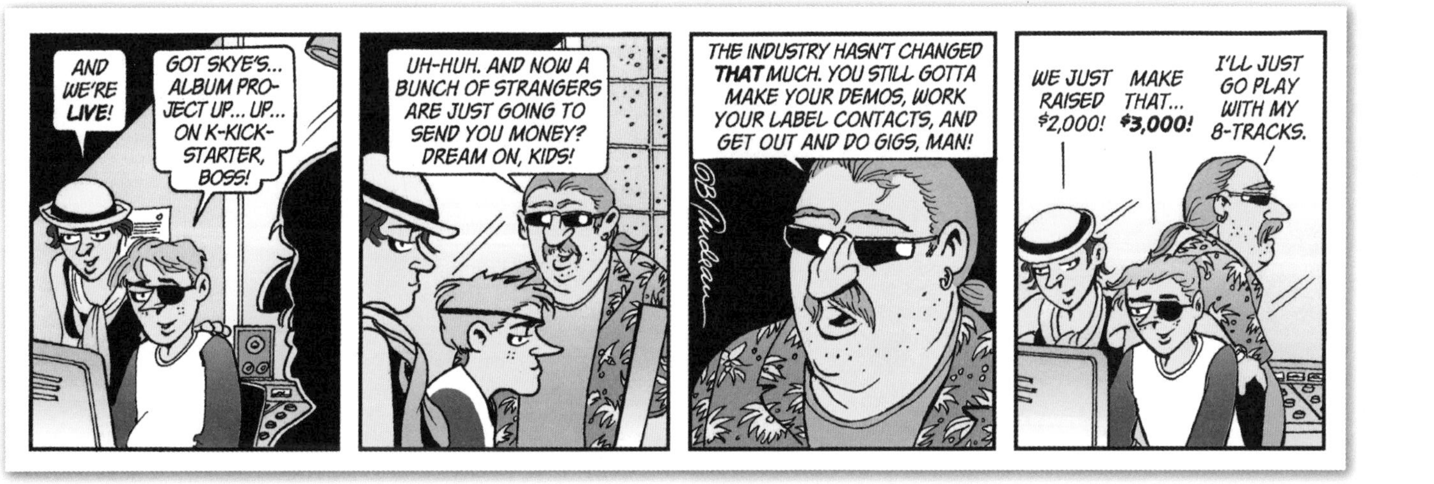
AND WE'RE LIVE!
GOT SKYE'S... ALBUM PRO-JECT UP... UP... ON K-KICK-STARTER, BOSS!
UH-HUH. AND NOW A BUNCH OF STRANGERS ARE JUST GOING TO SEND YOU MONEY? DREAM ON, KIDS!
THE INDUSTRY HASN'T CHANGED THAT MUCH. YOU STILL GOTTA MAKE YOUR DEMOS, WORK YOUR LABEL CONTACTS, AND GET OUT AND DO GIGS, MAN!
WE JUST RAISED $2,000!
MAKE THAT... $3,000!
I'LL JUST GO PLAY WITH MY 8-TRACKS.

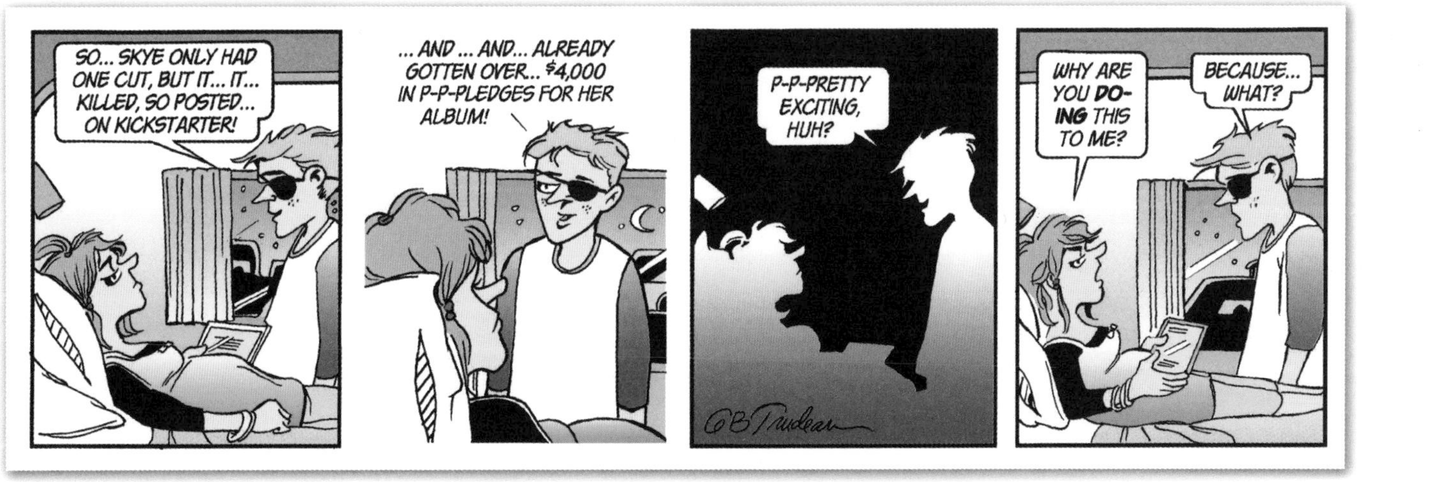
SO... SKYE ONLY HAD ONE CUT, BUT IT... IT... KILLED, SO POSTED... ON KICKSTARTER!
... AND ... AND... ALREADY GOTTEN OVER... $4,000 IN P-P-PLEDGES FOR HER ALBUM!
P-P-PRETTY EXCITING, HUH?
WHY ARE YOU DO-ING THIS TO ME?
BECAUSE... WHAT?

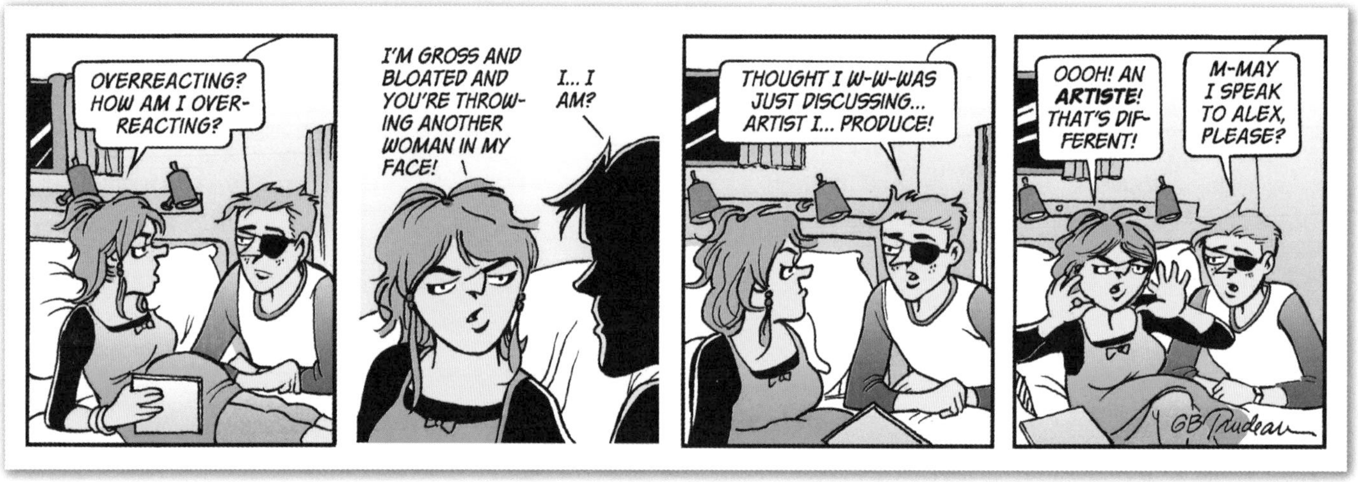
OVERREACTING? HOW AM I OVER-REACTING?
I'M GROSS AND BLOATED AND YOU'RE THROW-ING ANOTHER WOMAN IN MY FACE!
I... I AM?
THOUGHT I W-W-WAS JUST DISCUSSING... ARTIST I... PRODUCE!
OOOH! AN **ARTISTE**! THAT'S DIF-FERENT!
M-MAY I SPEAK TO ALEX, PLEASE?
GB Trudeau

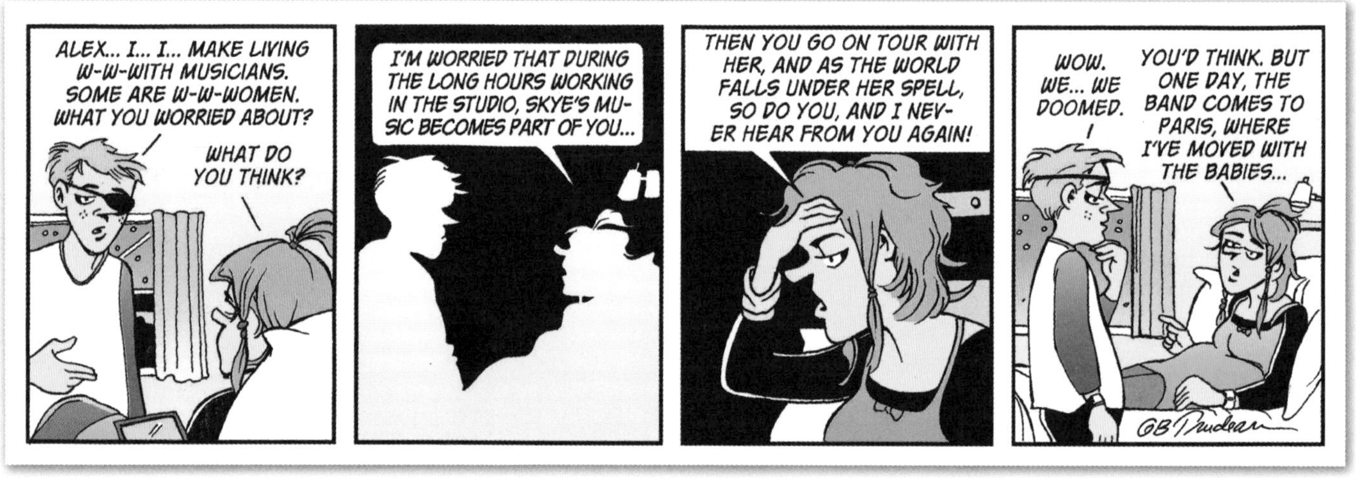
ALEX... I... I... MAKE LIVING W-W-WITH MUSICIANS. SOME ARE W-W-WOMEN. WHAT YOU WORRIED ABOUT?
WHAT DO YOU THINK?
I'M WORRIED THAT DURING THE LONG HOURS WORKING IN THE STUDIO, SKYE'S MU-SIC BECOMES PART OF YOU...
THEN YOU GO ON TOUR WITH HER, AND AS THE WORLD FALLS UNDER HER SPELL, SO DO YOU, AND I NEV-ER HEAR FROM YOU AGAIN!
WOW. WE... WE DOOMED.
YOU'D THINK. BUT ONE DAY, THE BAND COMES TO PARIS, WHERE I'VE MOVED WITH THE BABIES...
GB Trudeau

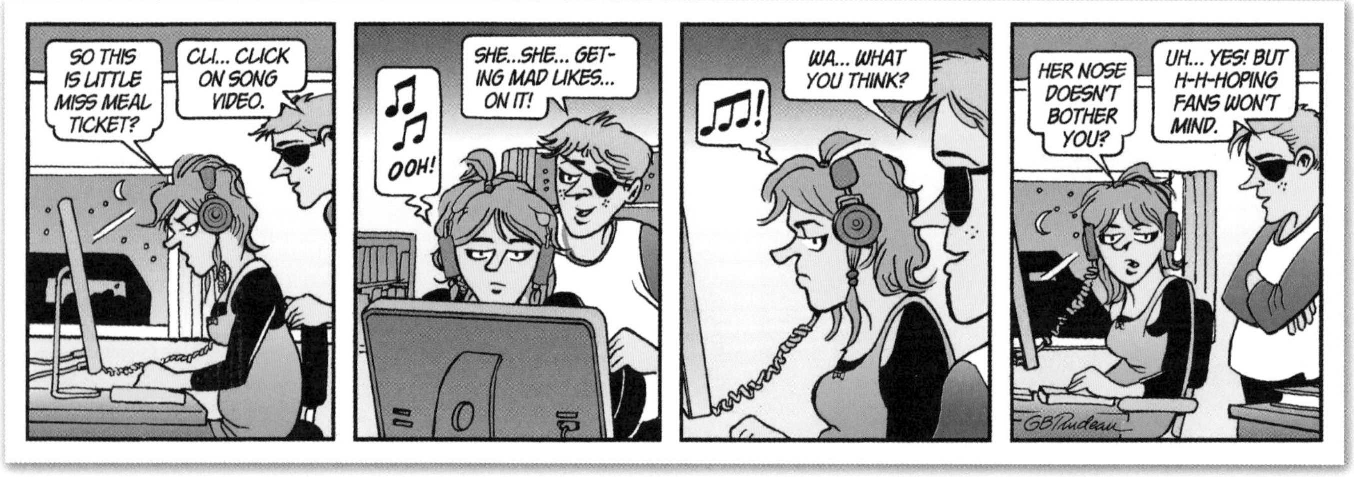
SO THIS IS LITTLE MISS MEAL TICKET?
CLI... CLICK ON SONG VIDEO.
OOH!
SHE...SHE... GET-ING MAD LIKES... ON IT!
WA... WHAT YOU THINK?
HER NOSE DOESN'T BOTHER YOU?
UH... YES! BUT H-H-HOPING FANS WON'T MIND.
GB Trudeau

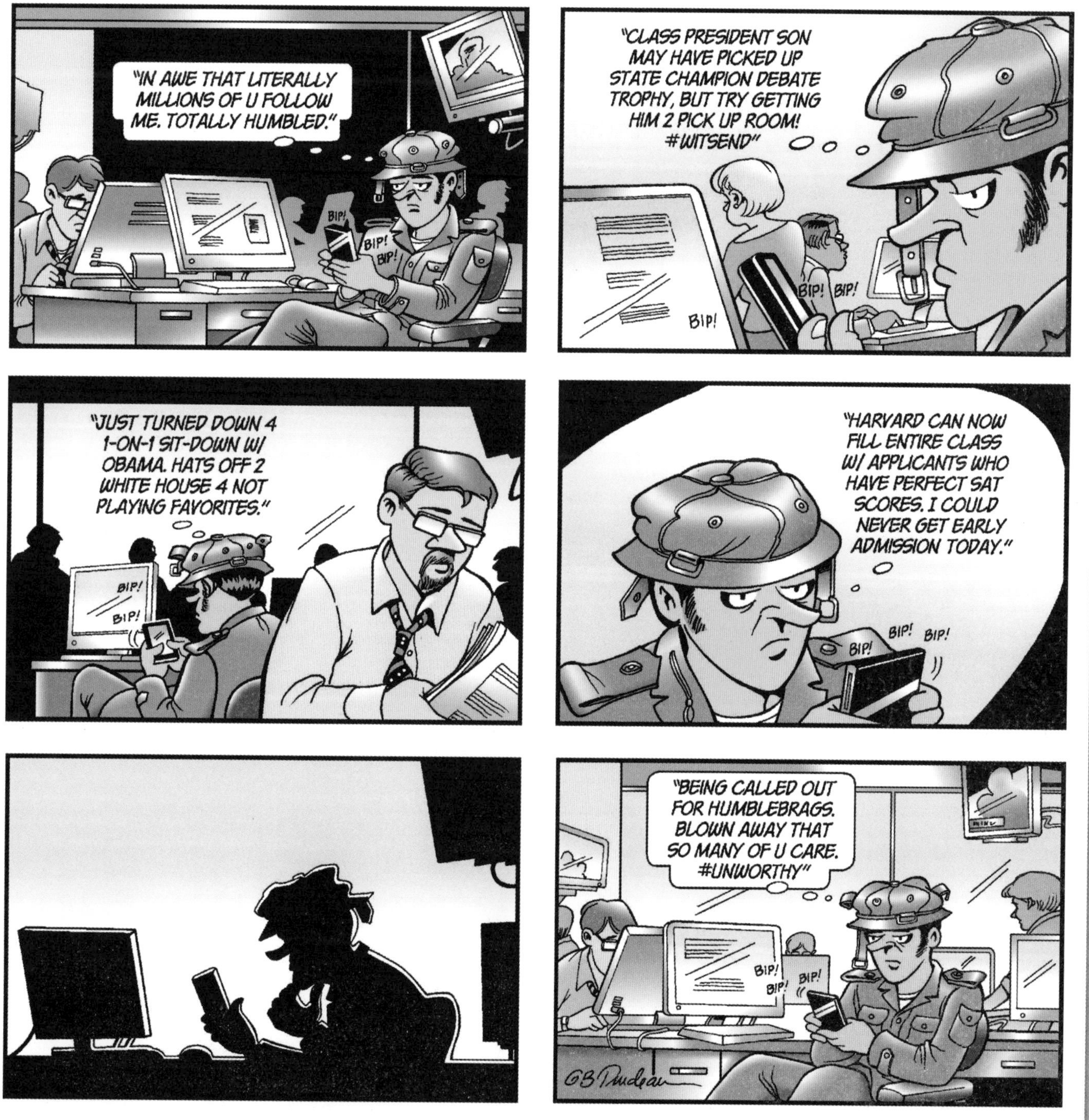
"IN AWE THAT LITERALLY MILLIONS OF U FOLLOW ME. TOTALLY HUMBLED."
BIP!
BIP!
BIP!
"CLASS PRESIDENT SON MAY HAVE PICKED UP STATE CHAMPION DEBATE TROPHY, BUT TRY GETTING HIM 2 PICK UP ROOM! #WITSEND"
BIP!
BIP!
BIP!
"JUST TURNED DOWN 4 1-ON-1 SIT-DOWN W/ OBAMA. HATS OFF 2 WHITE HOUSE 4 NOT PLAYING FAVORITES."
BIP!
BIP!
"HARVARD CAN NOW FILL ENTIRE CLASS W/ APPLICANTS WHO HAVE PERFECT SAT SCORES. I COULD NEVER GET EARLY ADMISSION TODAY."
BIP!
BIP!
BIP!
"BEING CALLED OUT FOR HUMBLEBRAGS. BLOWN AWAY THAT SO MANY OF U CARE. #UNWORTHY"
BIP!
BIP!
BIP!
GB Trudeau

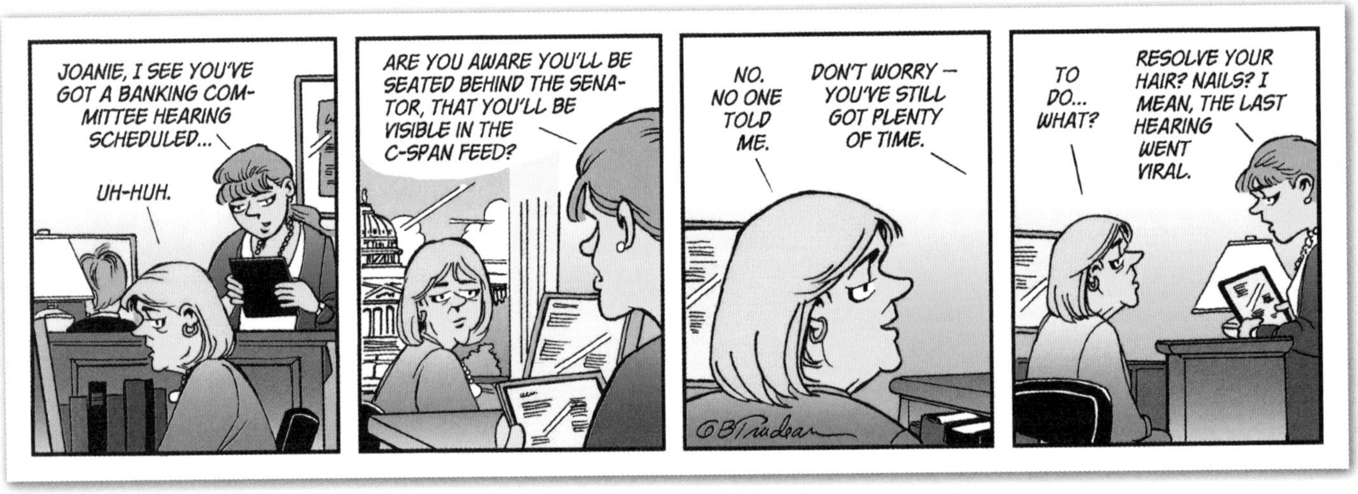
JOANIE, I SEE YOU'VE GOT A BANKING COMMITTEE HEARING SCHEDULED...
UH-HUH.
ARE YOU AWARE YOU'LL BE SEATED BEHIND THE SENATOR, THAT YOU'LL BE VISIBLE IN THE C-SPAN FEED?
NO. NO ONE TOLD ME.
DON'T WORRY — YOU'VE STILL GOT PLENTY OF TIME.
TO DO... WHAT?
RESOLVE YOUR HAIR? NAILS? I MEAN, THE LAST HEARING WENT VIRAL.

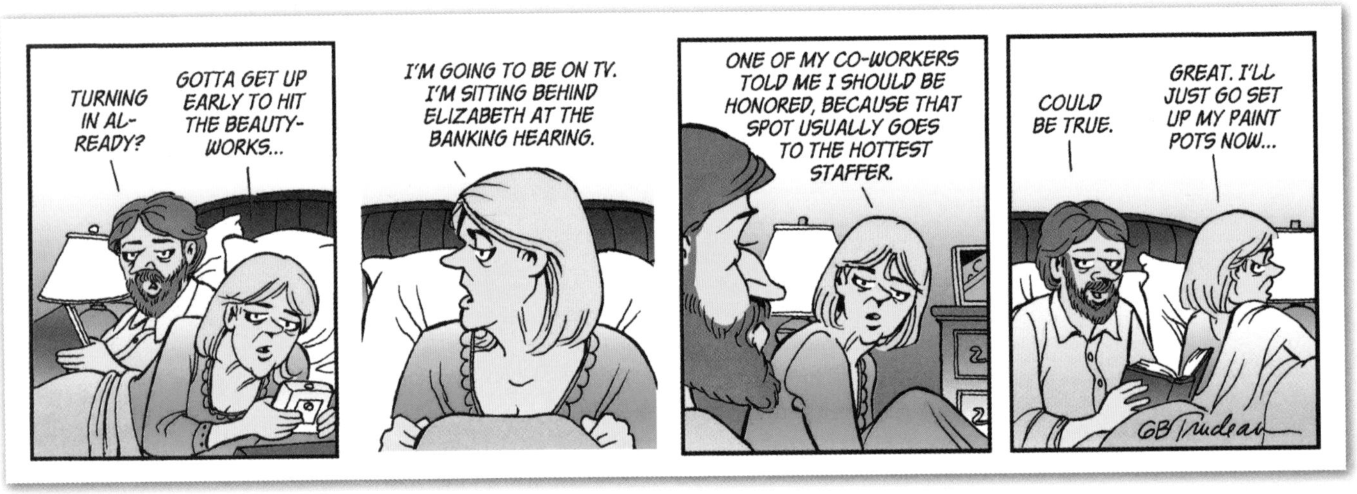
TURNING IN ALREADY?
GOTTA GET UP EARLY TO HIT THE BEAUTY-WORKS...
I'M GOING TO BE ON TV. I'M SITTING BEHIND ELIZABETH AT THE BANKING HEARING.
ONE OF MY CO-WORKERS TOLD ME I SHOULD BE HONORED, BECAUSE THAT SPOT USUALLY GOES TO THE HOTTEST STAFFER.
COULD BE TRUE.
GREAT. I'LL JUST GO SET UP MY PAINT POTS NOW...

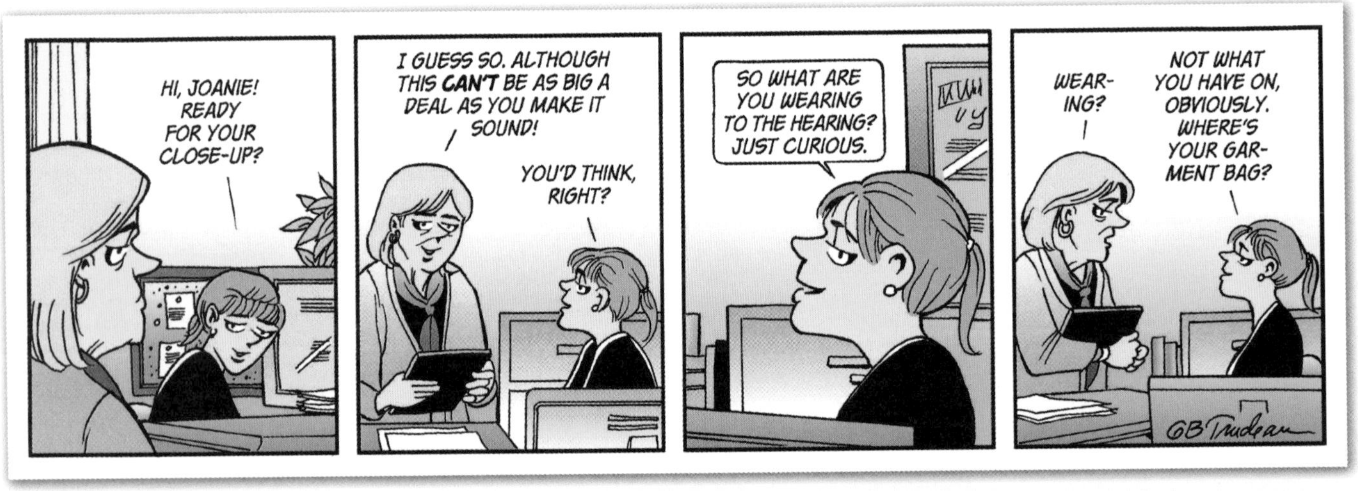
HI, JOANIE! READY FOR YOUR CLOSE-UP?
I GUESS SO. ALTHOUGH THIS **CAN'T** BE AS BIG A DEAL AS YOU MAKE IT SOUND!
YOU'D THINK, RIGHT?
SO WHAT ARE YOU WEARING TO THE HEARING? JUST CURIOUS.
WEARING?
NOT WHAT YOU HAVE ON, OBVIOUSLY. WHERE'S YOUR GARMENT BAG?

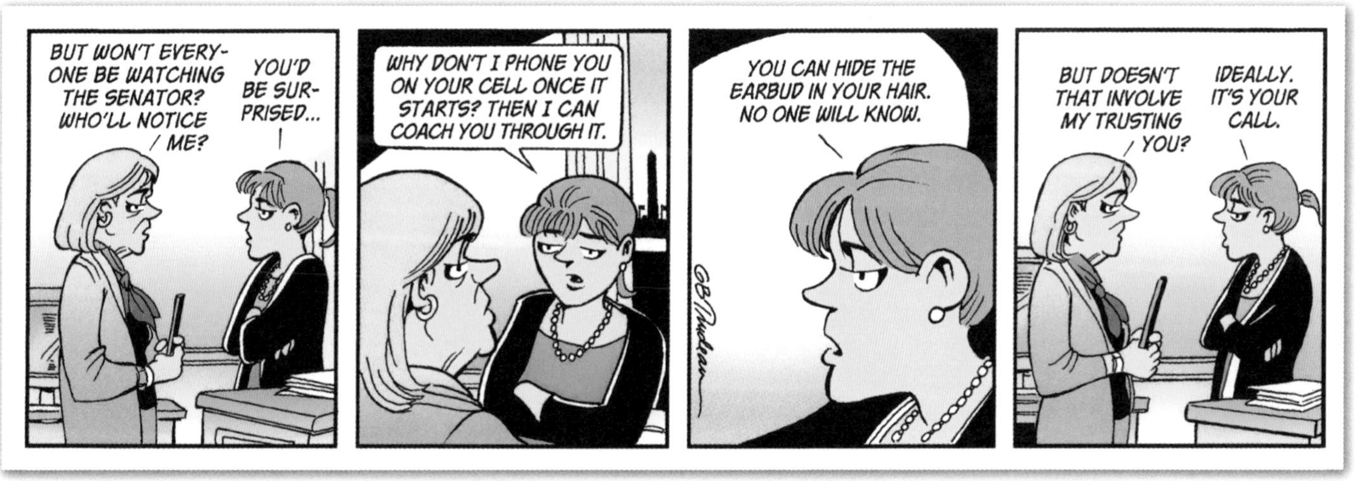
BUT WON'T EVERY-ONE BE WATCHING THE SENATOR? WHO'LL NOTICE ME?
YOU'D BE SUR-PRISED...
WHY DON'T I PHONE YOU ON YOUR CELL ONCE IT STARTS? THEN I CAN COACH YOU THROUGH IT.
YOU CAN HIDE THE EARBUD IN YOUR HAIR. NO ONE WILL KNOW.
BUT DOESN'T THAT INVOLVE MY TRUSTING YOU?
IDEALLY. IT'S YOUR CALL.

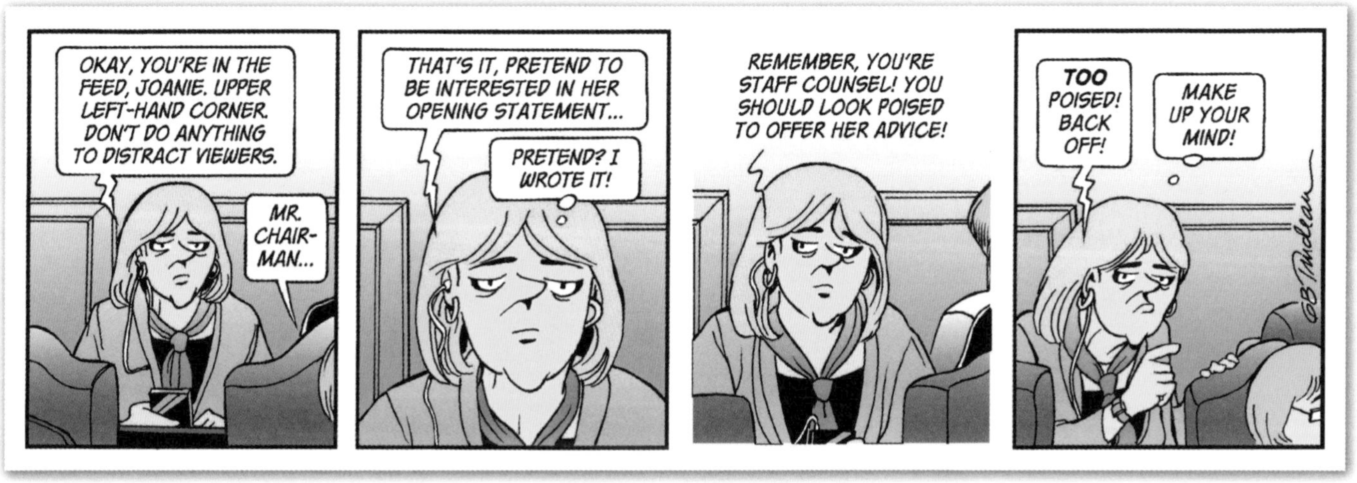
OKAY, YOU'RE IN THE FEED, JOANIE. UPPER LEFT-HAND CORNER. DON'T DO ANYTHING TO DISTRACT VIEWERS.
MR. CHAIR-MAN...
THAT'S IT, PRETEND TO BE INTERESTED IN HER OPENING STATEMENT...
PRETEND? I WROTE IT!
REMEMBER, YOU'RE STAFF COUNSEL! YOU SHOULD LOOK POISED TO OFFER HER ADVICE!
TOO POISED! BACK OFF!
MAKE UP YOUR MIND!

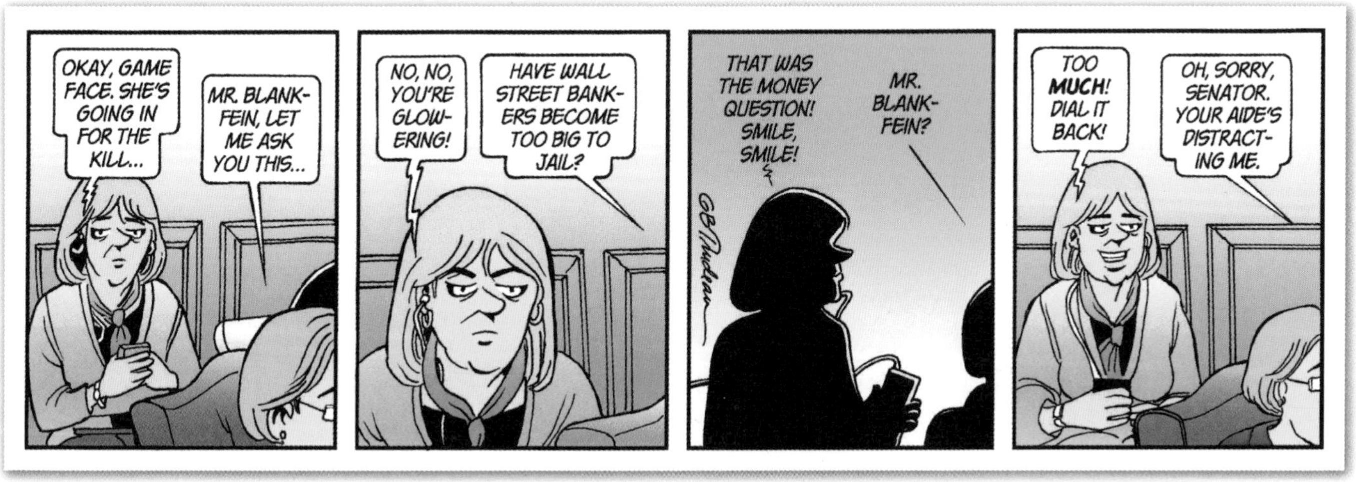
OKAY, GAME FACE. SHE'S GOING IN FOR THE KILL...
MR. BLANK-FEIN, LET ME ASK YOU THIS...
NO, NO, YOU'RE GLOW-ERING!
HAVE WALL STREET BANK-ERS BECOME TOO BIG TO JAIL?
THAT WAS THE MONEY QUESTION! SMILE, SMILE!
MR. BLANK-FEIN?
TOO **MUCH**! DIAL IT BACK!
OH, SORRY, SENATOR. YOUR AIDE'S DISTRACT-ING ME.

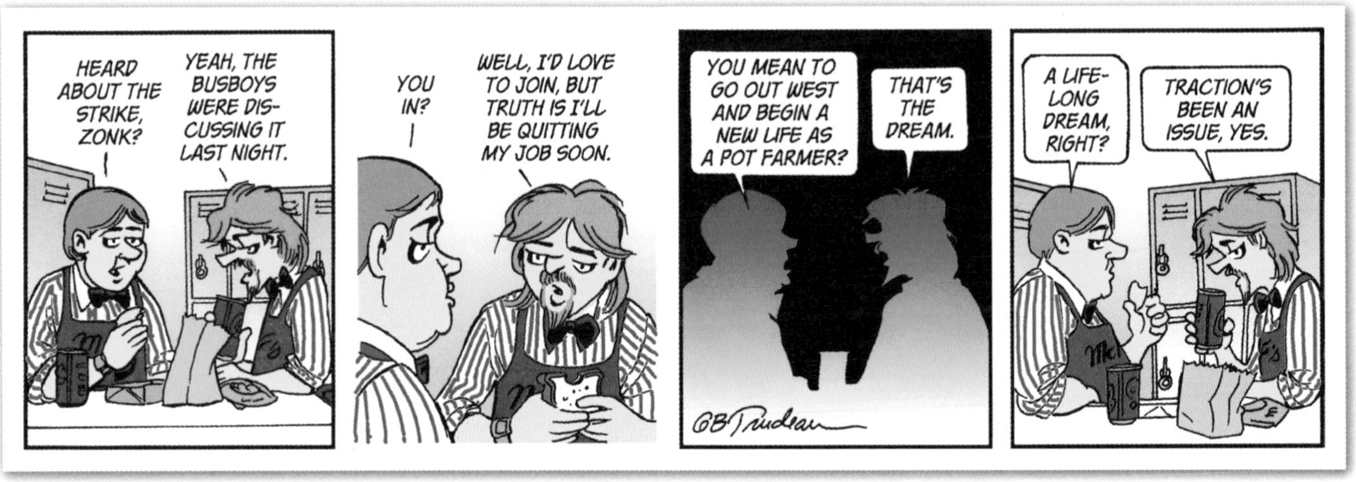
HEARD ABOUT THE STRIKE, ZONK?
YEAH, THE BUSBOYS WERE DISCUSSING IT LAST NIGHT.
YOU IN?
WELL, I'D LOVE TO JOIN, BUT TRUTH IS I'LL BE QUITTING MY JOB SOON.
YOU MEAN TO GO OUT WEST AND BEGIN A NEW LIFE AS A POT FARMER?
THAT'S THE DREAM.
A LIFE-LONG DREAM, RIGHT?
TRACTION'S BEEN AN ISSUE, YES.

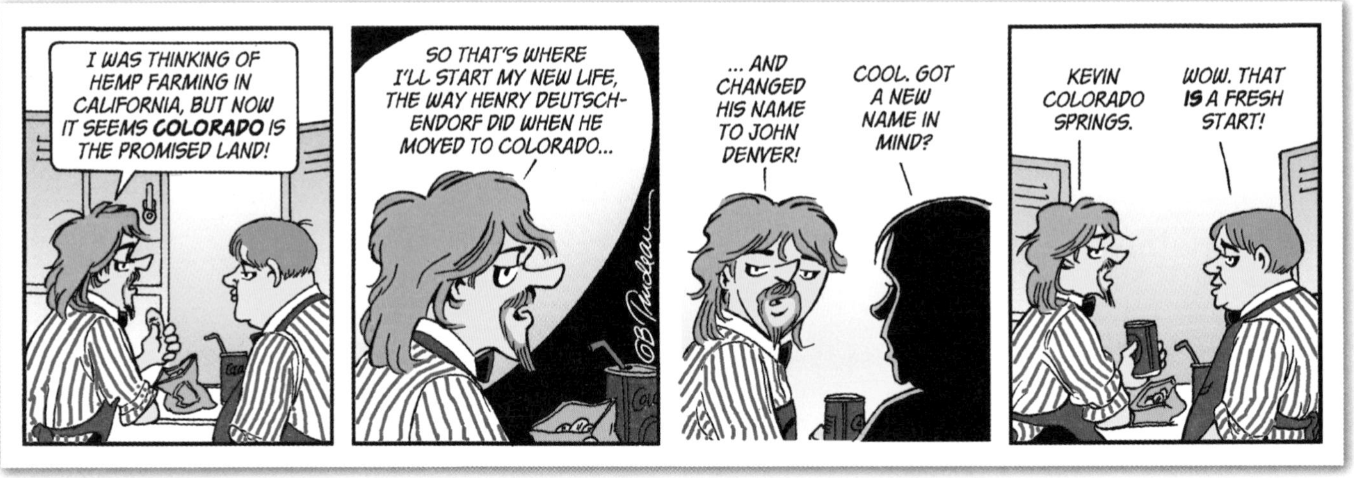
I WAS THINKING OF HEMP FARMING IN CALIFORNIA, BUT NOW IT SEEMS **COLORADO** IS THE PROMISED LAND!
SO THAT'S WHERE I'LL START MY NEW LIFE, THE WAY HENRY DEUTSCHENDORF DID WHEN HE MOVED TO COLORADO...
...AND CHANGED HIS NAME TO JOHN DENVER!
COOL. GOT A NEW NAME IN MIND?
KEVIN COLORADO SPRINGS.
WOW. THAT **IS** A FRESH START!

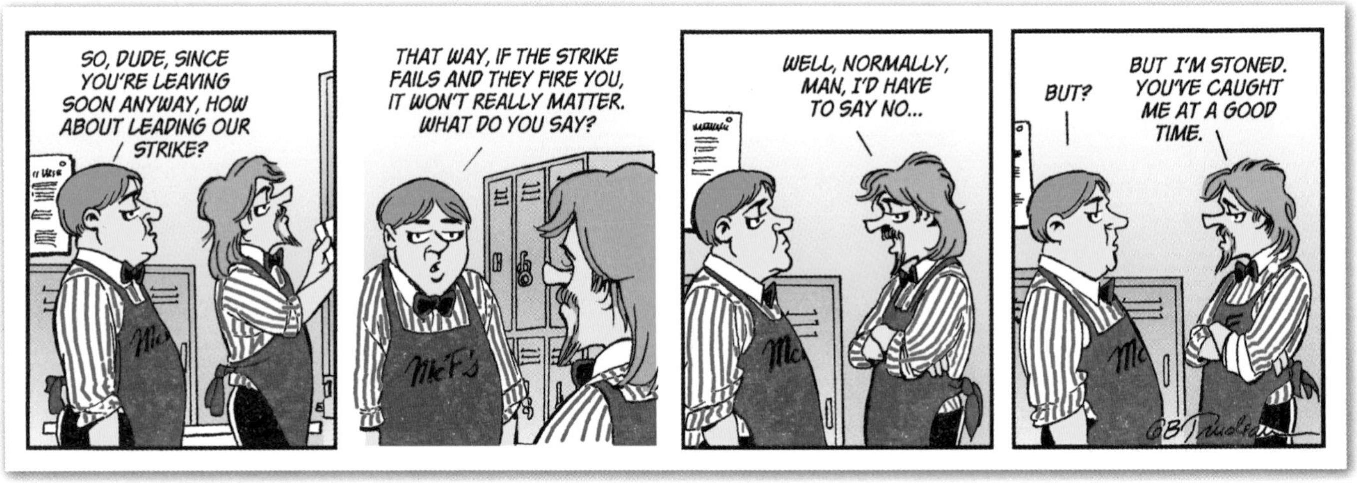
SO, DUDE, SINCE YOU'RE LEAVING SOON ANYWAY, HOW ABOUT LEADING OUR STRIKE?
THAT WAY, IF THE STRIKE FAILS AND THEY FIRE YOU, IT WON'T REALLY MATTER. WHAT DO YOU SAY?
WELL, NORMALLY, MAN, I'D HAVE TO SAY NO...
BUT?
BUT I'M STONED. YOU'VE CAUGHT ME AT A GOOD TIME.

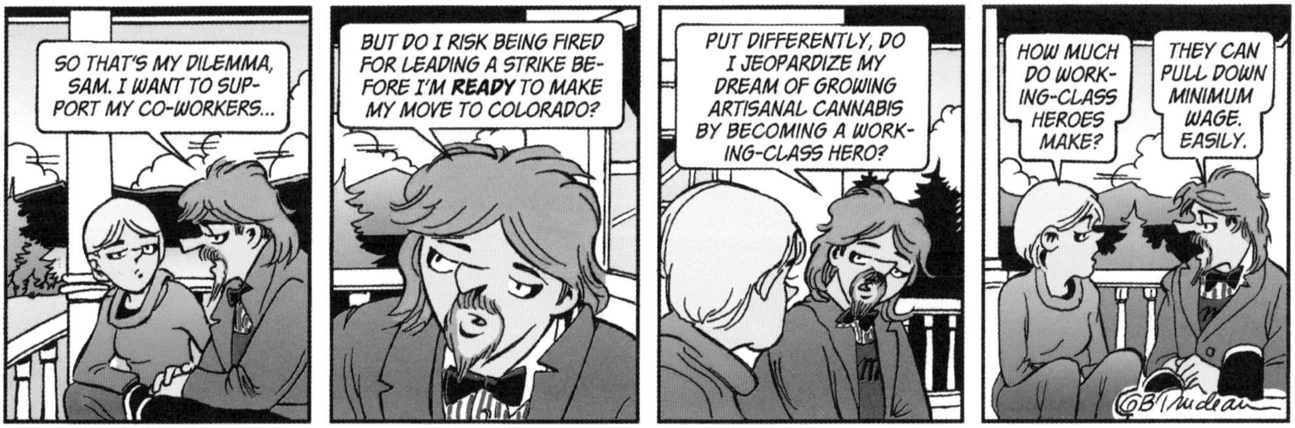
SO THAT'S MY DILEMMA, SAM. I WANT TO SUPPORT MY CO-WORKERS...
BUT DO I RISK BEING FIRED FOR LEADING A STRIKE BEFORE I'M **READY** TO MAKE MY MOVE TO COLORADO?
PUT DIFFERENTLY, DO I JEOPARDIZE MY DREAM OF GROWING ARTISANAL CANNABIS BY BECOMING A WORKING-CLASS HERO?
HOW MUCH DO WORKING-CLASS HEROES MAKE?
THEY CAN PULL DOWN MINIMUM WAGE. EASILY.

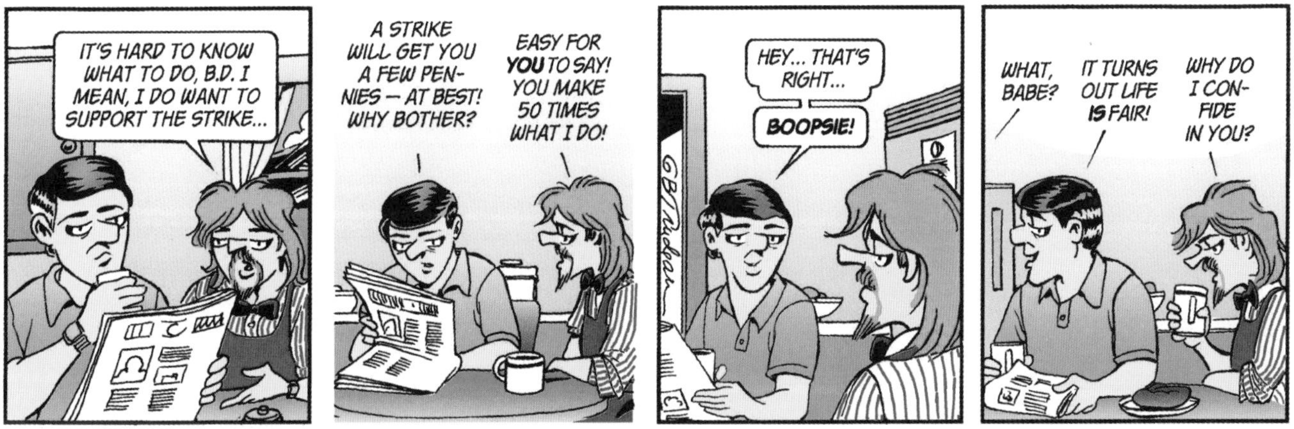
IT'S HARD TO KNOW WHAT TO DO, B.D. I MEAN, I DO WANT TO SUPPORT THE STRIKE...
A STRIKE WILL GET YOU A FEW PENNIES — AT BEST! WHY BOTHER?
EASY FOR **YOU** TO SAY! YOU MAKE 50 TIMES WHAT I DO!
HEY... THAT'S RIGHT...
BOOPSIE!
WHAT, BABE?
IT TURNS OUT LIFE **IS** FAIR!
WHY DO I CONFIDE IN YOU?

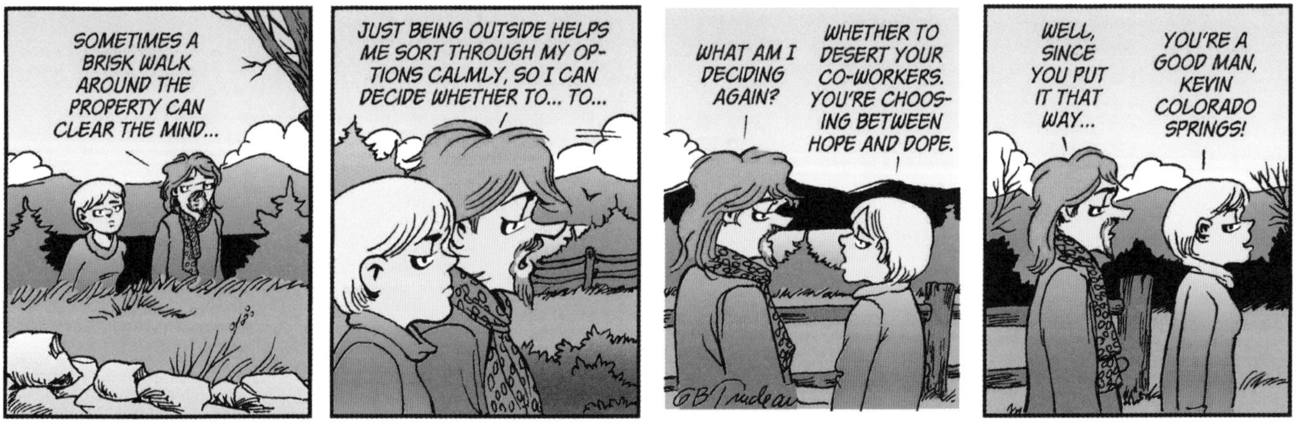
SOMETIMES A BRISK WALK AROUND THE PROPERTY CAN CLEAR THE MIND...
JUST BEING OUTSIDE HELPS ME SORT THROUGH MY OPTIONS CALMLY, SO I CAN DECIDE WHETHER TO... TO...
WHAT AM I DECIDING AGAIN?
WHETHER TO DESERT YOUR CO-WORKERS. YOU'RE CHOOSING BETWEEN HOPE AND DOPE.
WELL, SINCE YOU PUT IT THAT WAY...
YOU'RE A GOOD MAN, KEVIN COLORADO SPRINGS!

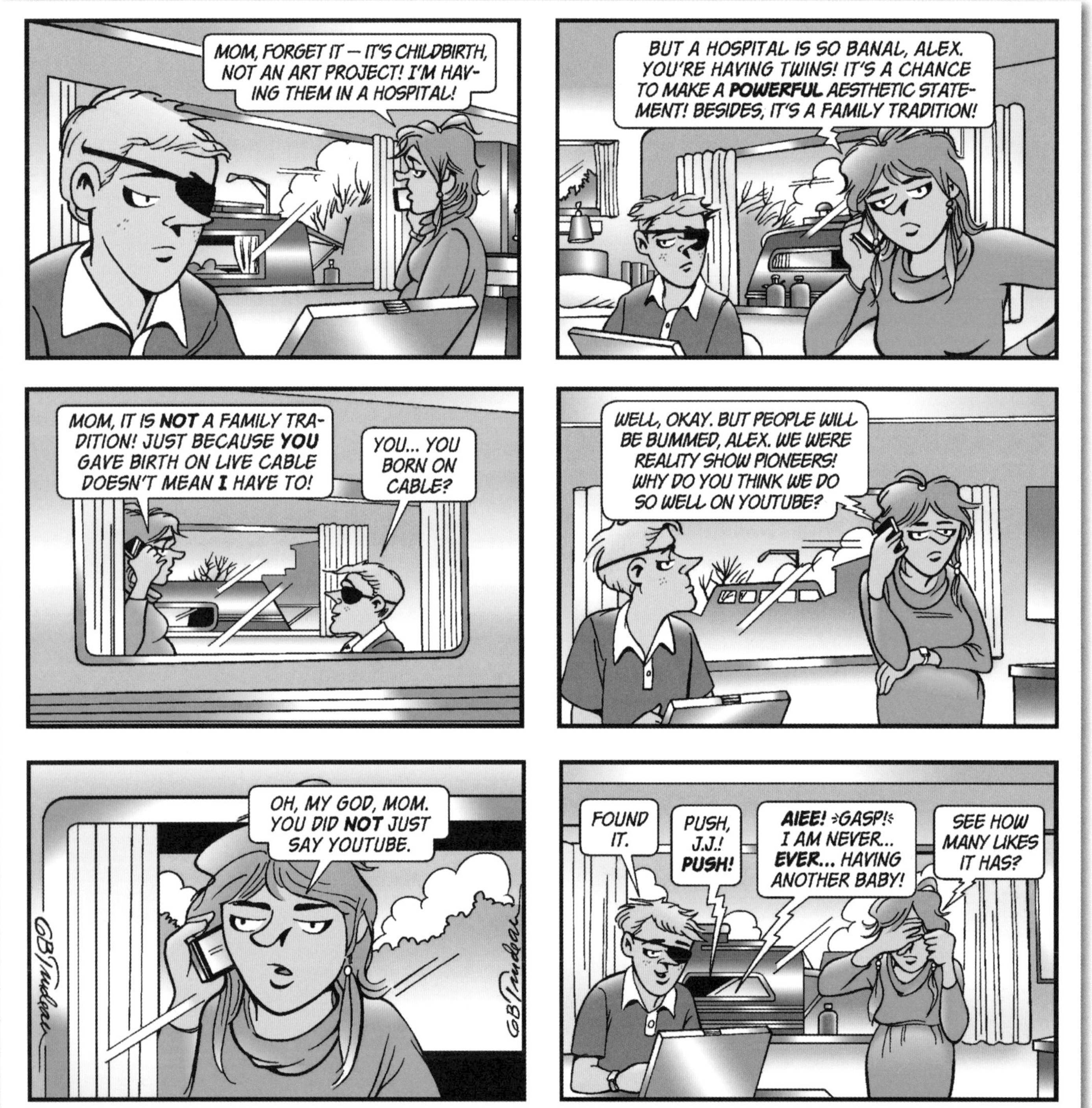
MOM, FORGET IT — IT'S CHILDBIRTH, NOT AN ART PROJECT! I'M HAVING THEM IN A HOSPITAL!
BUT A HOSPITAL IS SO BANAL, ALEX. YOU'RE HAVING TWINS! IT'S A CHANCE TO MAKE A **POWERFUL** AESTHETIC STATEMENT! BESIDES, IT'S A FAMILY TRADITION!
MOM, IT IS **NOT** A FAMILY TRADITION! JUST BECAUSE **YOU** GAVE BIRTH ON LIVE CABLE DOESN'T MEAN **I** HAVE TO!
YOU... YOU BORN ON CABLE?
WELL, OKAY. BUT PEOPLE WILL BE BUMMED, ALEX. WE WERE REALITY SHOW PIONEERS! WHY DO YOU THINK WE DO SO WELL ON YOUTUBE?
OH, MY GOD, MOM. YOU DID **NOT** JUST SAY YOUTUBE.
GBTrudeau
FOUND IT.
PUSH, J.J.! **PUSH!**
AIEE! GASP! I AM NEVER... **EVER...** HAVING ANOTHER BABY!
SEE HOW MANY LIKES IT HAS?

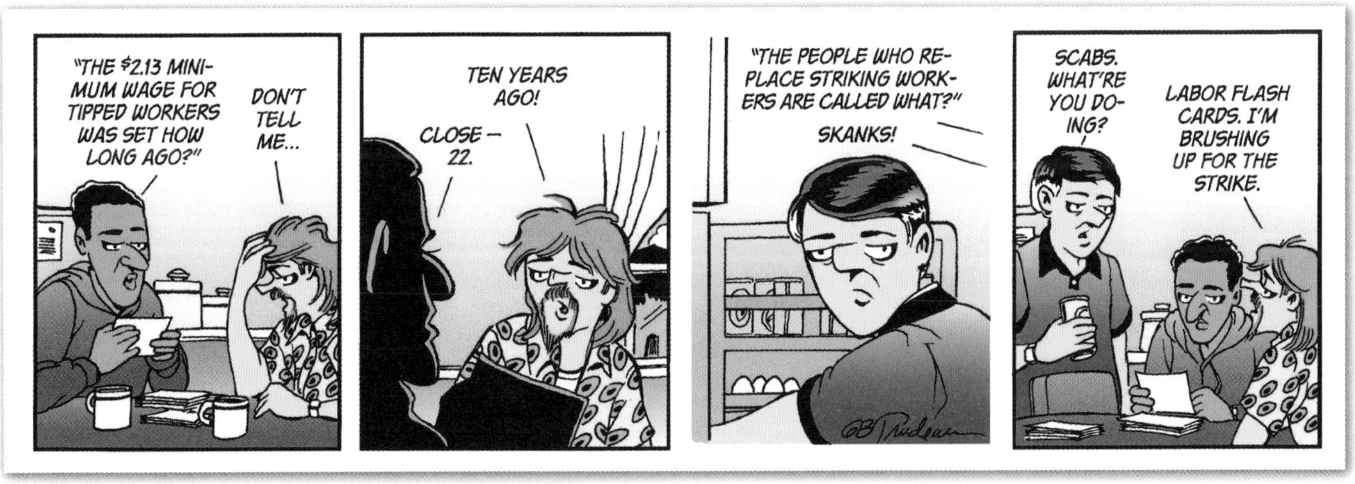
"THE $2.13 MINIMUM WAGE FOR TIPPED WORKERS WAS SET HOW LONG AGO?"
DON'T TELL ME...
CLOSE — 22.
TEN YEARS AGO!
"THE PEOPLE WHO REPLACE STRIKING WORKERS ARE CALLED WHAT?"
SKANKS!
SCABS. WHAT'RE YOU DOING?
LABOR FLASH CARDS. I'M BRUSHING UP FOR THE STRIKE.

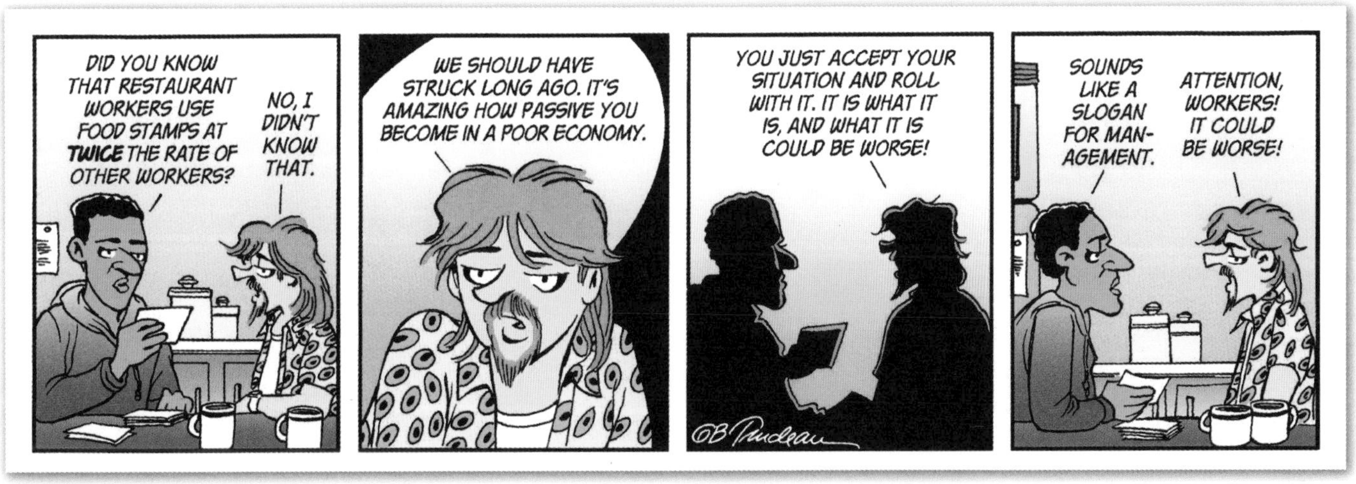
DID YOU KNOW THAT RESTAURANT WORKERS USE FOOD STAMPS AT TWICE THE RATE OF OTHER WORKERS?
NO, I DIDN'T KNOW THAT.
WE SHOULD HAVE STRUCK LONG AGO. IT'S AMAZING HOW PASSIVE YOU BECOME IN A POOR ECONOMY.
YOU JUST ACCEPT YOUR SITUATION AND ROLL WITH IT. IT IS WHAT IT IS, AND WHAT IT IS COULD BE WORSE!
SOUNDS LIKE A SLOGAN FOR MANAGEMENT.
ATTENTION, WORKERS! IT COULD BE WORSE!

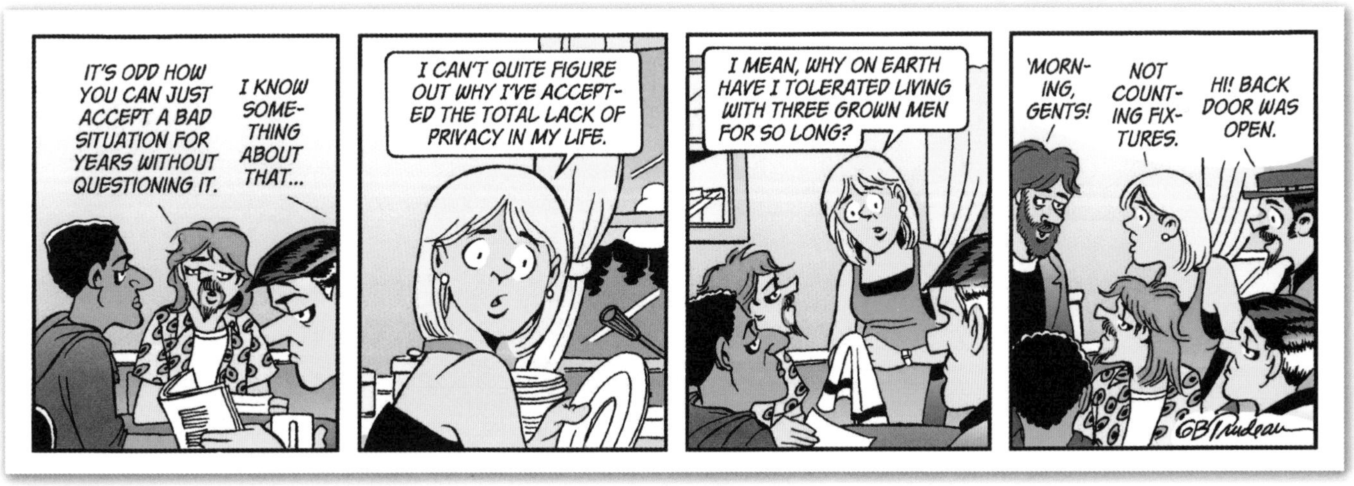
IT'S ODD HOW YOU CAN JUST ACCEPT A BAD SITUATION FOR YEARS WITHOUT QUESTIONING IT.
I KNOW SOMETHING ABOUT THAT...
I CAN'T QUITE FIGURE OUT WHY I'VE ACCEPTED THE TOTAL LACK OF PRIVACY IN MY LIFE.
I MEAN, WHY ON EARTH HAVE I TOLERATED LIVING WITH THREE GROWN MEN FOR SO LONG?
'MORNING, GENTS!
NOT COUNTING FIXTURES.
HI! BACK DOOR WAS OPEN.

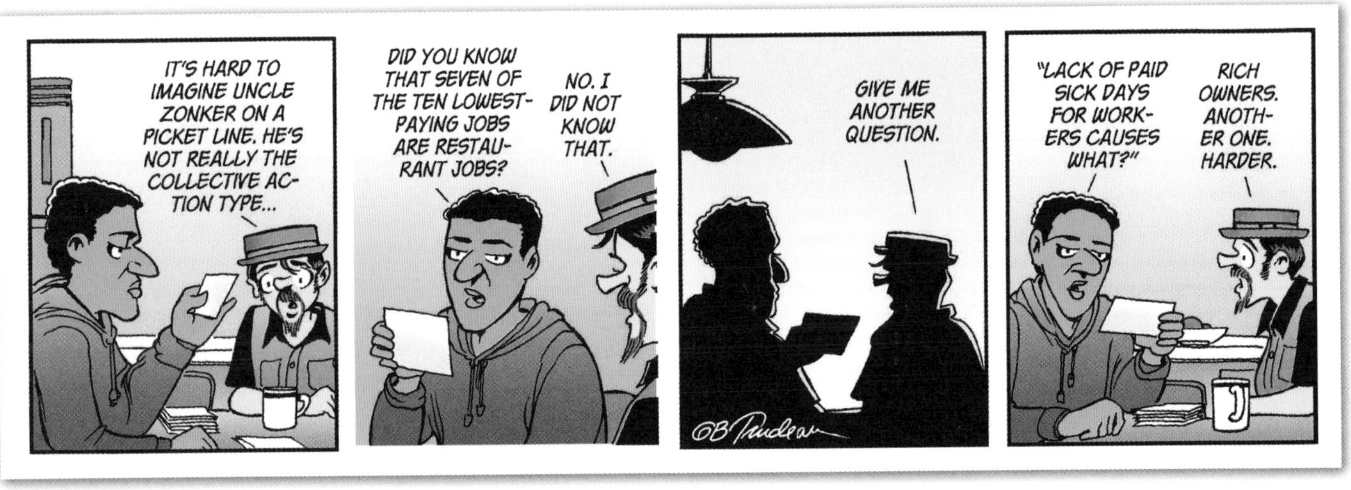
IT'S HARD TO IMAGINE UNCLE ZONKER ON A PICKET LINE. HE'S NOT REALLY THE COLLECTIVE ACTION TYPE...
DID YOU KNOW THAT SEVEN OF THE TEN LOWEST-PAYING JOBS ARE RESTAURANT JOBS?
NO. I DID NOT KNOW THAT.
GIVE ME ANOTHER QUESTION.
"LACK OF PAID SICK DAYS FOR WORKERS CAUSES WHAT?"
RICH OWNERS. ANOTHER ONE. HARDER.

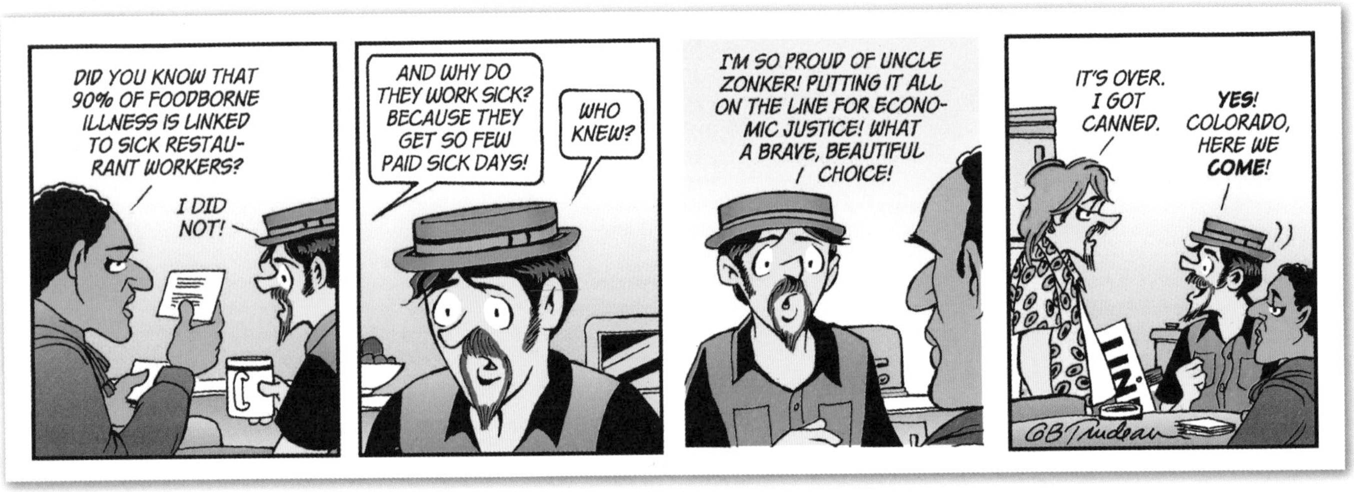
DID YOU KNOW THAT 90% OF FOODBORNE ILLNESS IS LINKED TO SICK RESTAURANT WORKERS?
I DID NOT!
AND WHY DO THEY WORK SICK? BECAUSE THEY GET SO FEW PAID SICK DAYS!
WHO KNEW?
I'M SO PROUD OF UNCLE ZONKER! PUTTING IT ALL ON THE LINE FOR ECONOMIC JUSTICE! WHAT A BRAVE, BEAUTIFUL CHOICE!
IT'S OVER. I GOT CANNED.
YES! COLORADO, HERE WE COME!

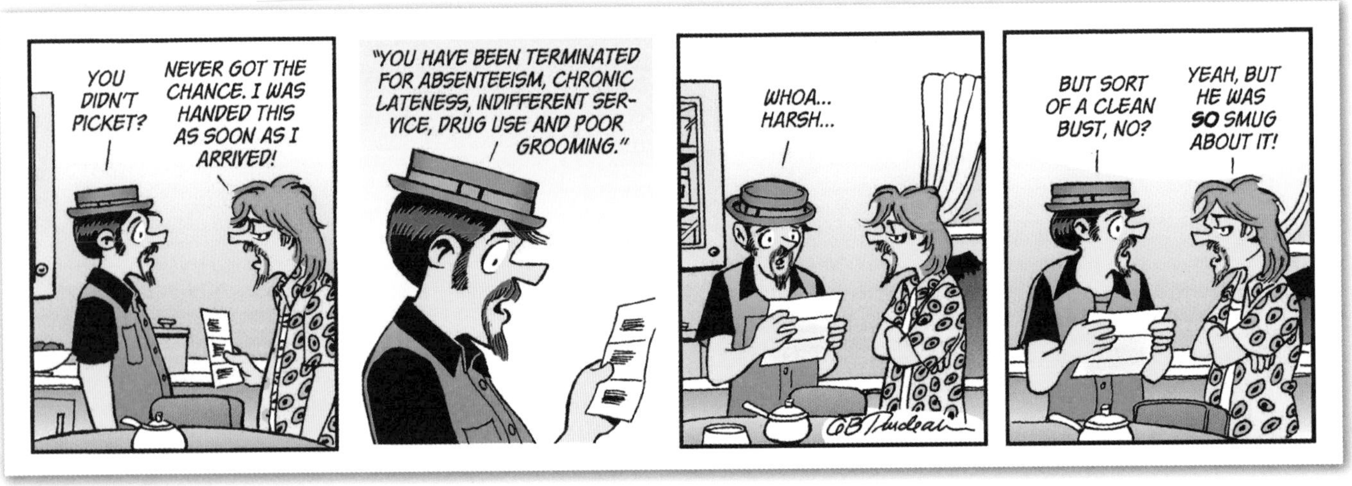
YOU DIDN'T PICKET?
NEVER GOT THE CHANCE. I WAS HANDED THIS AS SOON AS I ARRIVED!
"YOU HAVE BEEN TERMINATED FOR ABSENTEEISM, CHRONIC LATENESS, INDIFFERENT SERVICE, DRUG USE AND POOR GROOMING."
WHOA... HARSH...
BUT SORT OF A CLEAN BUST, NO?
YEAH, BUT HE WAS SO SMUG ABOUT IT!

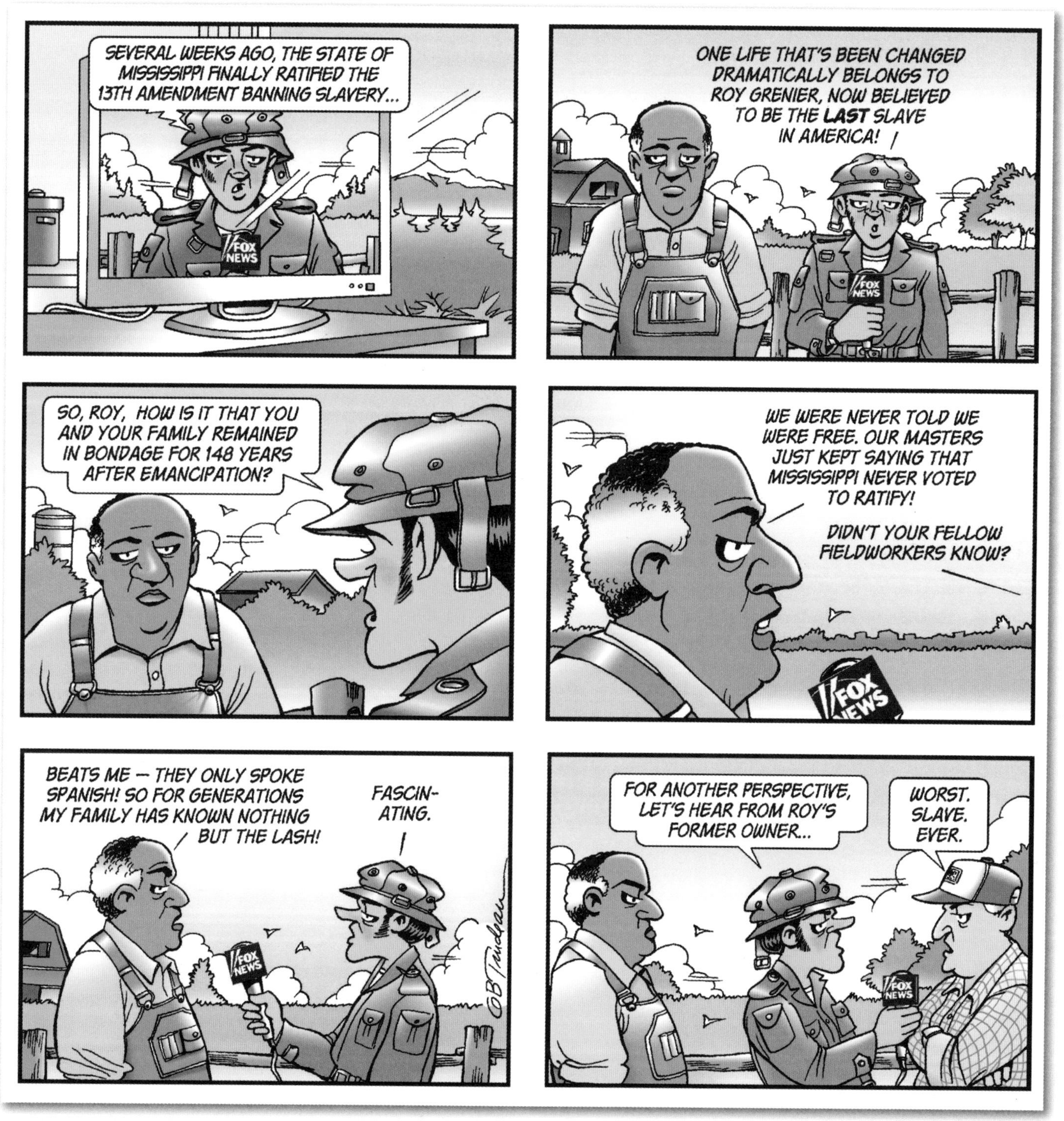
SEVERAL WEEKS AGO, THE STATE OF MISSISSIPPI FINALLY RATIFIED THE 13TH AMENDMENT BANNING SLAVERY...
ONE LIFE THAT'S BEEN CHANGED DRAMATICALLY BELONGS TO ROY GRENIER, NOW BELIEVED TO BE THE **LAST** SLAVE IN AMERICA!
SO, ROY, HOW IS IT THAT YOU AND YOUR FAMILY REMAINED IN BONDAGE FOR 148 YEARS AFTER EMANCIPATION?
WE WERE NEVER TOLD WE WERE FREE. OUR MASTERS JUST KEPT SAYING THAT MISSISSIPPI NEVER VOTED TO RATIFY!
DIDN'T YOUR FELLOW FIELDWORKERS KNOW?
BEATS ME — THEY ONLY SPOKE SPANISH! SO FOR GENERATIONS MY FAMILY HAS KNOWN NOTHING BUT THE LASH!
FASCIN-ATING.
FOR ANOTHER PERSPECTIVE, LET'S HEAR FROM ROY'S FORMER OWNER...
WORST. SLAVE. EVER.
FOX NEWS

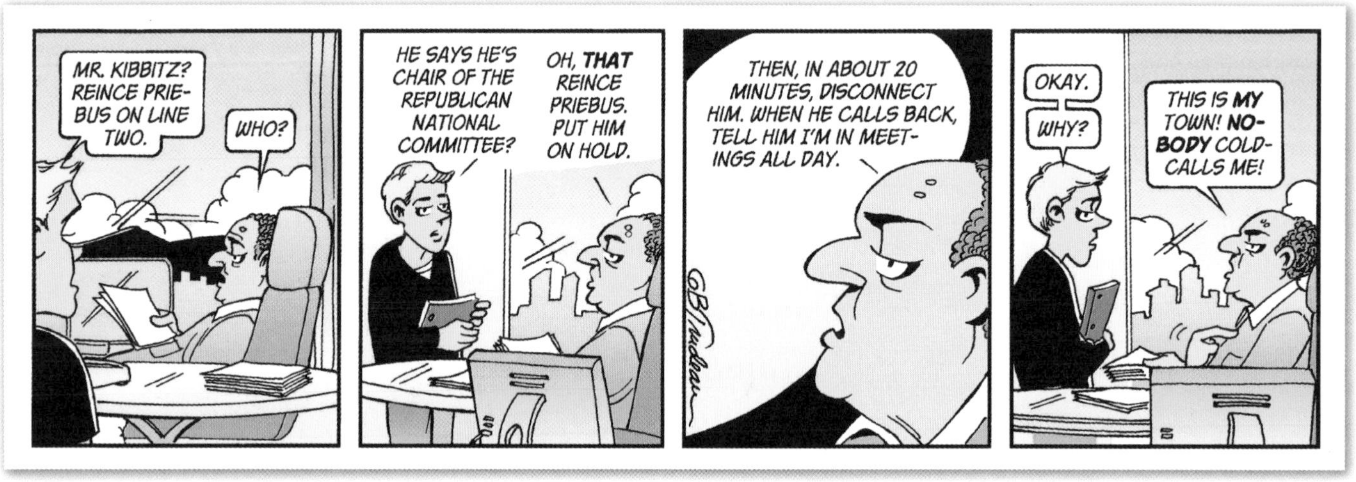
MR. KIBBITZ? REINCE PRIE-BUS ON LINE TWO.
WHO?
HE SAYS HE'S CHAIR OF THE REPUBLICAN NATIONAL COMMITTEE?
OH, THAT REINCE PRIEBUS. PUT HIM ON HOLD.
THEN, IN ABOUT 20 MINUTES, DISCONNECT HIM. WHEN HE CALLS BACK, TELL HIM I'M IN MEET-INGS ALL DAY.
OKAY.
WHY?
THIS IS MY TOWN! NO-BODY COLD-CALLS ME!

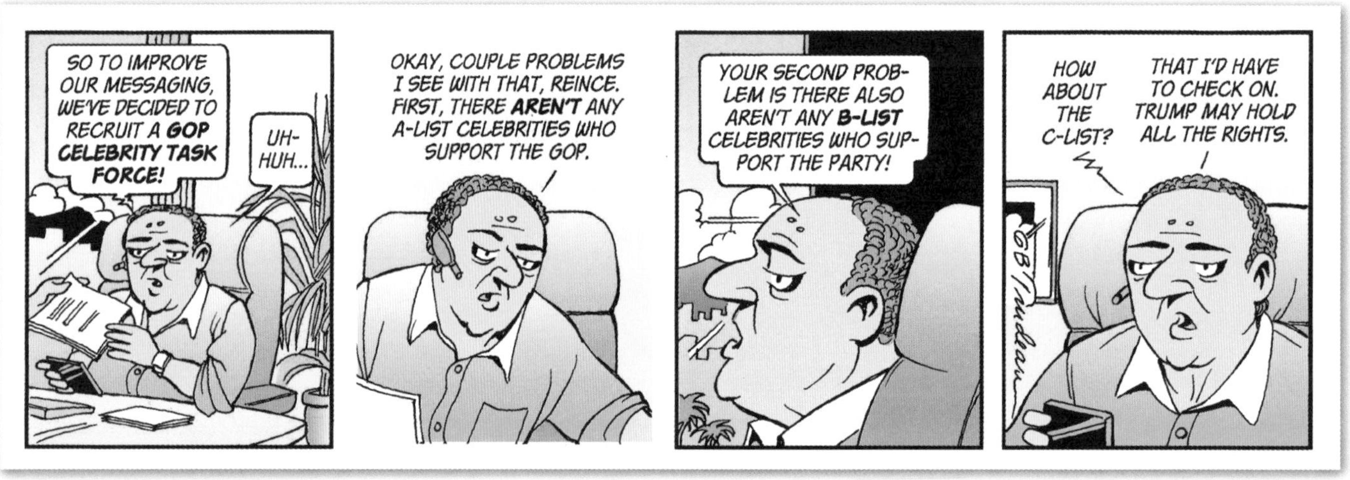
SO TO IMPROVE OUR MESSAGING, WE'VE DECIDED TO RECRUIT A GOP CELEBRITY TASK FORCE!
UH-HUH...
OKAY, COUPLE PROBLEMS I SEE WITH THAT, REINCE. FIRST, THERE AREN'T ANY A-LIST CELEBRITIES WHO SUPPORT THE GOP.
YOUR SECOND PROB-LEM IS THERE ALSO AREN'T ANY B-LIST CELEBRITIES WHO SUP-PORT THE PARTY!
HOW ABOUT THE C-LIST?
THAT I'D HAVE TO CHECK ON. TRUMP MAY HOLD ALL THE RIGHTS.

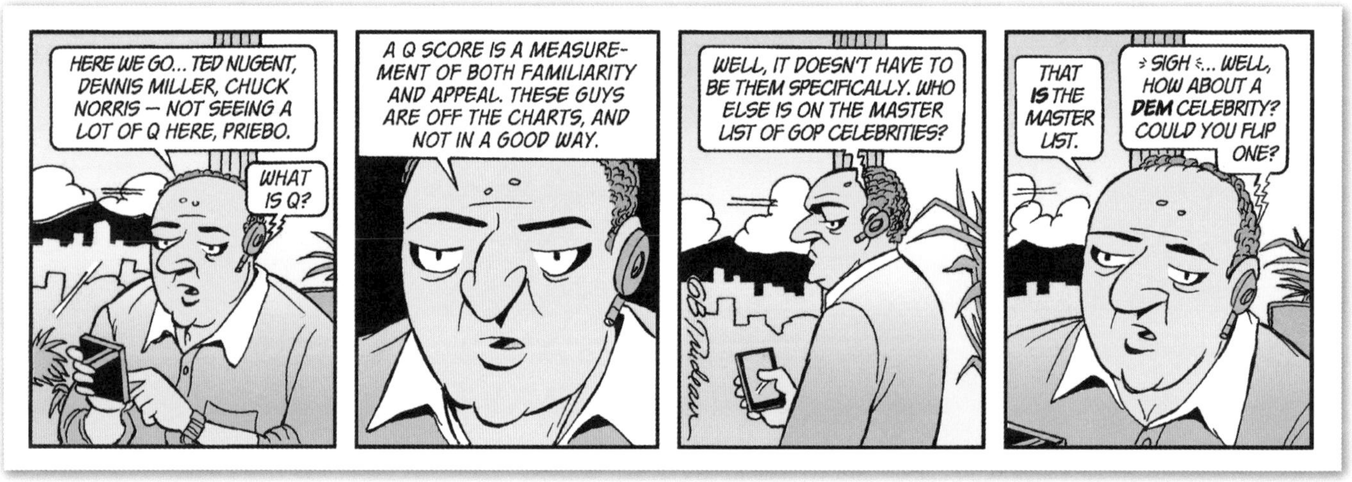
HERE WE GO... TED NUGENT, DENNIS MILLER, CHUCK NORRIS — NOT SEEING A LOT OF Q HERE, PRIEBO.
WHAT IS Q?
A Q SCORE IS A MEASURE-MENT OF BOTH FAMILIARITY AND APPEAL. THESE GUYS ARE OFF THE CHARTS, AND NOT IN A GOOD WAY.
WELL, IT DOESN'T HAVE TO BE THEM SPECIFICALLY. WHO ELSE IS ON THE MASTER LIST OF GOP CELEBRITIES?
THAT IS THE MASTER LIST.
SIGH... WELL, HOW ABOUT A DEM CELEBRITY? COULD YOU FLIP ONE?

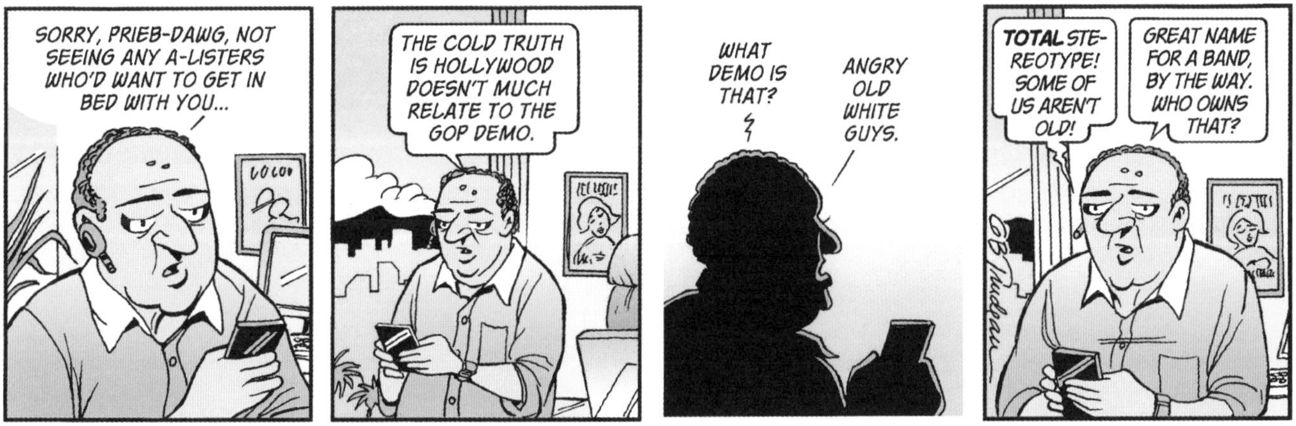
SORRY, PRIEB-DAWG, NOT SEEING ANY A-LISTERS WHO'D WANT TO GET IN BED WITH YOU...
THE COLD TRUTH IS HOLLYWOOD DOESN'T MUCH RELATE TO THE GOP DEMO.
WHAT DEMO IS THAT?
ANGRY OLD WHITE GUYS.
TOTAL STEREOTYPE! SOME OF US AREN'T OLD!
GREAT NAME FOR A BAND, BY THE WAY. WHO OWNS THAT?
GB Trudeau

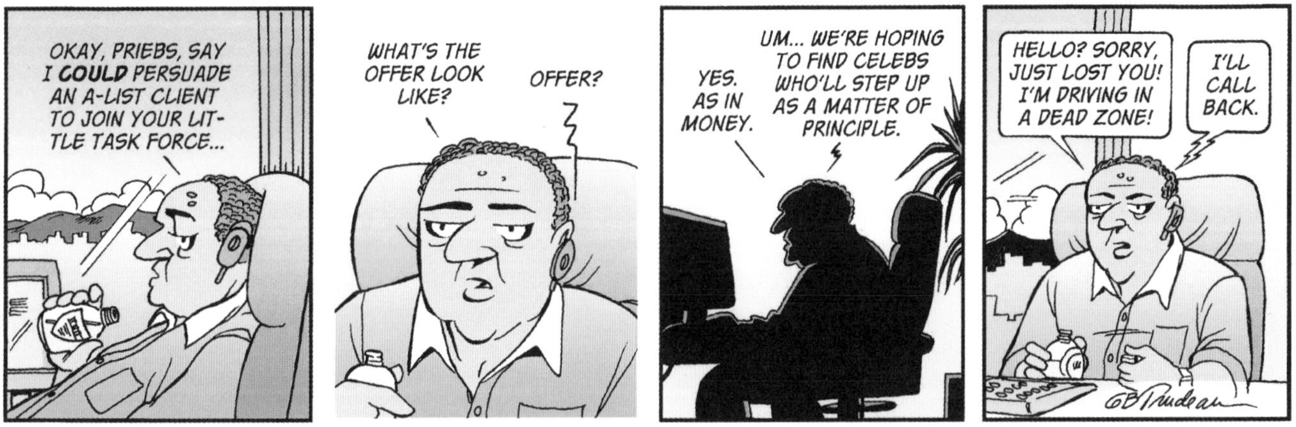
OKAY, PRIEBS, SAY I **COULD** PERSUADE AN A-LIST CLIENT TO JOIN YOUR LITTLE TASK FORCE...
WHAT'S THE OFFER LOOK LIKE?
OFFER?
YES. AS IN MONEY.
UM... WE'RE HOPING TO FIND CELEBS WHO'LL STEP UP AS A MATTER OF PRINCIPLE.
HELLO? SORRY, JUST LOST YOU! I'M DRIVING IN A DEAD ZONE!
I'LL CALL BACK.
GB Trudeau

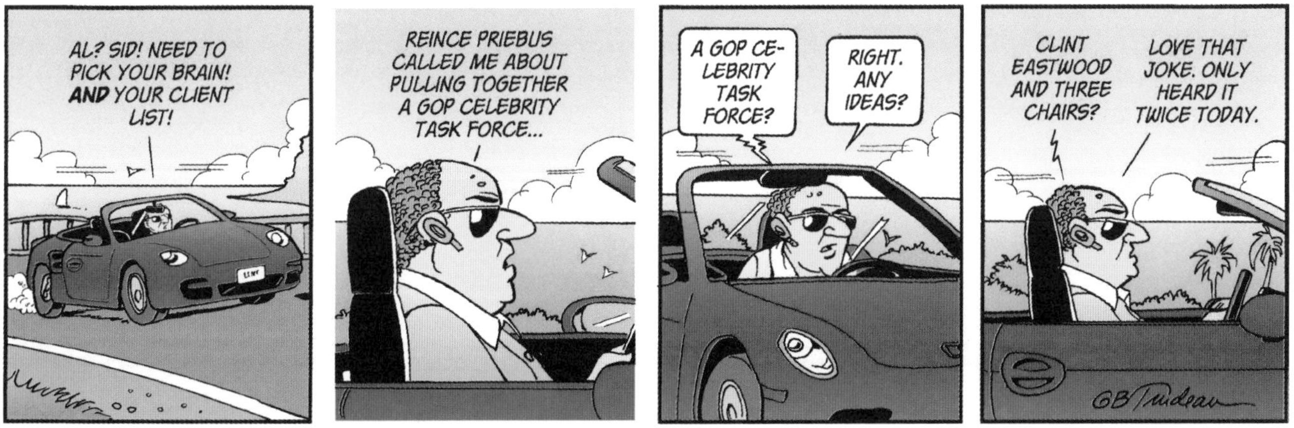
AL? SID! NEED TO PICK YOUR BRAIN! **AND** YOUR CLIENT LIST!
REINCE PRIEBUS CALLED ME ABOUT PULLING TOGETHER A GOP CELEBRITY TASK FORCE...
A GOP CELEBRITY TASK FORCE?
RIGHT. ANY IDEAS?
CLINT EASTWOOD AND THREE CHAIRS?
LOVE THAT JOKE. ONLY HEARD IT TWICE TODAY.
GB Trudeau

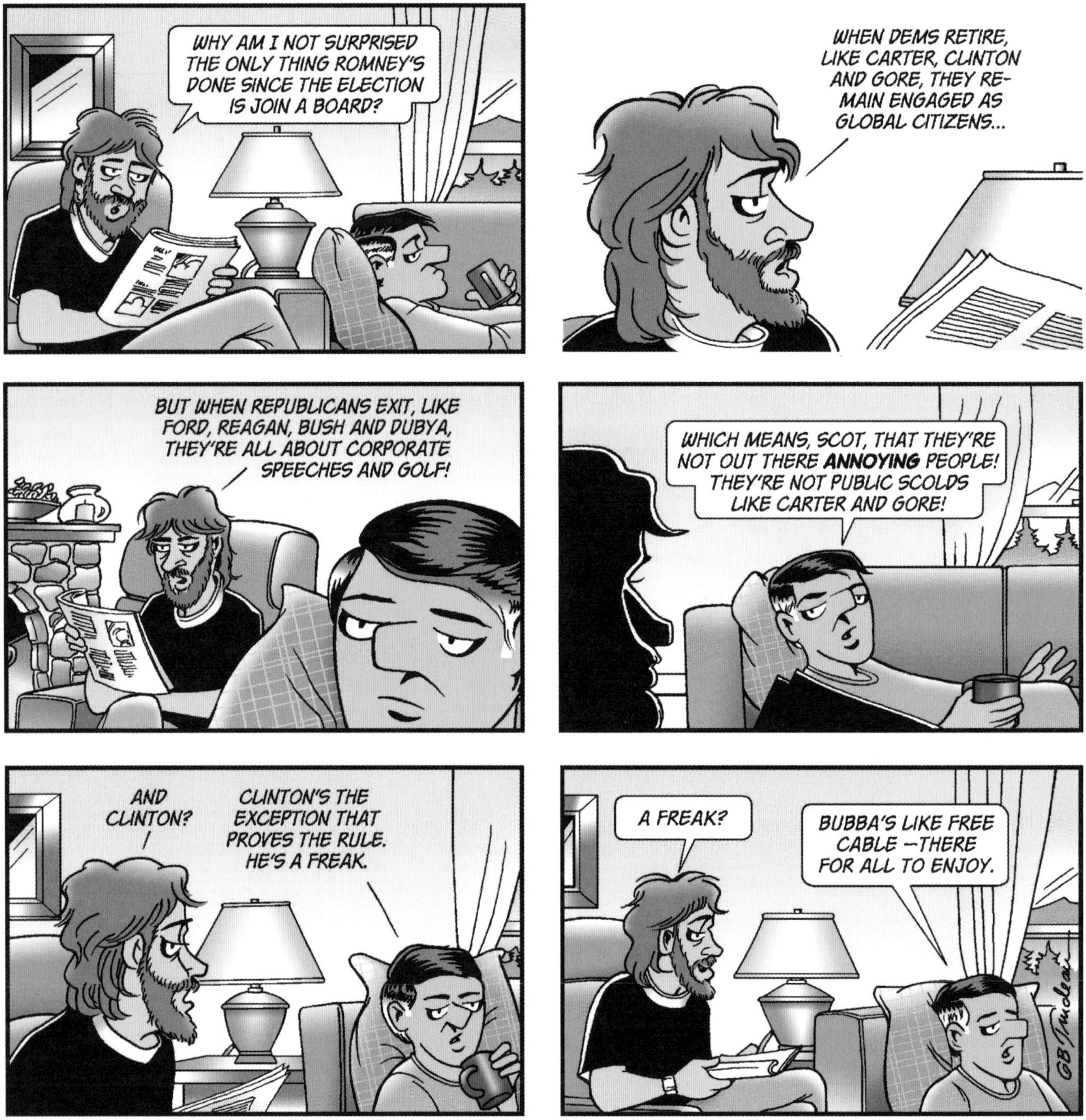
WHY AM I NOT SURPRISED THE ONLY THING ROMNEY'S DONE SINCE THE ELECTION IS JOIN A BOARD?
WHEN DEMS RETIRE, LIKE CARTER, CLINTON AND GORE, THEY RE-MAIN ENGAGED AS GLOBAL CITIZENS...
BUT WHEN REPUBLICANS EXIT, LIKE FORD, REAGAN, BUSH AND DUBYA, THEY'RE ALL ABOUT CORPORATE SPEECHES AND GOLF!
WHICH MEANS, SCOT, THAT THEY'RE NOT OUT THERE **ANNOYING** PEOPLE! THEY'RE NOT PUBLIC SCOLDS LIKE CARTER AND GORE!
AND CLINTON?
CLINTON'S THE EXCEPTION THAT PROVES THE RULE. HE'S A FREAK.
A FREAK?
BUBBA'S LIKE FREE CABLE —THERE FOR ALL TO ENJOY.
GBTrudeau

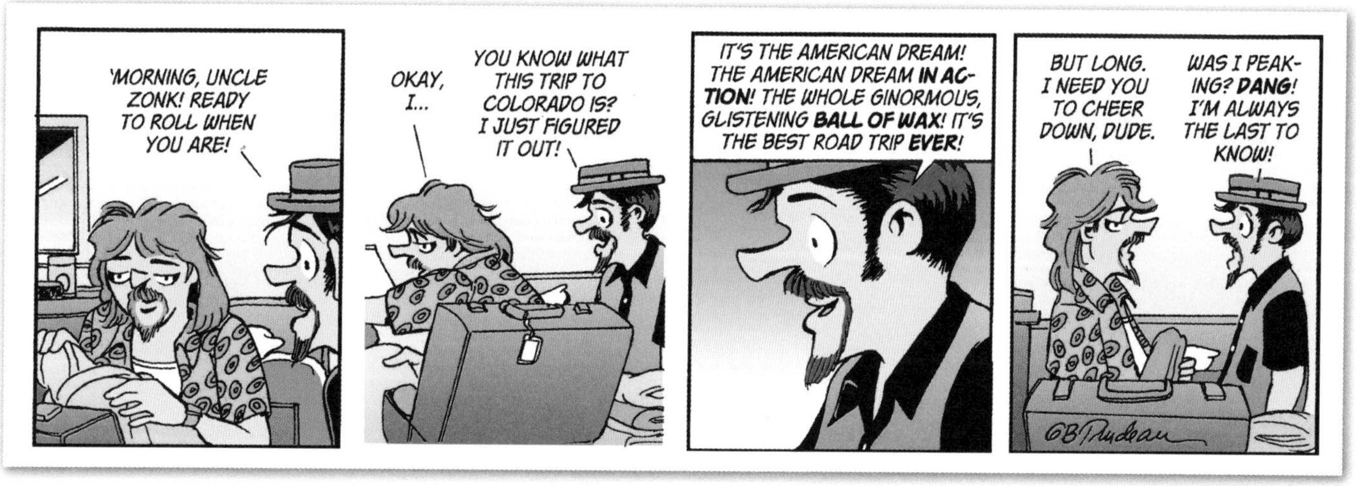
'MORNING, UNCLE ZONK! READY TO ROLL WHEN YOU ARE!
OKAY, I...
YOU KNOW WHAT THIS TRIP TO COLORADO IS? I JUST FIGURED IT OUT!
IT'S THE AMERICAN DREAM! THE AMERICAN DREAM **IN ACTION**! THE WHOLE GINORMOUS, GLISTENING **BALL OF WAX**! IT'S THE BEST ROAD TRIP **EVER**!
BUT LONG. I NEED YOU TO CHEER DOWN, DUDE.
WAS I PEAKING? **DANG**! I'M ALWAYS THE LAST TO KNOW!
©B Trudeau

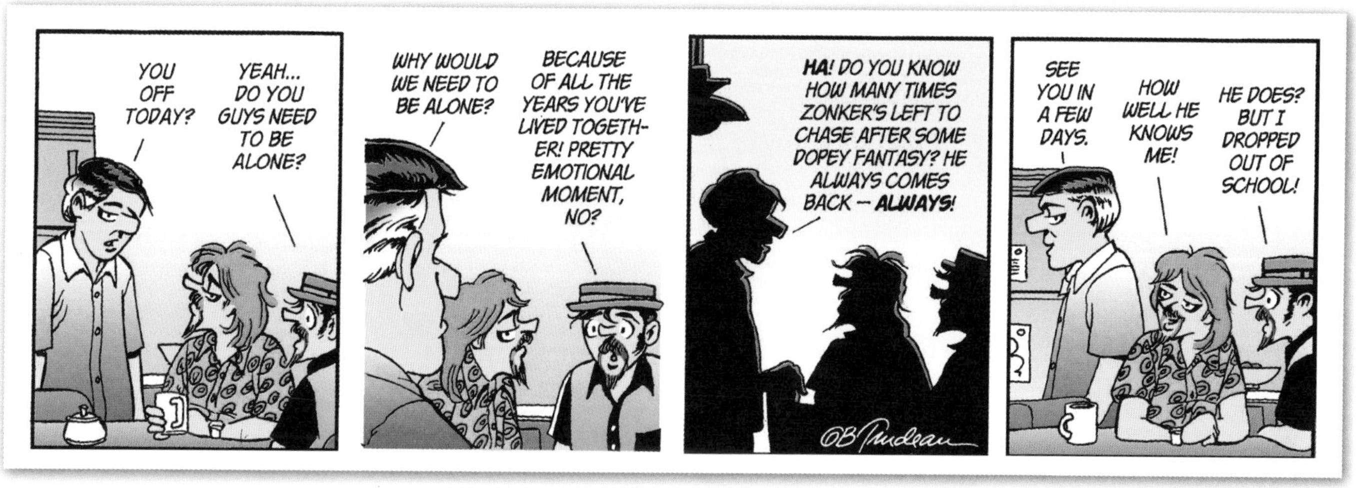
YOU OFF TODAY?
YEAH... DO YOU GUYS NEED TO BE ALONE?
WHY WOULD WE NEED TO BE ALONE?
BECAUSE OF ALL THE YEARS YOU'VE LIVED TOGETHER! PRETTY EMOTIONAL MOMENT, NO?
HA! DO YOU KNOW HOW MANY TIMES ZONKER'S LEFT TO CHASE AFTER SOME DOPEY FANTASY? HE ALWAYS COMES BACK -- **ALWAYS**!
©B Trudeau
SEE YOU IN A FEW DAYS.
HOW WELL HE KNOWS ME!
HE DOES? BUT I DROPPED OUT OF SCHOOL!

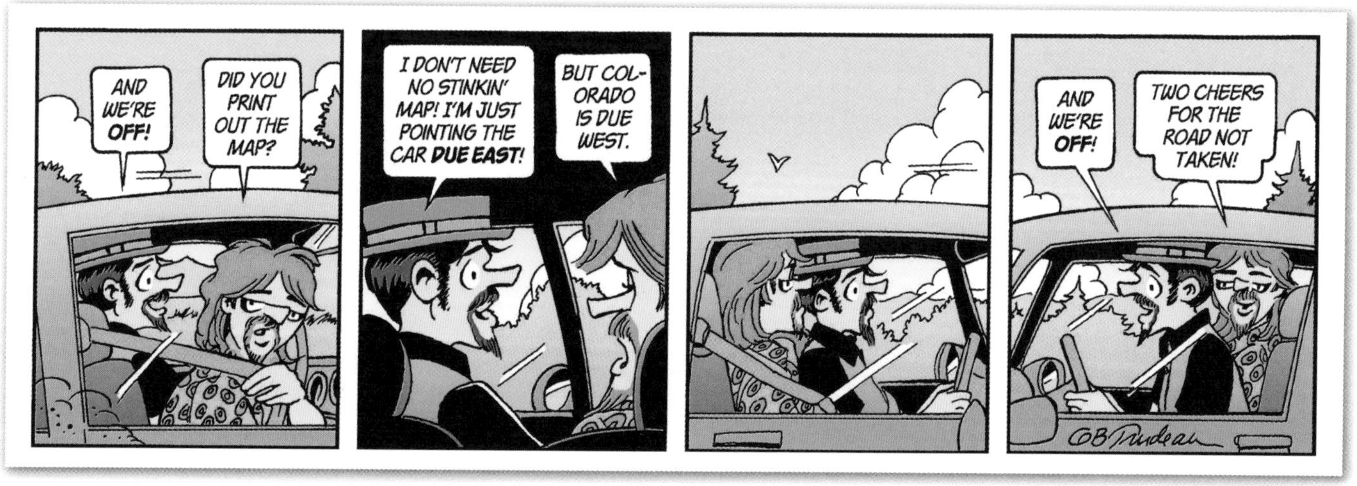
AND WE'RE **OFF**!
DID YOU PRINT OUT THE MAP?
I DON'T NEED NO STINKIN' MAP! I'M JUST POINTING THE CAR **DUE EAST**!
BUT COLORADO IS DUE WEST.
AND WE'RE **OFF**!
TWO CHEERS FOR THE ROAD NOT TAKEN!
©B Trudeau

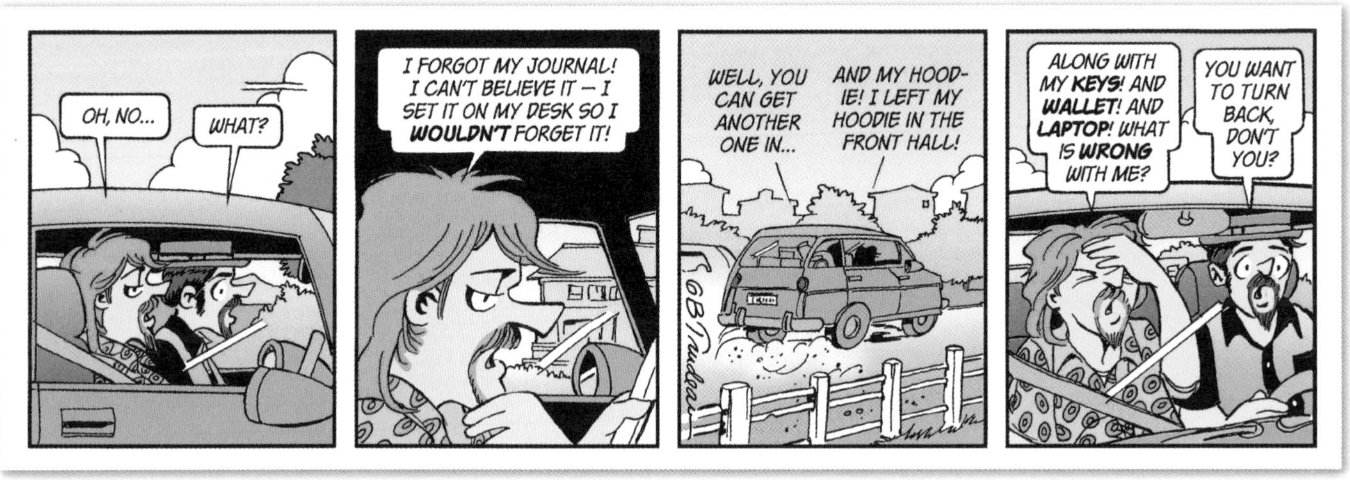
OH, NO...
WHAT?
I FORGOT MY JOURNAL! I CAN'T BELIEVE IT — I SET IT ON MY DESK SO I **WOULDN'T** FORGET IT!
WELL, YOU CAN GET ANOTHER ONE IN...
AND MY HOOD-IE! I LEFT MY HOODIE IN THE FRONT HALL!
ALONG WITH MY **KEYS**! AND **WALLET**! AND **LAPTOP**! WHAT IS **WRONG** WITH ME?
YOU WANT TO TURN BACK, DON'T YOU?

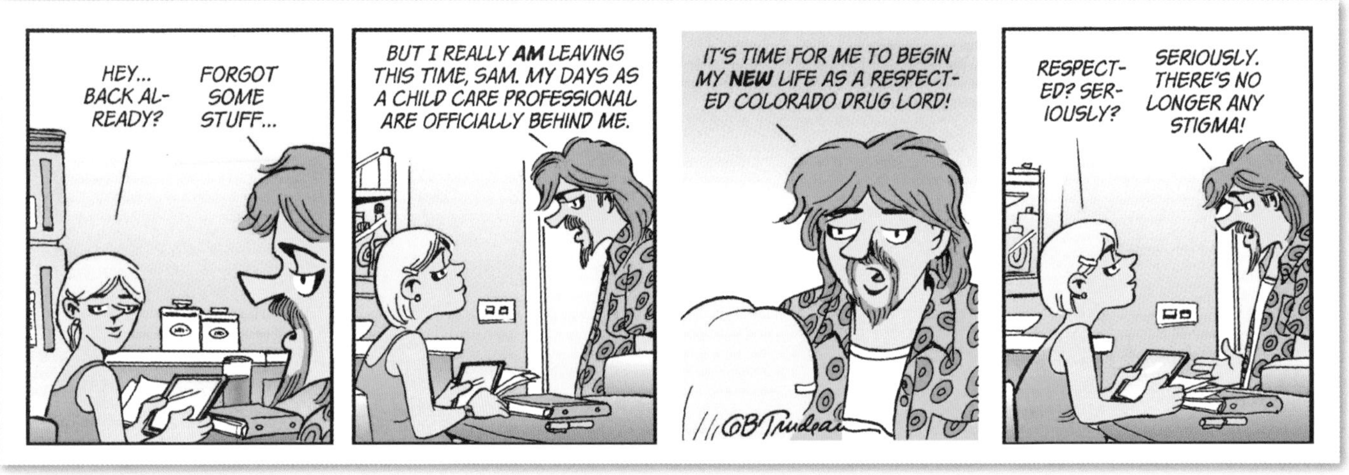
HEY... BACK AL-READY?
FORGOT SOME STUFF...
BUT I REALLY **AM** LEAVING THIS TIME, SAM. MY DAYS AS A CHILD CARE PROFESSIONAL ARE OFFICIALLY BEHIND ME.
IT'S TIME FOR ME TO BEGIN MY **NEW** LIFE AS A RESPECT-ED COLORADO DRUG LORD!
RESPECT-ED? SER-IOUSLY?
SERIOUSLY. THERE'S NO LONGER ANY STIGMA!

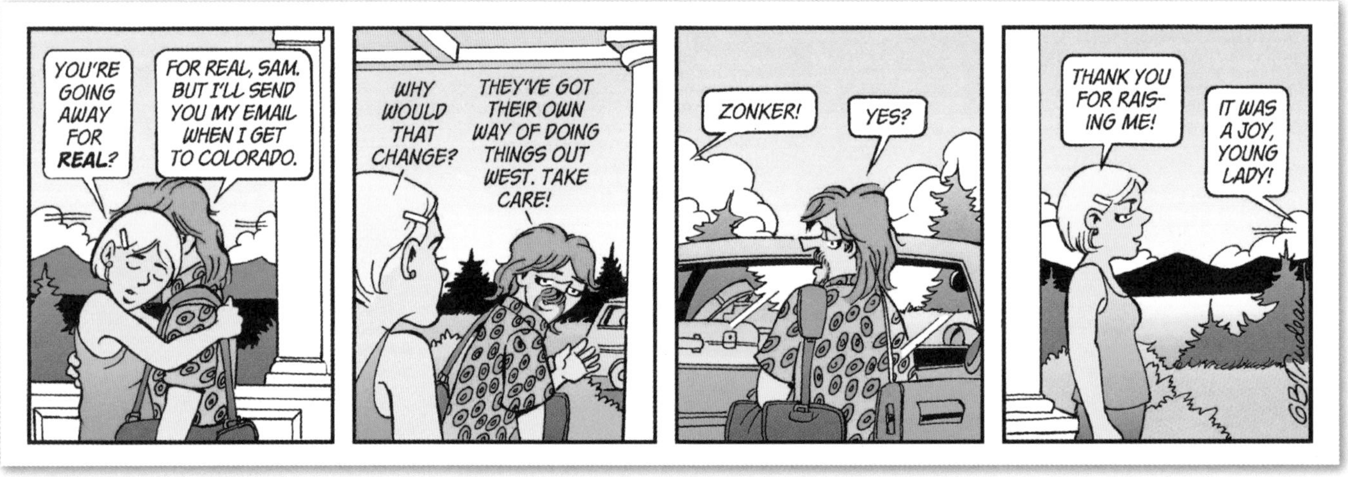
YOU'RE GOING AWAY FOR **REAL**?
FOR REAL, SAM. BUT I'LL SEND YOU MY EMAIL WHEN I GET TO COLORADO.
WHY WOULD THAT CHANGE?
THEY'VE GOT THEIR OWN WAY OF DOING THINGS OUT WEST. TAKE CARE!
ZONKER!
YES?
THANK YOU FOR RAIS-ING ME!
IT WAS A JOY, YOUNG LADY!

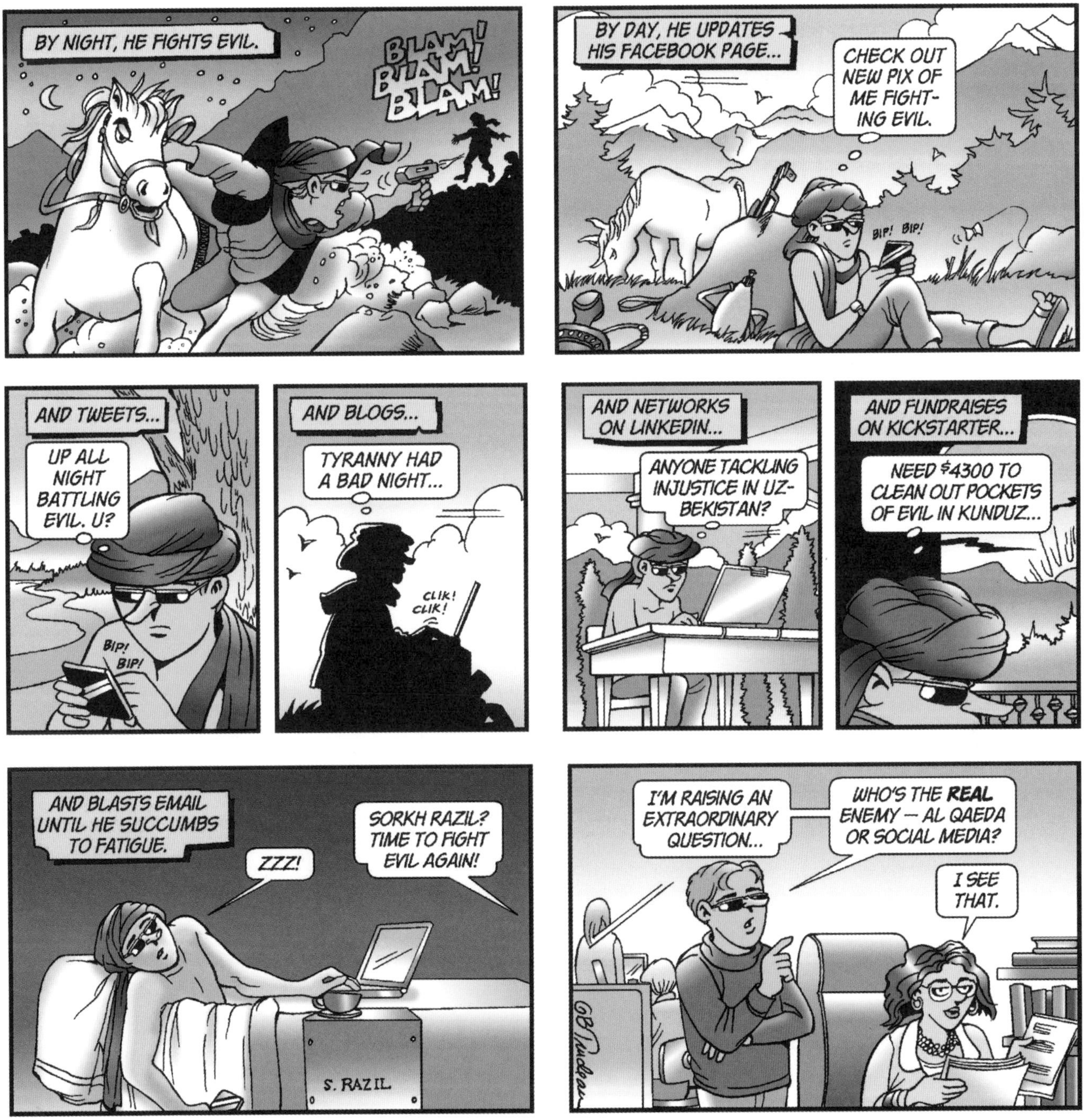
BY NIGHT, HE FIGHTS EVIL.
BLAM! BLAM! BLAM!
BY DAY, HE UPDATES HIS FACEBOOK PAGE...
CHECK OUT NEW PIX OF ME FIGHT-ING EVIL.
BIP! BIP!
AND TWEETS...
UP ALL NIGHT BATTLING EVIL. U?
BIP! BIP!
AND BLOGS...
TYRANNY HAD A BAD NIGHT...
CLIK! CLIK!
AND NETWORKS ON LINKEDIN...
ANYONE TACKLING INJUSTICE IN UZ-BEKISTAN?
AND FUNDRAISES ON KICKSTARTER...
NEED $4300 TO CLEAN OUT POCKETS OF EVIL IN KUNDUZ...
AND BLASTS EMAIL UNTIL HE SUCCUMBS TO FATIGUE.
ZZZ!
SORKH RAZIL? TIME TO FIGHT EVIL AGAIN!
S. RAZIL
I'M RAISING AN EXTRAORDINARY QUESTION...
WHO'S THE **REAL** ENEMY — AL QAEDA OR SOCIAL MEDIA?
I SEE THAT.
GBTrudeau

REALLY SPINNING MY WHEELS THIS WEEK...

ME, TOO. TOTALLY OFF MY GAME.

DONG!

WANT TO GO TO A MOVIE?

OKAY.

REALLY? AGAIN?

WHAT IS THIS, THE HOUSE OF SLACK?

SUR-PRISE!

DON'T WORRY — WE'LL BE GONE IN A WEEK!

SO WHERE YOU GUYS OFF TO?

COLORADO, DAWG — AND YOU SHOULD JOIN US!

UNCLE ZONK HAS SET HIS SIGHTS ON A SWEET LITTLE GROW OUTSIDE OF BOULDER! WE'RE GOING TO BECOME BAJILLIONAIRE PRODUCERS!

SOUNDS AWESOME.

IT IS! WE'RE NOT JUST CHASING THE AMERICAN DREAM, DUDE — IT'S CHASING US!

MAYBE I SHOULD JOIN THEM...

I'M GOING TO WORK.

SO, DUDE — DOES THIS MEAN YOU FINALLY FINISHED UP AT WALDEN?

NO... WHY?

WELL, YOU MIGHT FIND MORE OPPORTUNITIES IN COLORADO AS A COLLEGE GRAD.

GOOD POINT. AND I AM ONLY ONE ART PROJECT SHY OF COMPLETION...

MAYBE YOU COULD DO IT ON THE ROAD AND MAIL IT IN.

WHY NOT? ALL I NEED IS GLITTER AND POPSICLE STICKS!

WORTH A DETOUR. DEGREES ARE GOOD.

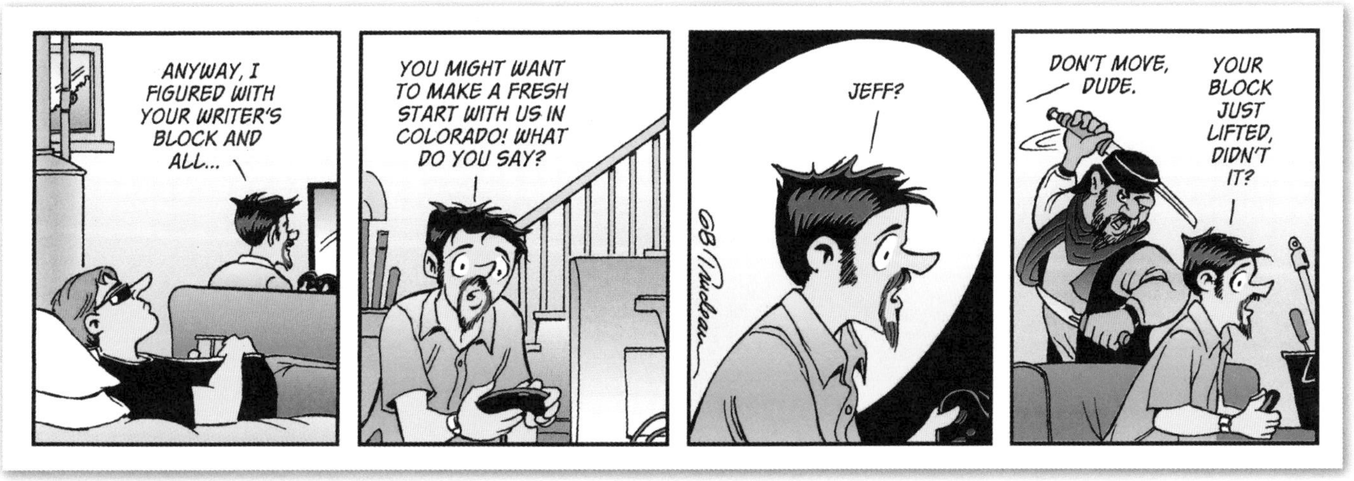
ANYWAY, I FIGURED WITH YOUR WRITER'S BLOCK AND ALL...
YOU MIGHT WANT TO MAKE A FRESH START WITH US IN COLORADO! WHAT DO YOU SAY?
JEFF?
DON'T MOVE, DUDE.
YOUR BLOCK JUST LIFTED, DIDN'T IT?
GB Trudeau

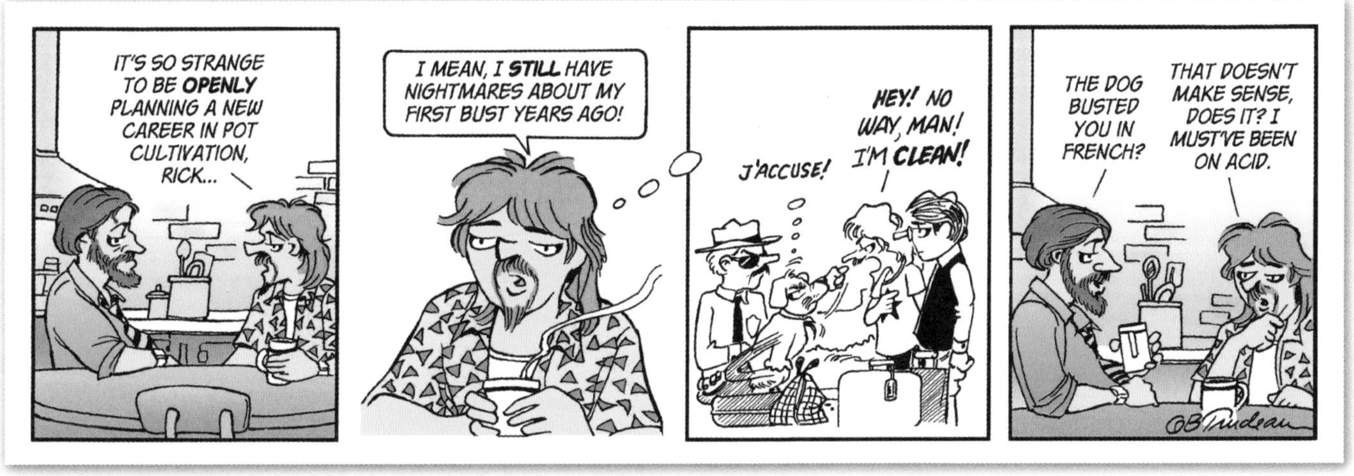
IT'S SO STRANGE TO BE OPENLY PLANNING A NEW CAREER IN POT CULTIVATION, RICK...
I MEAN, I STILL HAVE NIGHTMARES ABOUT MY FIRST BUST YEARS AGO!
J'ACCUSE!
HEY! NO WAY, MAN! I'M CLEAN!
THE DOG BUSTED YOU IN FRENCH?
THAT DOESN'T MAKE SENSE, DOES IT? I MUST'VE BEEN ON ACID.
GB Trudeau

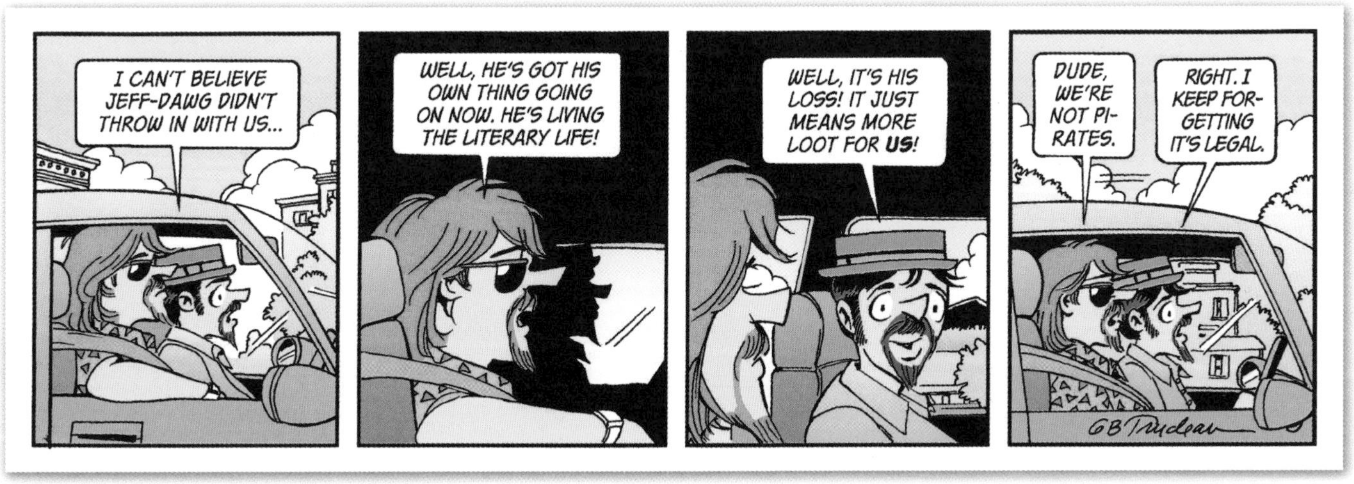
I CAN'T BELIEVE JEFF-DAWG DIDN'T THROW IN WITH US...
WELL, HE'S GOT HIS OWN THING GOING ON NOW. HE'S LIVING THE LITERARY LIFE!
WELL, IT'S HIS LOSS! IT JUST MEANS MORE LOOT FOR US!
DUDE, WE'RE NOT PI-RATES.
RIGHT. I KEEP FOR-GETTING IT'S LEGAL.
GB Trudeau

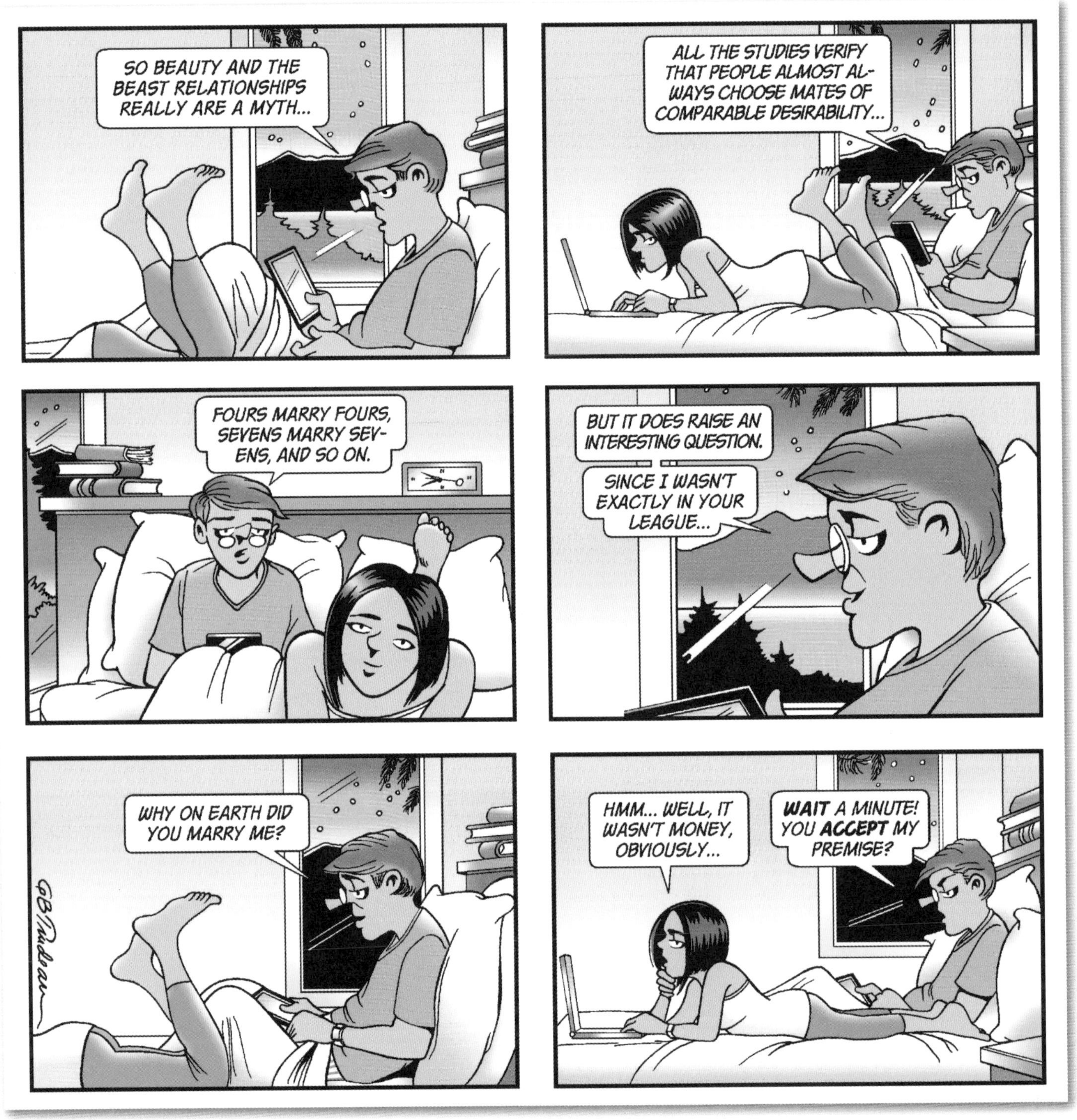
SO BEAUTY AND THE BEAST RELATIONSHIPS REALLY ARE A MYTH...
ALL THE STUDIES VERIFY THAT PEOPLE ALMOST AL-WAYS CHOOSE MATES OF COMPARABLE DESIRABILITY...
FOURS MARRY FOURS, SEVENS MARRY SEV-ENS, AND SO ON.
BUT IT DOES RAISE AN INTERESTING QUESTION.
SINCE I WASN'T EXACTLY IN YOUR LEAGUE...
WHY ON EARTH DID YOU MARRY ME?
HMM... WELL, IT WASN'T MONEY, OBVIOUSLY...
WAIT A MINUTE! YOU **ACCEPT** MY PREMISE?
GBTrudeau

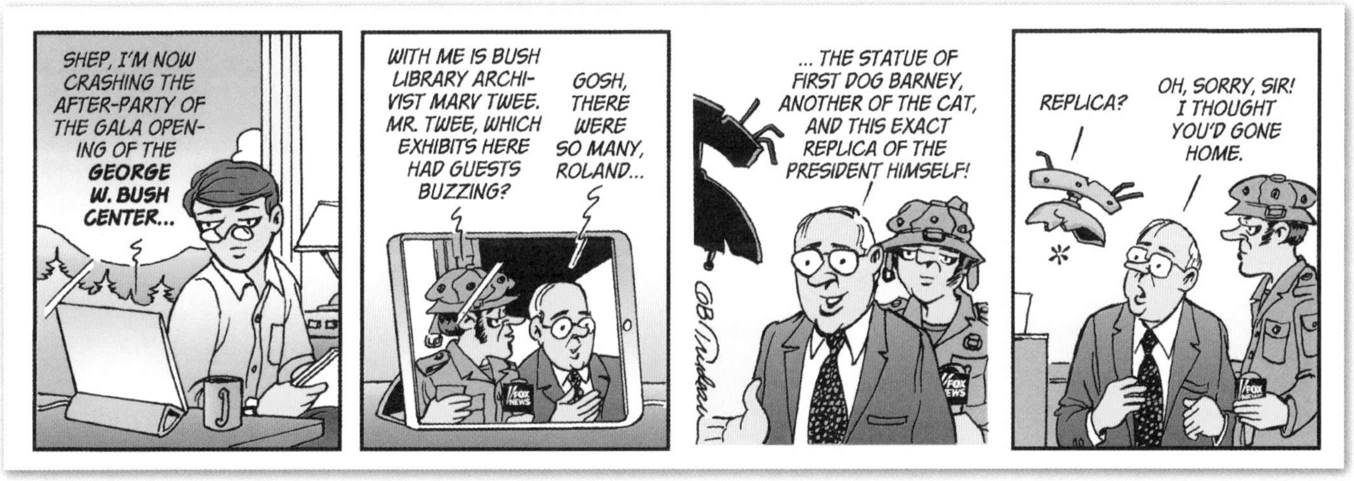
SHEP, I'M NOW CRASHING THE AFTER-PARTY OF THE GALA OPENING OF THE **GEORGE W. BUSH CENTER...**
WITH ME IS BUSH LIBRARY ARCHIVIST MARV TWEE. MR. TWEE, WHICH EXHIBITS HERE HAD GUESTS BUZZING?
GOSH, THERE WERE SO MANY, ROLAND...
... THE STATUE OF FIRST DOG BARNEY, ANOTHER OF THE CAT, AND THIS EXACT REPLICA OF THE PRESIDENT HIMSELF!
REPLICA?
OH, SORRY, SIR! I THOUGHT YOU'D GONE HOME.

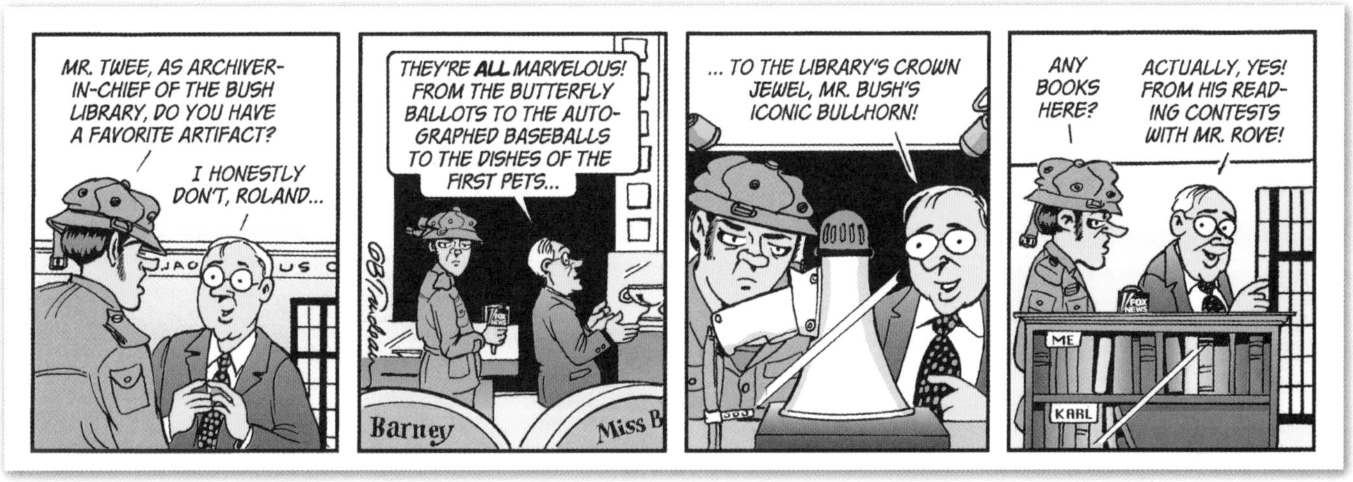
MR. TWEE, AS ARCHIVER-IN-CHIEF OF THE BUSH LIBRARY, DO YOU HAVE A FAVORITE ARTIFACT?
I HONESTLY DON'T, ROLAND...
THEY'RE **ALL** MARVELOUS! FROM THE BUTTERFLY BALLOTS TO THE AUTOGRAPHED BASEBALLS TO THE DISHES OF THE FIRST PETS...
Barney
Miss B
... TO THE LIBRARY'S CROWN JEWEL, MR. BUSH'S ICONIC BULLHORN!
ANY BOOKS HERE?
ACTUALLY, YES! FROM HIS READING CONTESTS WITH MR. ROVE!
ME
KARL

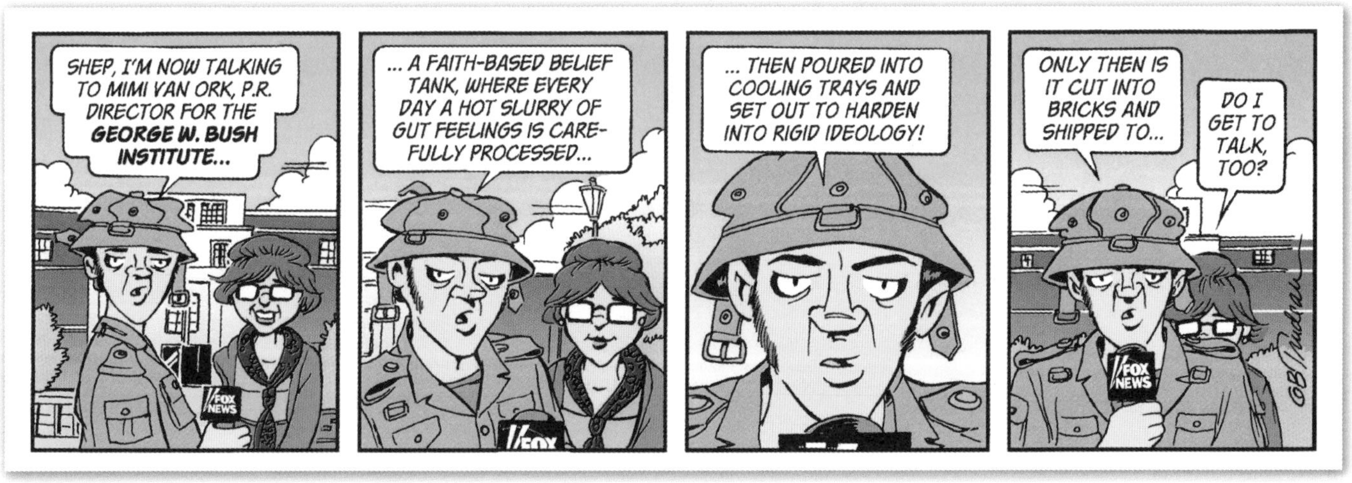
SHEP, I'M NOW TALKING TO MIMI VAN ORK, P.R. DIRECTOR FOR THE **GEORGE W. BUSH INSTITUTE...**
... A FAITH-BASED BELIEF TANK, WHERE EVERY DAY A HOT SLURRY OF GUT FEELINGS IS CAREFULLY PROCESSED...
... THEN POURED INTO COOLING TRAYS AND SET OUT TO HARDEN INTO RIGID IDEOLOGY!
ONLY THEN IS IT CUT INTO BRICKS AND SHIPPED TO...
DO I GET TO TALK, TOO?

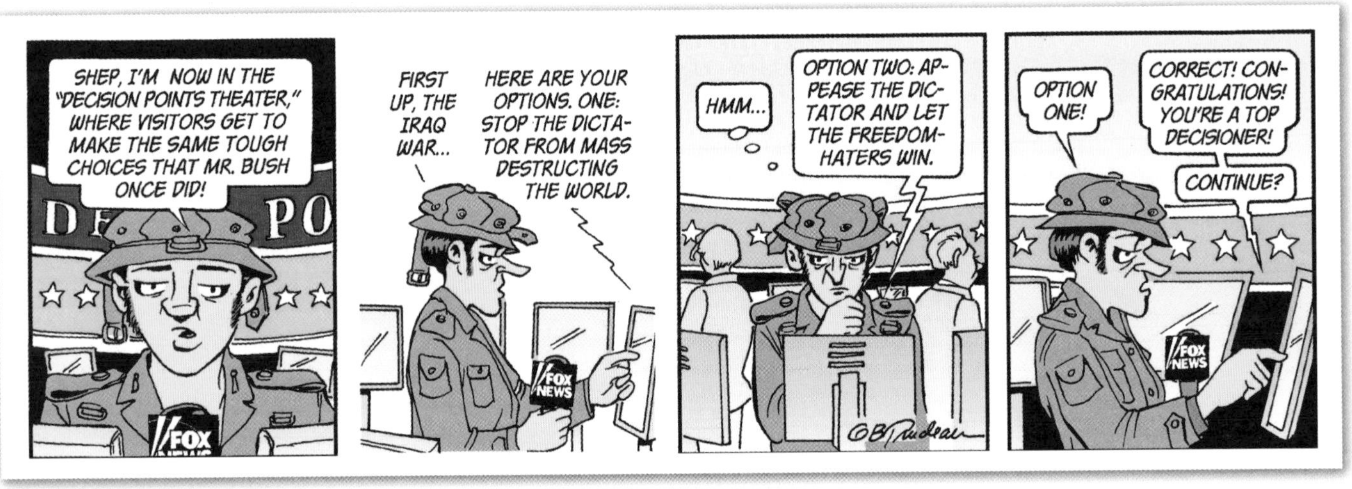
SHEP, I'M NOW IN THE "DECISION POINTS THEATER," WHERE VISITORS GET TO MAKE THE SAME TOUGH CHOICES THAT MR. BUSH ONCE DID!
FIRST UP, THE IRAQ WAR...
HERE ARE YOUR OPTIONS. ONE: STOP THE DICTATOR FROM MASS DESTRUCTING THE WORLD.
HMM...
OPTION TWO: APPEASE THE DICTATOR AND LET THE FREEDOM-HATERS WIN.
OPTION ONE!
CORRECT! CONGRATULATIONS! YOU'RE A TOP DECISIONER!
CONTINUE?

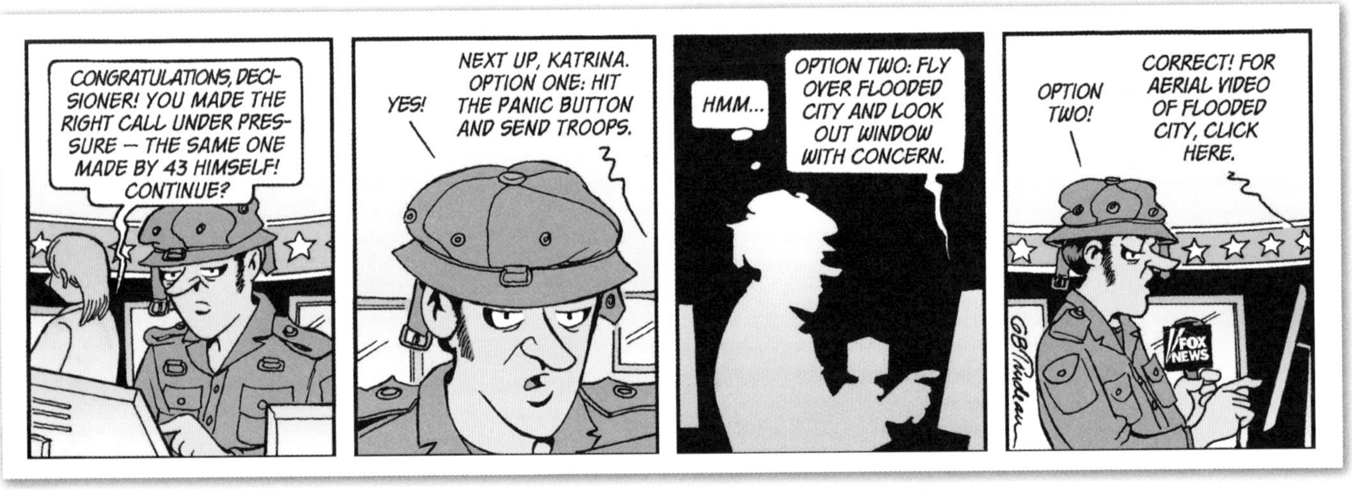
CONGRATULATIONS, DECISIONER! YOU MADE THE RIGHT CALL UNDER PRESSURE — THE SAME ONE MADE BY 43 HIMSELF! CONTINUE?
YES!
NEXT UP, KATRINA. OPTION ONE: HIT THE PANIC BUTTON AND SEND TROOPS.
HMM...
OPTION TWO: FLY OVER FLOODED CITY AND LOOK OUT WINDOW WITH CONCERN.
OPTION TWO!
CORRECT! FOR AERIAL VIDEO OF FLOODED CITY, CLICK HERE.

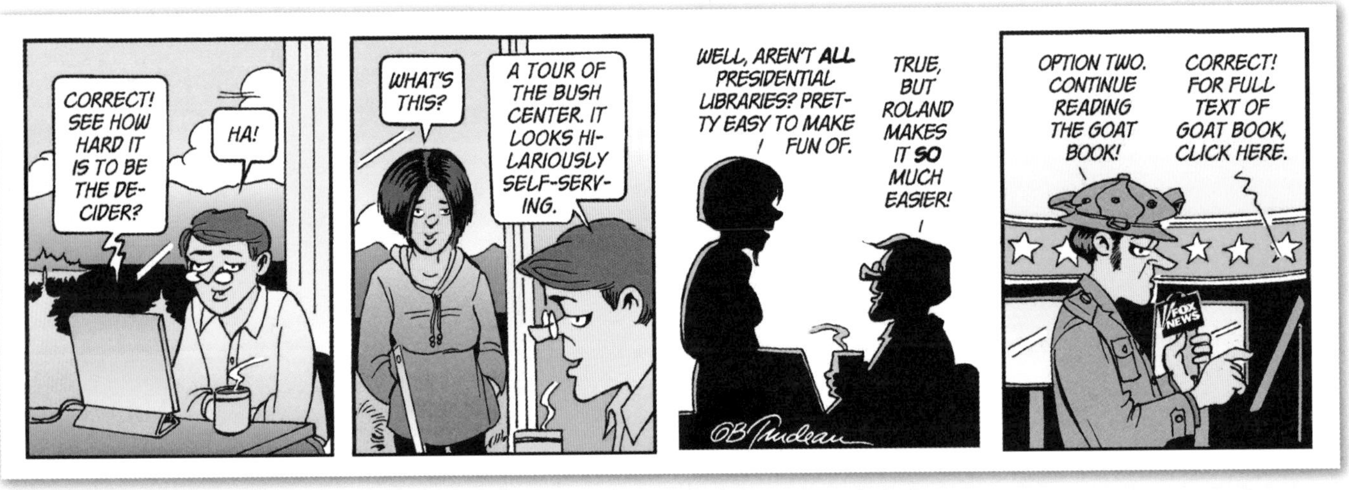
CORRECT! SEE HOW HARD IT IS TO BE THE DECIDER?
HA!
WHAT'S THIS?
A TOUR OF THE BUSH CENTER. IT LOOKS HILARIOUSLY SELF-SERVING.
WELL, AREN'T ALL PRESIDENTIAL LIBRARIES? PRETTY EASY TO MAKE FUN OF.
TRUE, BUT ROLAND MAKES IT SO MUCH EASIER!
OPTION TWO. CONTINUE READING THE GOAT BOOK!
CORRECT! FOR FULL TEXT OF GOAT BOOK, CLICK HERE.

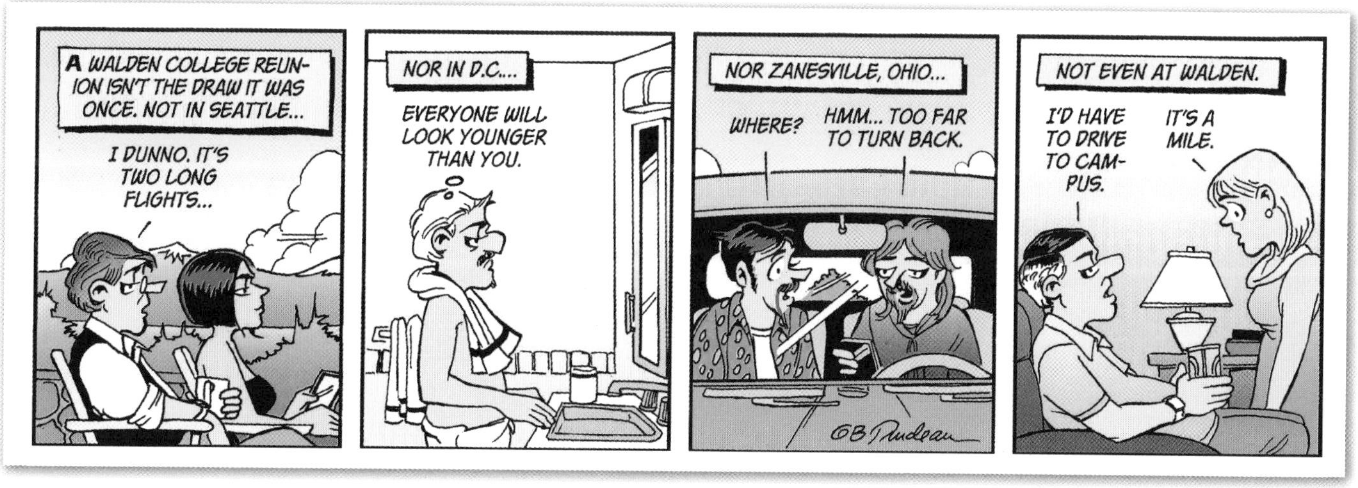
A WALDEN COLLEGE REUNION ISN'T THE DRAW IT WAS ONCE. NOT IN SEATTLE...
I DUNNO. IT'S TWO LONG FLIGHTS...
NOR IN D.C....
EVERYONE WILL LOOK YOUNGER THAN YOU.
NOR ZANESVILLE, OHIO...
WHERE?
HMM... TOO FAR TO TURN BACK.
NOT EVEN AT WALDEN.
I'D HAVE TO DRIVE TO CAMPUS.
IT'S A MILE.

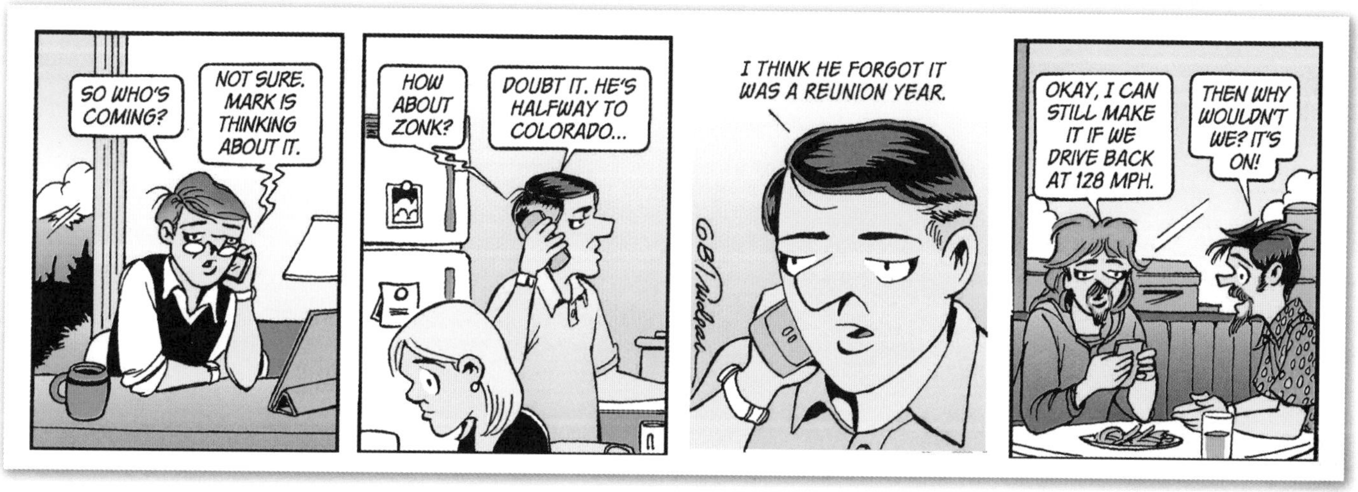
SO WHO'S COMING?
NOT SURE. MARK IS THINKING ABOUT IT.
HOW ABOUT ZONK?
DOUBT IT. HE'S HALFWAY TO COLORADO...
I THINK HE FORGOT IT WAS A REUNION YEAR.
OKAY, I CAN STILL MAKE IT IF WE DRIVE BACK AT 128 MPH.
THEN WHY WOULDN'T WE? IT'S ON!

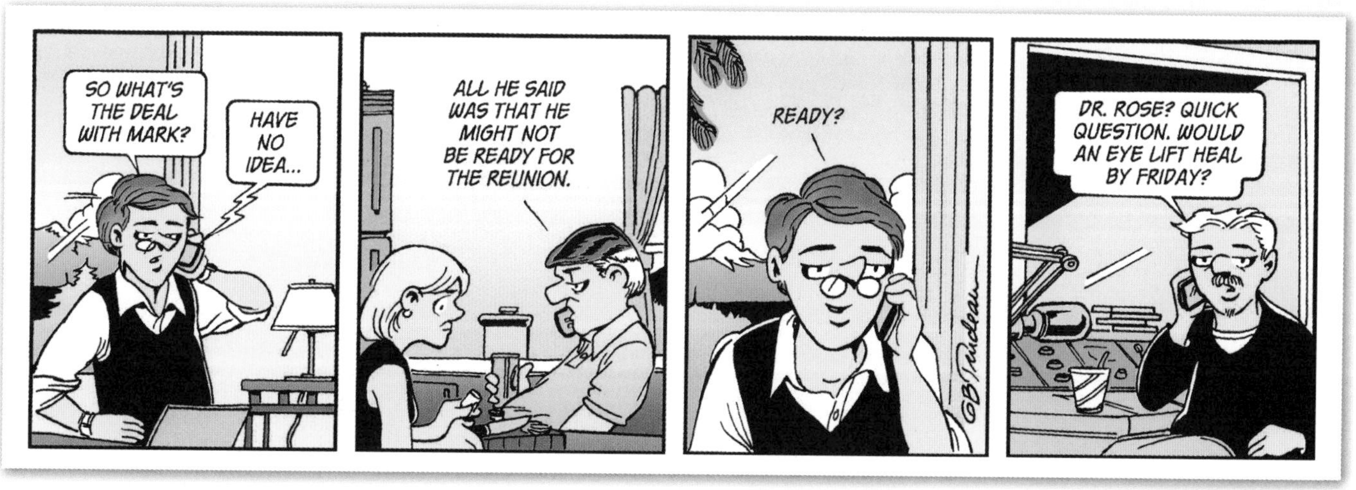
SO WHAT'S THE DEAL WITH MARK?
HAVE NO IDEA...
ALL HE SAID WAS THAT HE MIGHT NOT BE READY FOR THE REUNION.
READY?
DR. ROSE? QUICK QUESTION. WOULD AN EYE LIFT HEAL BY FRIDAY?

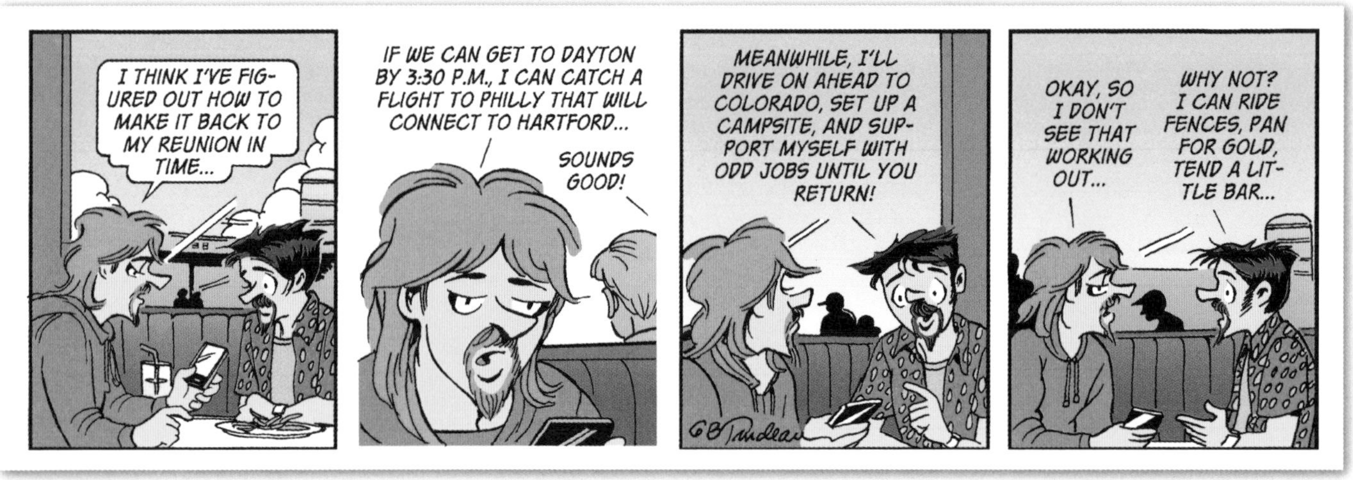
I THINK I'VE FIGURED OUT HOW TO MAKE IT BACK TO MY REUNION IN TIME...
IF WE CAN GET TO DAYTON BY 3:30 P.M., I CAN CATCH A FLIGHT TO PHILLY THAT WILL CONNECT TO HARTFORD...
SOUNDS GOOD!
MEANWHILE, I'LL DRIVE ON AHEAD TO COLORADO, SET UP A CAMPSITE, AND SUPPORT MYSELF WITH ODD JOBS UNTIL YOU RETURN!
OKAY, SO I DON'T SEE THAT WORKING OUT...
WHY NOT? I CAN RIDE FENCES, PAN FOR GOLD, TEND A LITTLE BAR...

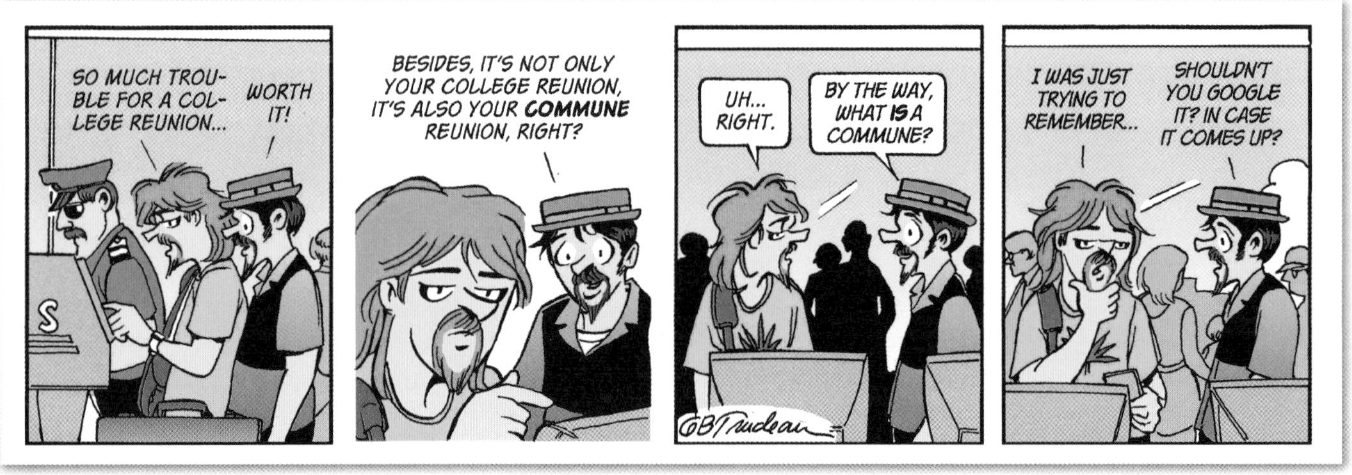
SO MUCH TROUBLE FOR A COLLEGE REUNION...
WORTH IT!
BESIDES, IT'S NOT ONLY YOUR COLLEGE REUNION, IT'S ALSO YOUR **COMMUNE** REUNION, RIGHT?
UH... RIGHT.
BY THE WAY, WHAT **IS** A COMMUNE?
I WAS JUST TRYING TO REMEMBER...
SHOULDN'T YOU GOOGLE IT? IN CASE IT COMES UP?

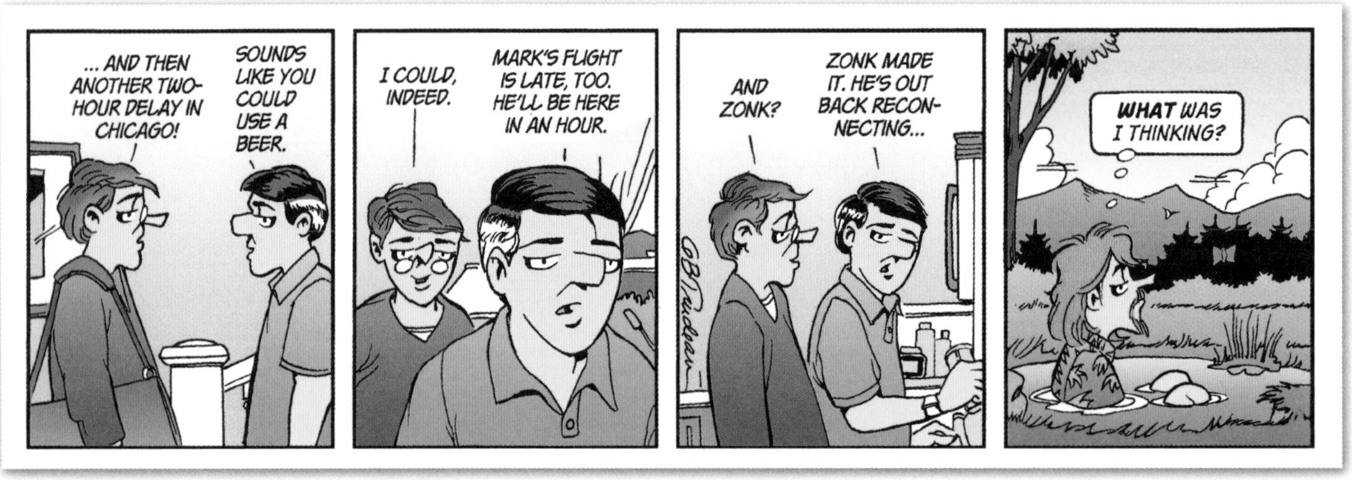
... AND THEN ANOTHER TWO-HOUR DELAY IN CHICAGO!
SOUNDS LIKE YOU COULD USE A BEER.
I COULD, INDEED.
MARK'S FLIGHT IS LATE, TOO. HE'LL BE HERE IN AN HOUR.
AND ZONK?
ZONK MADE IT. HE'S OUT BACK RECONNECTING...
WHAT WAS I THINKING?

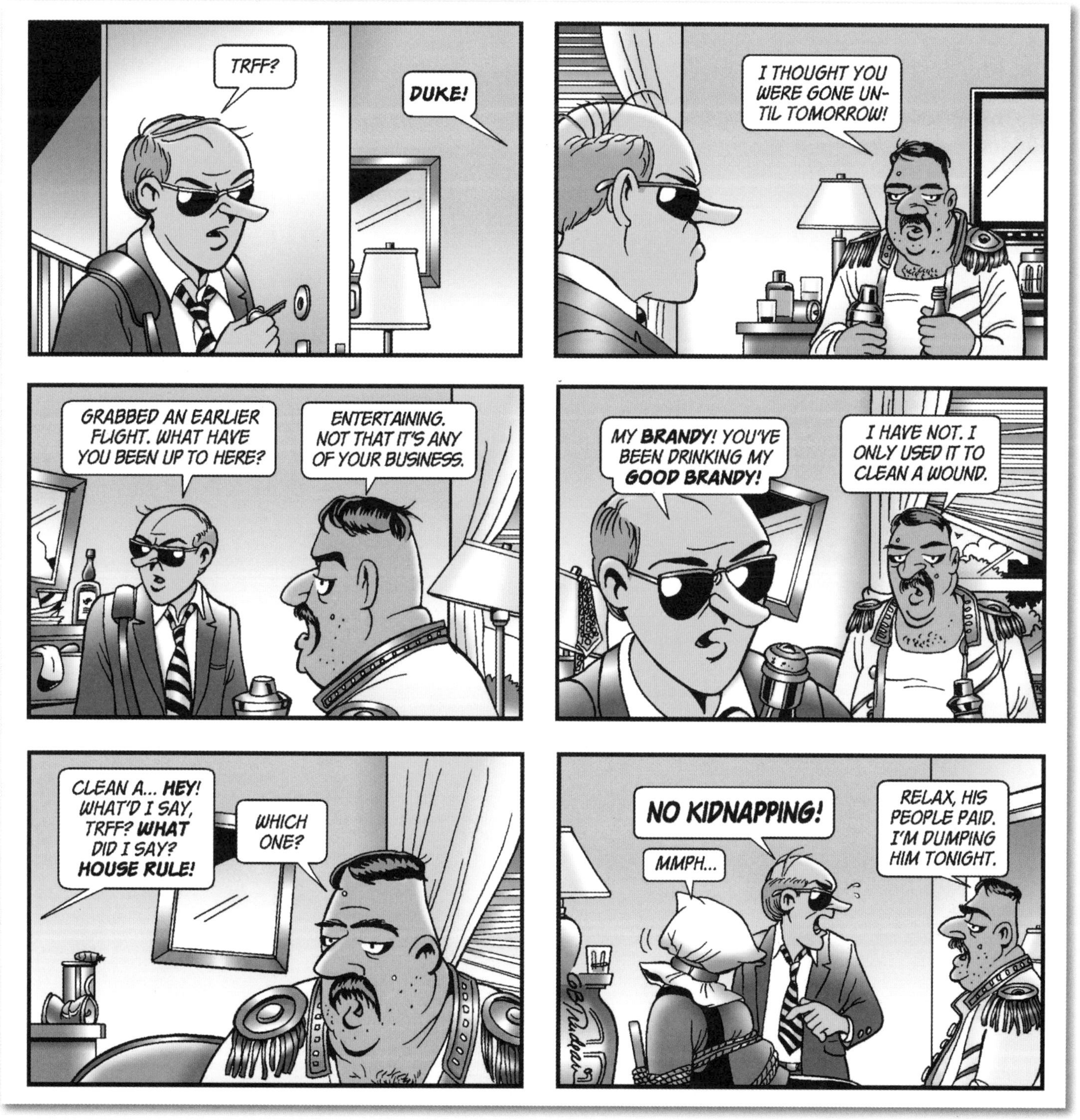
TRFF?
DUKE!
I THOUGHT YOU WERE GONE UN-TIL TOMORROW!
GRABBED AN EARLIER FLIGHT. WHAT HAVE YOU BEEN UP TO HERE?
ENTERTAINING. NOT THAT IT'S ANY OF YOUR BUSINESS.
MY BRANDY! YOU'VE BEEN DRINKING MY GOOD BRANDY!
I HAVE NOT. I ONLY USED IT TO CLEAN A WOUND.
CLEAN A... HEY! WHAT'D I SAY, TRFF? WHAT DID I SAY? HOUSE RULE!
WHICH ONE?
NO KIDNAPPING!
MMPH...
RELAX, HIS PEOPLE PAID. I'M DUMPING HIM TONIGHT.

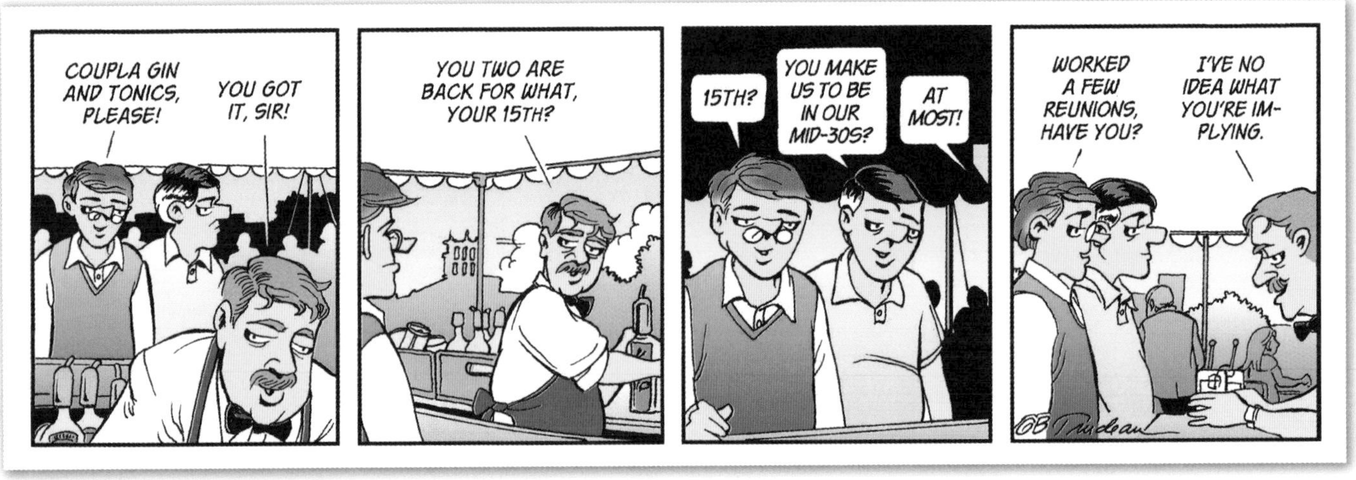
COUPLA GIN AND TONICS, PLEASE!
YOU GOT IT, SIR!
YOU TWO ARE BACK FOR WHAT, YOUR 15TH?
15TH?
YOU MAKE US TO BE IN OUR MID-30S?
AT MOST!
WORKED A FEW REUNIONS, HAVE YOU?
I'VE NO IDEA WHAT YOU'RE IMPLYING.
GB Trudeau

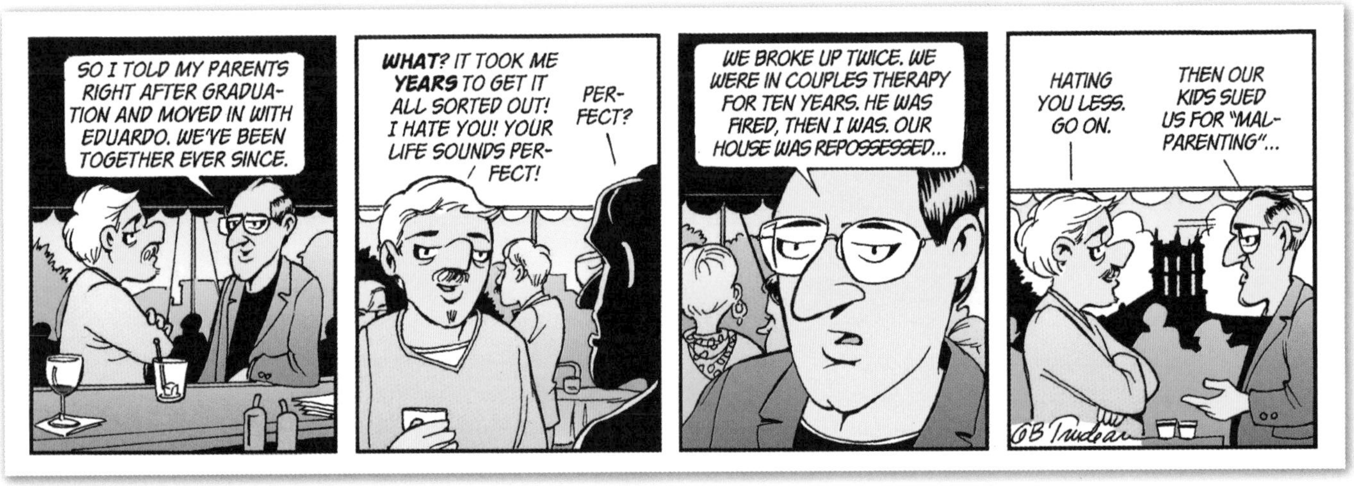
SO I TOLD MY PARENTS RIGHT AFTER GRADUATION AND MOVED IN WITH EDUARDO. WE'VE BEEN TOGETHER EVER SINCE.
WHAT? IT TOOK ME **YEARS** TO GET IT ALL SORTED OUT! I HATE YOU! YOUR LIFE SOUNDS PERFECT!
PERFECT?
WE BROKE UP TWICE. WE WERE IN COUPLES THERAPY FOR TEN YEARS. HE WAS FIRED, THEN I WAS. OUR HOUSE WAS REPOSSESSED...
HATING YOU LESS. GO ON.
THEN OUR KIDS SUED US FOR "MALPARENTING"...
GB Trudeau

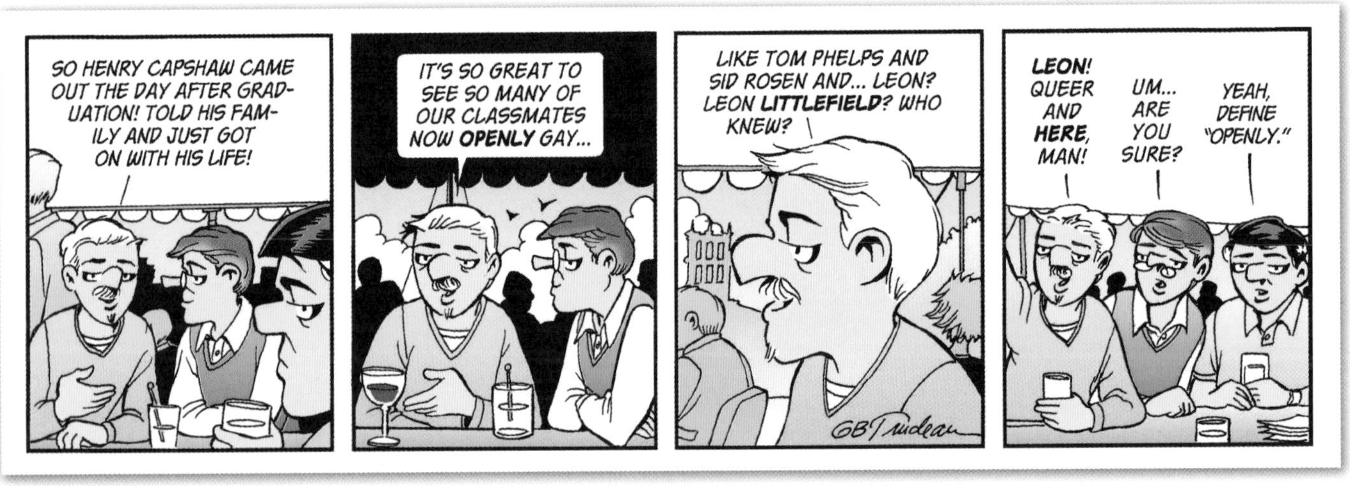
SO HENRY CAPSHAW CAME OUT THE DAY AFTER GRADUATION! TOLD HIS FAMILY AND JUST GOT ON WITH HIS LIFE!
IT'S SO GREAT TO SEE SO MANY OF OUR CLASSMATES NOW **OPENLY** GAY...
LIKE TOM PHELPS AND SID ROSEN AND... LEON? LEON **LITTLEFIELD**? WHO KNEW?
GB Trudeau
LEON! QUEER AND **HERE**, MAN!
UM... ARE YOU SURE?
YEAH, DEFINE "OPENLY."

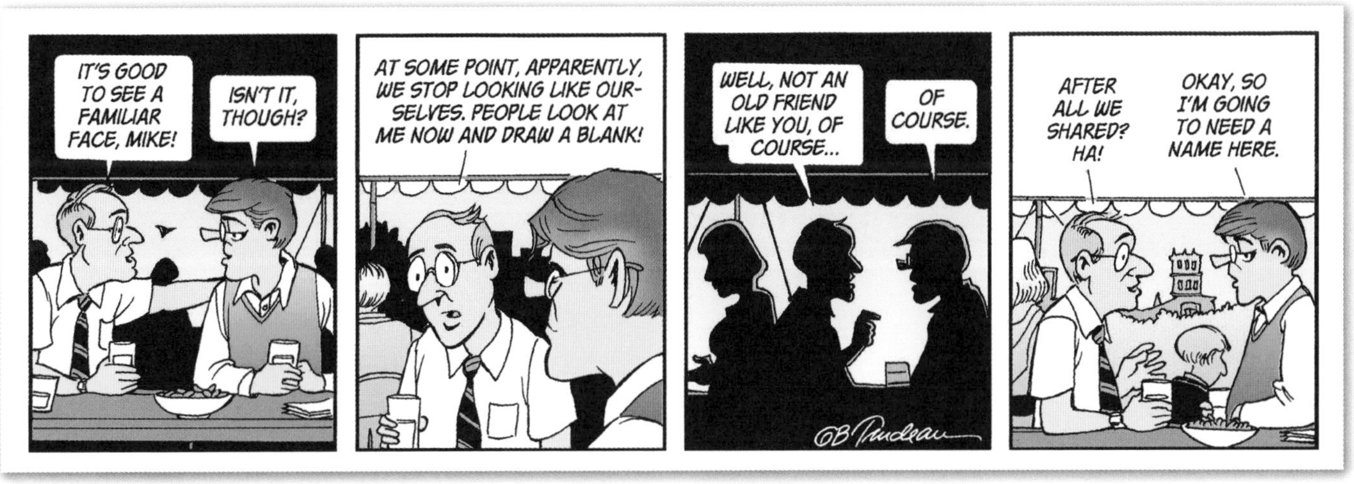
IT'S GOOD TO SEE A FAMILIAR FACE, MIKE!
ISN'T IT, THOUGH?
AT SOME POINT, APPARENTLY, WE STOP LOOKING LIKE OUR-SELVES. PEOPLE LOOK AT ME NOW AND DRAW A BLANK!
WELL, NOT AN OLD FRIEND LIKE YOU, OF COURSE...
OF COURSE.
AFTER ALL WE SHARED? HA!
OKAY, SO I'M GOING TO NEED A NAME HERE.

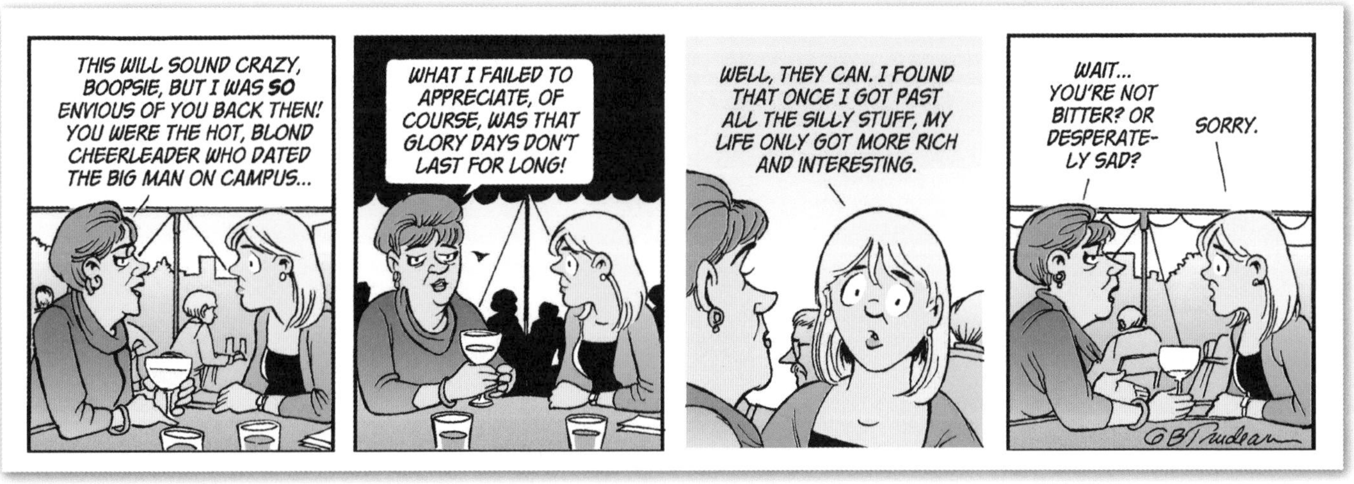
THIS WILL SOUND CRAZY, BOOPSIE, BUT I WAS **SO** ENVIOUS OF YOU BACK THEN! YOU WERE THE HOT, BLOND CHEERLEADER WHO DATED THE BIG MAN ON CAMPUS...
WHAT I FAILED TO APPRECIATE, OF COURSE, WAS THAT GLORY DAYS DON'T LAST FOR LONG!
WELL, THEY CAN. I FOUND THAT ONCE I GOT PAST ALL THE SILLY STUFF, MY LIFE ONLY GOT MORE RICH AND INTERESTING.
WAIT... YOU'RE NOT BITTER? OR DESPERATE-LY SAD?
SORRY.

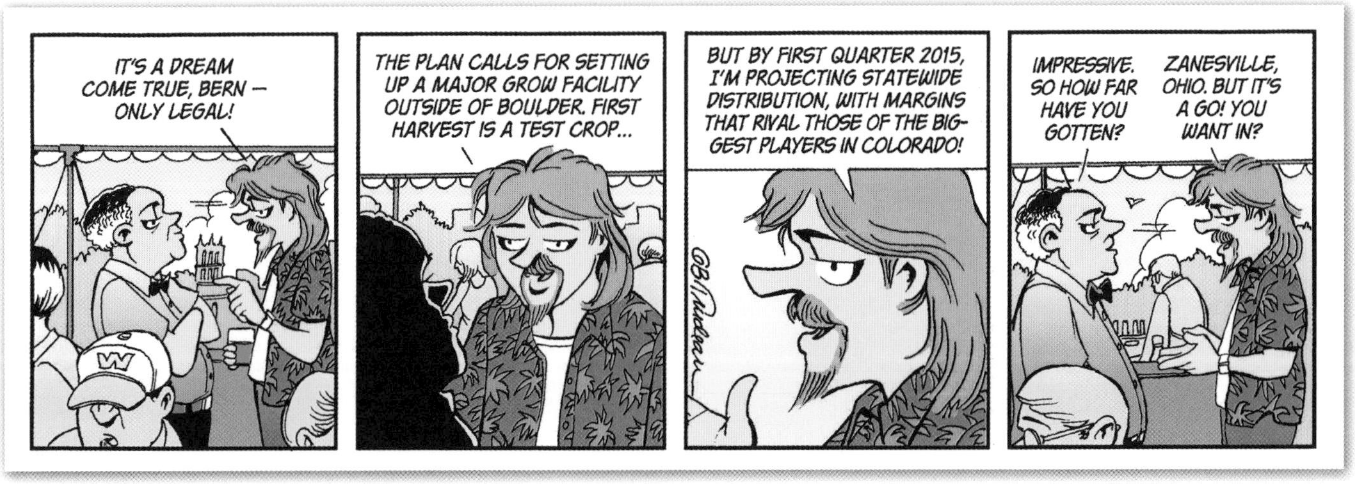
IT'S A DREAM COME TRUE, BERN — ONLY LEGAL!
THE PLAN CALLS FOR SETTING UP A MAJOR GROW FACILITY OUTSIDE OF BOULDER. FIRST HARVEST IS A TEST CROP...
BUT BY FIRST QUARTER 2015, I'M PROJECTING STATEWIDE DISTRIBUTION, WITH MARGINS THAT RIVAL THOSE OF THE BIG-GEST PLAYERS IN COLORADO!
IMPRESSIVE. SO HOW FAR HAVE YOU GOTTEN?
ZANESVILLE, OHIO. BUT IT'S A GO! YOU WANT IN?

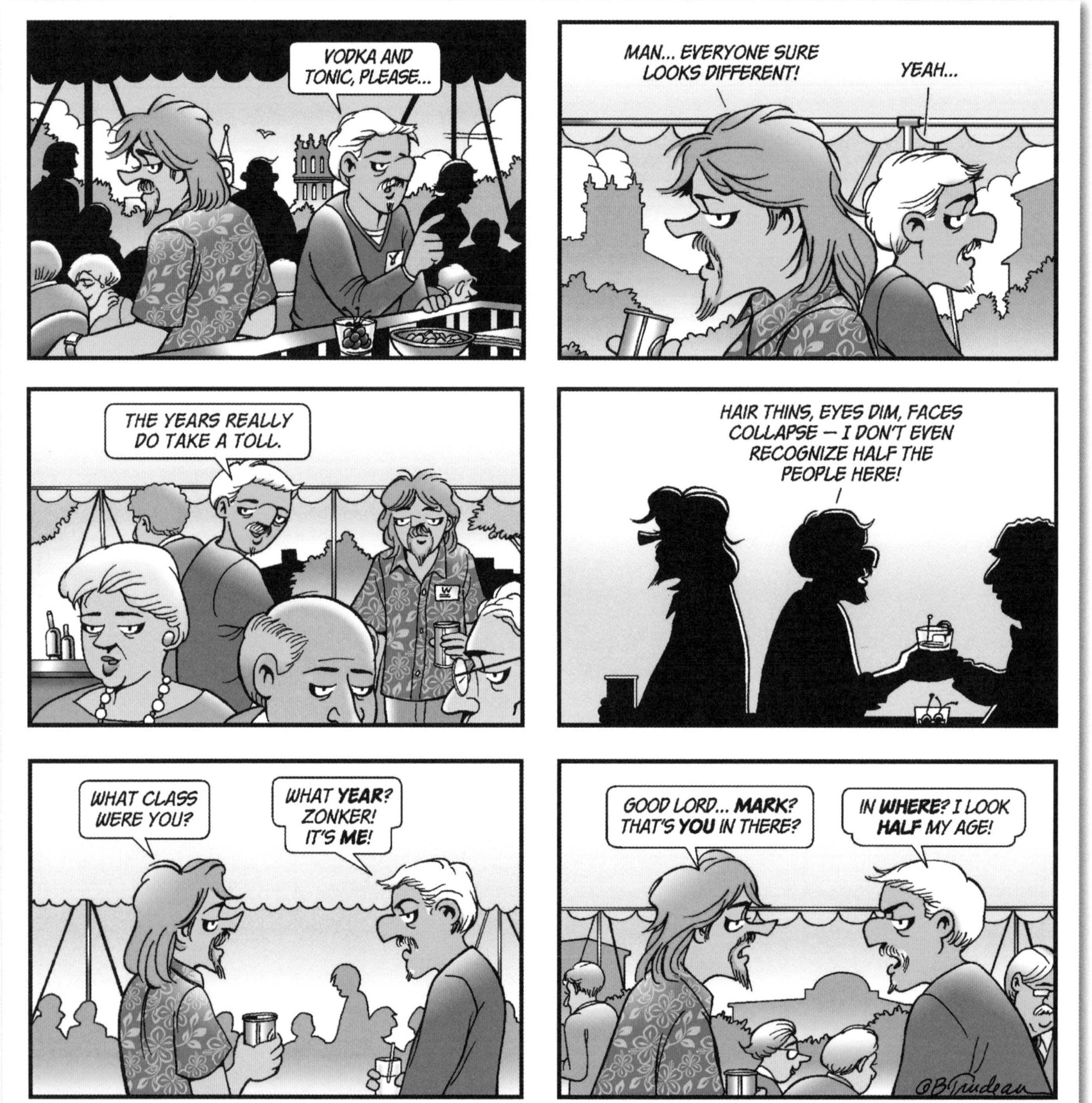
VODKA AND TONIC, PLEASE...
MAN... EVERYONE SURE LOOKS DIFFERENT!
YEAH...
THE YEARS REALLY DO TAKE A TOLL.
HAIR THINS, EYES DIM, FACES COLLAPSE — I DON'T EVEN RECOGNIZE HALF THE PEOPLE HERE!
WHAT CLASS WERE YOU?
WHAT YEAR? ZONKER! IT'S ME!
GOOD LORD... MARK? THAT'S YOU IN THERE?
IN WHERE? I LOOK HALF MY AGE!
©B. Trudeau

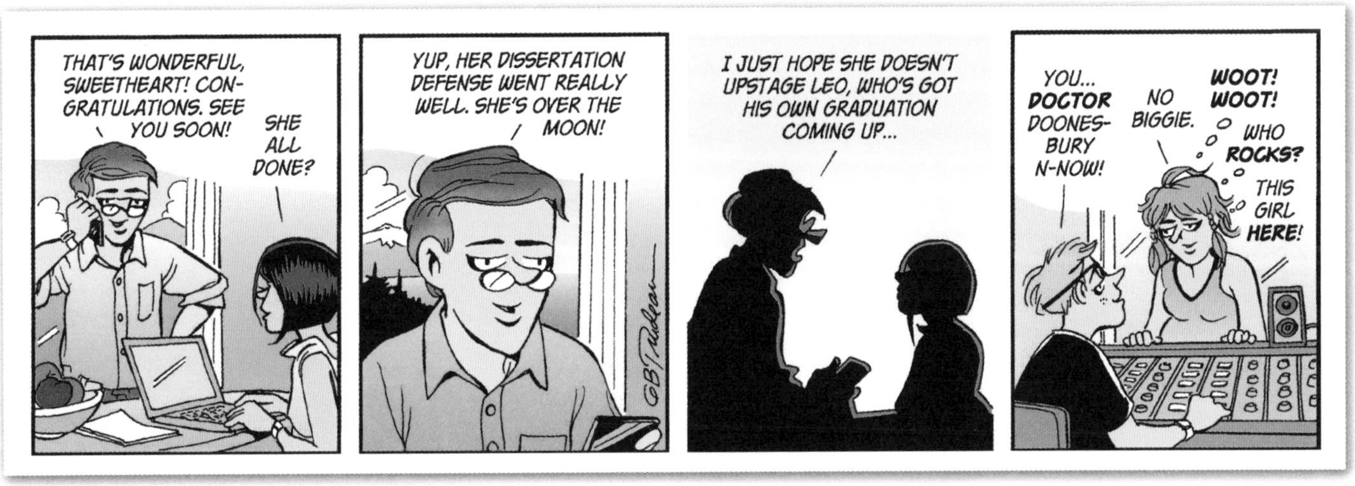
THAT'S WONDERFUL, SWEETHEART! CONGRATULATIONS. SEE YOU SOON!
SHE ALL DONE?
YUP, HER DISSERTATION DEFENSE WENT REALLY WELL. SHE'S OVER THE MOON!
I JUST HOPE SHE DOESN'T UPSTAGE LEO, WHO'S GOT HIS OWN GRADUATION COMING UP...
YOU... DOCTOR DOONESBURY N-NOW!
NO BIGGIE.
WOOT! WOOT!
WHO ROCKS?
THIS GIRL HERE!

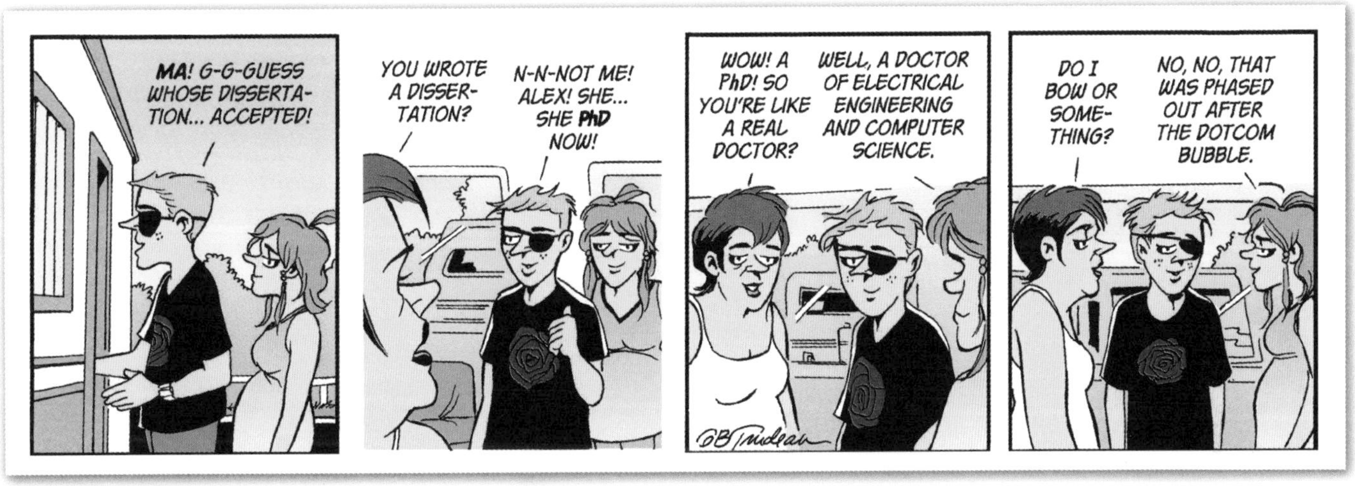
MA! G-G-GUESS WHOSE DISSERTATION... ACCEPTED!
YOU WROTE A DISSERTATION?
N-N-NOT ME! ALEX! SHE... SHE PhD NOW!
WOW! A PhD! SO YOU'RE LIKE A REAL DOCTOR?
WELL, A DOCTOR OF ELECTRICAL ENGINEERING AND COMPUTER SCIENCE.
DO I BOW OR SOMETHING?
NO, NO, THAT WAS PHASED OUT AFTER THE DOTCOM BUBBLE.

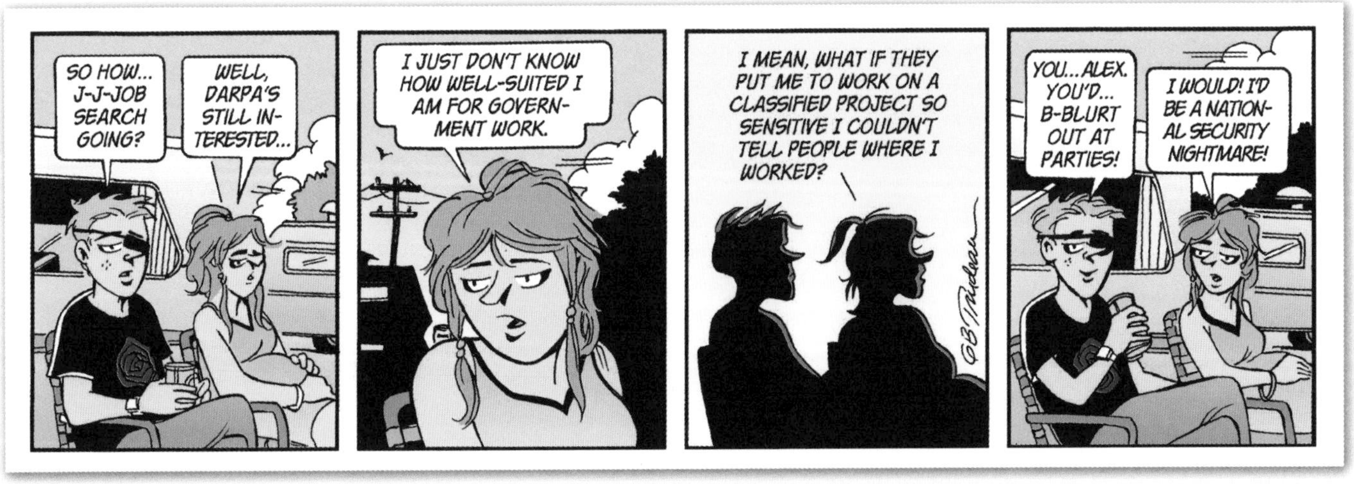
SO HOW... J-J-JOB SEARCH GOING?
WELL, DARPA'S STILL INTERESTED...
I JUST DON'T KNOW HOW WELL-SUITED I AM FOR GOVERNMENT WORK.
I MEAN, WHAT IF THEY PUT ME TO WORK ON A CLASSIFIED PROJECT SO SENSITIVE I COULDN'T TELL PEOPLE WHERE I WORKED?
YOU...ALEX. YOU'D... B-BLURT OUT AT PARTIES!
I WOULD! I'D BE A NATIONAL SECURITY NIGHTMARE!

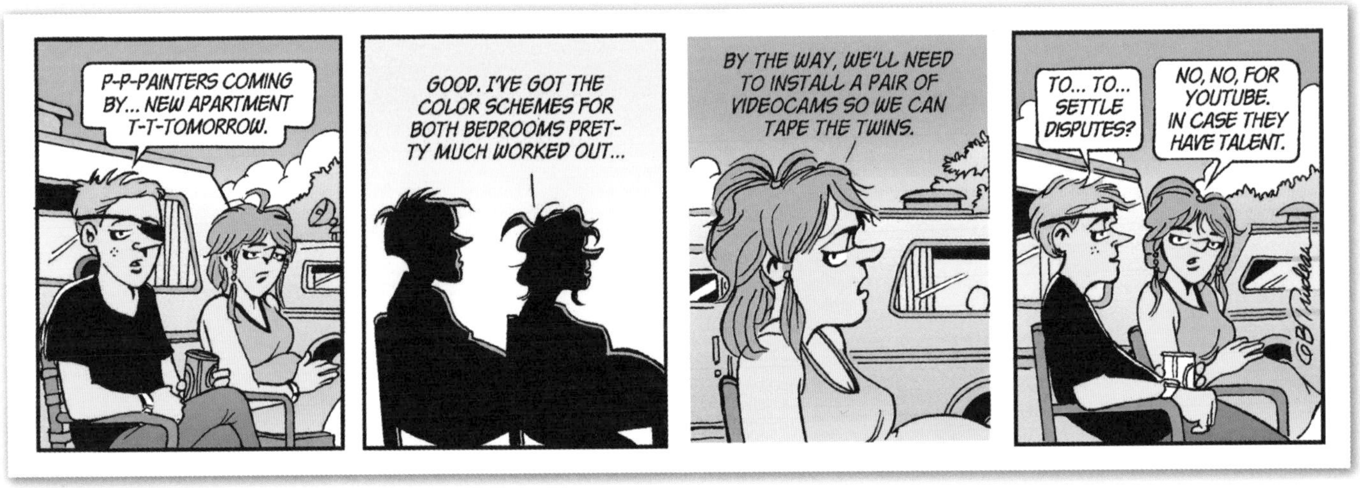
P-P-PAINTERS COMING BY... NEW APARTMENT T-T-TOMORROW.
GOOD. I'VE GOT THE COLOR SCHEMES FOR BOTH BEDROOMS PRETTY MUCH WORKED OUT...
BY THE WAY, WE'LL NEED TO INSTALL A PAIR OF VIDEOCAMS SO WE CAN TAPE THE TWINS.
TO... TO... SETTLE DISPUTES?
NO, NO, FOR YOUTUBE. IN CASE THEY HAVE TALENT.
GB Trudeau

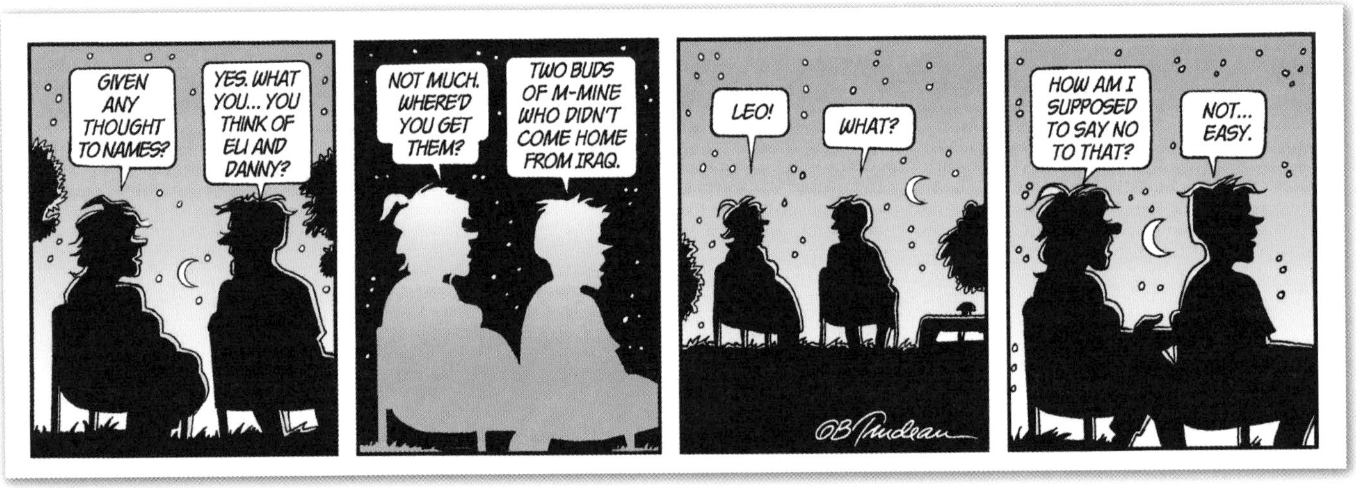
GIVEN ANY THOUGHT TO NAMES?
YES. WHAT YOU... YOU THINK OF ELI AND DANNY?
NOT MUCH. WHERE'D YOU GET THEM?
TWO BUDS OF M-MINE WHO DIDN'T COME HOME FROM IRAQ.
LEO!
WHAT?
HOW AM I SUPPOSED TO SAY NO TO THAT?
NOT... EASY.
GB Trudeau

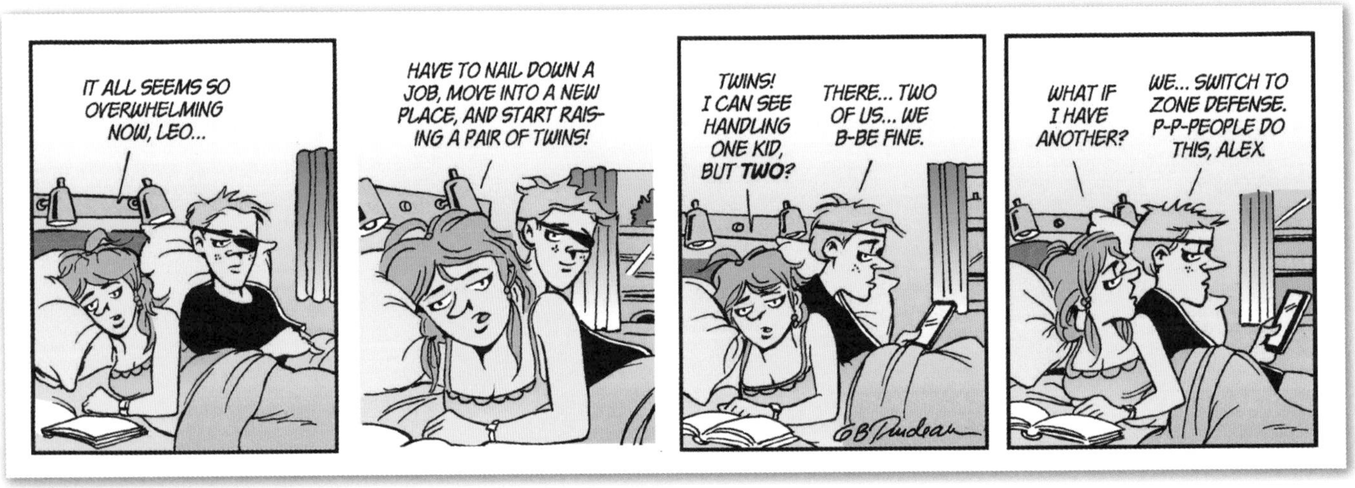
IT ALL SEEMS SO OVERWHELMING NOW, LEO...
HAVE TO NAIL DOWN A JOB, MOVE INTO A NEW PLACE, AND START RAISING A PAIR OF TWINS!
TWINS! I CAN SEE HANDLING ONE KID, BUT **TWO**?
THERE... TWO OF US... WE B-BE FINE.
WHAT IF I HAVE ANOTHER?
WE... SWITCH TO ZONE DEFENSE. P-P-PEOPLE DO THIS, ALEX.
GB Trudeau

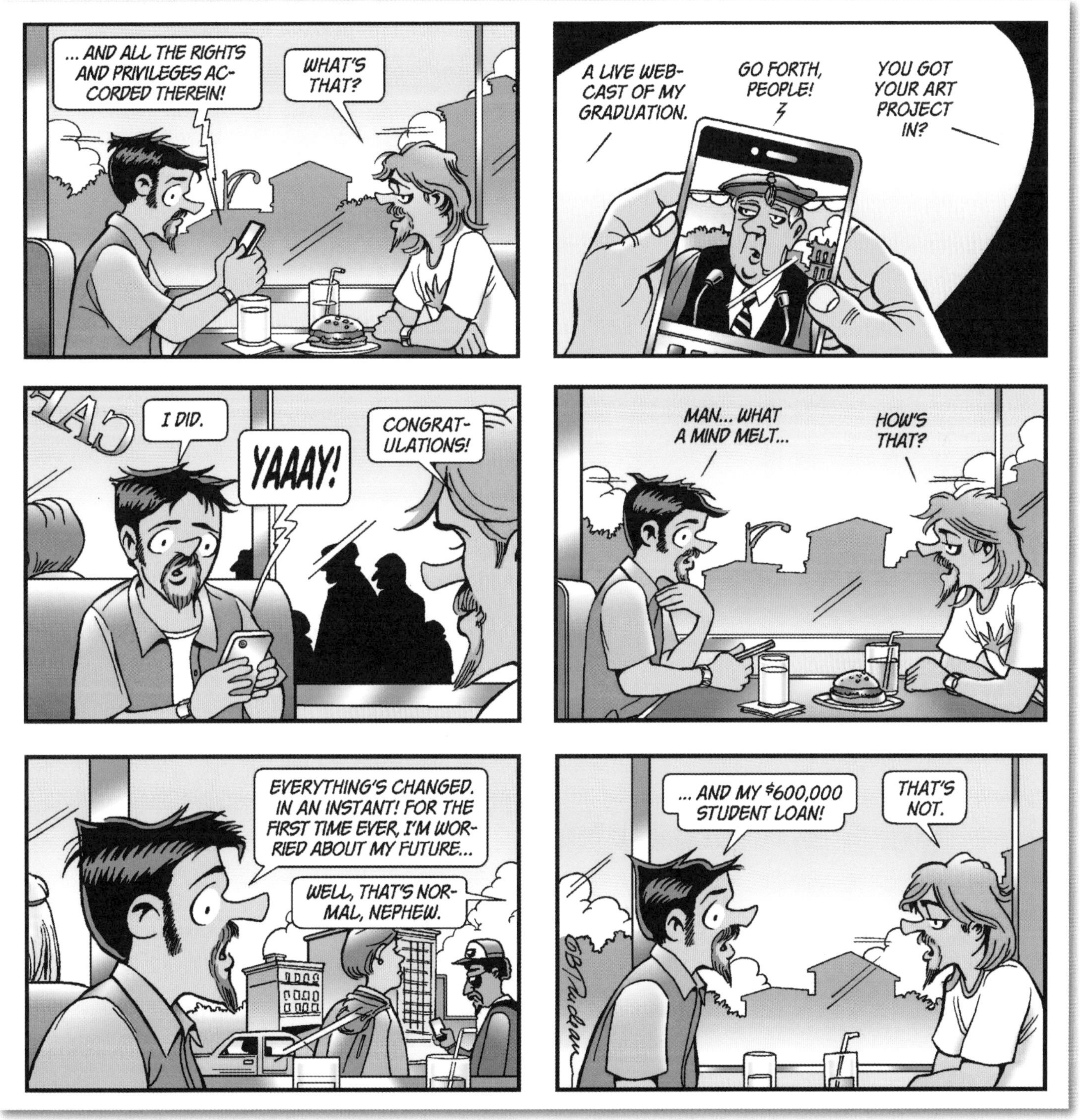
... AND ALL THE RIGHTS AND PRIVILEGES ACCORDED THEREIN!
WHAT'S THAT?
A LIVE WEBCAST OF MY GRADUATION.
GO FORTH, PEOPLE!
YOU GOT YOUR ART PROJECT IN?
I DID.
YAAAY!
CONGRATULATIONS!
MAN... WHAT A MIND MELT...
HOW'S THAT?
EVERYTHING'S CHANGED. IN AN INSTANT! FOR THE FIRST TIME EVER, I'M WORRIED ABOUT MY FUTURE...
WELL, THAT'S NORMAL, NEPHEW.
... AND MY $600,000 STUDENT LOAN!
THAT'S NOT.

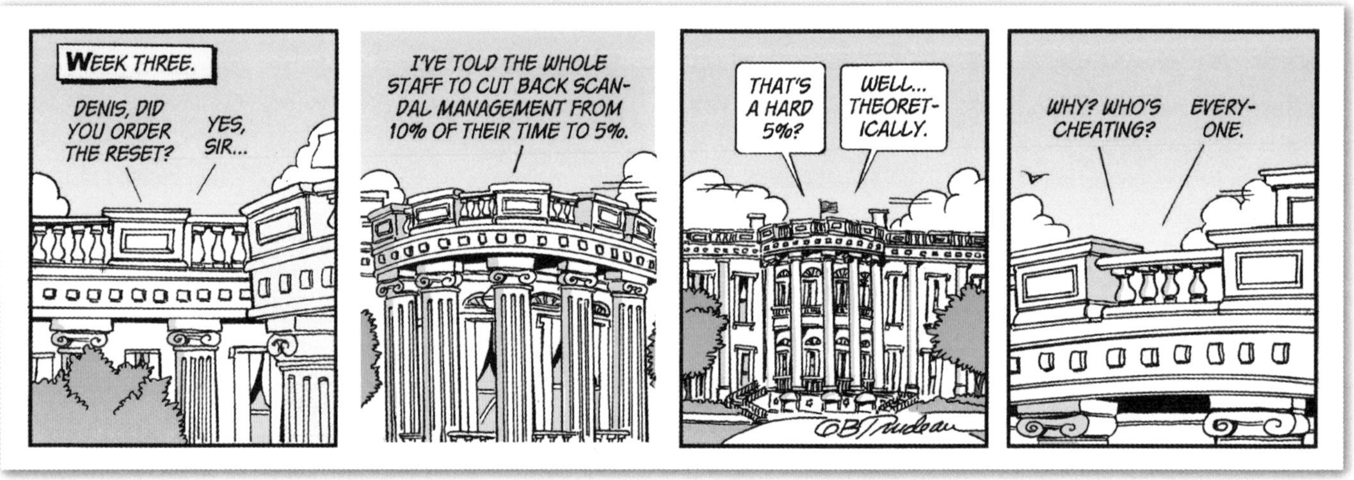
WEEK THREE.
DENIS, DID YOU ORDER THE RESET?
YES, SIR...
I'VE TOLD THE WHOLE STAFF TO CUT BACK SCANDAL MANAGEMENT FROM 10% OF THEIR TIME TO 5%.
THAT'S A HARD 5%?
WELL... THEORETICALLY.
WHY? WHO'S CHEATING?
EVERYONE.
GBTrudeau

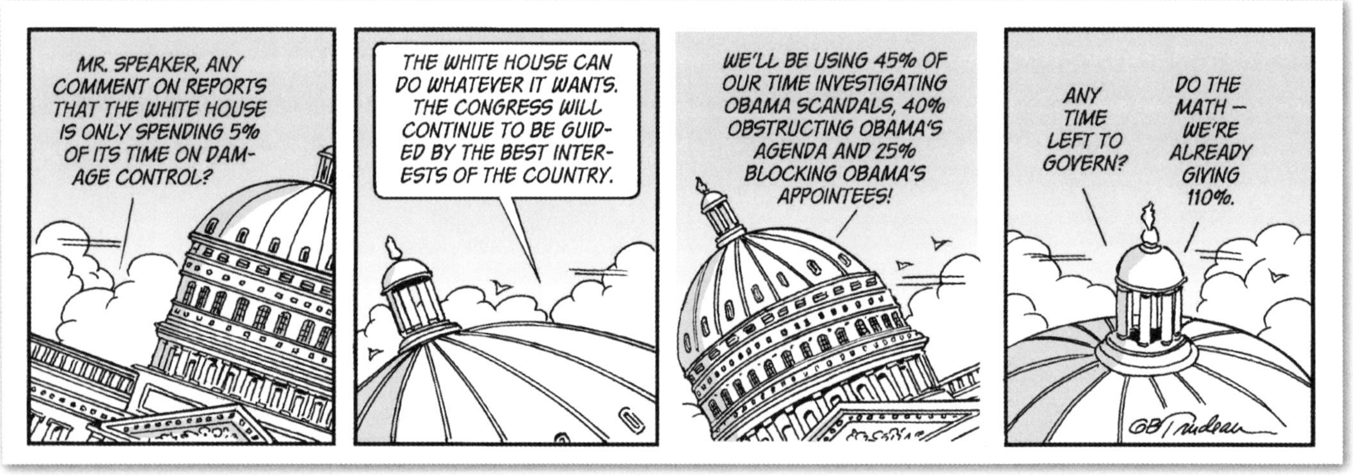
MR. SPEAKER, ANY COMMENT ON REPORTS THAT THE WHITE HOUSE IS ONLY SPENDING 5% OF ITS TIME ON DAMAGE CONTROL?
THE WHITE HOUSE CAN DO WHATEVER IT WANTS. THE CONGRESS WILL CONTINUE TO BE GUIDED BY THE BEST INTERESTS OF THE COUNTRY.
WE'LL BE USING 45% OF OUR TIME INVESTIGATING OBAMA SCANDALS, 40% OBSTRUCTING OBAMA'S AGENDA AND 25% BLOCKING OBAMA'S APPOINTEES!
ANY TIME LEFT TO GOVERN?
DO THE MATH — WE'RE ALREADY GIVING 110%.
GBTrudeau

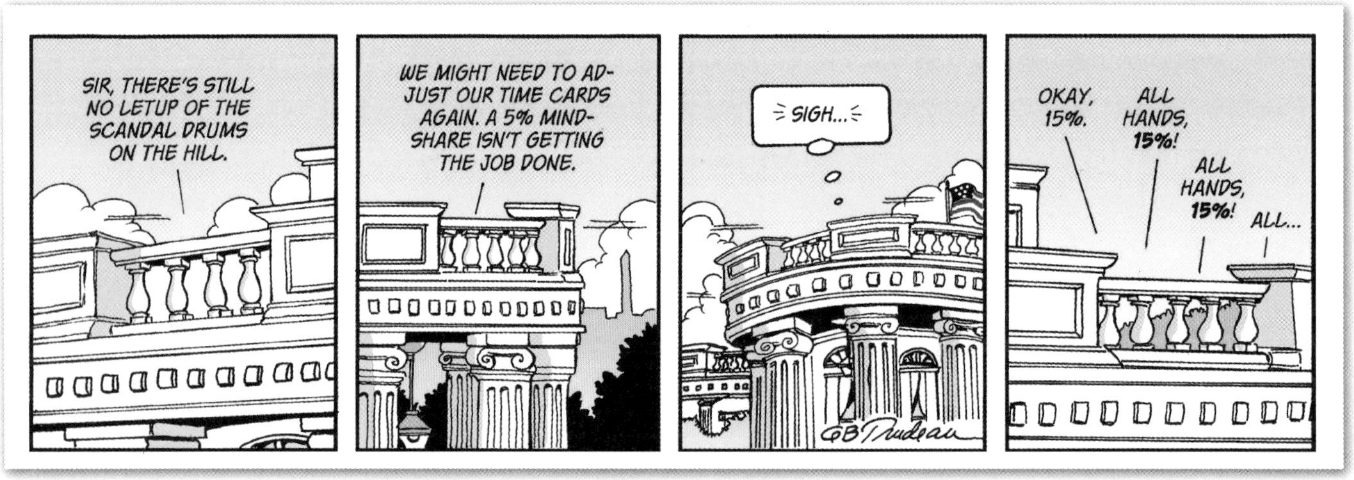
SIR, THERE'S STILL NO LETUP OF THE SCANDAL DRUMS ON THE HILL.
WE MIGHT NEED TO ADJUST OUR TIME CARDS AGAIN. A 5% MINDSHARE ISN'T GETTING THE JOB DONE.
SIGH...
OKAY, 15%.
ALL HANDS, 15%!
ALL HANDS, 15%!
ALL...
GBTrudeau

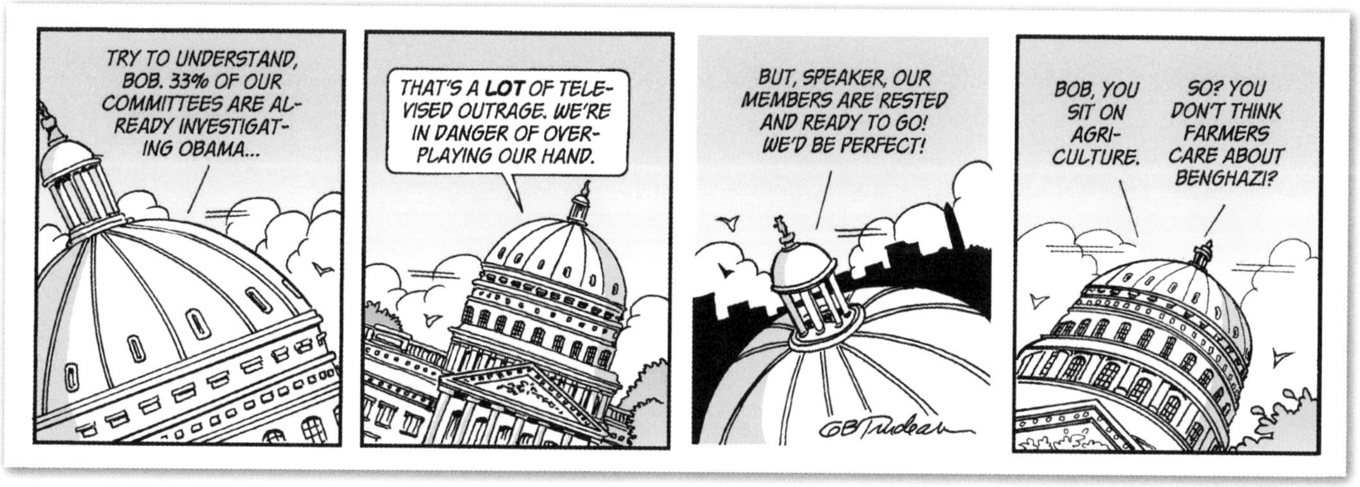
TRY TO UNDERSTAND, BOB. 33% OF OUR COMMITTEES ARE ALREADY INVESTIGATING OBAMA...
THAT'S A **LOT** OF TELEVISED OUTRAGE. WE'RE IN DANGER OF OVERPLAYING OUR HAND.
BUT, SPEAKER, OUR MEMBERS ARE RESTED AND READY TO GO! WE'D BE PERFECT!
BOB, YOU SIT ON AGRICULTURE.
SO? YOU DON'T THINK FARMERS CARE ABOUT BENGHAZI?
GBTrudeau

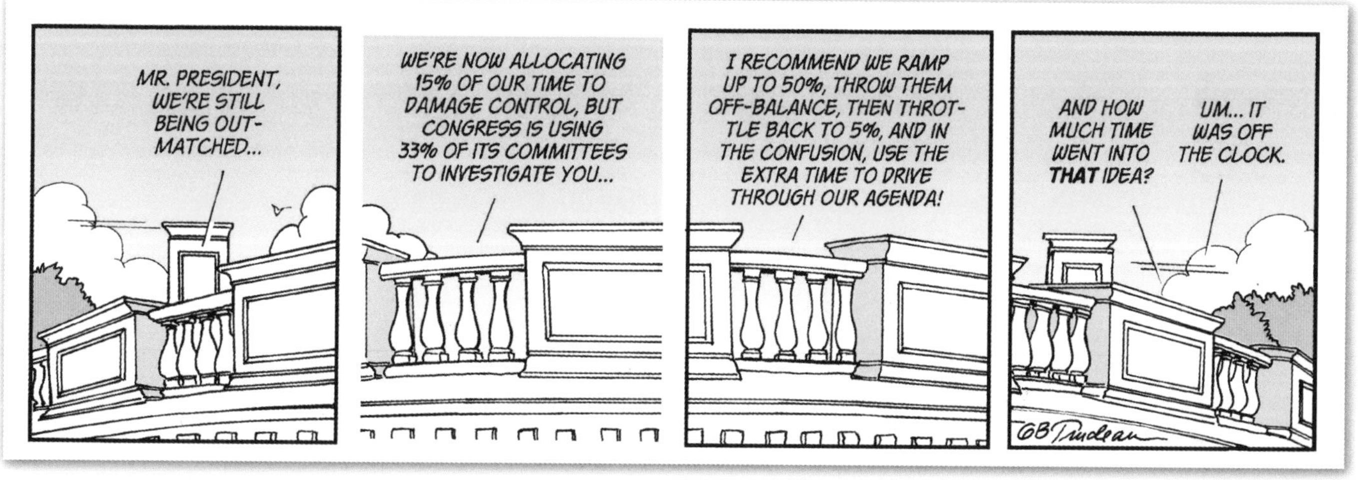
MR. PRESIDENT, WE'RE STILL BEING OUTMATCHED...
WE'RE NOW ALLOCATING 15% OF OUR TIME TO DAMAGE CONTROL, BUT CONGRESS IS USING 33% OF ITS COMMITTEES TO INVESTIGATE YOU...
I RECOMMEND WE RAMP UP TO 50%, THROW THEM OFF-BALANCE, THEN THROTTLE BACK TO 5%, AND IN THE CONFUSION, USE THE EXTRA TIME TO DRIVE THROUGH OUR AGENDA!
AND HOW MUCH TIME WENT INTO **THAT** IDEA?
UM... IT WAS OFF THE CLOCK.
GBTrudeau

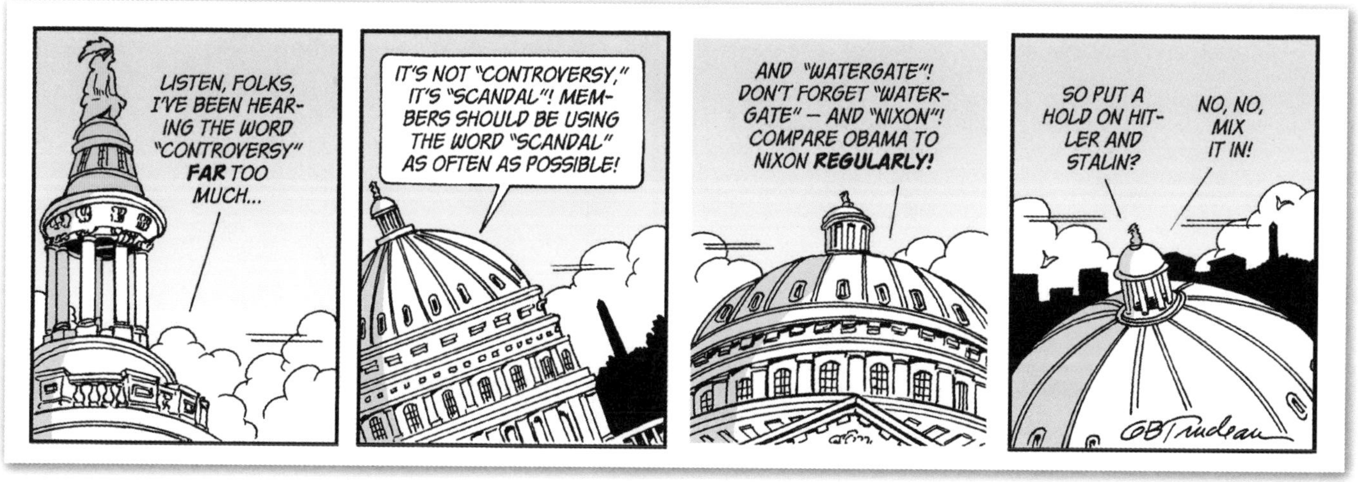
LISTEN, FOLKS, I'VE BEEN HEARING THE WORD "CONTROVERSY" **FAR** TOO MUCH...
IT'S NOT "CONTROVERSY," IT'S "SCANDAL"! MEMBERS SHOULD BE USING THE WORD "SCANDAL" AS OFTEN AS POSSIBLE!
AND "WATERGATE"! DON'T FORGET "WATERGATE" — AND "NIXON"! COMPARE OBAMA TO NIXON **REGULARLY!**
SO PUT A HOLD ON HITLER AND STALIN?
NO, NO, MIX IT IN!
GBTrudeau

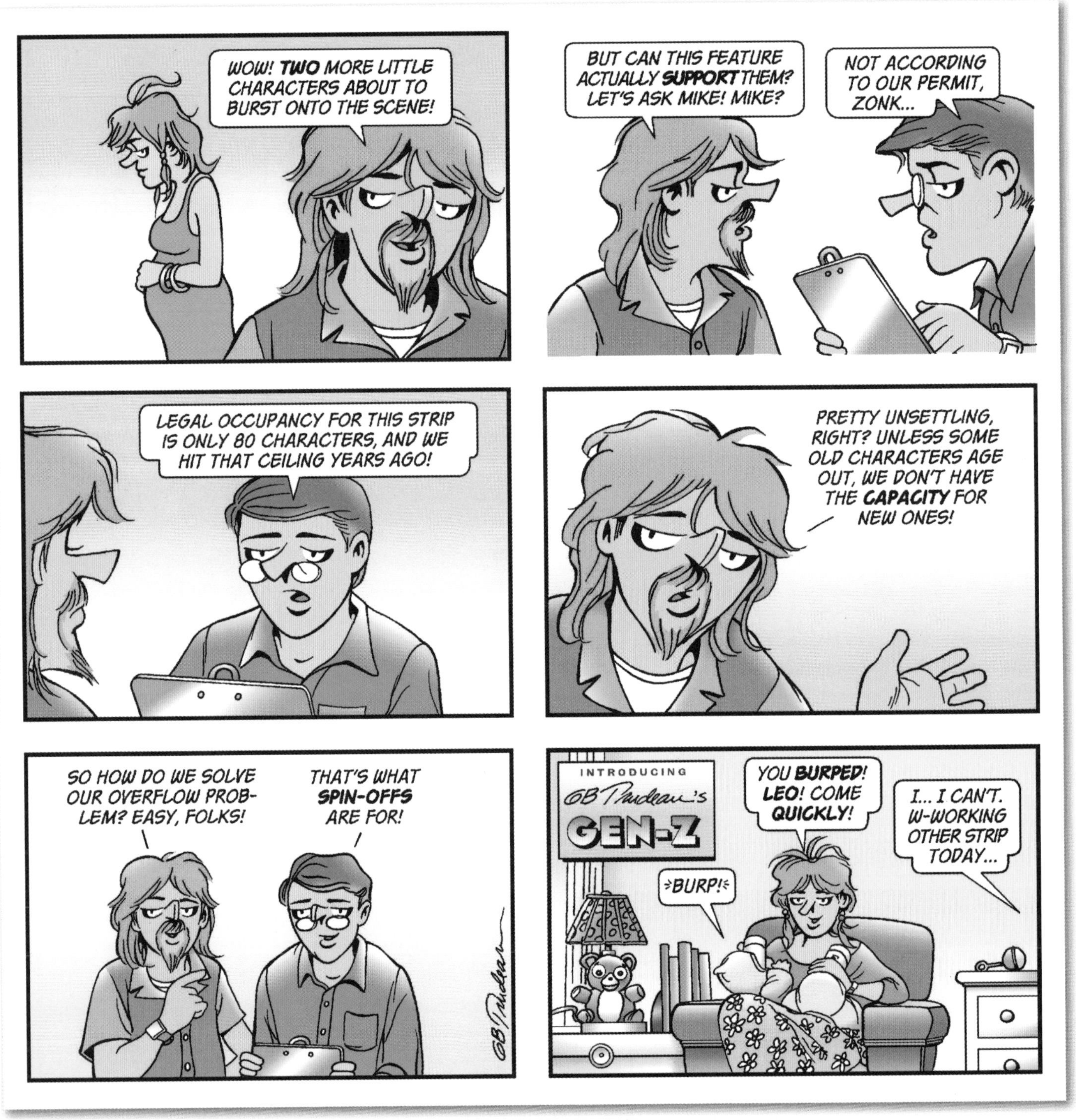
WOW! TWO MORE LITTLE CHARACTERS ABOUT TO BURST ONTO THE SCENE!
BUT CAN THIS FEATURE ACTUALLY SUPPORT THEM? LET'S ASK MIKE! MIKE?
NOT ACCORDING TO OUR PERMIT, ZONK...
LEGAL OCCUPANCY FOR THIS STRIP IS ONLY 80 CHARACTERS, AND WE HIT THAT CEILING YEARS AGO!
PRETTY UNSETTLING, RIGHT? UNLESS SOME OLD CHARACTERS AGE OUT, WE DON'T HAVE THE CAPACITY FOR NEW ONES!
SO HOW DO WE SOLVE OUR OVERFLOW PROB-LEM? EASY, FOLKS!
THAT'S WHAT SPIN-OFFS ARE FOR!
INTRODUCING
GB Trudeau's
GEN-Z
YOU BURPED! LEO! COME QUICKLY!
I... I CAN'T. W-WORKING OTHER STRIP TODAY...
BURP!

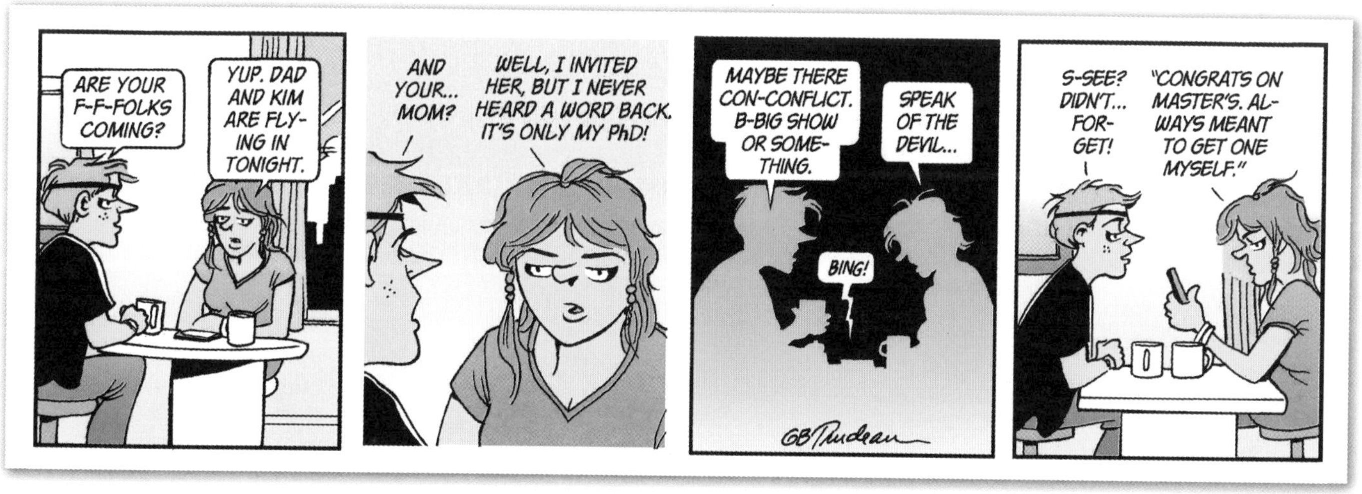
ARE YOUR F-F-FOLKS COMING?
YUP. DAD AND KIM ARE FLYING IN TONIGHT.
AND YOUR... MOM?
WELL, I INVITED HER, BUT I NEVER HEARD A WORD BACK. IT'S ONLY MY PhD!
MAYBE THERE CON-CONFLICT. B-BIG SHOW OR SOMETHING.
SPEAK OF THE DEVIL...
BING!
S-SEE? DIDN'T... FORGET!
"CONGRATS ON MASTER'S. ALWAYS MEANT TO GET ONE MYSELF."
GB Trudeau

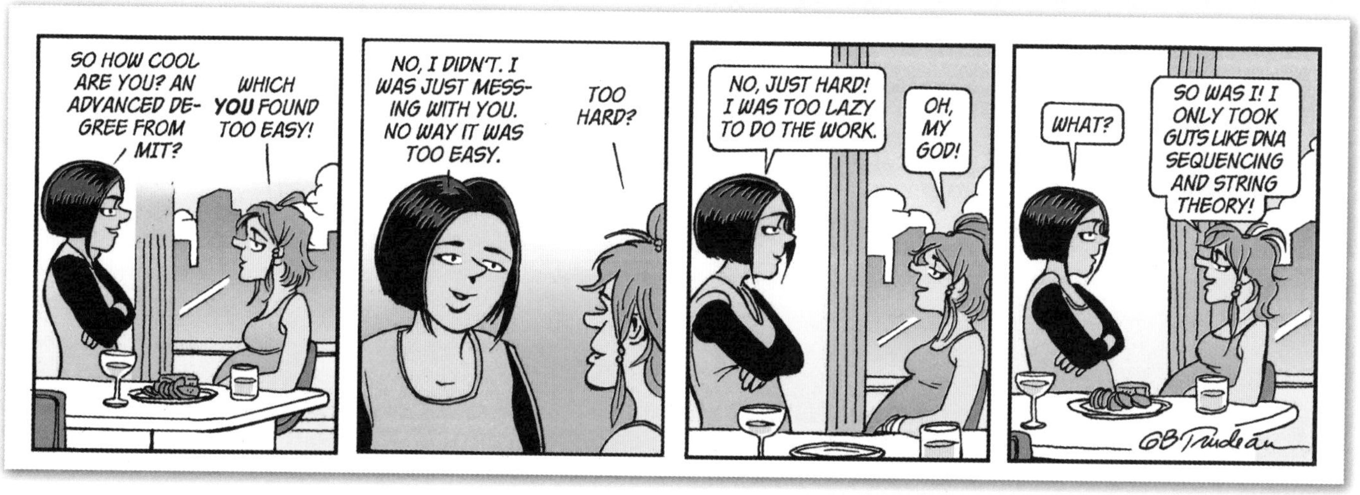
SO HOW COOL ARE YOU? AN ADVANCED DEGREE FROM MIT?
WHICH YOU FOUND TOO EASY!
NO, I DIDN'T. I WAS JUST MESSING WITH YOU. NO WAY IT WAS TOO EASY.
TOO HARD?
NO, JUST HARD! I WAS TOO LAZY TO DO THE WORK.
OH, MY GOD!
WHAT?
SO WAS I! I ONLY TOOK GUTS LIKE DNA SEQUENCING AND STRING THEORY!
GB Trudeau

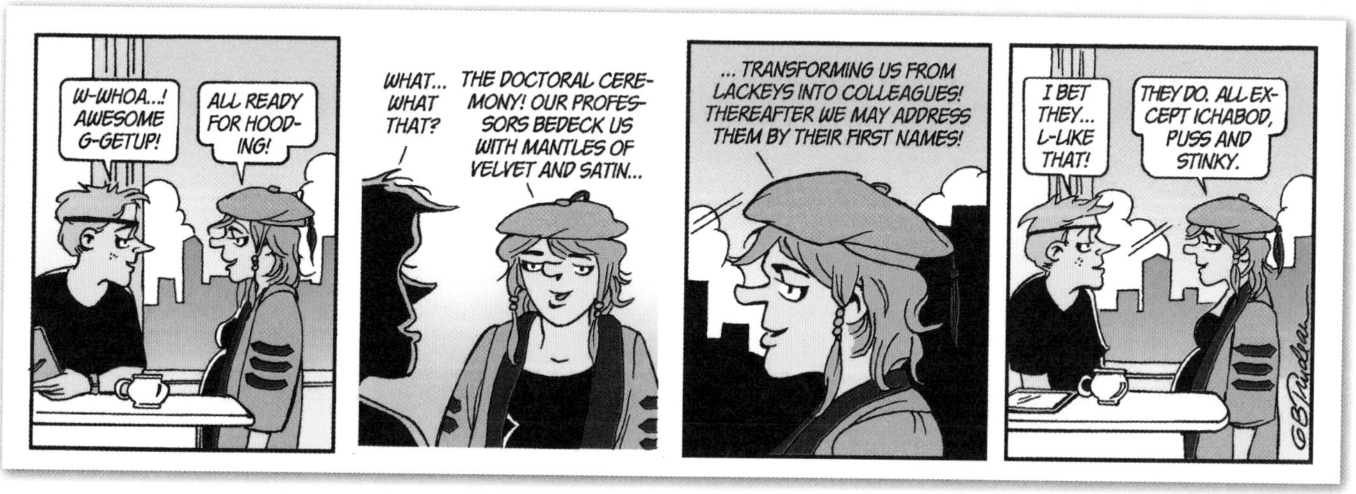
W-WHOA...! AWESOME G-GETUP!
ALL READY FOR HOODING!
WHAT... WHAT THAT?
THE DOCTORAL CEREMONY! OUR PROFESSORS BEDECK US WITH MANTLES OF VELVET AND SATIN...
... TRANSFORMING US FROM LACKEYS INTO COLLEAGUES! THEREAFTER WE MAY ADDRESS THEM BY THEIR FIRST NAMES!
I BET THEY... L-LIKE THAT!
THEY DO. ALL EXCEPT ICHABOD, PUSS AND STINKY.
GB Trudeau

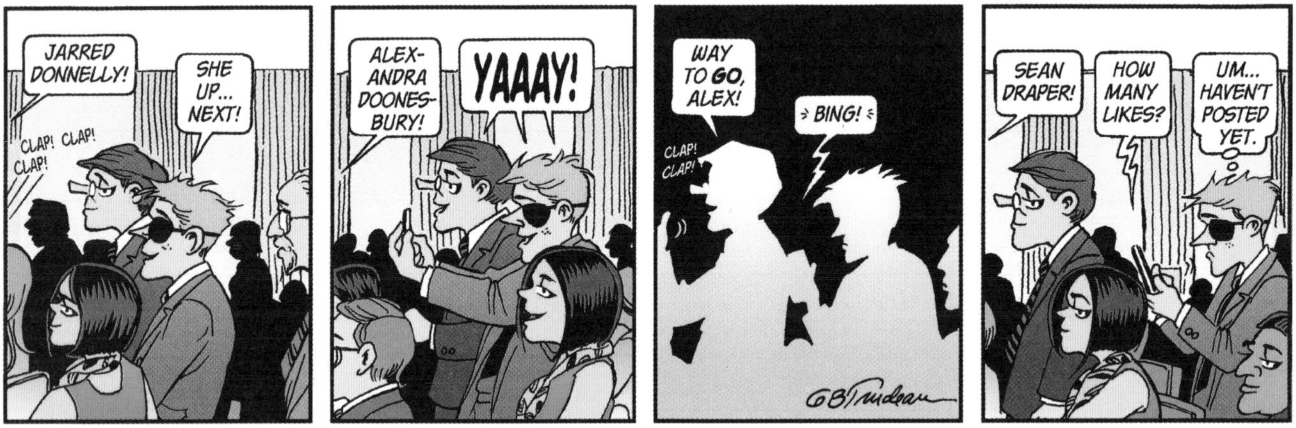
JARRED DONNELLY!
SHE UP... NEXT!
CLAP! CLAP! CLAP!
ALEX-ANDRA DOONES-BURY!
YAAAY!
WAY TO GO, ALEX!
CLAP! CLAP!
BING!
SEAN DRAPER!
HOW MANY LIKES?
UM... HAVEN'T POSTED YET.

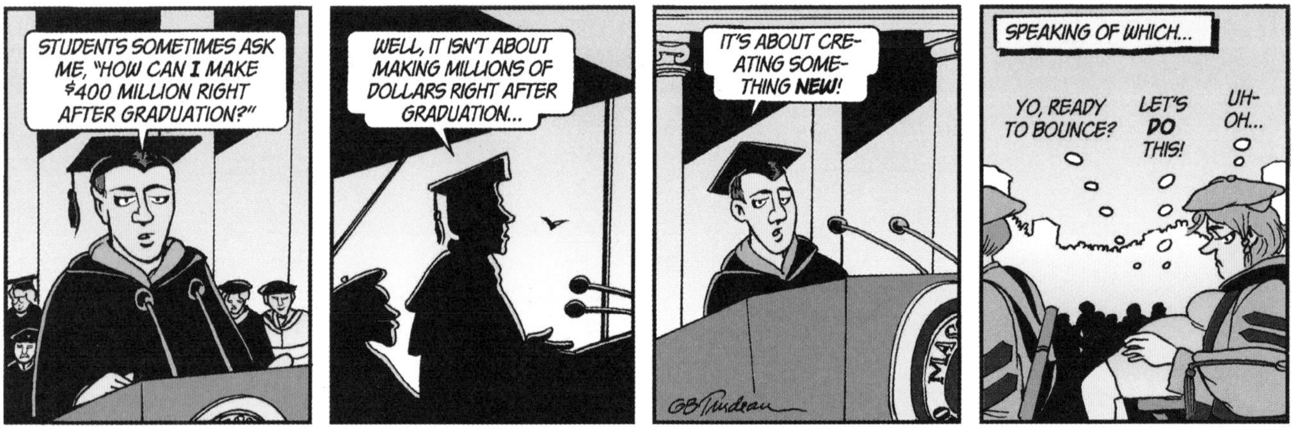
STUDENTS SOMETIMES ASK ME, "HOW CAN I MAKE $400 MILLION RIGHT AFTER GRADUATION?"
WELL, IT ISN'T ABOUT MAKING MILLIONS OF DOLLARS RIGHT AFTER GRADUATION...
IT'S ABOUT CRE-ATING SOME-THING NEW!
SPEAKING OF WHICH...
YO, READY TO BOUNCE?
LET'S DO THIS!
UH-OH...

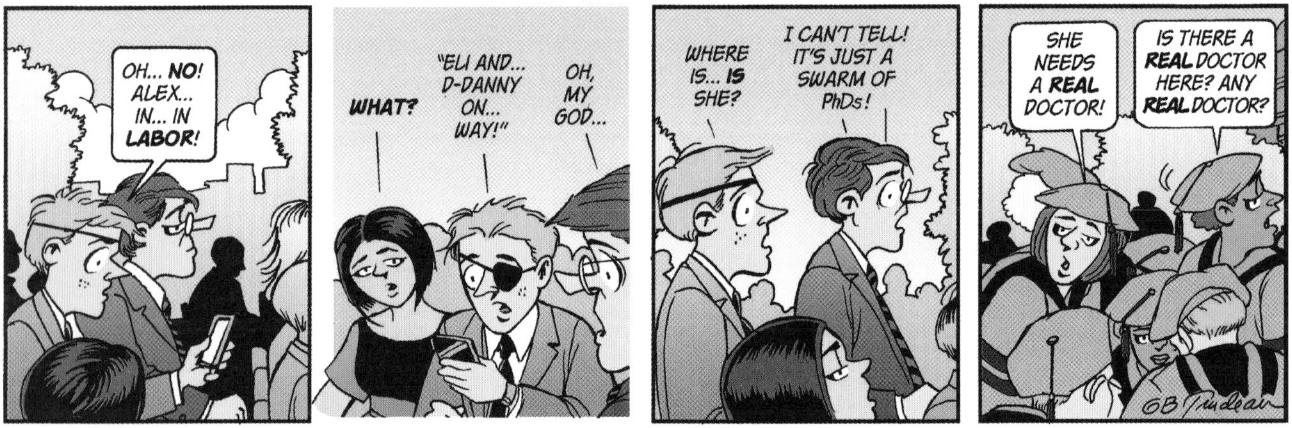
OH... NO! ALEX... IN... IN LABOR!
WHAT?
"ELI AND... D-DANNY ON... WAY!"
OH, MY GOD...
WHERE IS... IS SHE?
I CAN'T TELL! IT'S JUST A SWARM OF PhDs!
SHE NEEDS A REAL DOCTOR!
IS THERE A REAL DOCTOR HERE? ANY REAL DOCTOR?

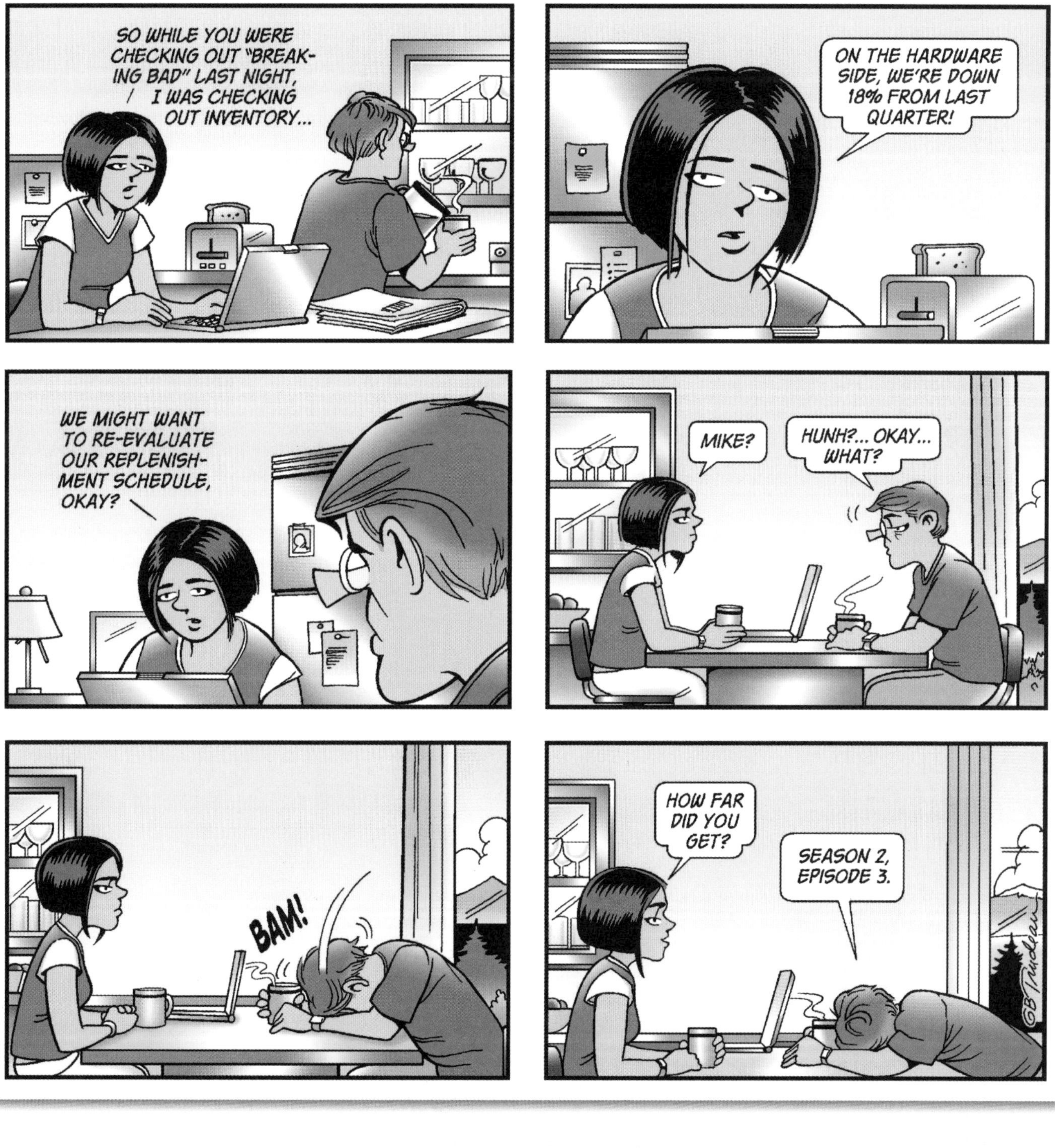
SO WHILE YOU WERE CHECKING OUT "BREAKING BAD" LAST NIGHT,
I WAS CHECKING OUT INVENTORY...
ON THE HARDWARE SIDE, WE'RE DOWN 18% FROM LAST QUARTER!
WE MIGHT WANT TO RE-EVALUATE OUR REPLENISHMENT SCHEDULE, OKAY?
MIKE?
HUNH?... OKAY... WHAT?
BAM!
HOW FAR DID YOU GET?
SEASON 2, EPISODE 3.
©GBTrudeau

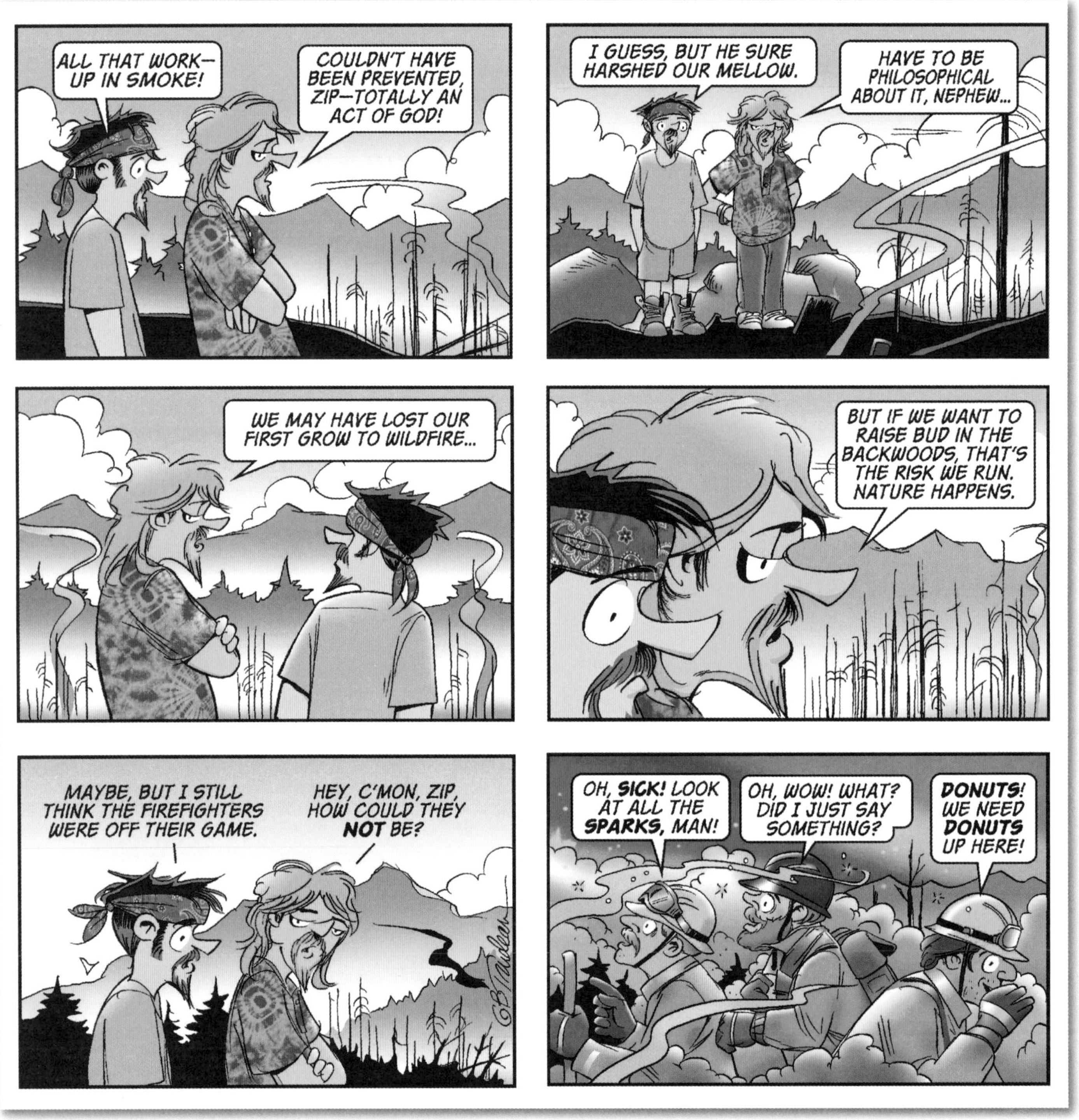
ALL THAT WORK—UP IN SMOKE!
COULDN'T HAVE BEEN PREVENTED, ZIP—TOTALLY AN ACT OF GOD!
I GUESS, BUT HE SURE HARSHED OUR MELLOW.
HAVE TO BE PHILOSOPHICAL ABOUT IT, NEPHEW...
WE MAY HAVE LOST OUR FIRST GROW TO WILDFIRE...
BUT IF WE WANT TO RAISE BUD IN THE BACKWOODS, THAT'S THE RISK WE RUN. NATURE HAPPENS.
MAYBE, BUT I STILL THINK THE FIREFIGHTERS WERE OFF THEIR GAME.
HEY, C'MON, ZIP, HOW COULD THEY **NOT** BE?
©B Trudeau
OH, **SICK!** LOOK AT ALL THE **SPARKS,** MAN!
OH, WOW! WHAT? DID I JUST SAY SOMETHING?
DONUTS! WE NEED **DONUTS** UP HERE!

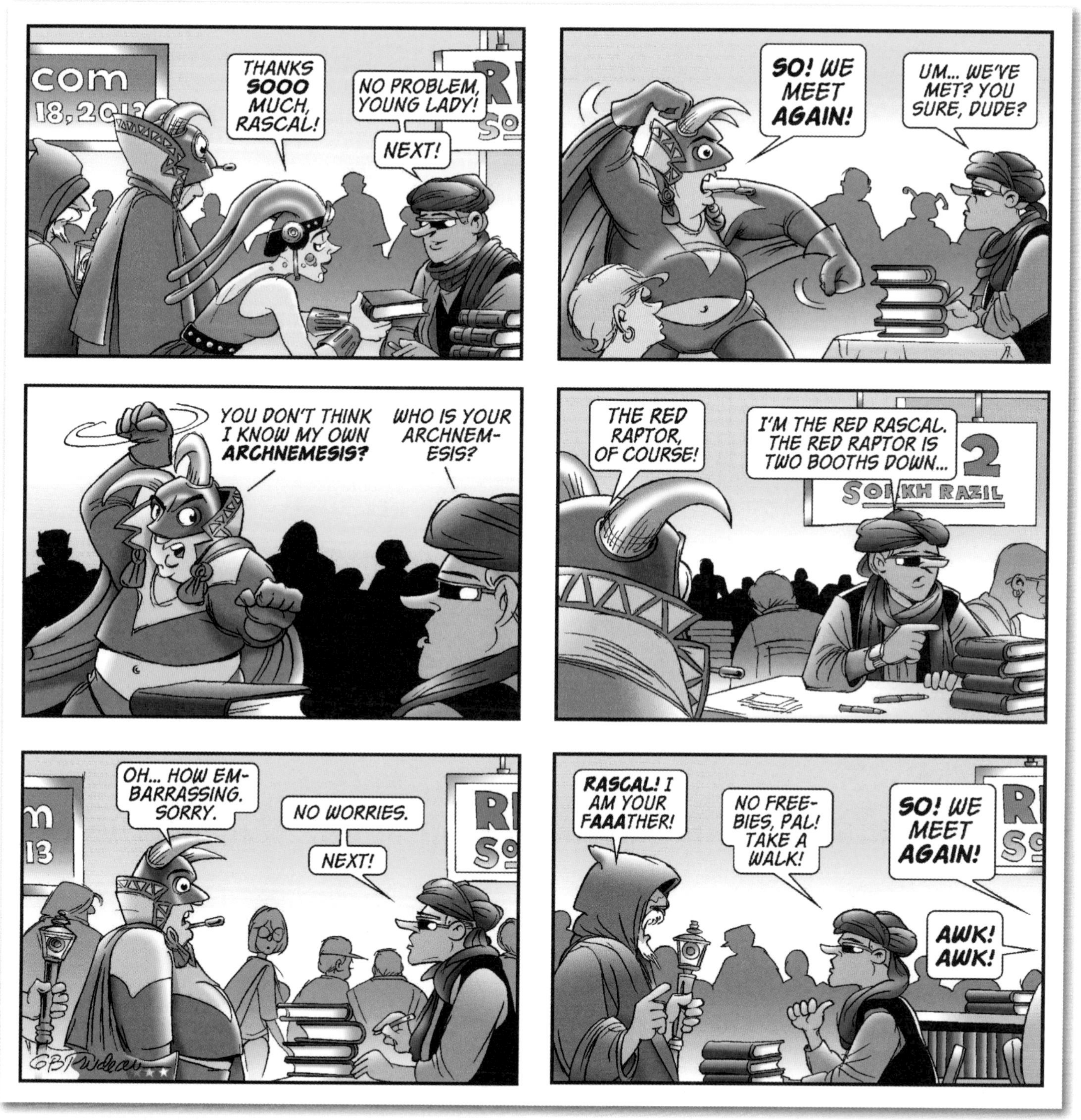
THANKS **SOOO** MUCH, RASCAL!
NO PROBLEM, YOUNG LADY!
NEXT!
SO! WE MEET AGAIN!
UM... WE'VE MET? YOU SURE, DUDE?
YOU DON'T THINK I KNOW MY OWN **ARCHNEMESIS?**
WHO IS YOUR ARCHNEM- ESIS?
THE RED RAPTOR, OF COURSE!
I'M THE RED RASCAL. THE RED RAPTOR IS TWO BOOTHS DOWN...
OH... HOW EM- BARRASSING. SORRY.
NO WORRIES.
NEXT!
RASCAL! I AM YOUR **FAAA**THER!
NO FREE- BIES, PAL! TAKE A WALK!
SO! WE MEET AGAIN!
AWK! AWK!

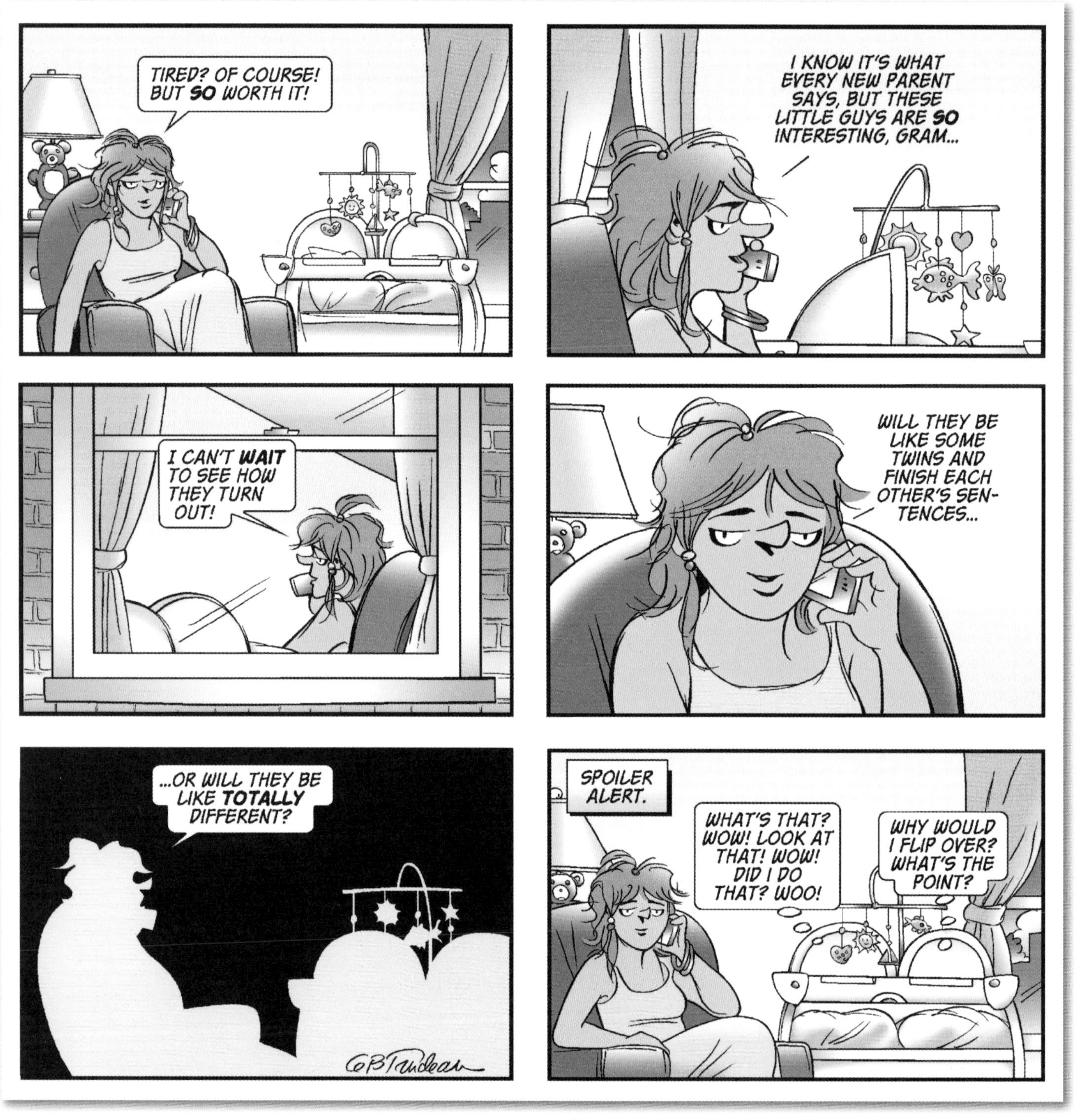
TIRED? OF COURSE! BUT **SO** WORTH IT!
I KNOW IT'S WHAT EVERY NEW PARENT SAYS, BUT THESE LITTLE GUYS ARE **SO** INTERESTING, GRAM...
I CAN'T **WAIT** TO SEE HOW THEY TURN OUT!
WILL THEY BE LIKE SOME TWINS AND FINISH EACH OTHER'S SEN-TENCES...
...OR WILL THEY BE LIKE **TOTALLY** DIFFERENT?
SPOILER ALERT.
WHAT'S THAT? WOW! LOOK AT THAT! WOW! DID I DO THAT? WOO!
WHY WOULD I FLIP OVER? WHAT'S THE POINT?
GBTrudeau

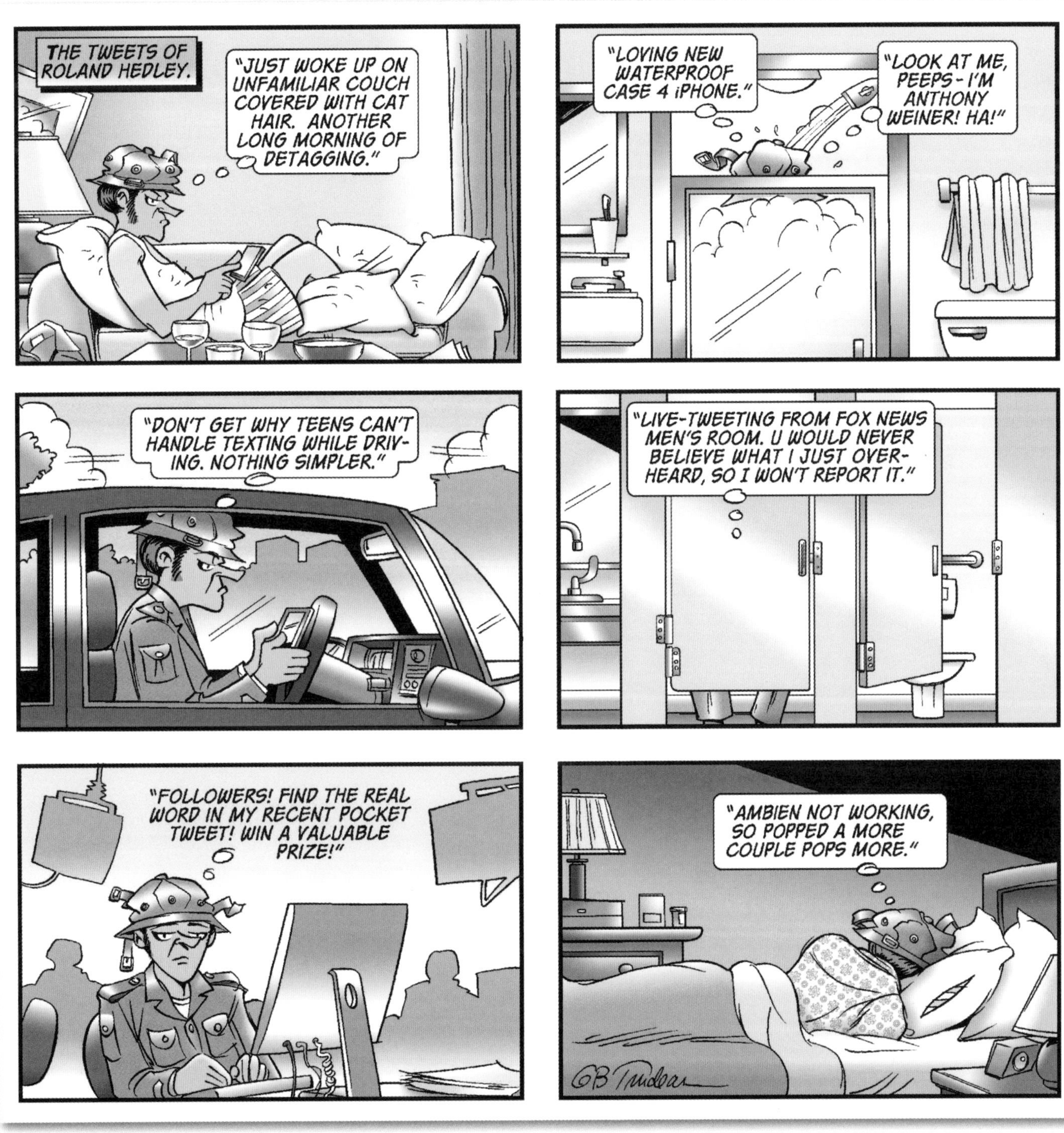
THE TWEETS OF ROLAND HEDLEY.
"JUST WOKE UP ON UNFAMILIAR COUCH COVERED WITH CAT HAIR. ANOTHER LONG MORNING OF DETAGGING."
"LOVING NEW WATERPROOF CASE 4 iPHONE."
"LOOK AT ME, PEEPS - I'M ANTHONY WEINER! HA!"
"DON'T GET WHY TEENS CAN'T HANDLE TEXTING WHILE DRIV-ING. NOTHING SIMPLER."
"LIVE-TWEETING FROM FOX NEWS MEN'S ROOM. U WOULD NEVER BELIEVE WHAT I JUST OVER-HEARD, SO I WON'T REPORT IT."
"FOLLOWERS! FIND THE REAL WORD IN MY RECENT POCKET TWEET! WIN A VALUABLE PRIZE!"
"AMBIEN NOT WORKING, SO POPPED A MORE COUPLE POPS MORE."
GB Trudeau

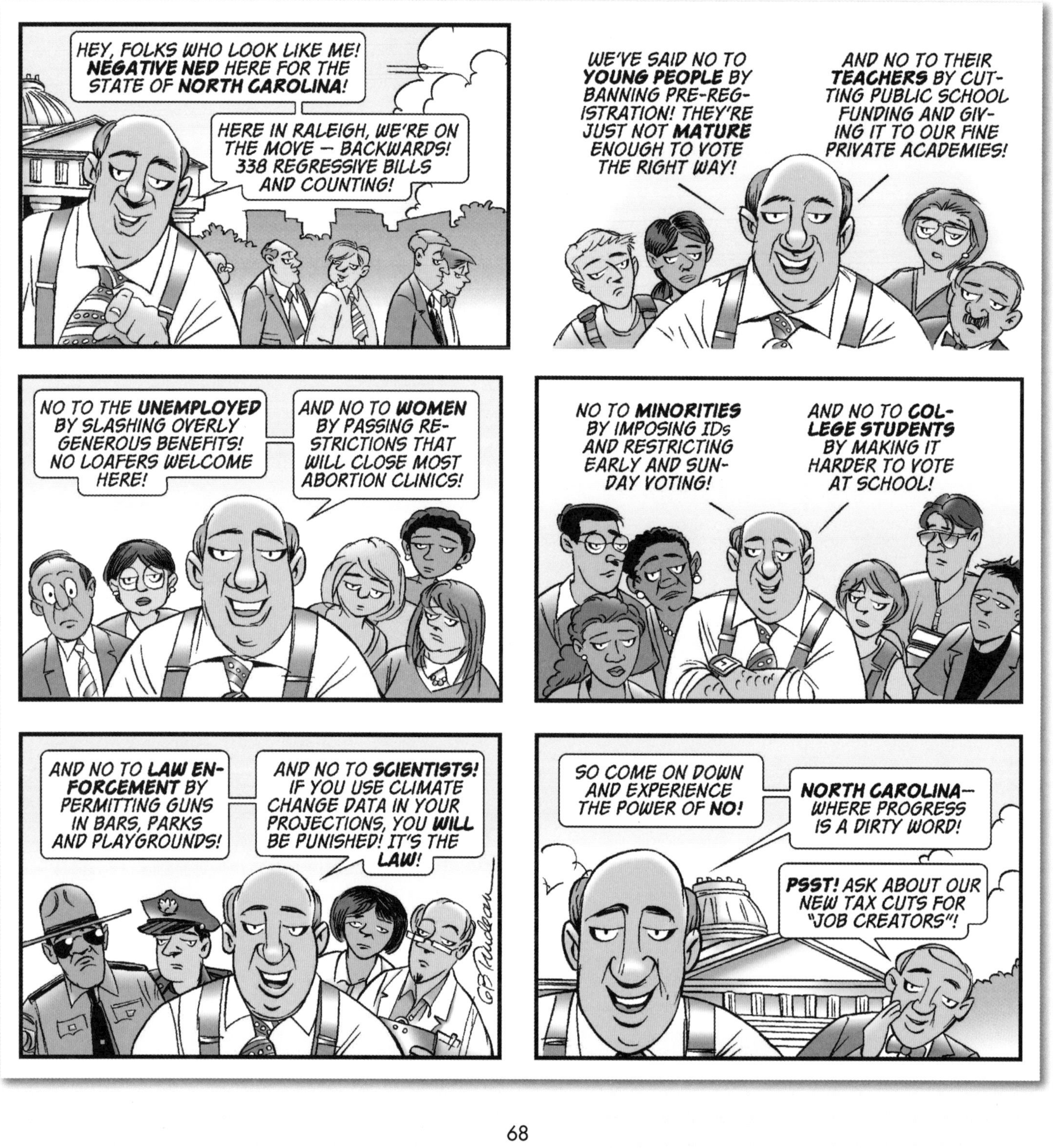
HEY, FOLKS WHO LOOK LIKE ME! NEGATIVE NED HERE FOR THE STATE OF NORTH CAROLINA!
HERE IN RALEIGH, WE'RE ON THE MOVE — BACKWARDS! 338 REGRESSIVE BILLS AND COUNTING!
WE'VE SAID NO TO YOUNG PEOPLE BY BANNING PRE-REGISTRATION! THEY'RE JUST NOT MATURE ENOUGH TO VOTE THE RIGHT WAY!
AND NO TO THEIR TEACHERS BY CUTTING PUBLIC SCHOOL FUNDING AND GIVING IT TO OUR FINE PRIVATE ACADEMIES!
NO TO THE UNEMPLOYED BY SLASHING OVERLY GENEROUS BENEFITS! NO LOAFERS WELCOME HERE!
AND NO TO WOMEN BY PASSING RESTRICTIONS THAT WILL CLOSE MOST ABORTION CLINICS!
NO TO MINORITIES BY IMPOSING IDs AND RESTRICTING EARLY AND SUNDAY VOTING!
AND NO TO COLLEGE STUDENTS BY MAKING IT HARDER TO VOTE AT SCHOOL!
AND NO TO LAW ENFORCEMENT BY PERMITTING GUNS IN BARS, PARKS AND PLAYGROUNDS!
AND NO TO SCIENTISTS! IF YOU USE CLIMATE CHANGE DATA IN YOUR PROJECTIONS, YOU WILL BE PUNISHED! IT'S THE LAW!
GBTrudeau
SO COME ON DOWN AND EXPERIENCE THE POWER OF NO!
NORTH CAROLINA— WHERE PROGRESS IS A DIRTY WORD!
PSST! ASK ABOUT OUR NEW TAX CUTS FOR "JOB CREATORS"!

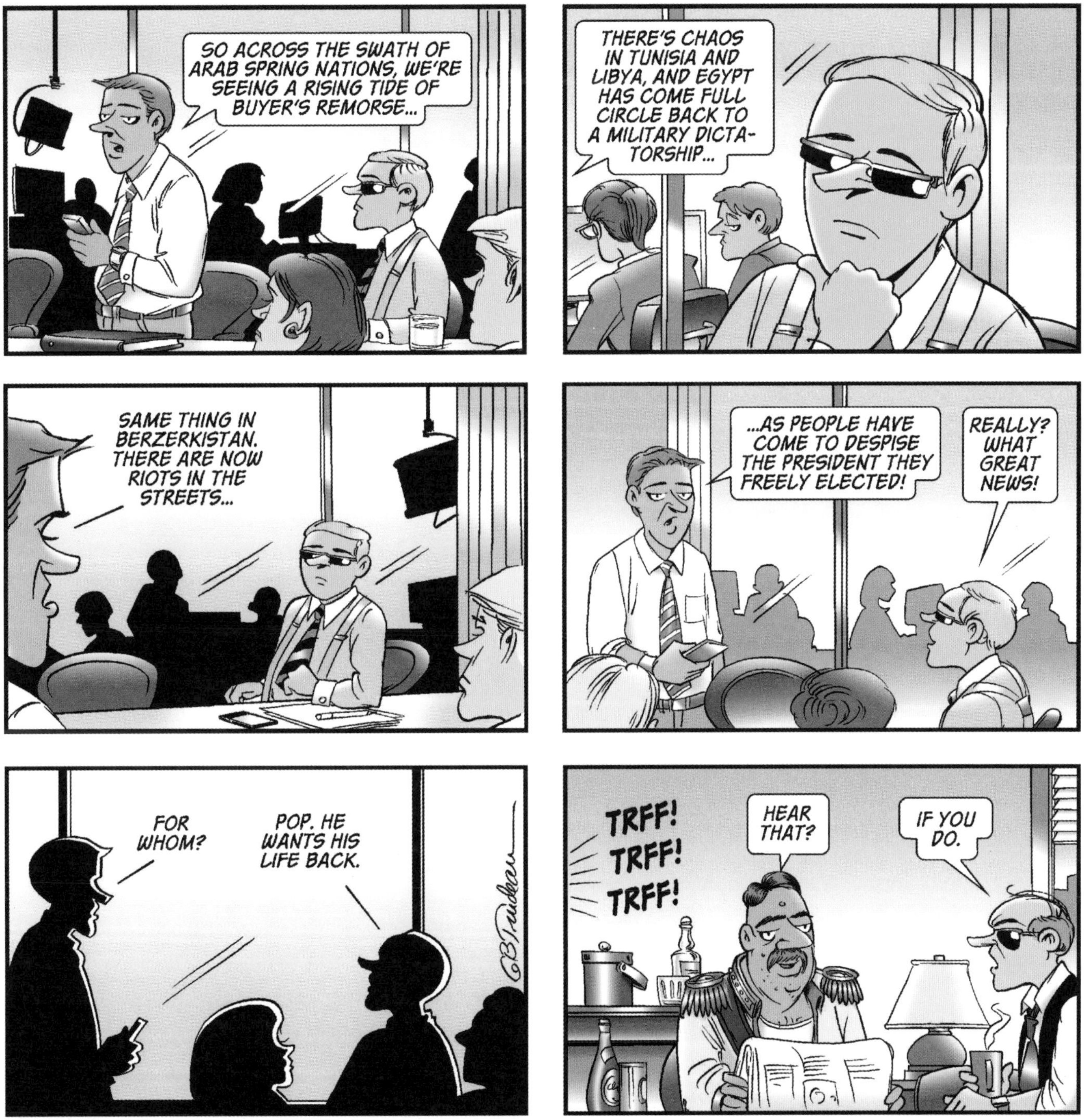
SO ACROSS THE SWATH OF ARAB SPRING NATIONS, WE'RE SEEING A RISING TIDE OF BUYER'S REMORSE...
THERE'S CHAOS IN TUNISIA AND LIBYA, AND EGYPT HAS COME FULL CIRCLE BACK TO A MILITARY DICTATORSHIP...
SAME THING IN BERZERKISTAN. THERE ARE NOW RIOTS IN THE STREETS...
...AS PEOPLE HAVE COME TO DESPISE THE PRESIDENT THEY FREELY ELECTED!
REALLY? WHAT GREAT NEWS!
FOR WHOM?
POP. HE WANTS HIS LIFE BACK.
GBTrudeau
TRFF!
TRFF!
TRFF!
HEAR THAT?
IF YOU DO.

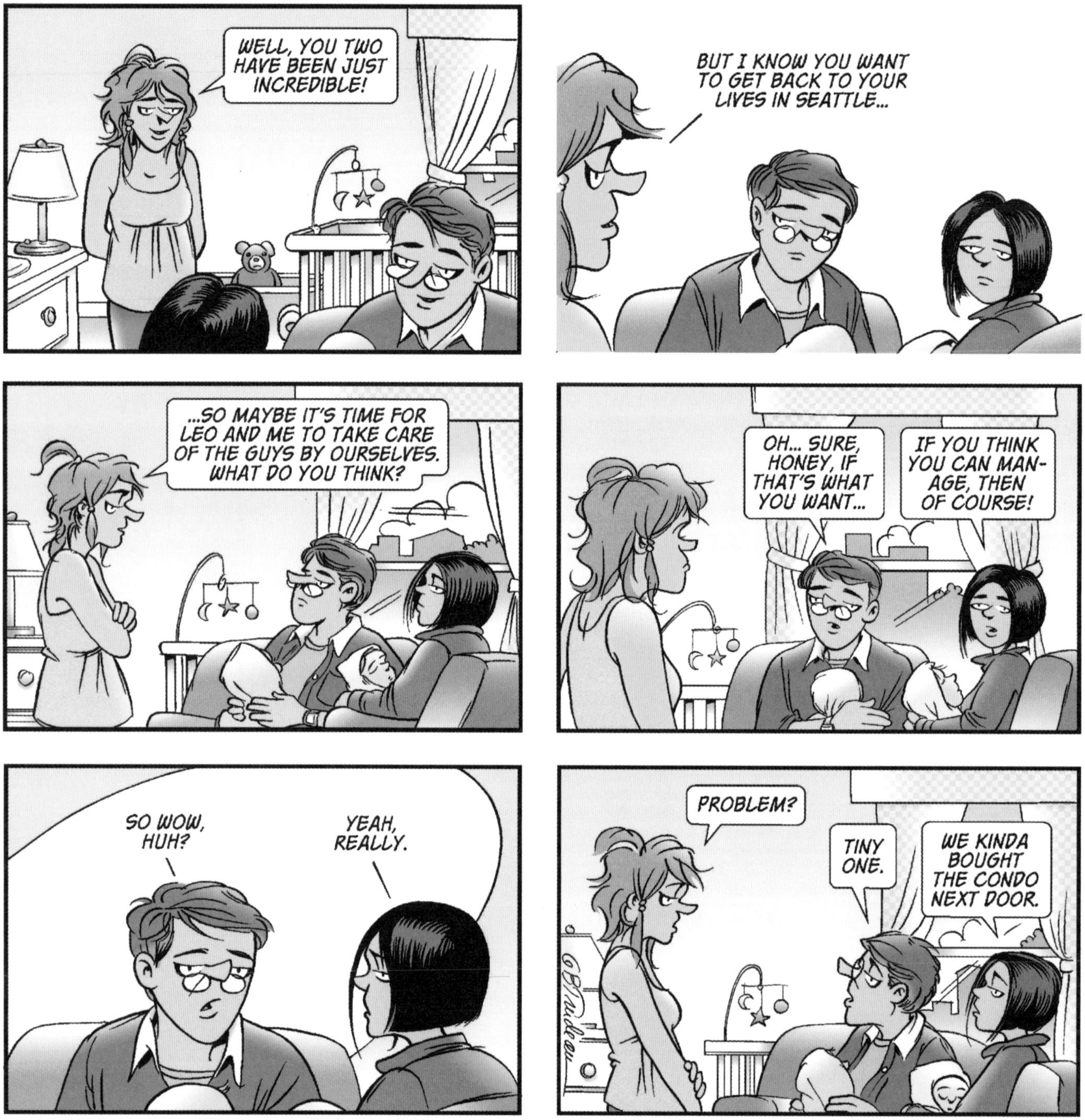
WELL, YOU TWO HAVE BEEN JUST INCREDIBLE!
BUT I KNOW YOU WANT TO GET BACK TO YOUR LIVES IN SEATTLE...
...SO MAYBE IT'S TIME FOR LEO AND ME TO TAKE CARE OF THE GUYS BY OURSELVES. WHAT DO YOU THINK?
OH... SURE, HONEY, IF THAT'S WHAT YOU WANT...
IF YOU THINK YOU CAN MAN-AGE, THEN OF COURSE!
SO WOW, HUH?
YEAH, REALLY.
PROBLEM?
TINY ONE.
WE KINDA BOUGHT THE CONDO NEXT DOOR.

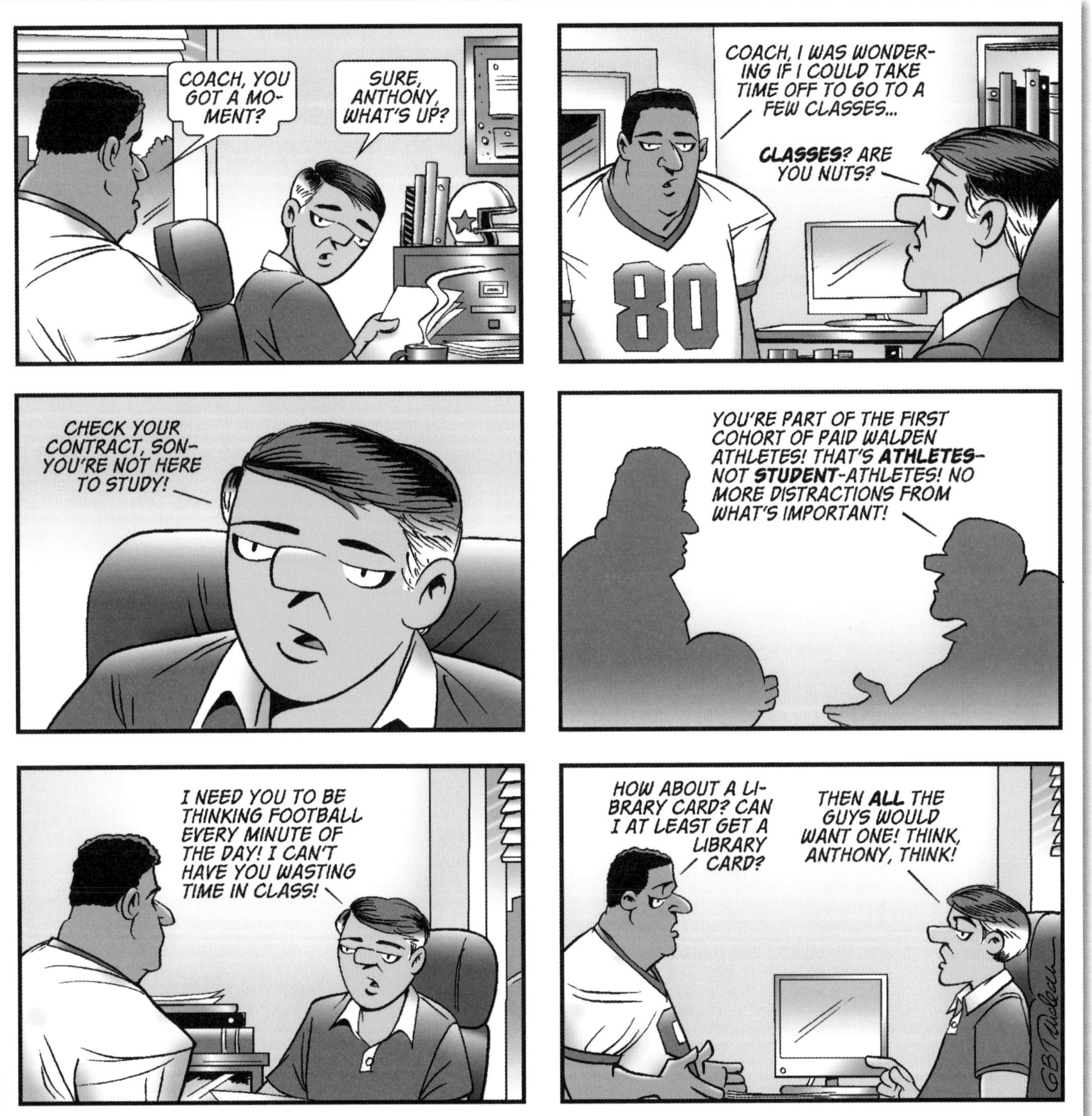
COACH, YOU GOT A MOMENT?
SURE, ANTHONY, WHAT'S UP?
COACH, I WAS WONDERING IF I COULD TAKE TIME OFF TO GO TO A FEW CLASSES...
CLASSES? ARE YOU NUTS?
80
CHECK YOUR CONTRACT, SON–YOU'RE NOT HERE TO STUDY!
YOU'RE PART OF THE FIRST COHORT OF PAID WALDEN ATHLETES! THAT'S **ATHLETES**–NOT **STUDENT**-ATHLETES! NO MORE DISTRACTIONS FROM WHAT'S IMPORTANT!
I NEED YOU TO BE THINKING FOOTBALL EVERY MINUTE OF THE DAY! I CAN'T HAVE YOU WASTING TIME IN CLASS!
HOW ABOUT A LIBRARY CARD? CAN I AT LEAST GET A LIBRARY CARD?
THEN **ALL** THE GUYS WOULD WANT ONE! THINK, ANTHONY, THINK!
GBTrudeau

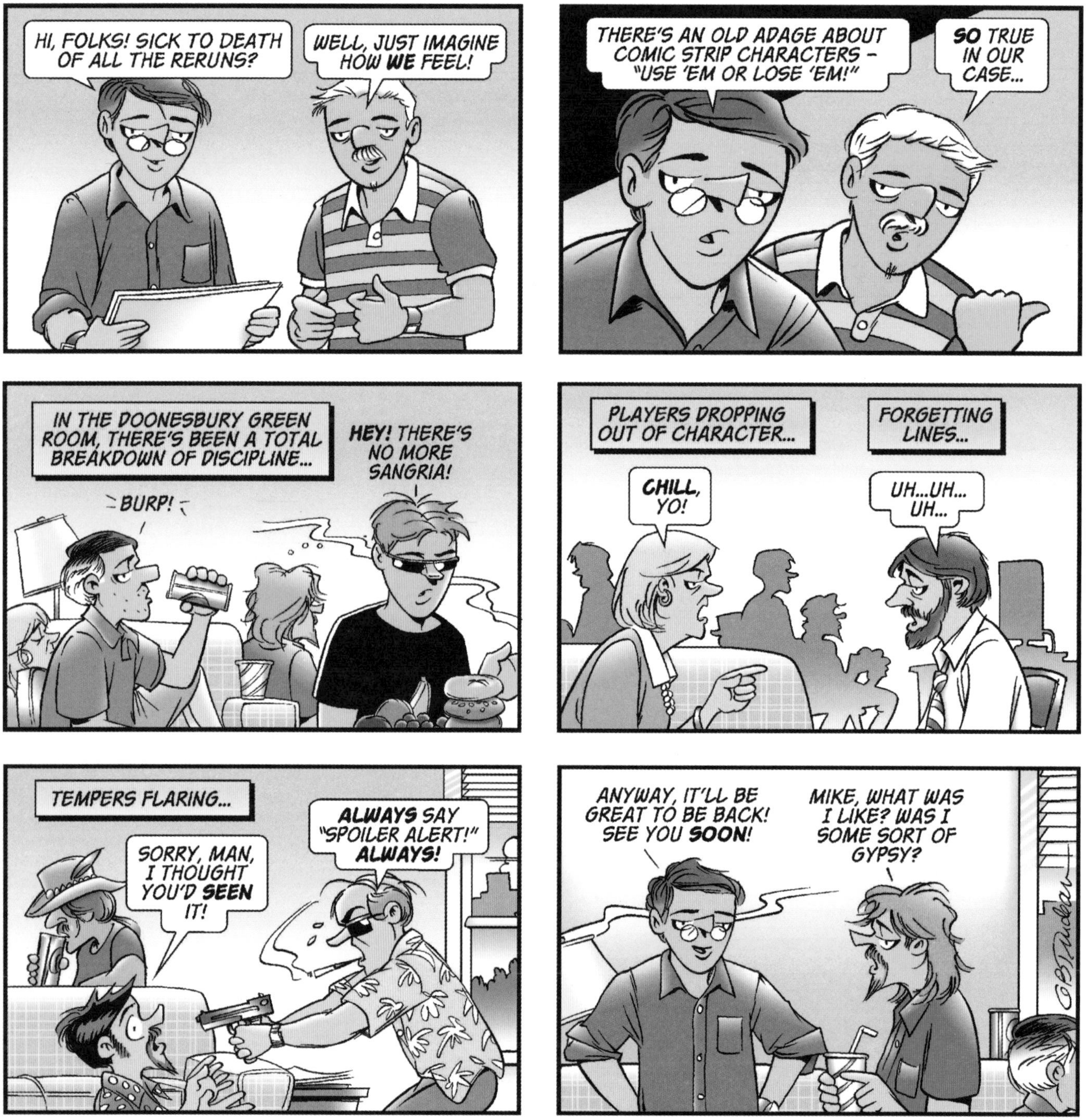
HI, FOLKS! SICK TO DEATH OF ALL THE RERUNS?
WELL, JUST IMAGINE HOW **WE** FEEL!
THERE'S AN OLD ADAGE ABOUT COMIC STRIP CHARACTERS – "USE 'EM OR LOSE 'EM!"
SO TRUE IN OUR CASE...
IN THE DOONESBURY GREEN ROOM, THERE'S BEEN A TOTAL BREAKDOWN OF DISCIPLINE...
BURP!
HEY! THERE'S NO MORE SANGRIA!
PLAYERS DROPPING OUT OF CHARACTER...
CHILL, YO!
FORGETTING LINES...
UH...UH... UH...
TEMPERS FLARING...
SORRY, MAN, I THOUGHT YOU'D **SEEN** IT!
ALWAYS SAY "SPOILER ALERT!" **ALWAYS!**
ANYWAY, IT'LL BE GREAT TO BE BACK! SEE YOU **SOON**!
MIKE, WHAT WAS I LIKE? WAS I SOME SORT OF GYPSY?

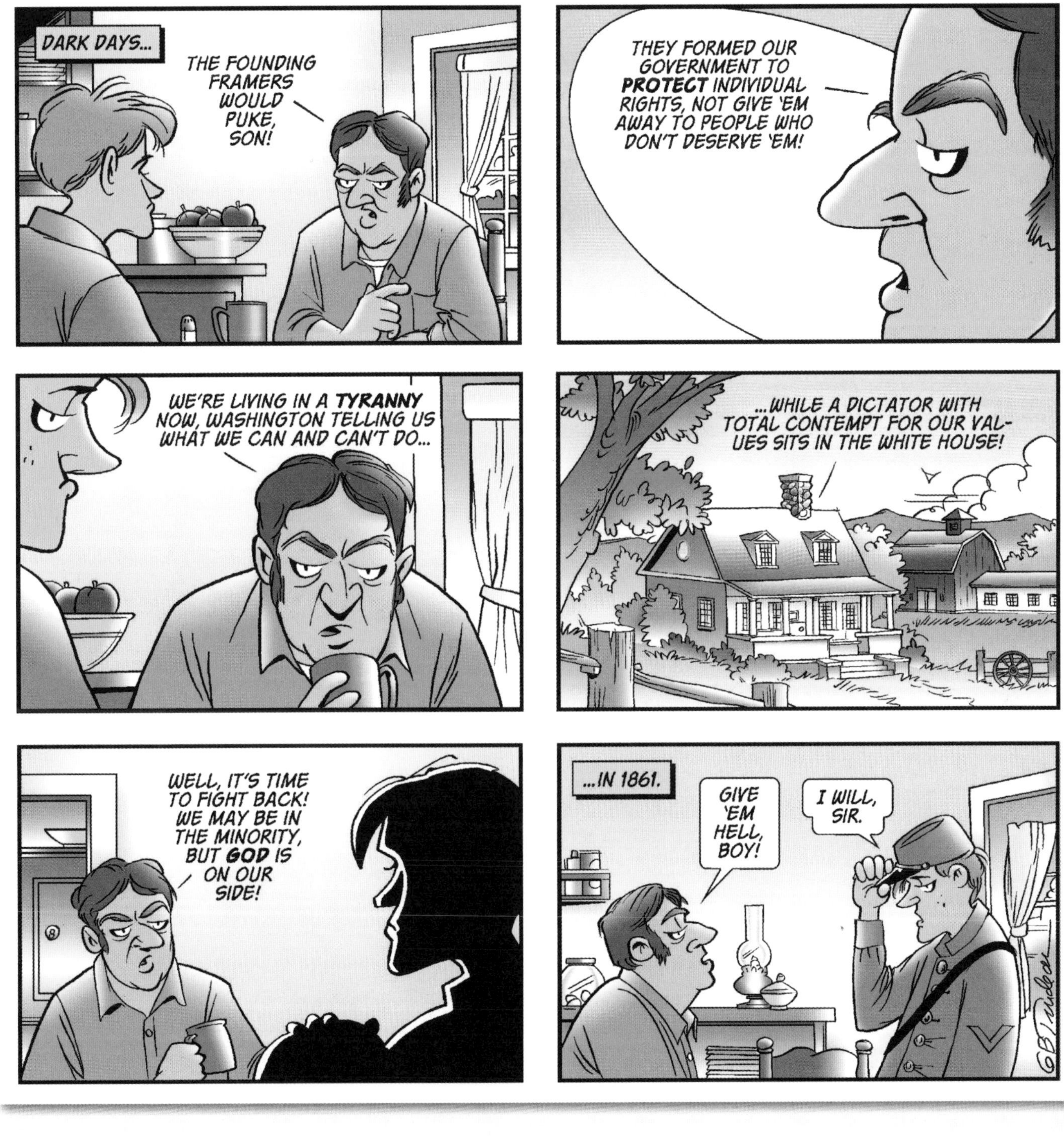
DARK DAYS...
THE FOUNDING FRAMERS WOULD PUKE, SON!
THEY FORMED OUR GOVERNMENT TO **PROTECT** INDIVIDUAL RIGHTS, NOT GIVE 'EM AWAY TO PEOPLE WHO DON'T DESERVE 'EM!
WE'RE LIVING IN A **TYRANNY** NOW, WASHINGTON TELLING US WHAT WE CAN AND CAN'T DO...
...WHILE A DICTATOR WITH TOTAL CONTEMPT FOR OUR VAL-UES SITS IN THE WHITE HOUSE!
WELL, IT'S TIME TO FIGHT BACK! WE MAY BE IN THE MINORITY, BUT **GOD** IS ON OUR SIDE!
...IN 1861.
GIVE 'EM HELL, BOY!
I WILL, SIR.

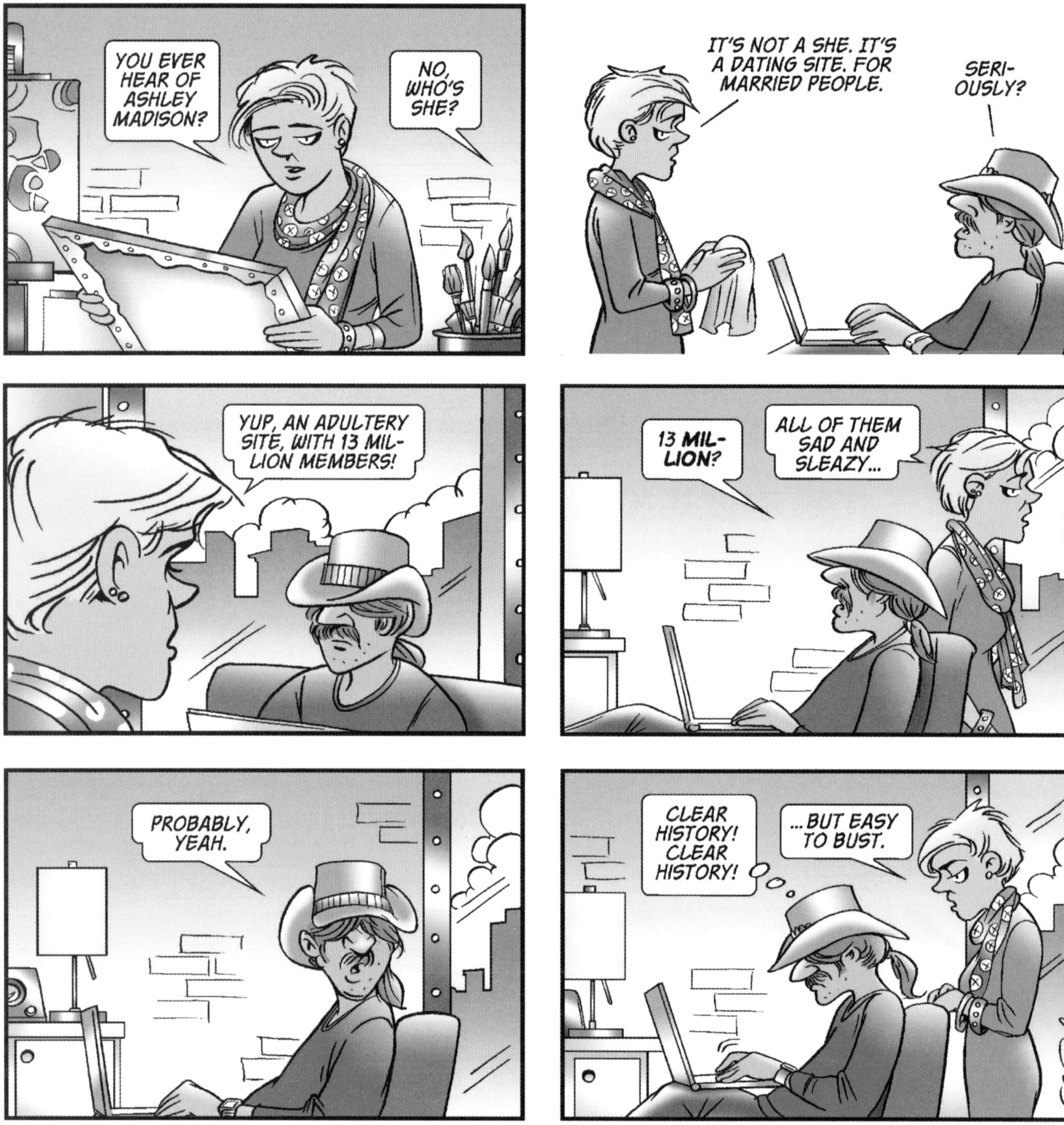
YOU EVER HEAR OF ASHLEY MADISON?
NO, WHO'S SHE?
IT'S NOT A SHE. IT'S A DATING SITE. FOR MARRIED PEOPLE.
SERI-OUSLY?
YUP, AN ADULTERY SITE, WITH 13 MIL-LION MEMBERS!
13 **MIL-LION**?
ALL OF THEM SAD AND SLEAZY...
PROBABLY, YEAH.
CLEAR HISTORY! CLEAR HISTORY!
...BUT EASY TO BUST.
GBTrudeau

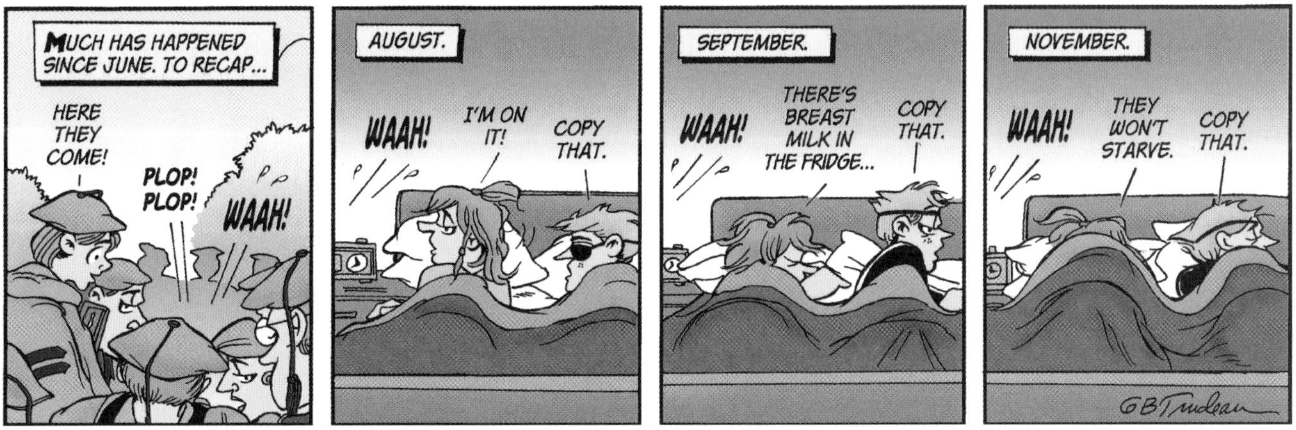
MUCH HAS HAPPENED SINCE JUNE. TO RECAP...
HERE THEY COME!
PLOP! PLOP!
WAAH!
AUGUST.
WAAH!
I'M ON IT!
COPY THAT.
SEPTEMBER.
WAAH!
THERE'S BREAST MILK IN THE FRIDGE...
COPY THAT.
NOVEMBER.
WAAH!
THEY WON'T STARVE.
COPY THAT.
GBTrudeau

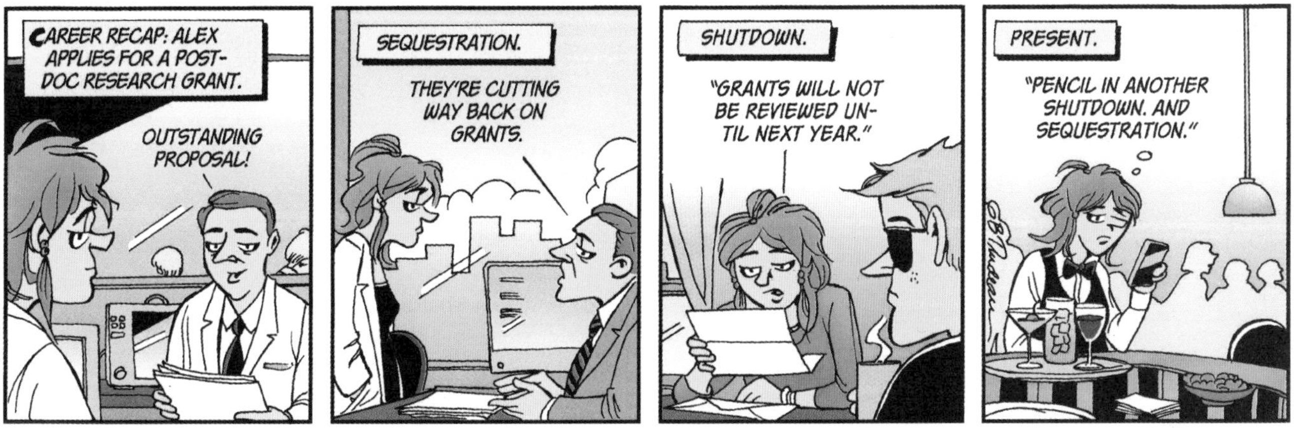
CAREER RECAP: ALEX APPLIES FOR A POST-DOC RESEARCH GRANT.
OUTSTANDING PROPOSAL!
SEQUESTRATION.
THEY'RE CUTTING WAY BACK ON GRANTS.
SHUTDOWN.
"GRANTS WILL NOT BE REVIEWED UNTIL NEXT YEAR."
PRESENT.
"PENCIL IN ANOTHER SHUTDOWN. AND SEQUESTRATION."
GBTrudeau

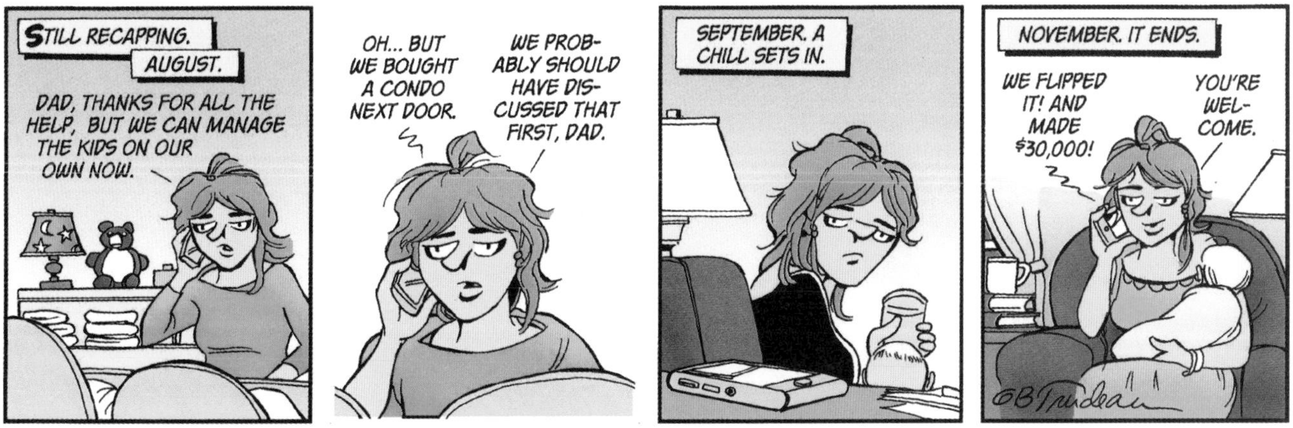
STILL RECAPPING.
AUGUST.
DAD, THANKS FOR ALL THE HELP, BUT WE CAN MANAGE THE KIDS ON OUR OWN NOW.
OH... BUT WE BOUGHT A CONDO NEXT DOOR.
WE PROBABLY SHOULD HAVE DISCUSSED THAT FIRST, DAD.
SEPTEMBER. A CHILL SETS IN.
NOVEMBER. IT ENDS.
WE FLIPPED IT! AND MADE $30,000!
YOU'RE WELCOME.
GBTrudeau

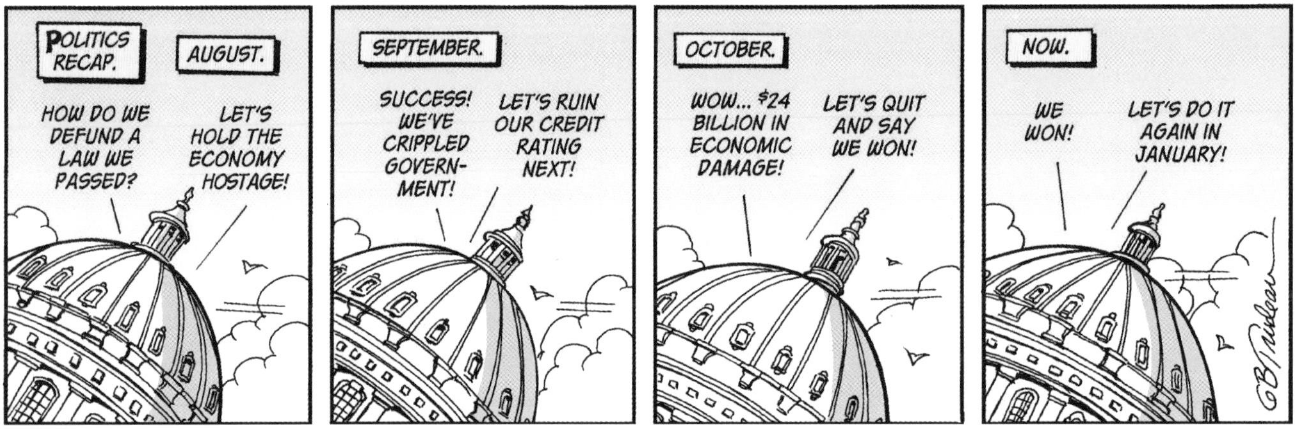
POLITICS RECAP.
AUGUST.
HOW DO WE DEFUND A LAW WE PASSED?
LET'S HOLD THE ECONOMY HOSTAGE!
SEPTEMBER.
SUCCESS! WE'VE CRIPPLED GOVERN-MENT!
LET'S RUIN OUR CREDIT RATING NEXT!
OCTOBER.
WOW... $24 BILLION IN ECONOMIC DAMAGE!
LET'S QUIT AND SAY WE WON!
NOW.
WE WON!
LET'S DO IT AGAIN IN JANUARY!

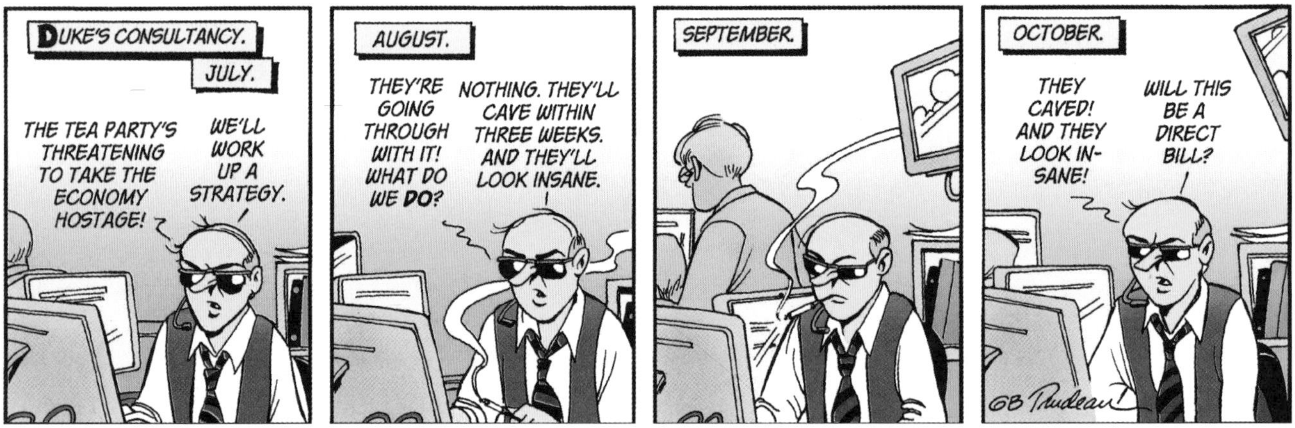
DUKE'S CONSULTANCY.
JULY.
THE TEA PARTY'S THREATENING TO TAKE THE ECONOMY HOSTAGE!
WE'LL WORK UP A STRATEGY.
AUGUST.
THEY'RE GOING THROUGH WITH IT! WHAT DO WE DO?
NOTHING. THEY'LL CAVE WITHIN THREE WEEKS. AND THEY'LL LOOK INSANE.
SEPTEMBER.
OCTOBER.
THEY CAVED! AND THEY LOOK IN-SANE!
WILL THIS BE A DIRECT BILL?

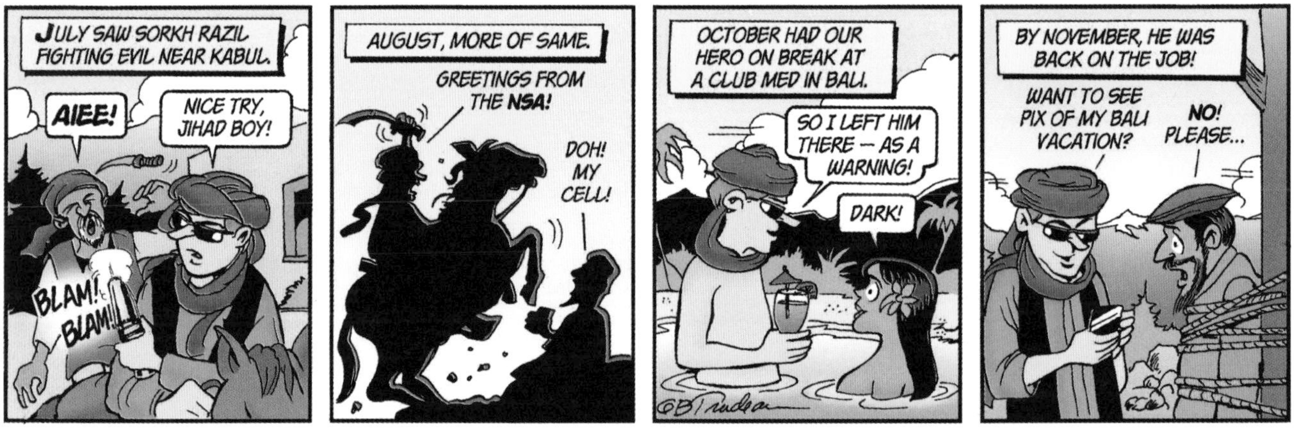
JULY SAW SORKH RAZIL FIGHTING EVIL NEAR KABUL.
AIEE!
NICE TRY, JIHAD BOY!
BLAM! BLAM!
AUGUST, MORE OF SAME.
GREETINGS FROM THE NSA!
DOH! MY CELL!
OCTOBER HAD OUR HERO ON BREAK AT A CLUB MED IN BALI.
SO I LEFT HIM THERE — AS A WARNING!
DARK!
BY NOVEMBER, HE WAS BACK ON THE JOB!
WANT TO SEE PIX OF MY BALI VACATION?
NO! PLEASE...

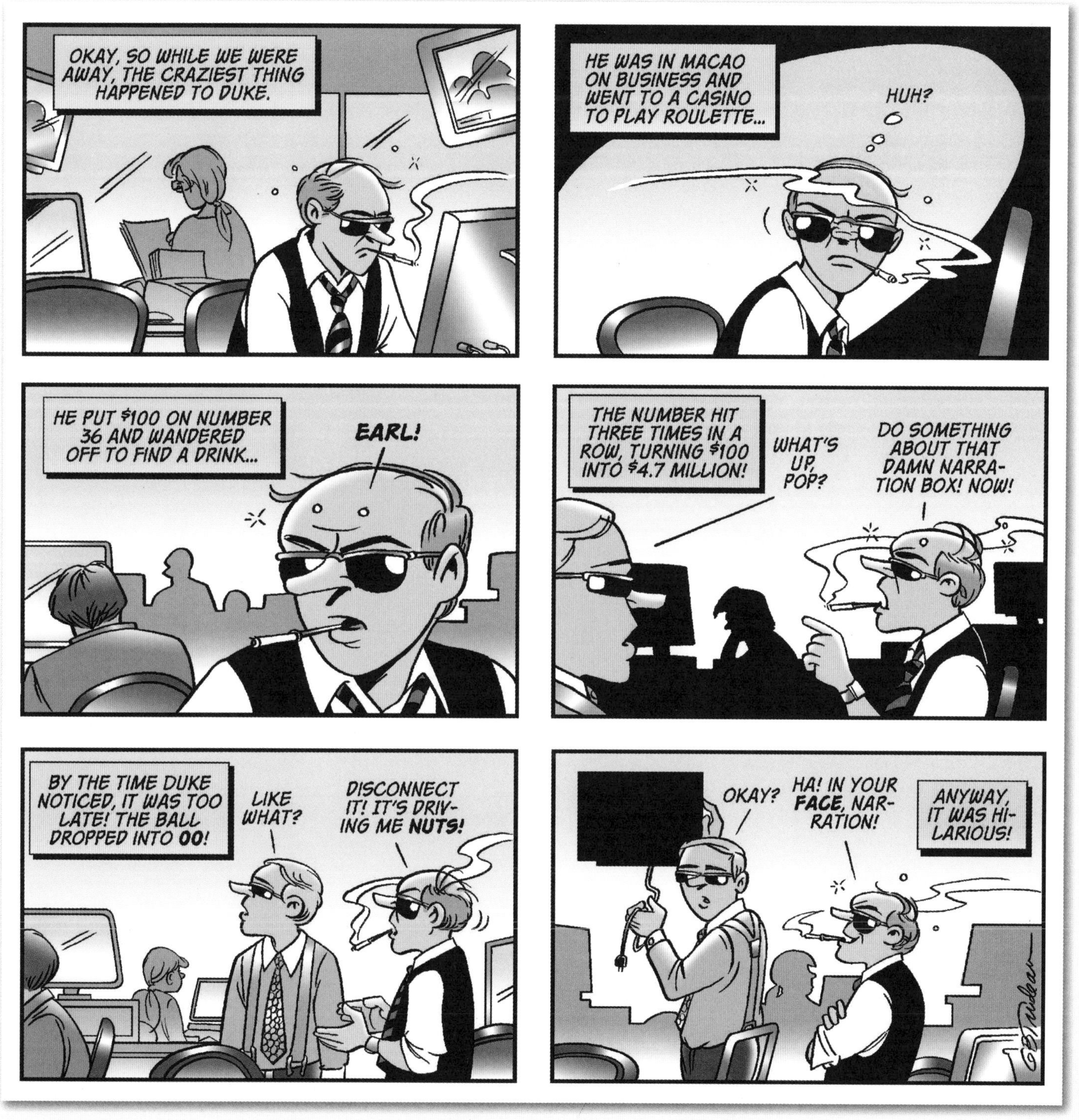
OKAY, SO WHILE WE WERE AWAY, THE CRAZIEST THING HAPPENED TO DUKE.
HE WAS IN MACAO ON BUSINESS AND WENT TO A CASINO TO PLAY ROULETTE...
HUH?
HE PUT $100 ON NUMBER 36 AND WANDERED OFF TO FIND A DRINK...
EARL!
THE NUMBER HIT THREE TIMES IN A ROW, TURNING $100 INTO $4.7 MILLION!
WHAT'S UP, POP?
DO SOMETHING ABOUT THAT DAMN NARRATION BOX! NOW!
BY THE TIME DUKE NOTICED, IT WAS TOO LATE! THE BALL DROPPED INTO 00!
LIKE WHAT?
DISCONNECT IT! IT'S DRIVING ME NUTS!
OKAY?
HA! IN YOUR FACE, NARRATION!
ANYWAY, IT WAS HILARIOUS!

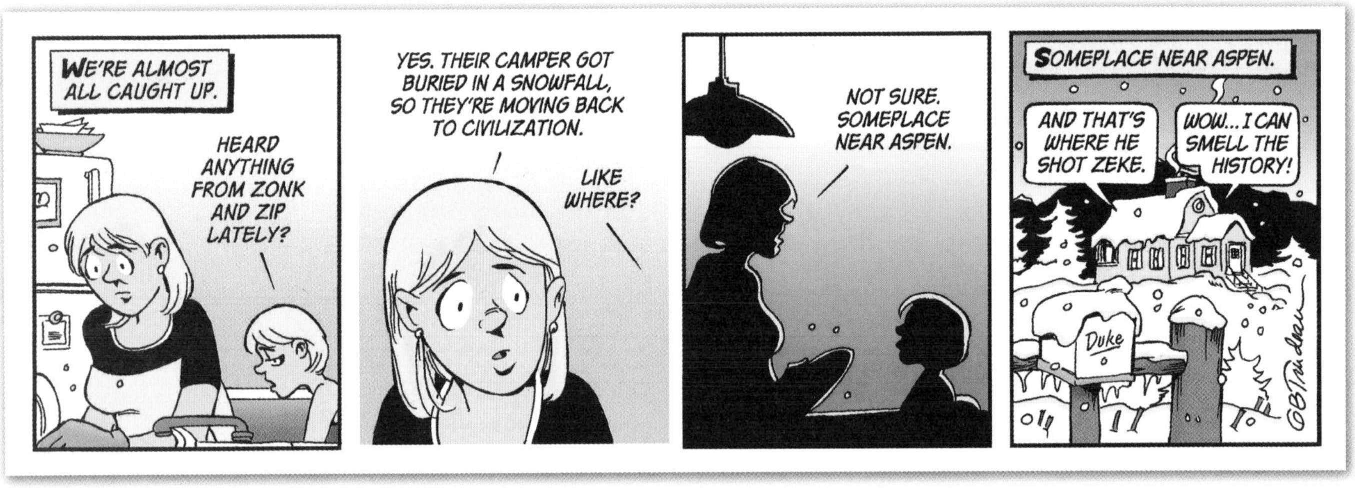
WE'RE ALMOST ALL CAUGHT UP.
HEARD ANYTHING FROM ZONK AND ZIP LATELY?
YES. THEIR CAMPER GOT BURIED IN A SNOWFALL, SO THEY'RE MOVING BACK TO CIVILIZATION.
LIKE WHERE?
NOT SURE. SOMEPLACE NEAR ASPEN.
SOMEPLACE NEAR ASPEN.
AND THAT'S WHERE HE SHOT ZEKE.
WOW... I CAN SMELL THE HISTORY!
Duke

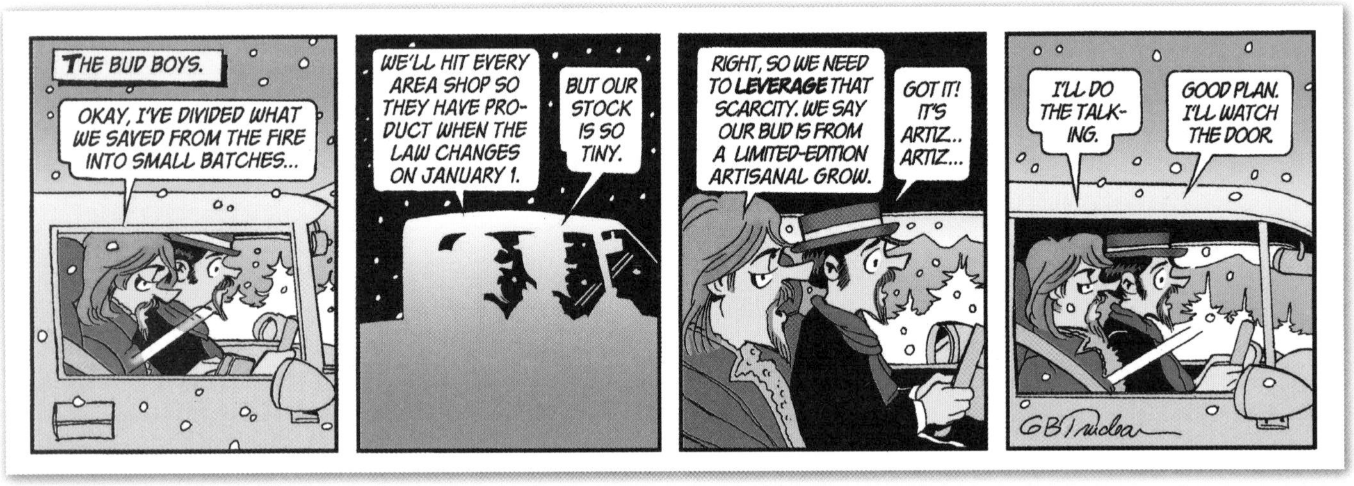
THE BUD BOYS.
OKAY, I'VE DIVIDED WHAT WE SAVED FROM THE FIRE INTO SMALL BATCHES...
WE'LL HIT EVERY AREA SHOP SO THEY HAVE PRODUCT WHEN THE LAW CHANGES ON JANUARY 1.
BUT OUR STOCK IS SO TINY.
RIGHT, SO WE NEED TO LEVERAGE THAT SCARCITY. WE SAY OUR BUD IS FROM A LIMITED-EDITION ARTISANAL GROW.
GOT IT! IT'S ARTIZ... ARTIZ...
I'LL DO THE TALKING.
GOOD PLAN. I'LL WATCH THE DOOR.

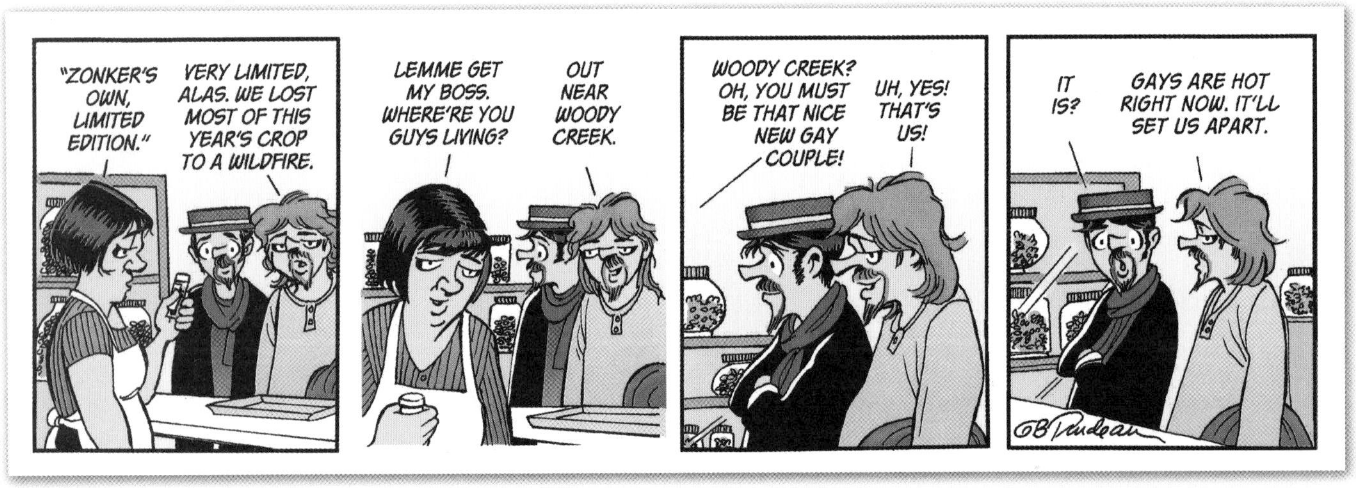
"ZONKER'S OWN, LIMITED EDITION."
VERY LIMITED, ALAS. WE LOST MOST OF THIS YEAR'S CROP TO A WILDFIRE.
LEMME GET MY BOSS. WHERE'RE YOU GUYS LIVING?
OUT NEAR WOODY CREEK.
WOODY CREEK? OH, YOU MUST BE THAT NICE NEW GAY COUPLE!
UH, YES! THAT'S US!
IT IS?
GAYS ARE HOT RIGHT NOW. IT'LL SET US APART.

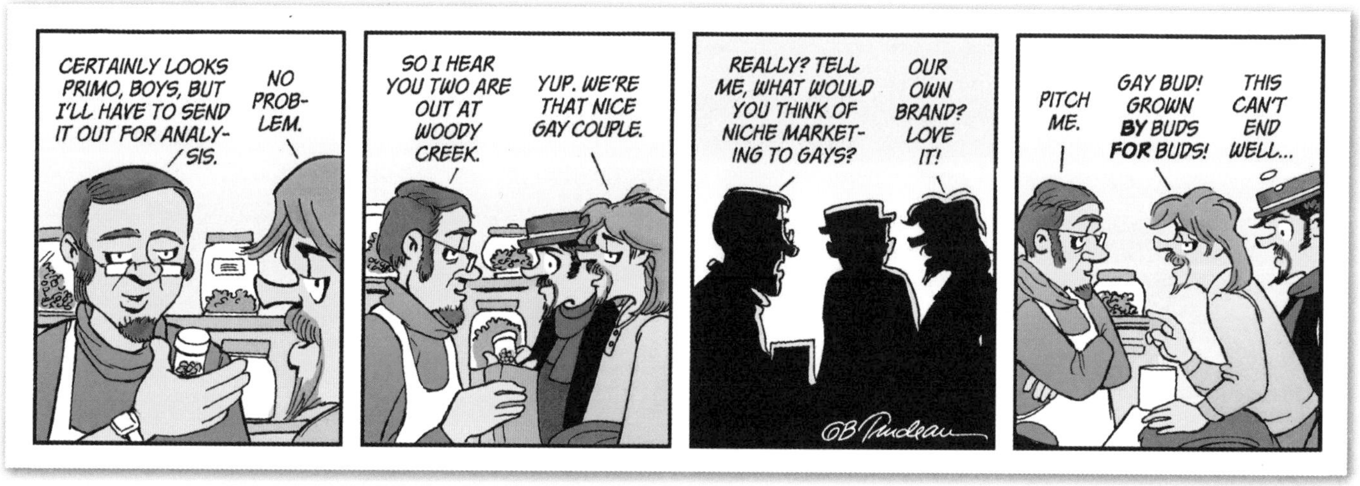
CERTAINLY LOOKS PRIMO, BOYS, BUT I'LL HAVE TO SEND IT OUT FOR ANALY-SIS.
NO PROB-LEM.
SO I HEAR YOU TWO ARE OUT AT WOODY CREEK.
YUP. WE'RE THAT NICE GAY COUPLE.
REALLY? TELL ME, WHAT WOULD YOU THINK OF NICHE MARKET-ING TO GAYS?
OUR OWN BRAND? LOVE IT!
GB Trudeau
PITCH ME.
GAY BUD! GROWN **BY** BUDS **FOR** BUDS!
THIS CAN'T END WELL...

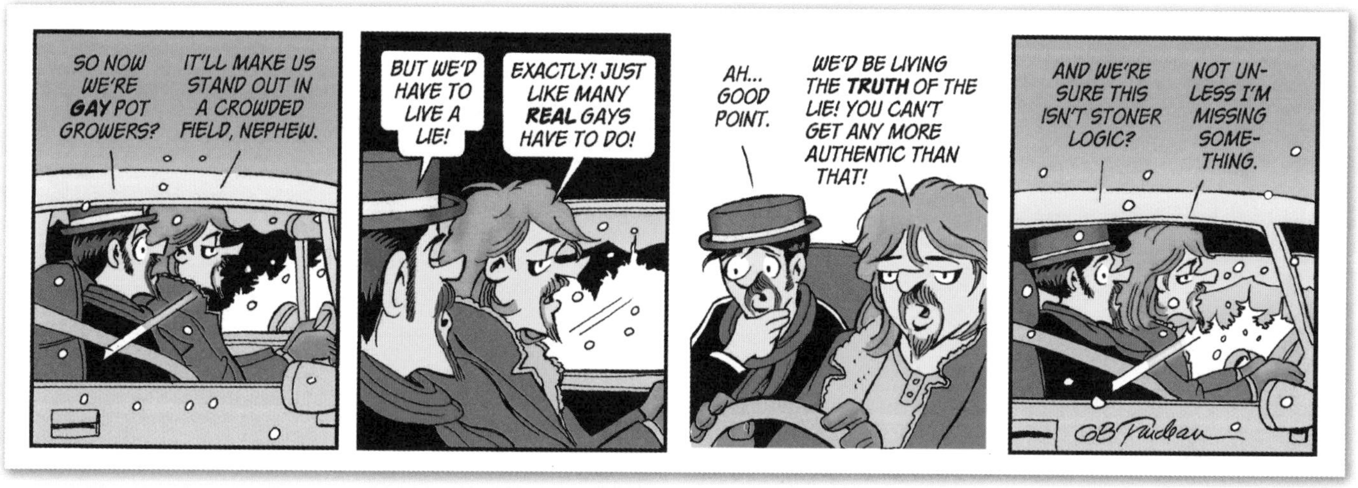
SO NOW WE'RE **GAY** POT GROWERS?
IT'LL MAKE US STAND OUT IN A CROWDED FIELD, NEPHEW.
BUT WE'D HAVE TO LIVE A LIE!
EXACTLY! JUST LIKE MANY **REAL** GAYS HAVE TO DO!
AH... GOOD POINT.
WE'D BE LIVING THE **TRUTH** OF THE LIE! YOU CAN'T GET ANY MORE AUTHENTIC THAN THAT!
AND WE'RE SURE THIS ISN'T STONER LOGIC?
NOT UN-LESS I'M MISSING SOME-THING.
GB Trudeau

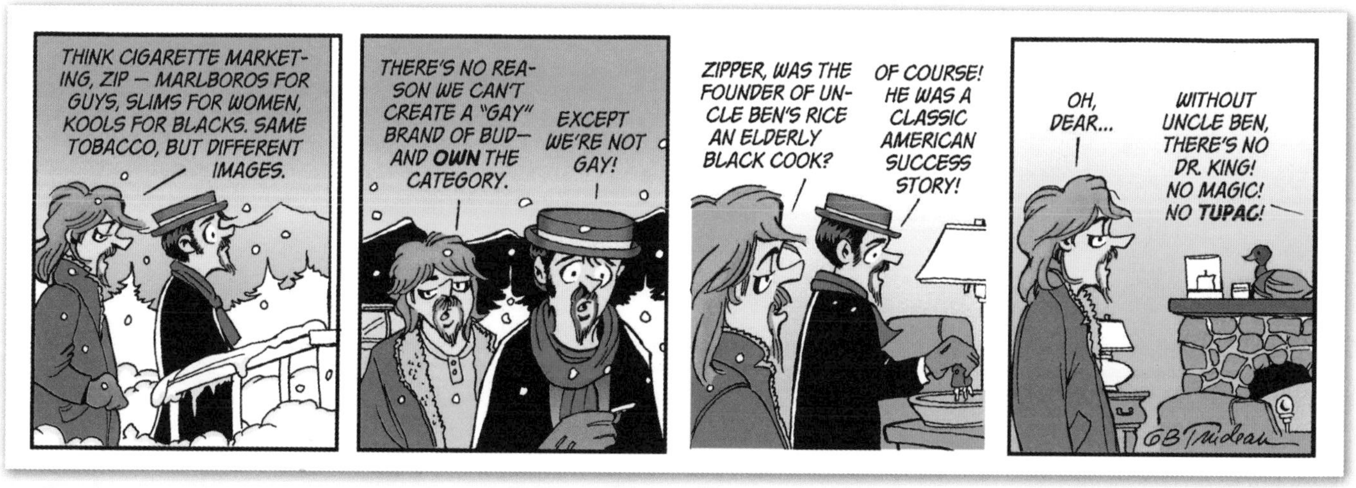
THINK CIGARETTE MARKET-ING, ZIP — MARLBOROS FOR GUYS, SLIMS FOR WOMEN, KOOLS FOR BLACKS. SAME TOBACCO, BUT DIFFERENT IMAGES.
THERE'S NO REA-SON WE CAN'T CREATE A "GAY" BRAND OF BUD— AND **OWN** THE CATEGORY.
EXCEPT WE'RE NOT GAY!
ZIPPER, WAS THE FOUNDER OF UN-CLE BEN'S RICE AN ELDERLY BLACK COOK?
OF COURSE! HE WAS A CLASSIC AMERICAN SUCCESS STORY!
OH, DEAR...
WITHOUT UNCLE BEN, THERE'S NO DR. KING! NO MAGIC! NO **TUPAC**!
GB Trudeau

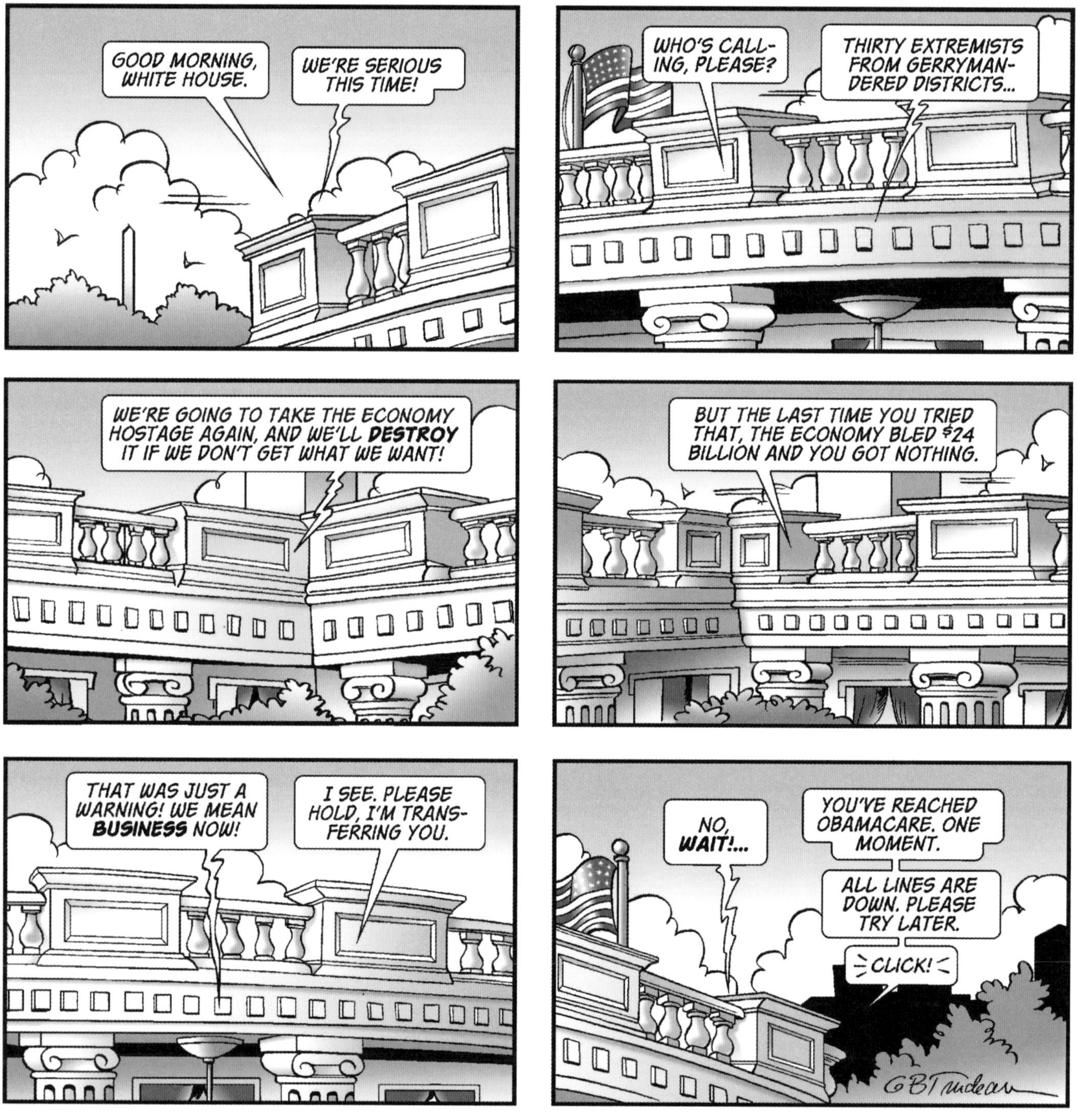
GOOD MORNING, WHITE HOUSE.
WE'RE SERIOUS THIS TIME!
WHO'S CALL-ING, PLEASE?
THIRTY EXTREMISTS FROM GERRYMAN-DERED DISTRICTS...
WE'RE GOING TO TAKE THE ECONOMY HOSTAGE AGAIN, AND WE'LL **DESTROY** IT IF WE DON'T GET WHAT WE WANT!
BUT THE LAST TIME YOU TRIED THAT, THE ECONOMY BLED $24 BILLION AND YOU GOT NOTHING.
THAT WAS JUST A WARNING! WE MEAN **BUSINESS** NOW!
I SEE. PLEASE HOLD, I'M TRANS-FERRING YOU.
NO, **WAIT!...**
YOU'VE REACHED OBAMACARE. ONE MOMENT.
ALL LINES ARE DOWN. PLEASE TRY LATER.
CLICK!
GBTrudeau

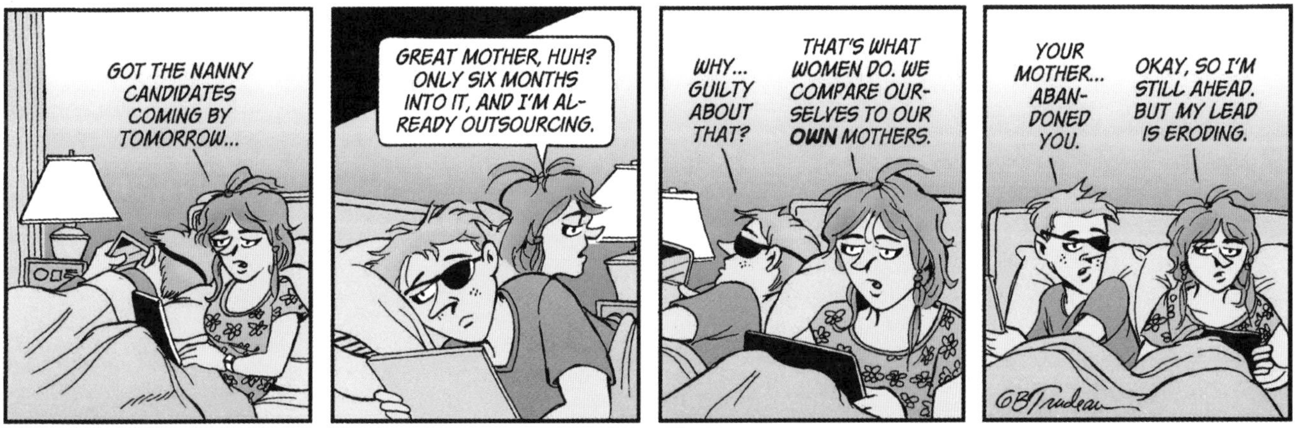

GOT THE NANNY CANDIDATES COMING BY TOMORROW...
GREAT MOTHER, HUH? ONLY SIX MONTHS INTO IT, AND I'M AL-READY OUTSOURCING.
WHY... GUILTY ABOUT THAT?
THAT'S WHAT WOMEN DO. WE COMPARE OUR-SELVES TO OUR **OWN** MOTHERS.
YOUR MOTHER... ABAN-DONED YOU.
OKAY, SO I'M STILL AHEAD. BUT MY LEAD IS ERODING.
GBTrudeau

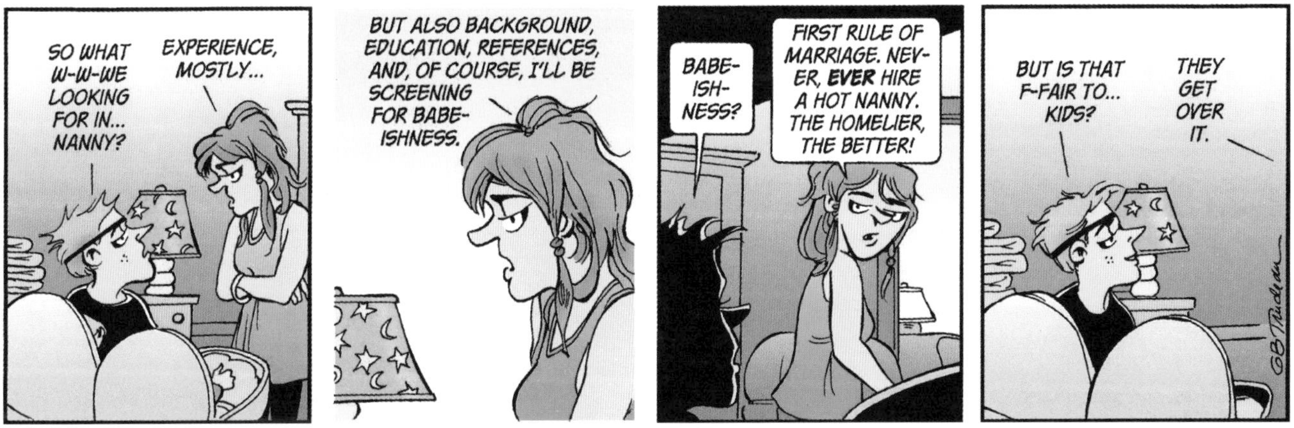

SO WHAT W-W-WE LOOKING FOR IN... NANNY?
EXPERIENCE, MOSTLY...
BUT ALSO BACKGROUND, EDUCATION, REFERENCES, AND, OF COURSE, I'LL BE SCREENING FOR BABE-ISHNESS.
BABE-ISH-NESS?
FIRST RULE OF MARRIAGE. NEV-ER, **EVER** HIRE A HOT NANNY. THE HOMELIER, THE BETTER!
BUT IS THAT F-FAIR TO... KIDS?
THEY GET OVER IT.
GBTrudeau

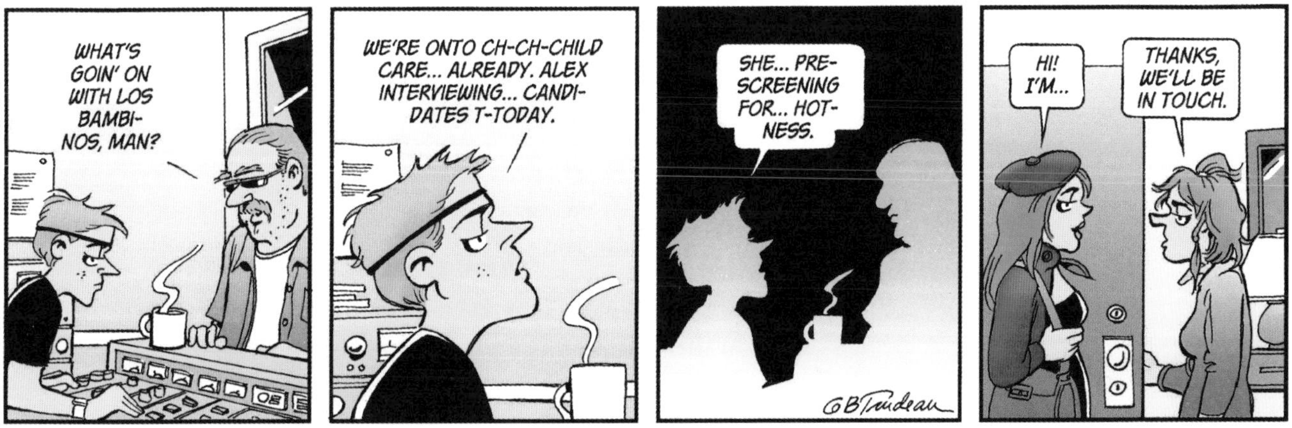

WHAT'S GOIN' ON WITH LOS BAMBI-NOS, MAN?
WE'RE ONTO CH-CH-CHILD CARE... ALREADY. ALEX INTERVIEWING... CANDI-DATES T-TODAY.
SHE... PRE-SCREENING FOR... HOT-NESS.
GBTrudeau
HI! I'M...
THANKS, WE'LL BE IN TOUCH.

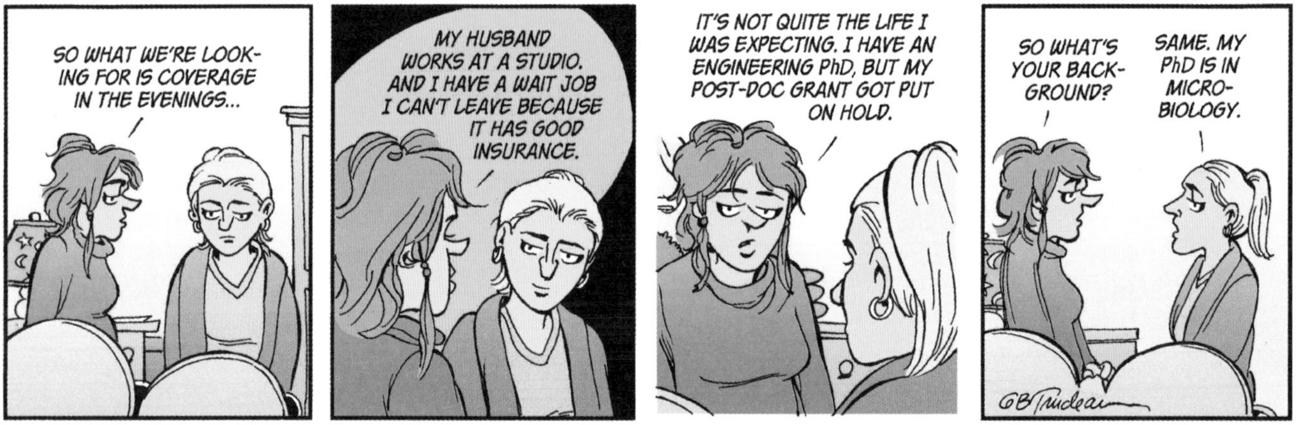
SO WHAT WE'RE LOOKING FOR IS COVERAGE IN THE EVENINGS...
MY HUSBAND WORKS AT A STUDIO. AND I HAVE A WAIT JOB I CAN'T LEAVE BECAUSE IT HAS GOOD INSURANCE.
IT'S NOT QUITE THE LIFE I WAS EXPECTING. I HAVE AN ENGINEERING PhD, BUT MY POST-DOC GRANT GOT PUT ON HOLD.
SO WHAT'S YOUR BACKGROUND?
SAME. MY PhD IS IN MICROBIOLOGY.

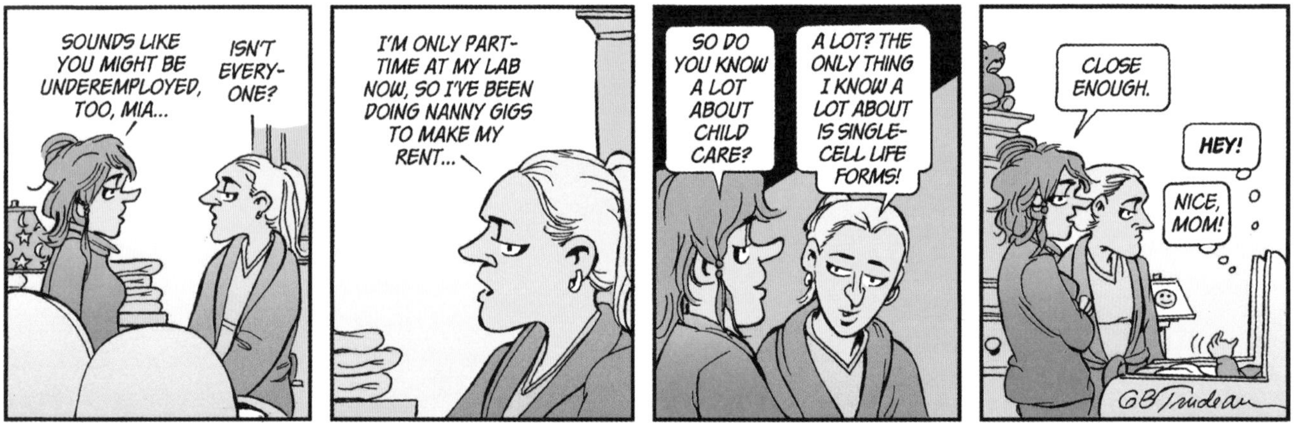
SOUNDS LIKE YOU MIGHT BE UNDEREMPLOYED, TOO, MIA...
ISN'T EVERYONE?
I'M ONLY PART-TIME AT MY LAB NOW, SO I'VE BEEN DOING NANNY GIGS TO MAKE MY RENT...
SO DO YOU KNOW A LOT ABOUT CHILD CARE?
A LOT? THE ONLY THING I KNOW A LOT ABOUT IS SINGLE-CELL LIFE FORMS!
CLOSE ENOUGH.
HEY!
NICE, MOM!

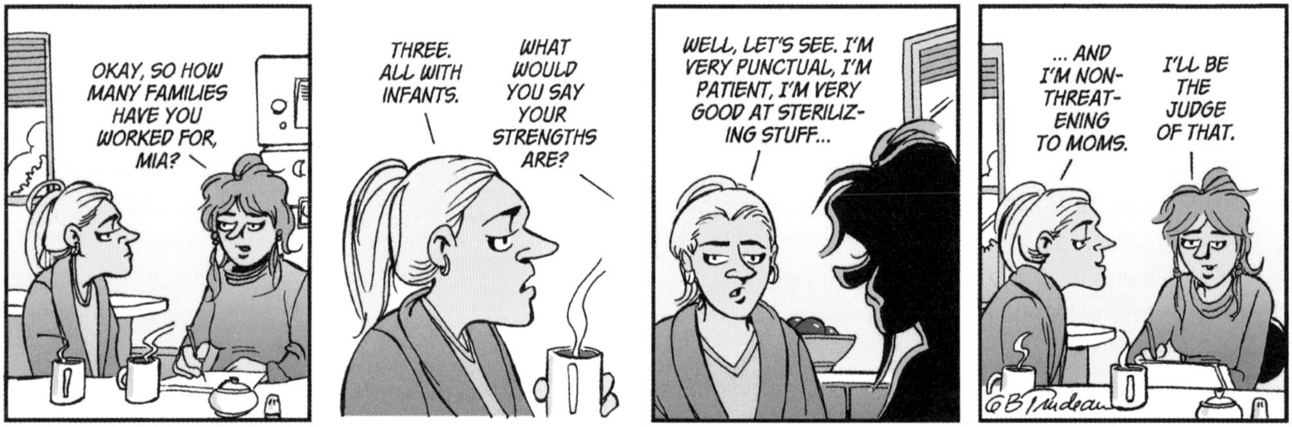
OKAY, SO HOW MANY FAMILIES HAVE YOU WORKED FOR, MIA?
THREE. ALL WITH INFANTS.
WHAT WOULD YOU SAY YOUR STRENGTHS ARE?
WELL, LET'S SEE. I'M VERY PUNCTUAL, I'M PATIENT, I'M VERY GOOD AT STERILIZING STUFF...
... AND I'M NON-THREATENING TO MOMS.
I'LL BE THE JUDGE OF THAT.

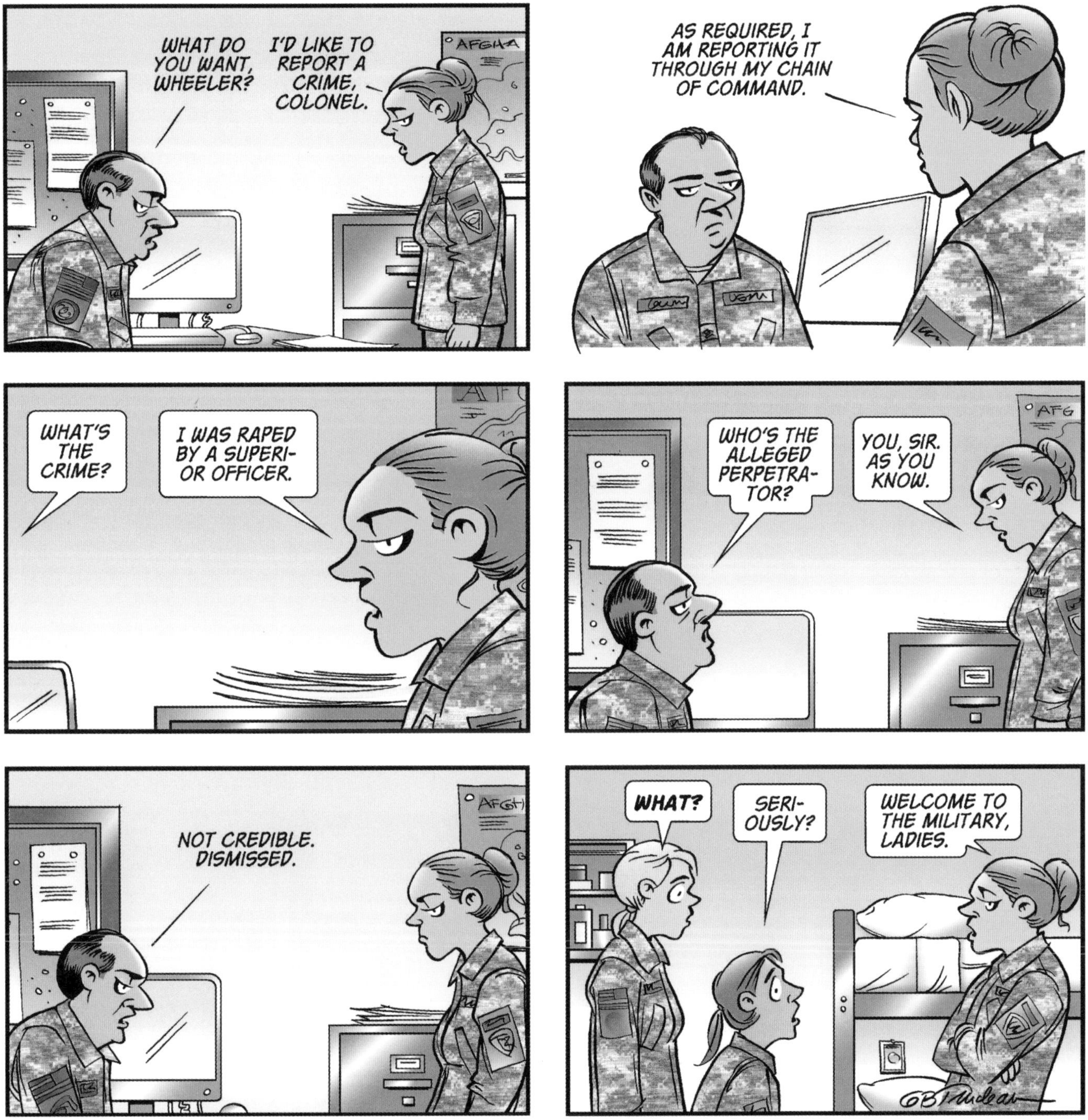

WHAT DO YOU WANT, WHEELER?
I'D LIKE TO REPORT A CRIME, COLONEL.
AFGHA
AS REQUIRED, I AM REPORTING IT THROUGH MY CHAIN OF COMMAND.
WHAT'S THE CRIME?
I WAS RAPED BY A SUPERIOR OFFICER.
WHO'S THE ALLEGED PERPETRATOR?
YOU, SIR. AS YOU KNOW.
AFG
NOT CREDIBLE. DISMISSED.
AFGH
WHAT?
SERIOUSLY?
WELCOME TO THE MILITARY, LADIES.
GBTrudeau

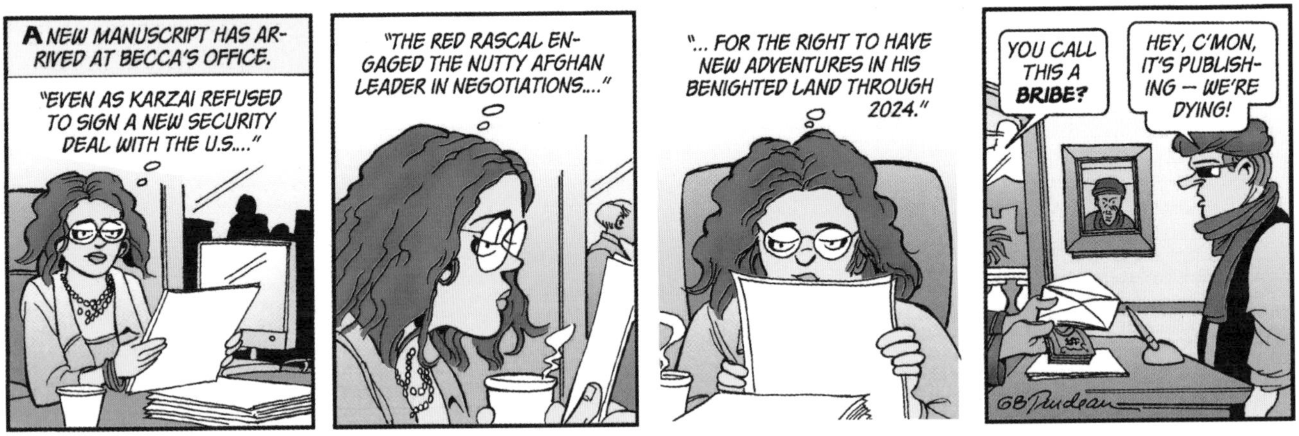
A NEW MANUSCRIPT HAS ARRIVED AT BECCA'S OFFICE.
"EVEN AS KARZAI REFUSED TO SIGN A NEW SECURITY DEAL WITH THE U.S...."
"THE RED RASCAL ENGAGED THE NUTTY AFGHAN LEADER IN NEGOTIATIONS...."
"... FOR THE RIGHT TO HAVE NEW ADVENTURES IN HIS BENIGHTED LAND THROUGH 2024."
YOU CALL THIS A **BRIBE?**
HEY, C'MON, IT'S PUBLISHING — WE'RE DYING!
GBTrudeau

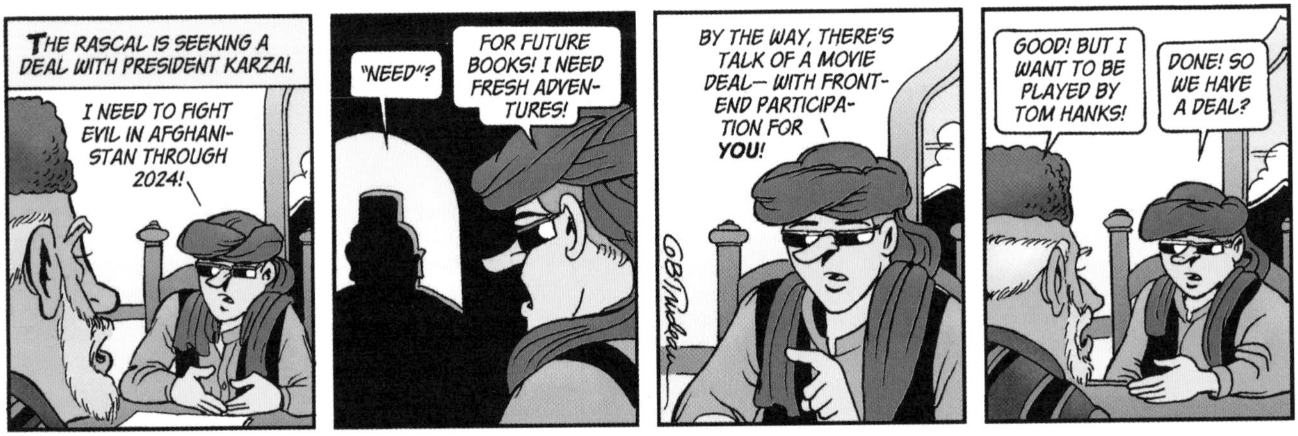
THE RASCAL IS SEEKING A DEAL WITH PRESIDENT KARZAI.
I NEED TO FIGHT EVIL IN AFGHANISTAN THROUGH 2024!
"NEED"?
FOR FUTURE BOOKS! I NEED FRESH ADVENTURES!
BY THE WAY, THERE'S TALK OF A MOVIE DEAL— WITH FRONT-END PARTICIPATION FOR **YOU**!
GBTrudeau
GOOD! BUT I WANT TO BE PLAYED BY TOM HANKS!
DONE! SO WE HAVE A DEAL?

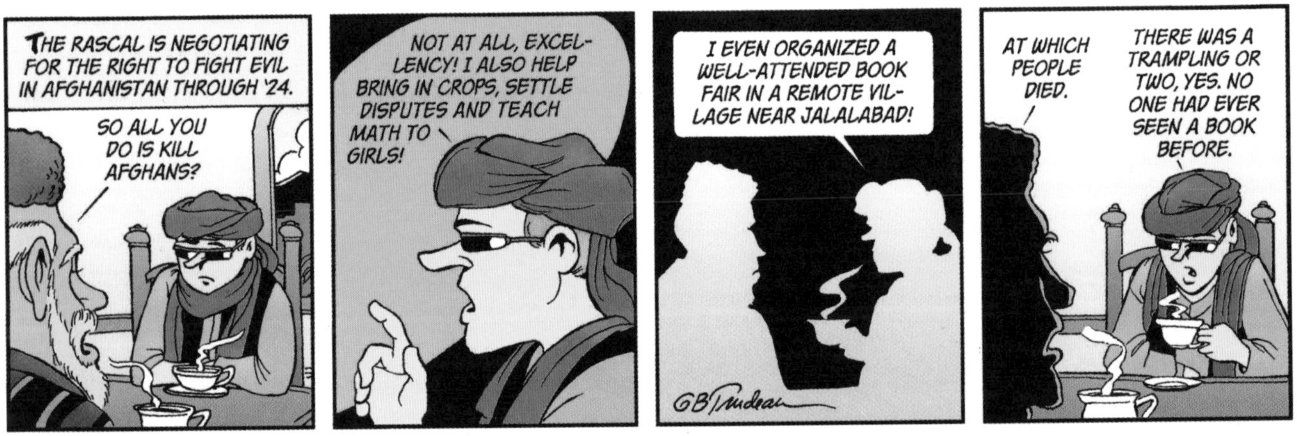
THE RASCAL IS NEGOTIATING FOR THE RIGHT TO FIGHT EVIL IN AFGHANISTAN THROUGH '24.
SO ALL YOU DO IS KILL AFGHANS?
NOT AT ALL, EXCELLENCY! I ALSO HELP BRING IN CROPS, SETTLE DISPUTES AND TEACH MATH TO GIRLS!
I EVEN ORGANIZED A WELL-ATTENDED BOOK FAIR IN A REMOTE VILLAGE NEAR JALALABAD!
GBTrudeau
AT WHICH PEOPLE DIED.
THERE WAS A TRAMPLING OR TWO, YES. NO ONE HAD EVER SEEN A BOOK BEFORE.

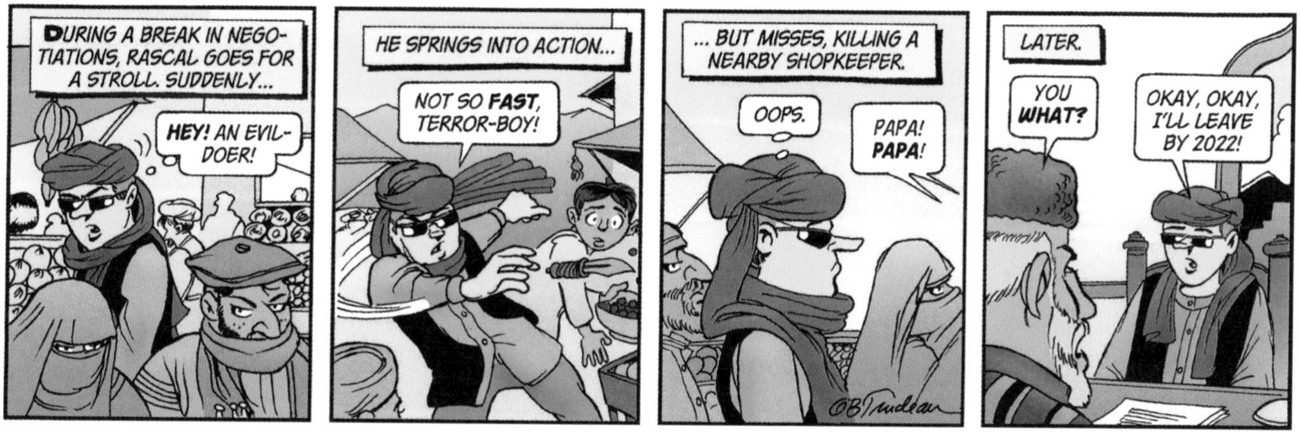
DURING A BREAK IN NEGOTIATIONS, RASCAL GOES FOR A STROLL. SUDDENLY...
HEY! AN EVILDOER!
HE SPRINGS INTO ACTION...
NOT SO FAST, TERROR-BOY!
... BUT MISSES, KILLING A NEARBY SHOPKEEPER.
OOPS.
PAPA! PAPA!
GB Trudeau
LATER.
YOU WHAT?
OKAY, OKAY, I'LL LEAVE BY 2022!

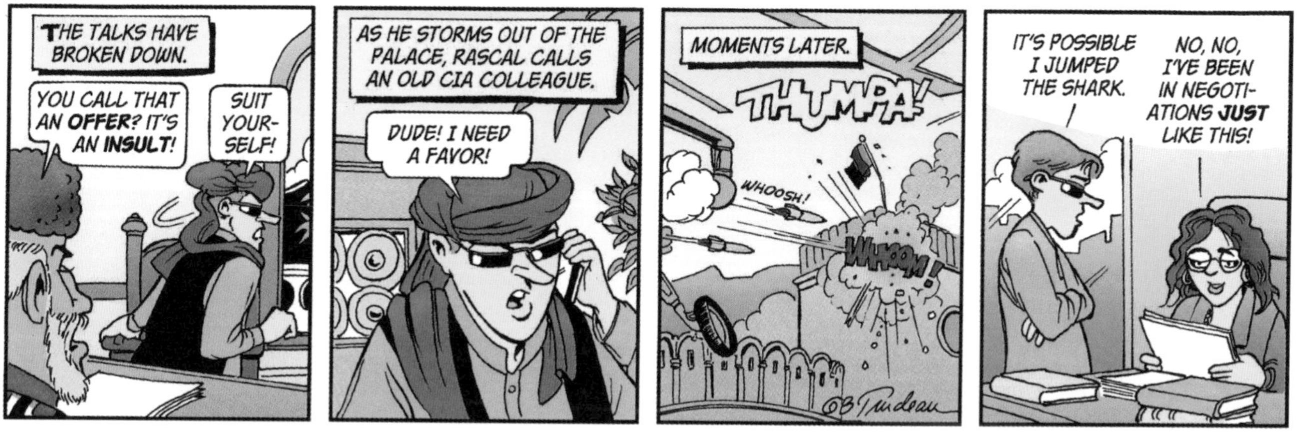
THE TALKS HAVE BROKEN DOWN.
YOU CALL THAT AN OFFER? IT'S AN INSULT!
SUIT YOURSELF!
AS HE STORMS OUT OF THE PALACE, RASCAL CALLS AN OLD CIA COLLEAGUE.
DUDE! I NEED A FAVOR!
MOMENTS LATER.
THUMPA!
WHOOSH!
WHOOM!
GB Trudeau
IT'S POSSIBLE I JUMPED THE SHARK.
NO, NO, I'VE BEEN IN NEGOTIATIONS JUST LIKE THIS!

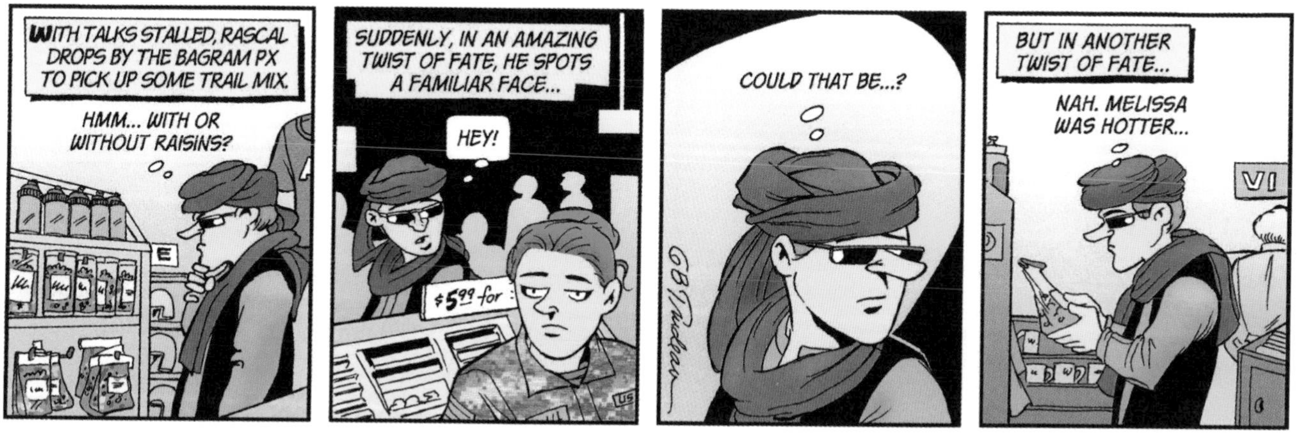
WITH TALKS STALLED, RASCAL DROPS BY THE BAGRAM PX TO PICK UP SOME TRAIL MIX.
HMM... WITH OR WITHOUT RAISINS?
SUDDENLY, IN AN AMAZING TWIST OF FATE, HE SPOTS A FAMILIAR FACE...
HEY!
$5.99 for
COULD THAT BE...?
GB Trudeau
BUT IN ANOTHER TWIST OF FATE...
NAH. MELISSA WAS HOTTER...

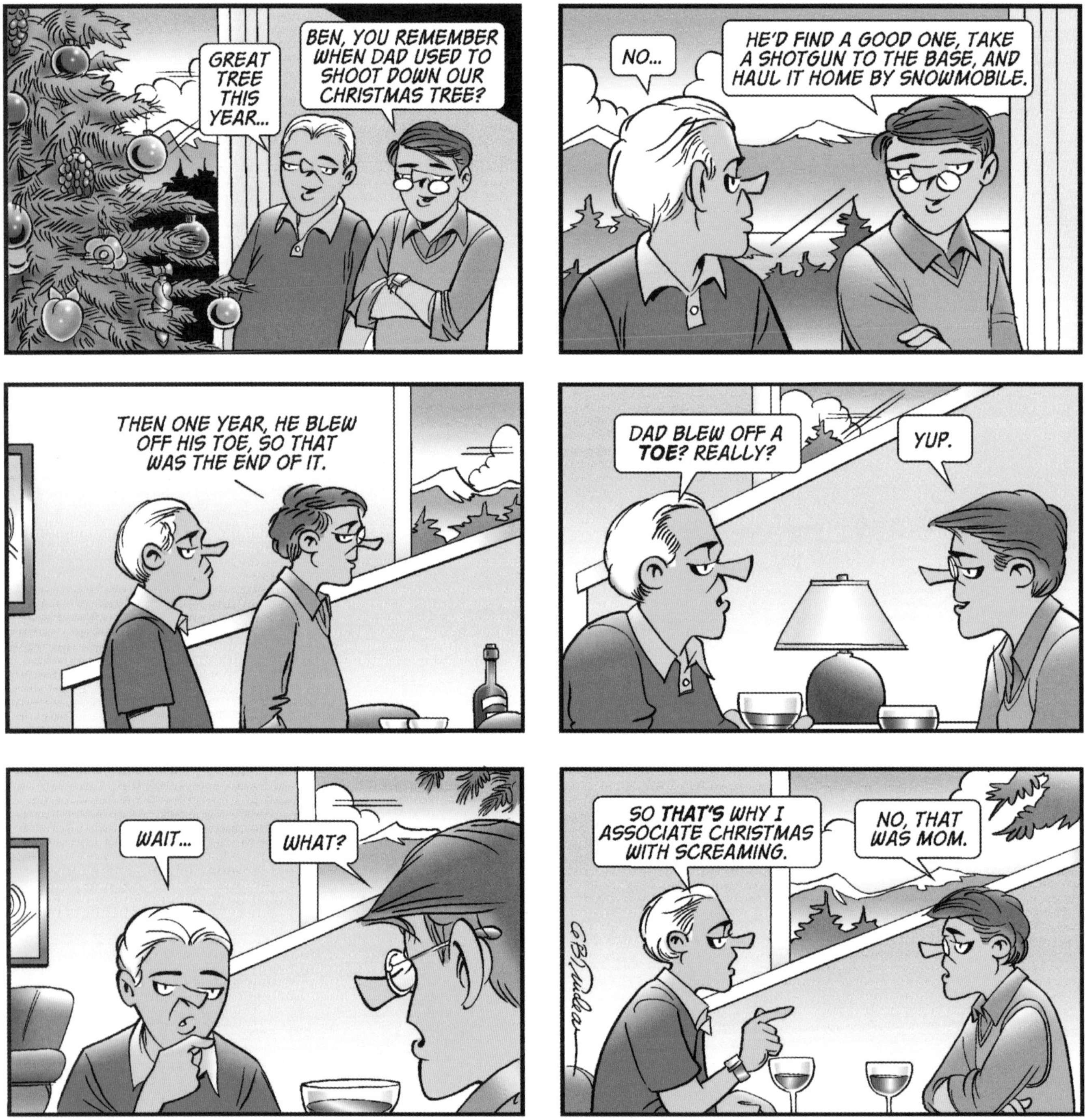
GREAT TREE THIS YEAR...
BEN, YOU REMEMBER WHEN DAD USED TO SHOOT DOWN OUR CHRISTMAS TREE?
NO...
HE'D FIND A GOOD ONE, TAKE A SHOTGUN TO THE BASE, AND HAUL IT HOME BY SNOWMOBILE.
THEN ONE YEAR, HE BLEW OFF HIS TOE, SO THAT WAS THE END OF IT.
DAD BLEW OFF A TOE? REALLY?
YUP.
WAIT...
WHAT?
SO THAT'S WHY I ASSOCIATE CHRISTMAS WITH SCREAMING.
NO, THAT WAS MOM.

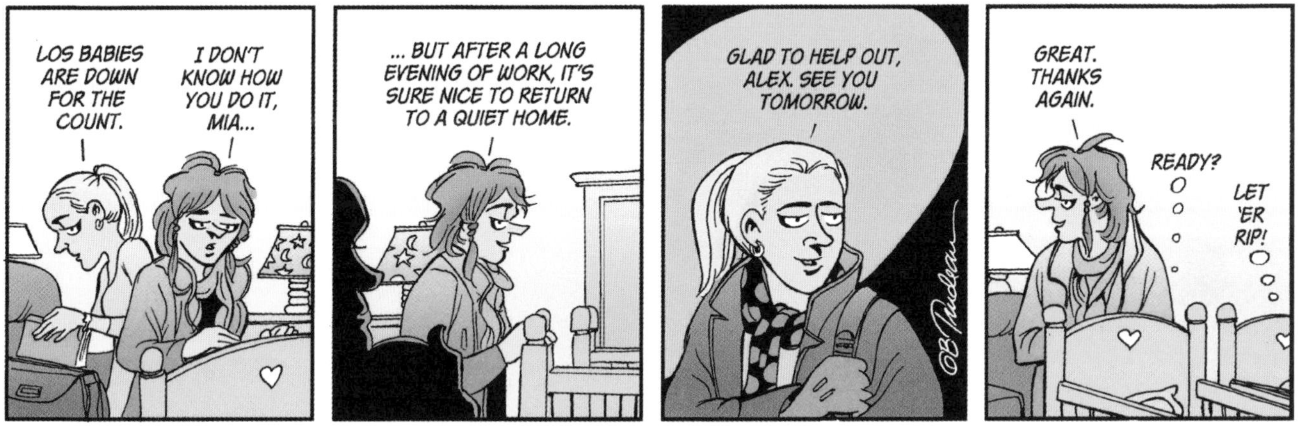
LOS BABIES ARE DOWN FOR THE COUNT.
I DON'T KNOW HOW YOU DO IT, MIA...
... BUT AFTER A LONG EVENING OF WORK, IT'S SURE NICE TO RETURN TO A QUIET HOME.
GLAD TO HELP OUT, ALEX. SEE YOU TOMORROW.
GREAT. THANKS AGAIN.
READY?
LET 'ER RIP!

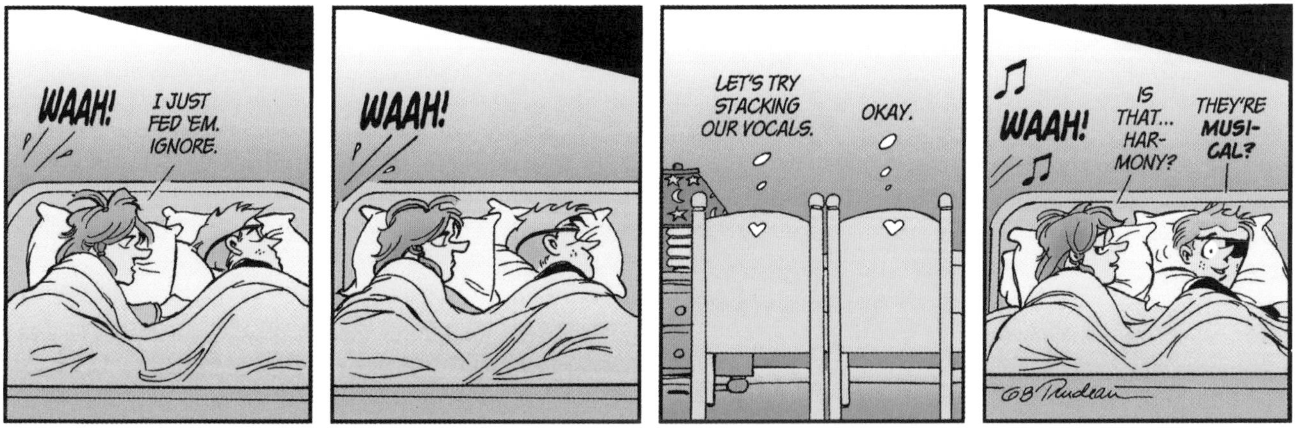
WAAH!
I JUST FED 'EM. IGNORE.
WAAH!
LET'S TRY STACKING OUR VOCALS.
OKAY.
WAAH!
IS THAT... HAR-MONY?
THEY'RE **MUSI-CAL?**

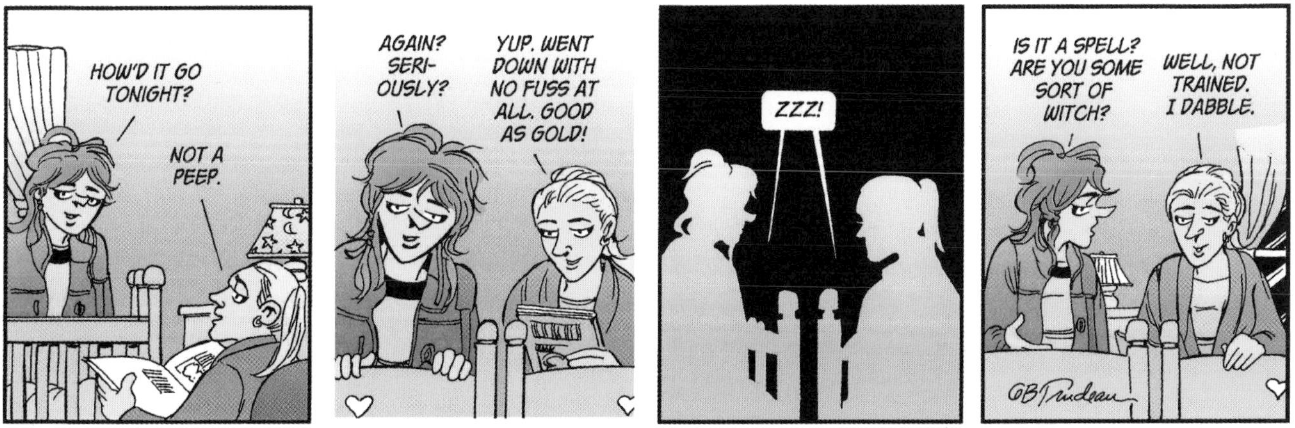
HOW'D IT GO TONIGHT?
NOT A PEEP.
AGAIN? SERI-OUSLY?
YUP. WENT DOWN WITH NO FUSS AT ALL. GOOD AS GOLD!
ZZZ!
IS IT A SPELL? ARE YOU SOME SORT OF WITCH?
WELL, NOT TRAINED. I DABBLE.

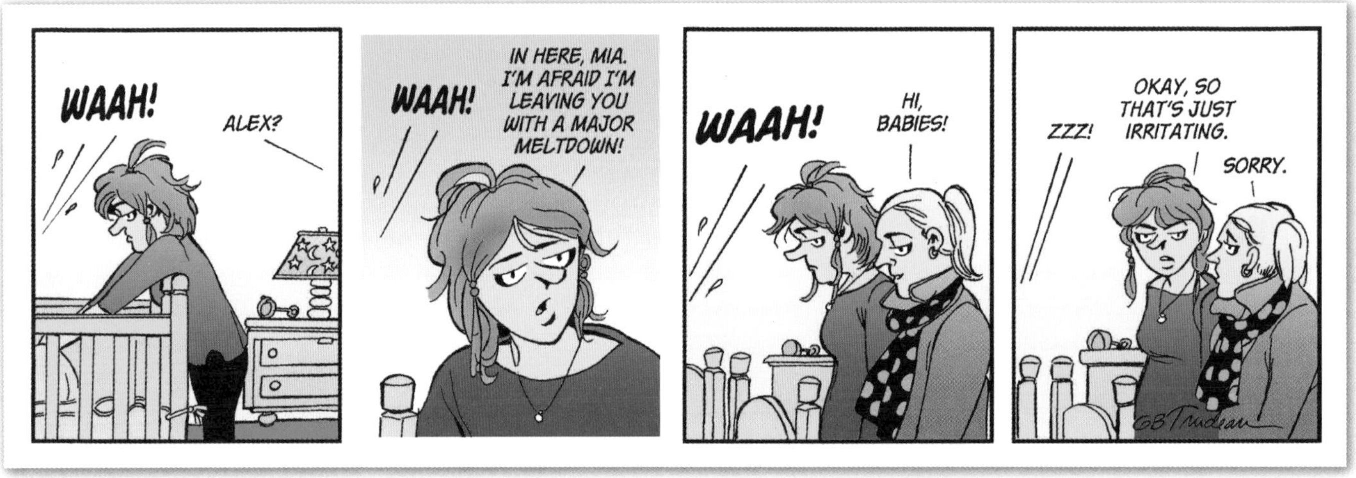
WAAH!
ALEX?
WAAH!
IN HERE, MIA. I'M AFRAID I'M LEAVING YOU WITH A MAJOR MELTDOWN!
WAAH!
HI, BABIES!
ZZZ!
OKAY, SO THAT'S JUST IRRITATING.
SORRY.
GB Trudeau

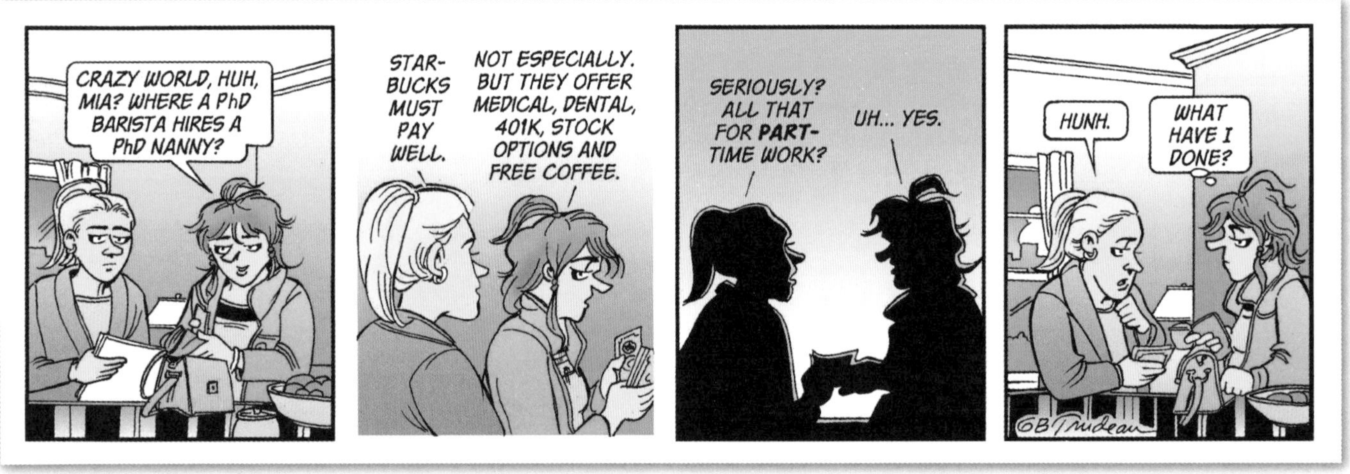
CRAZY WORLD, HUH, MIA? WHERE A PhD BARISTA HIRES A PhD NANNY?
STAR-BUCKS MUST PAY WELL.
NOT ESPECIALLY. BUT THEY OFFER MEDICAL, DENTAL, 401K, STOCK OPTIONS AND FREE COFFEE.
SERIOUSLY? ALL THAT FOR PART-TIME WORK?
UH... YES.
HUNH.
WHAT HAVE I DONE?
GB Trudeau

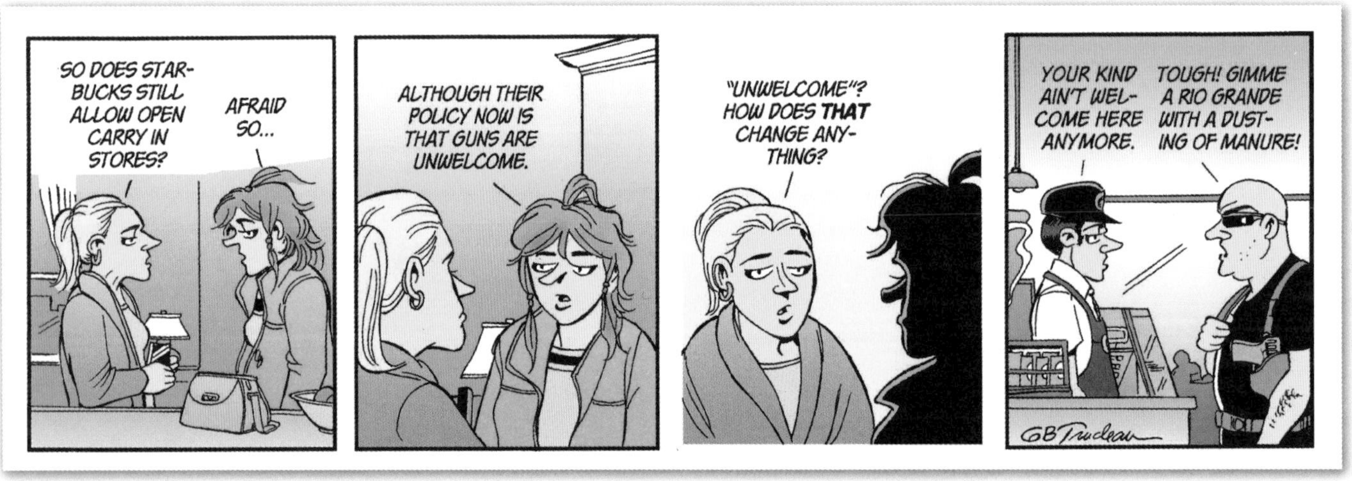
SO DOES STAR-BUCKS STILL ALLOW OPEN CARRY IN STORES?
AFRAID SO...
ALTHOUGH THEIR POLICY NOW IS THAT GUNS ARE UNWELCOME.
"UNWELCOME"? HOW DOES THAT CHANGE ANY-THING?
YOUR KIND AIN'T WEL-COME HERE ANYMORE.
TOUGH! GIMME A RIO GRANDE WITH A DUST-ING OF MANURE!
GB Trudeau

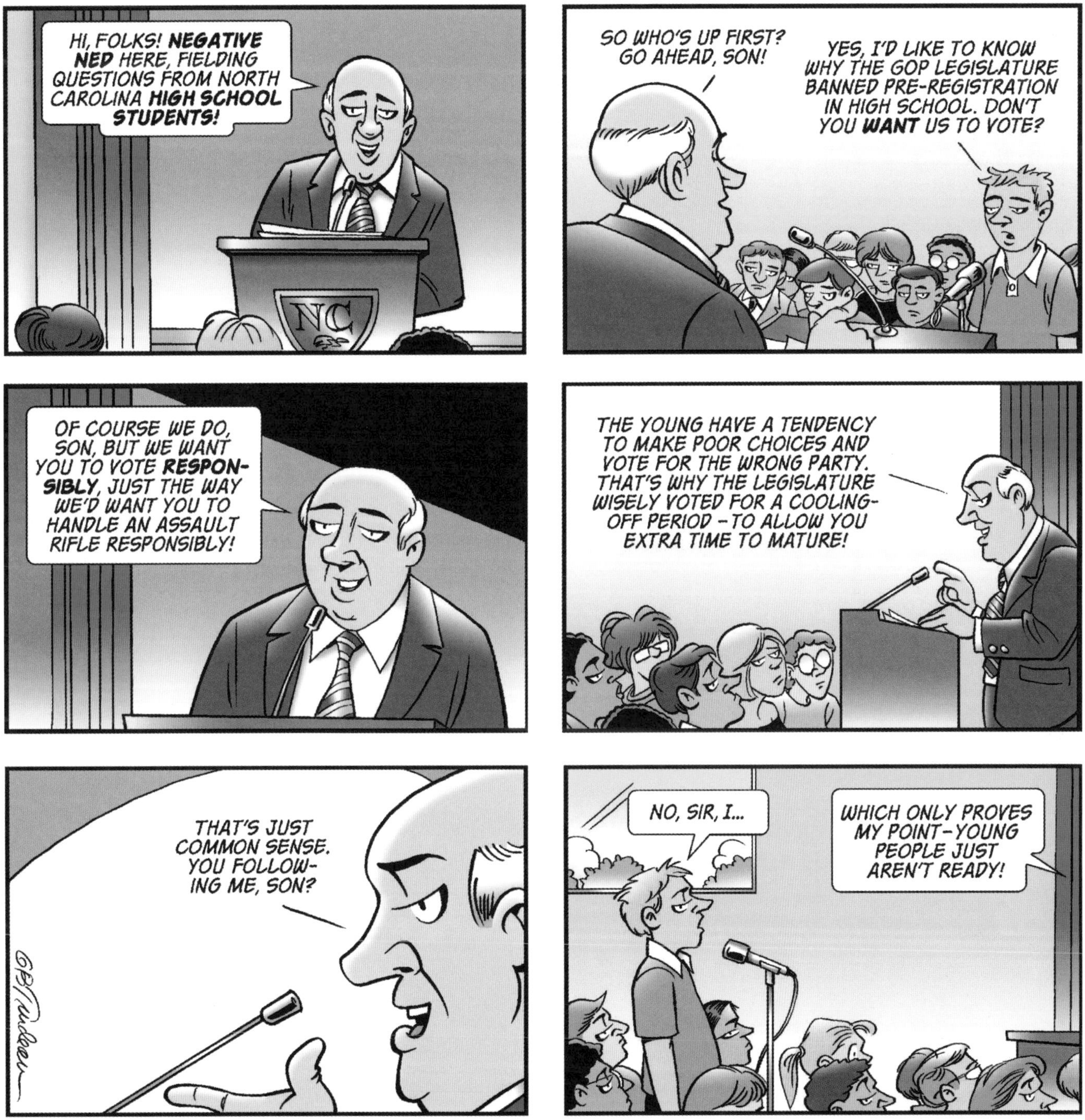
HI, FOLKS! NEGATIVE NED HERE, FIELDING QUESTIONS FROM NORTH CAROLINA HIGH SCHOOL STUDENTS!
NC
SO WHO'S UP FIRST? GO AHEAD, SON!
YES, I'D LIKE TO KNOW WHY THE GOP LEGISLATURE BANNED PRE-REGISTRATION IN HIGH SCHOOL. DON'T YOU WANT US TO VOTE?
OF COURSE WE DO, SON, BUT WE WANT YOU TO VOTE RESPONSIBLY, JUST THE WAY WE'D WANT YOU TO HANDLE AN ASSAULT RIFLE RESPONSIBLY!
THE YOUNG HAVE A TENDENCY TO MAKE POOR CHOICES AND VOTE FOR THE WRONG PARTY. THAT'S WHY THE LEGISLATURE WISELY VOTED FOR A COOLING-OFF PERIOD – TO ALLOW YOU EXTRA TIME TO MATURE!
THAT'S JUST COMMON SENSE. YOU FOLLOWING ME, SON?
NO, SIR, I...
WHICH ONLY PROVES MY POINT – YOUNG PEOPLE JUST AREN'T READY!

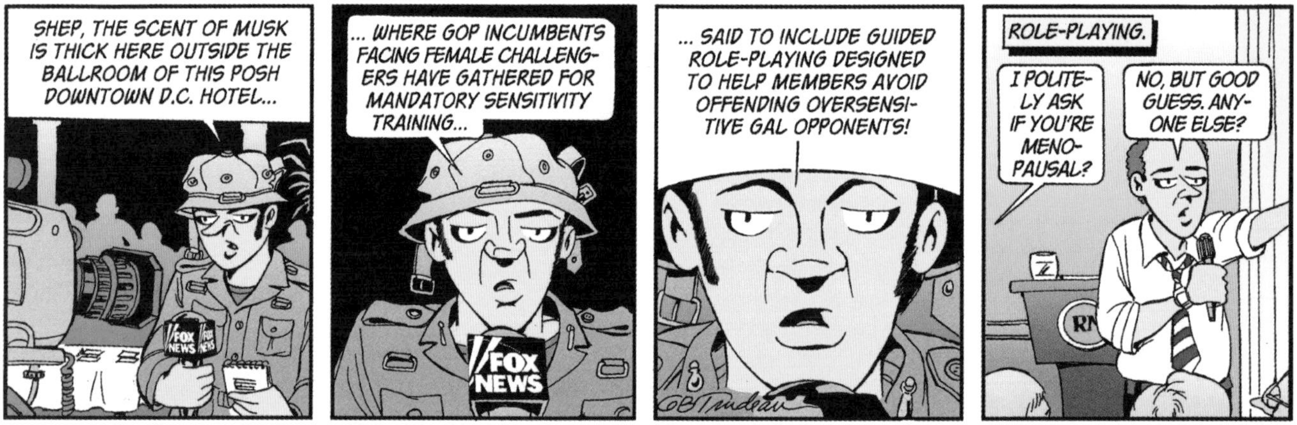
SHEP, THE SCENT OF MUSK IS THICK HERE OUTSIDE THE BALLROOM OF THIS POSH DOWNTOWN D.C. HOTEL...
FOX NEWS
... WHERE GOP INCUMBENTS FACING FEMALE CHALLENGERS HAVE GATHERED FOR MANDATORY SENSITIVITY TRAINING...
FOX NEWS
... SAID TO INCLUDE GUIDED ROLE-PLAYING DESIGNED TO HELP MEMBERS AVOID OFFENDING OVERSENSITIVE GAL OPPONENTS!
ROLE-PLAYING.
I POLITELY ASK IF YOU'RE MENOPAUSAL?
NO, BUT GOOD GUESS. ANYONE ELSE?

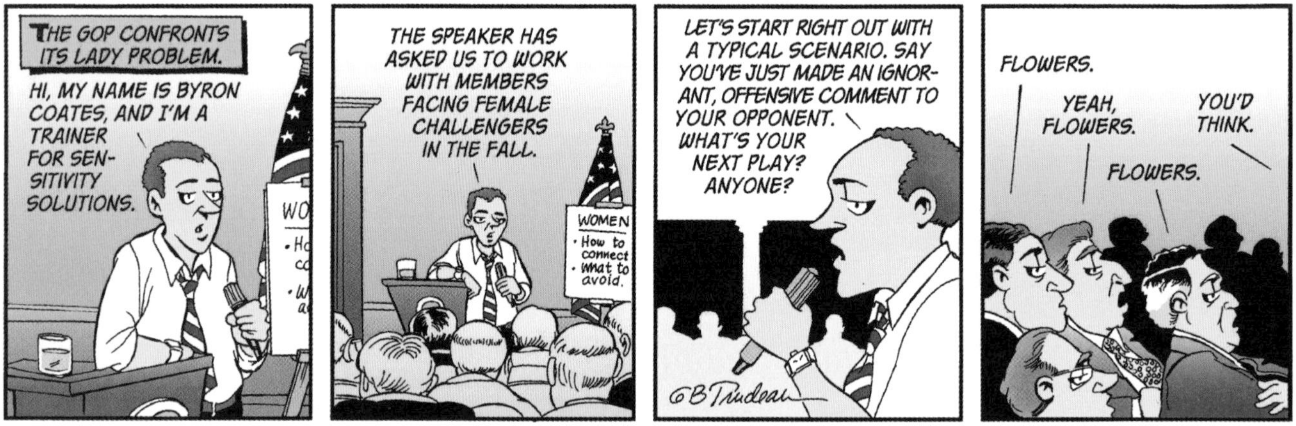
THE GOP CONFRONTS ITS LADY PROBLEM.
HI, MY NAME IS BYRON COATES, AND I'M A TRAINER FOR SENSITIVITY SOLUTIONS.
THE SPEAKER HAS ASKED US TO WORK WITH MEMBERS FACING FEMALE CHALLENGERS IN THE FALL.
WOMEN
• How to connect
• What to avoid.
LET'S START RIGHT OUT WITH A TYPICAL SCENARIO. SAY YOU'VE JUST MADE AN IGNORANT, OFFENSIVE COMMENT TO YOUR OPPONENT. WHAT'S YOUR NEXT PLAY? ANYONE?
FLOWERS.
YEAH, FLOWERS.
FLOWERS.
YOU'D THINK.

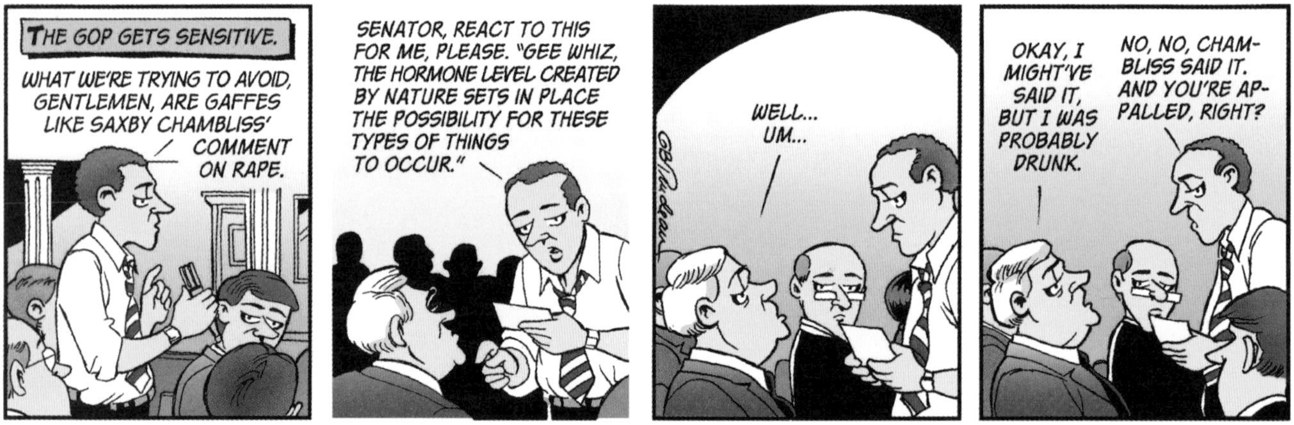
THE GOP GETS SENSITIVE.
WHAT WE'RE TRYING TO AVOID, GENTLEMEN, ARE GAFFES LIKE SAXBY CHAMBLISS' COMMENT ON RAPE.
SENATOR, REACT TO THIS FOR ME, PLEASE. "GEE WHIZ, THE HORMONE LEVEL CREATED BY NATURE SETS IN PLACE THE POSSIBILITY FOR THESE TYPES OF THINGS TO OCCUR."
WELL... UM...
OKAY, I MIGHT'VE SAID IT, BUT I WAS PROBABLY DRUNK.
NO, NO, CHAMBLISS SAID IT. AND YOU'RE APPALLED, RIGHT?

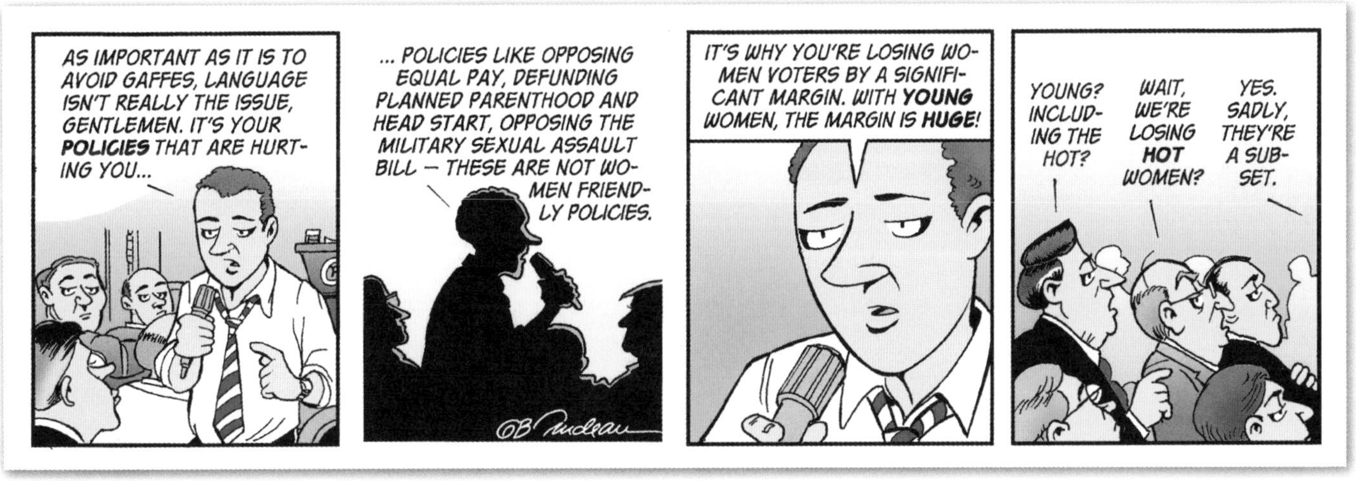
AS IMPORTANT AS IT IS TO AVOID GAFFES, LANGUAGE ISN'T REALLY THE ISSUE, GENTLEMEN. IT'S YOUR **POLICIES** THAT ARE HURTING YOU...
... POLICIES LIKE OPPOSING EQUAL PAY, DEFUNDING PLANNED PARENTHOOD AND HEAD START, OPPOSING THE MILITARY SEXUAL ASSAULT BILL — THESE ARE NOT WOMEN FRIENDLY POLICIES.
GB Trudeau
IT'S WHY YOU'RE LOSING WOMEN VOTERS BY A SIGNIFICANT MARGIN. WITH **YOUNG** WOMEN, THE MARGIN IS **HUGE**!
YOUNG? INCLUDING THE HOT?
WAIT, WE'RE LOSING **HOT** WOMEN?
YES. SADLY, THEY'RE A SUBSET.

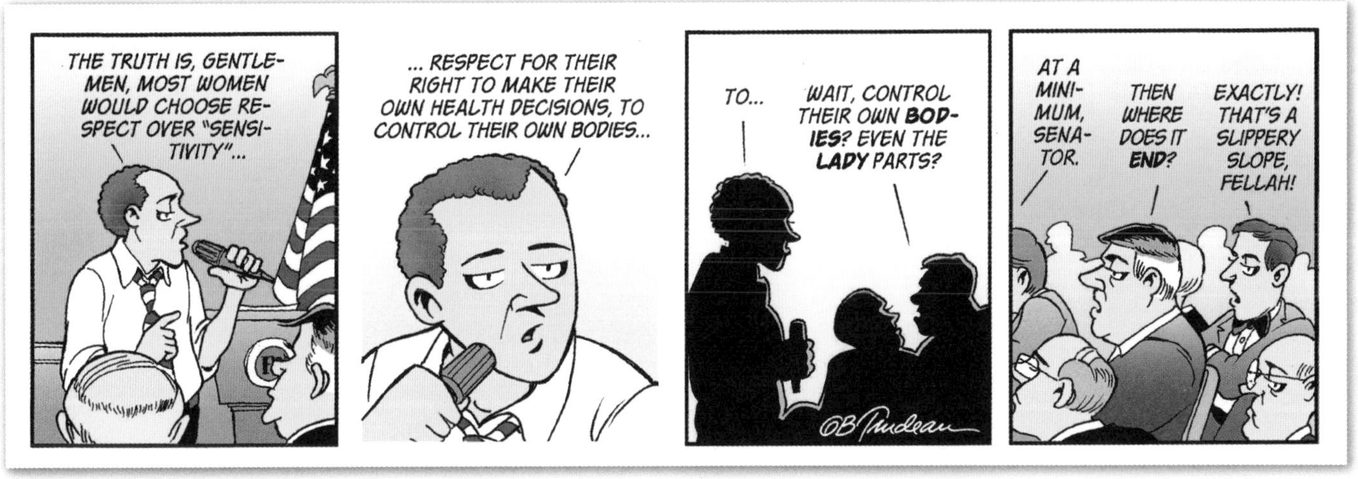
THE TRUTH IS, GENTLEMEN, MOST WOMEN WOULD CHOOSE RESPECT OVER "SENSITIVITY"...
... RESPECT FOR THEIR RIGHT TO MAKE THEIR OWN HEALTH DECISIONS, TO CONTROL THEIR OWN BODIES...
TO...
WAIT, CONTROL THEIR OWN **BODIES**? EVEN THE **LADY** PARTS?
GB Trudeau
AT A MINIMUM, SENATOR.
THEN WHERE DOES IT **END**?
EXACTLY! THAT'S A SLIPPERY SLOPE, FELLAH!

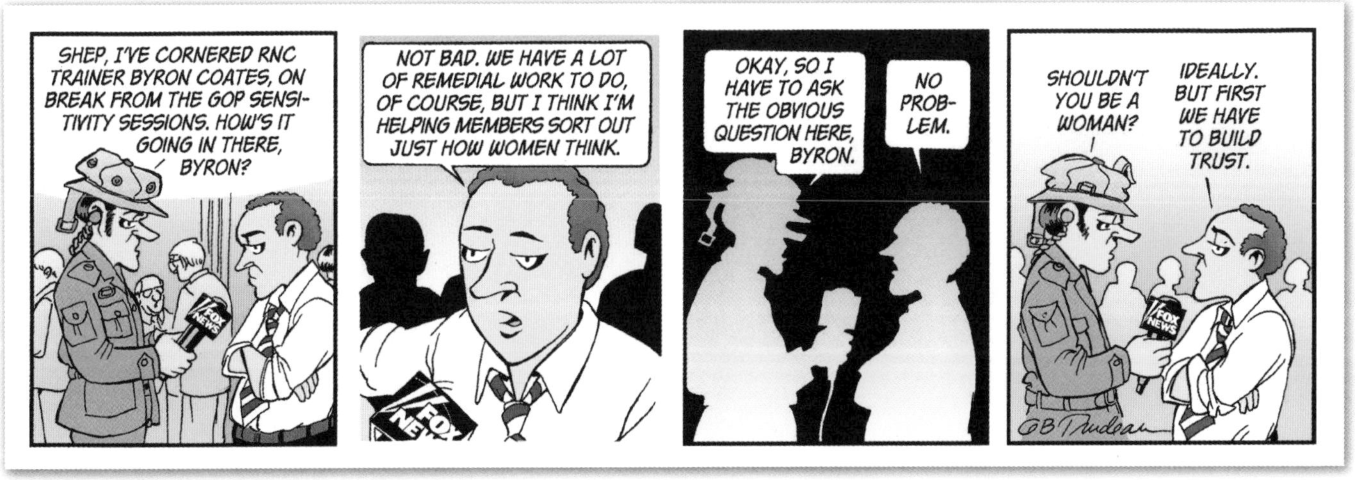
SHEP, I'VE CORNERED RNC TRAINER BYRON COATES, ON BREAK FROM THE GOP SENSITIVITY SESSIONS. HOW'S IT GOING IN THERE, BYRON?
FOX NEWS
NOT BAD. WE HAVE A LOT OF REMEDIAL WORK TO DO, OF COURSE, BUT I THINK I'M HELPING MEMBERS SORT OUT JUST HOW WOMEN THINK.
OKAY, SO I HAVE TO ASK THE OBVIOUS QUESTION HERE, BYRON.
NO PROBLEM.
SHOULDN'T YOU BE A WOMAN?
IDEALLY. BUT FIRST WE HAVE TO BUILD TRUST.
GB Trudeau

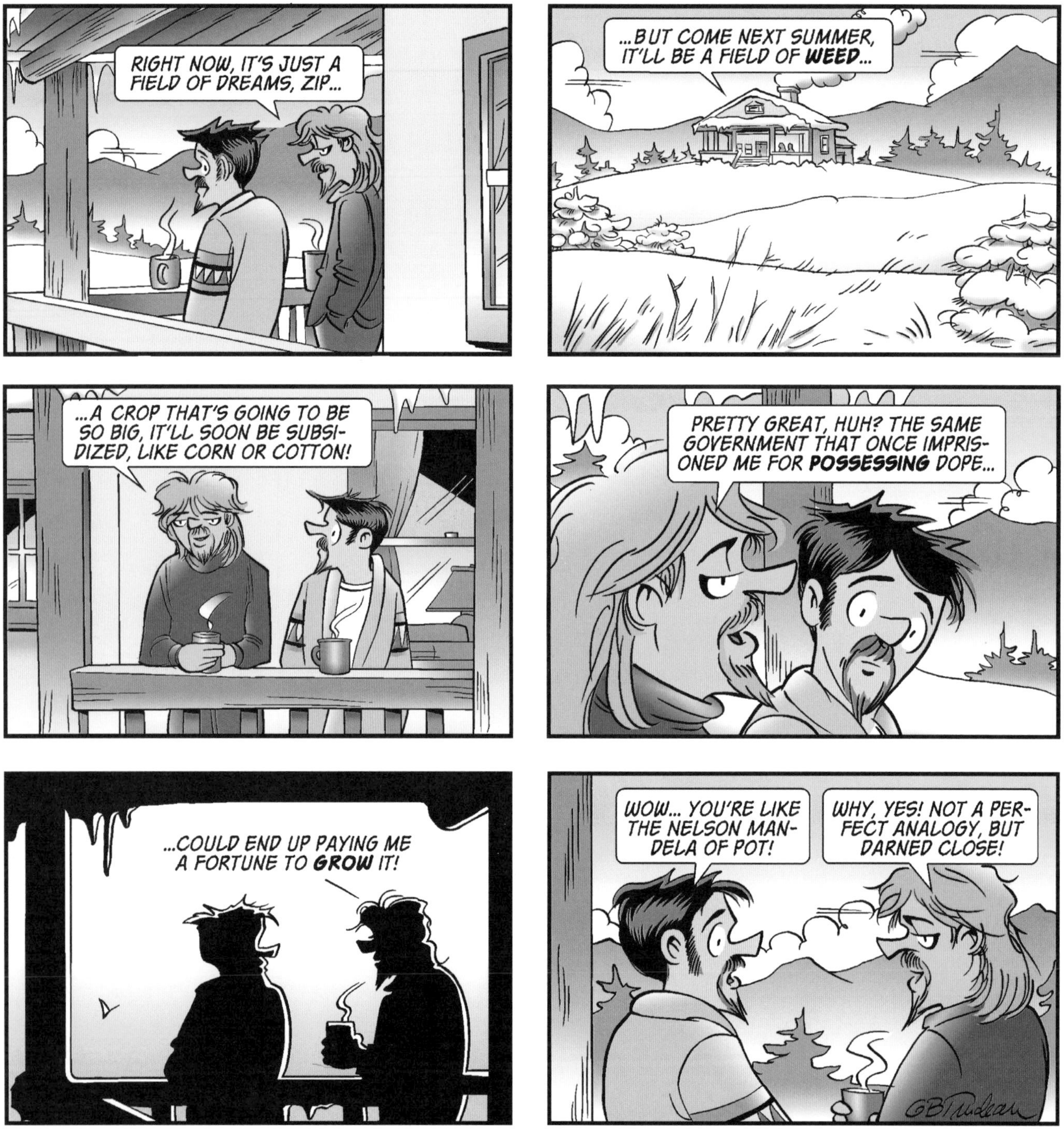
RIGHT NOW, IT'S JUST A FIELD OF DREAMS, ZIP...
...BUT COME NEXT SUMMER, IT'LL BE A FIELD OF **WEED**...
...A CROP THAT'S GOING TO BE SO BIG, IT'LL SOON BE SUBSIDIZED, LIKE CORN OR COTTON!
PRETTY GREAT, HUH? THE SAME GOVERNMENT THAT ONCE IMPRISONED ME FOR **POSSESSING** DOPE...
...COULD END UP PAYING ME A FORTUNE TO **GROW** IT!
WOW... YOU'RE LIKE THE NELSON MANDELA OF POT!
WHY, YES! NOT A PERFECT ANALOGY, BUT DARNED CLOSE!
GBTrudeau

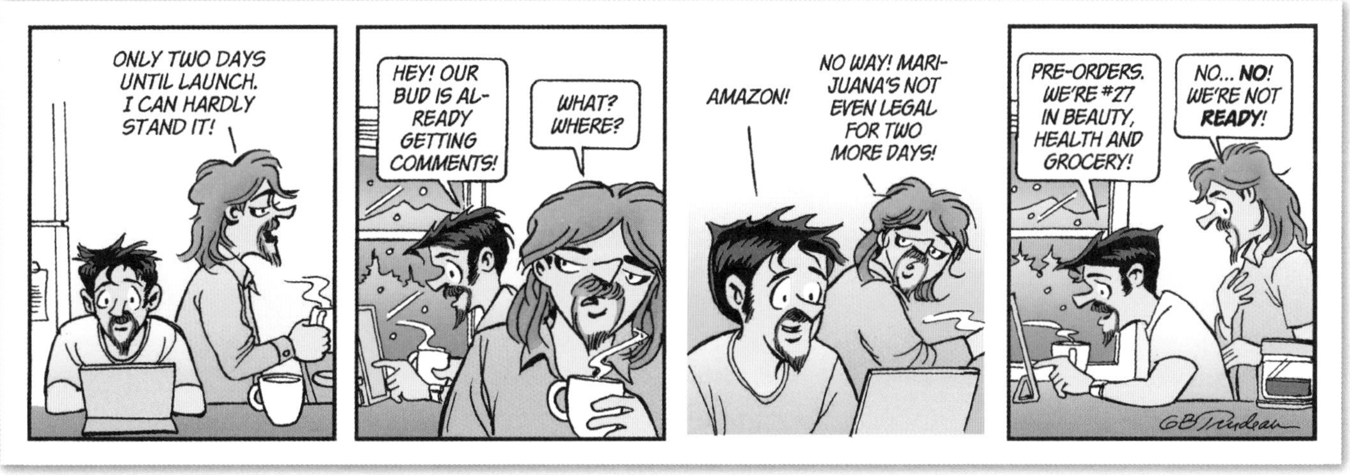
ONLY TWO DAYS UNTIL LAUNCH. I CAN HARDLY STAND IT!
HEY! OUR BUD IS AL-READY GETTING COMMENTS!
WHAT? WHERE?
AMAZON!
NO WAY! MARI-JUANA'S NOT EVEN LEGAL FOR TWO MORE DAYS!
PRE-ORDERS. WE'RE #27 IN BEAUTY, HEALTH AND GROCERY!
NO... NO! WE'RE NOT READY!
GB Trudeau

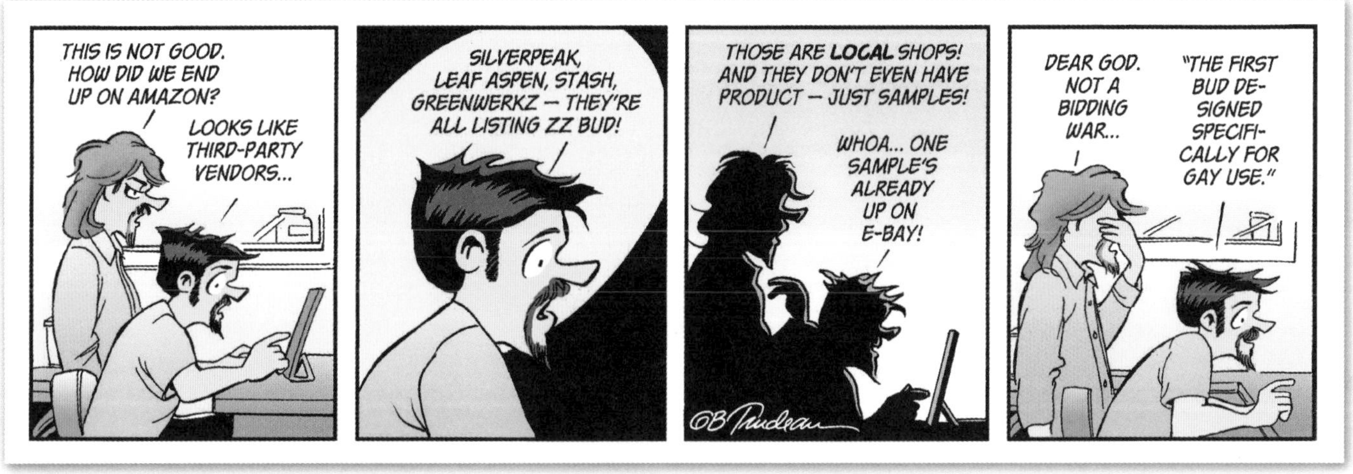
THIS IS NOT GOOD. HOW DID WE END UP ON AMAZON?
LOOKS LIKE THIRD-PARTY VENDORS...
SILVERPEAK, LEAF ASPEN, STASH, GREENWERKZ — THEY'RE ALL LISTING ZZ BUD!
THOSE ARE LOCAL SHOPS! AND THEY DON'T EVEN HAVE PRODUCT — JUST SAMPLES!
WHOA... ONE SAMPLE'S ALREADY UP ON E-BAY!
GB Trudeau
DEAR GOD. NOT A BIDDING WAR...
"THE FIRST BUD DE-SIGNED SPECIFI-CALLY FOR GAY USE."

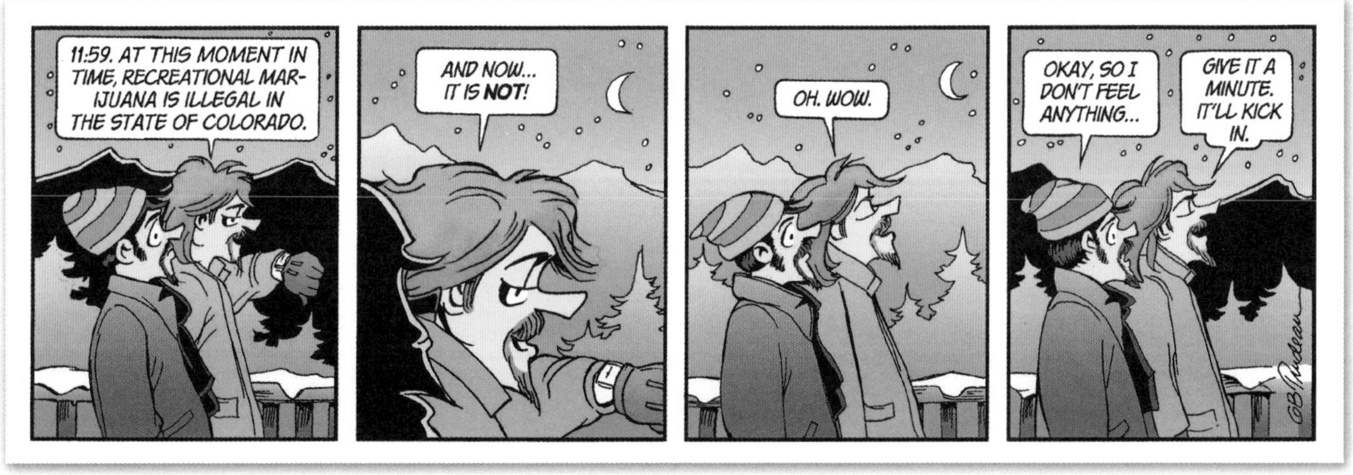
11:59. AT THIS MOMENT IN TIME, RECREATIONAL MAR-IJUANA IS ILLEGAL IN THE STATE OF COLORADO.
AND NOW... IT IS NOT!
OH. WOW.
OKAY, SO I DON'T FEEL ANYTHING...
GIVE IT A MINUTE. IT'LL KICK IN.
GB Trudeau

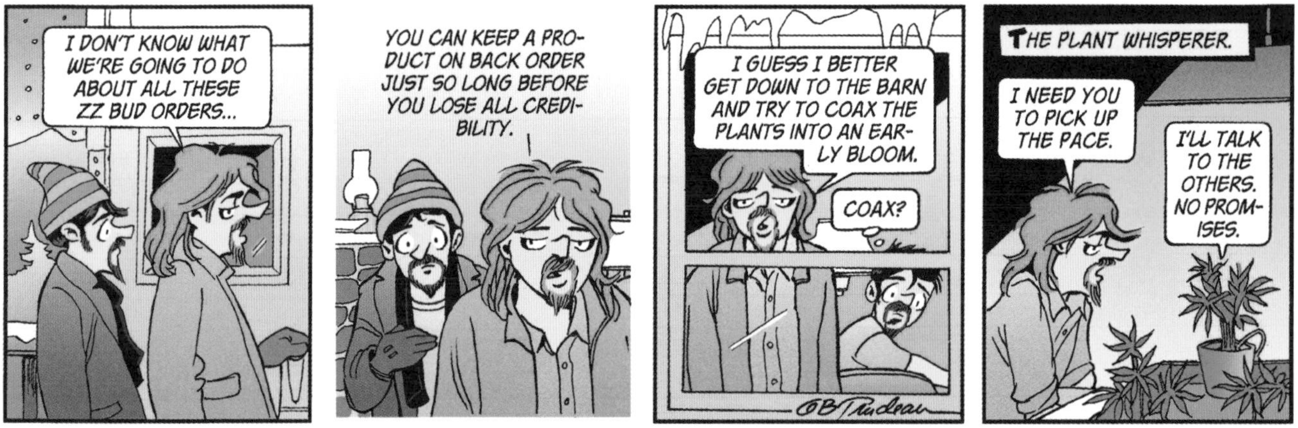
I DON'T KNOW WHAT WE'RE GOING TO DO ABOUT ALL THESE ZZ BUD ORDERS...
YOU CAN KEEP A PRODUCT ON BACK ORDER JUST SO LONG BEFORE YOU LOSE ALL CREDIBILITY.
I GUESS I BETTER GET DOWN TO THE BARN AND TRY TO COAX THE PLANTS INTO AN EARLY BLOOM.
COAX?
THE PLANT WHISPERER.
I NEED YOU TO PICK UP THE PACE.
I'LL TALK TO THE OTHERS. NO PROMISES.
GBTrudeau

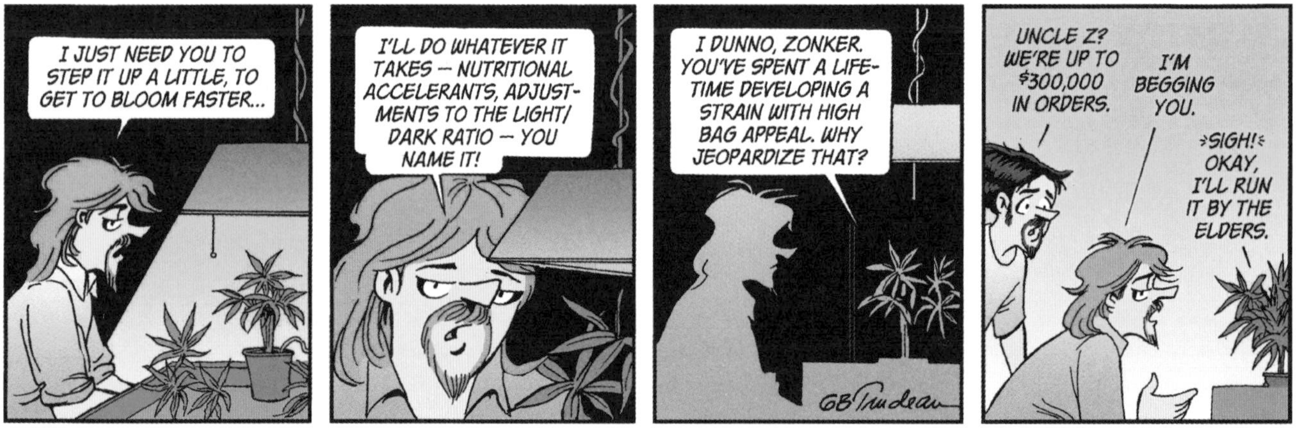
I JUST NEED YOU TO STEP IT UP A LITTLE, TO GET TO BLOOM FASTER...
I'LL DO WHATEVER IT TAKES — NUTRITIONAL ACCELERANTS, ADJUSTMENTS TO THE LIGHT/DARK RATIO — YOU NAME IT!
I DUNNO, ZONKER. YOU'VE SPENT A LIFETIME DEVELOPING A STRAIN WITH HIGH BAG APPEAL. WHY JEOPARDIZE THAT?
UNCLE Z? WE'RE UP TO $300,000 IN ORDERS.
I'M BEGGING YOU.
SIGH! OKAY, I'LL RUN IT BY THE ELDERS.
GBTrudeau

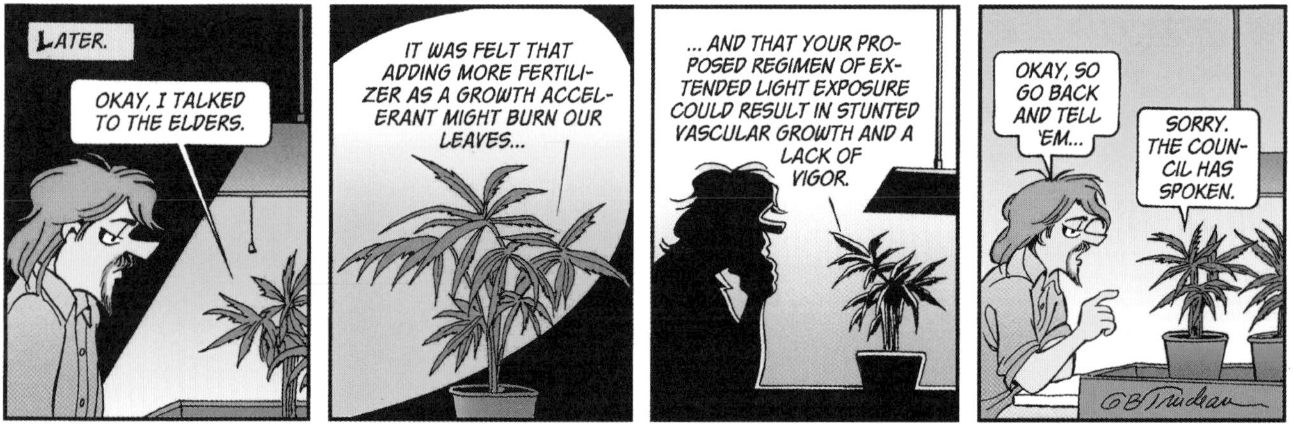
LATER.
OKAY, I TALKED TO THE ELDERS.
IT WAS FELT THAT ADDING MORE FERTILIZER AS A GROWTH ACCELERANT MIGHT BURN OUR LEAVES...
... AND THAT YOUR PROPOSED REGIMEN OF EXTENDED LIGHT EXPOSURE COULD RESULT IN STUNTED VASCULAR GROWTH AND A LACK OF VIGOR.
OKAY, SO GO BACK AND TELL 'EM...
SORRY. THE COUNCIL HAS SPOKEN.
GBTrudeau

UNCLE ZONKER! OUR FIRST **RE-VIEW!** FROM THE DENVER POST POT CRITIC!

READ! READ!

"ZZ-BUD, A DELIGHTFUL NEWCOMER OUT OF WOODY CREEK, LIVES UP TO ALL THE PRE-LEGALIZATION BUZZ..."

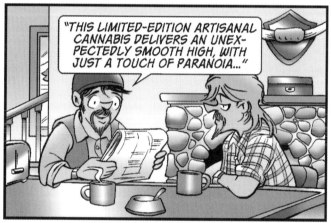

"THIS LIMITED-EDITION ARTISANAL CANNABIS DELIVERS AN UNEX-PECTEDLY SMOOTH HIGH, WITH JUST A TOUCH OF PARANOIA..."

"WHILE PITCHED TO THE GAY USER, ZZ-BUD SHOULD AP-PEAL TO DISCRIMINATING STRAIGHTS AS WELL! **FOUR STARS!**"

GASP!

UNCLE Z...? YOU OKAY?

I'M FINE... FINE... JUST OVERCOME...

MY LIFE'S WORK HAS BEEN... VIN-DICATED!

NICE. SO WHAT'S OUR EXIT STRATEGY?

SAVOR, KID, SAVOR! YOU'RE **SUCH** A MILLENNIAL!

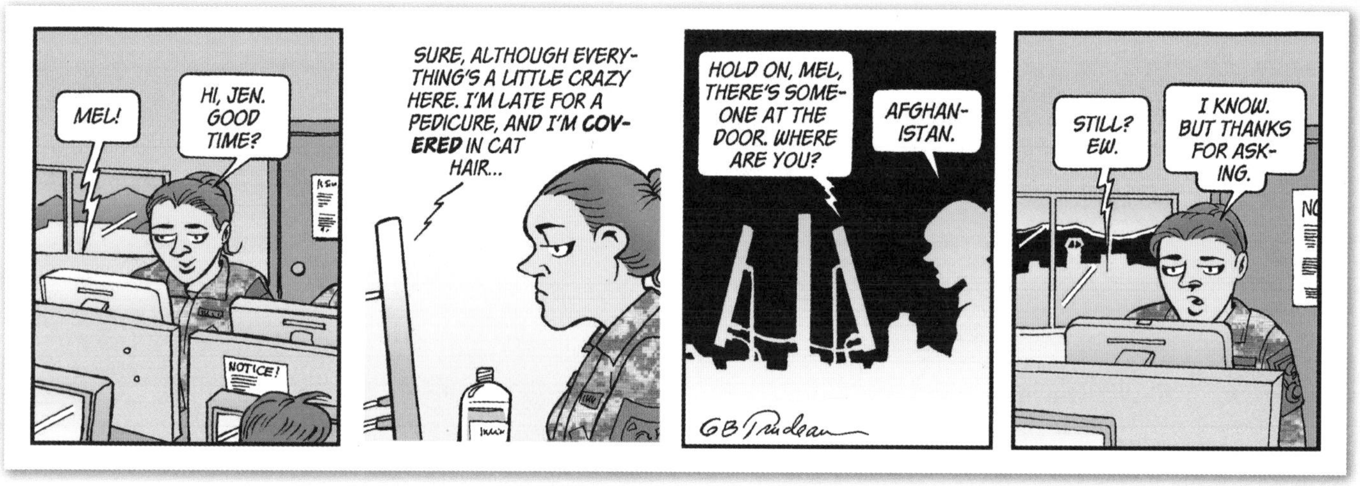
MEL!
HI, JEN. GOOD TIME?
SURE, ALTHOUGH EVERYTHING'S A LITTLE CRAZY HERE. I'M LATE FOR A PEDICURE, AND I'M **COVERED** IN CAT HAIR...
HOLD ON, MEL, THERE'S SOMEONE AT THE DOOR. WHERE ARE YOU?
AFGHANISTAN.
STILL? EW.
I KNOW. BUT THANKS FOR ASKING.
NOTICE!
GB Trudeau

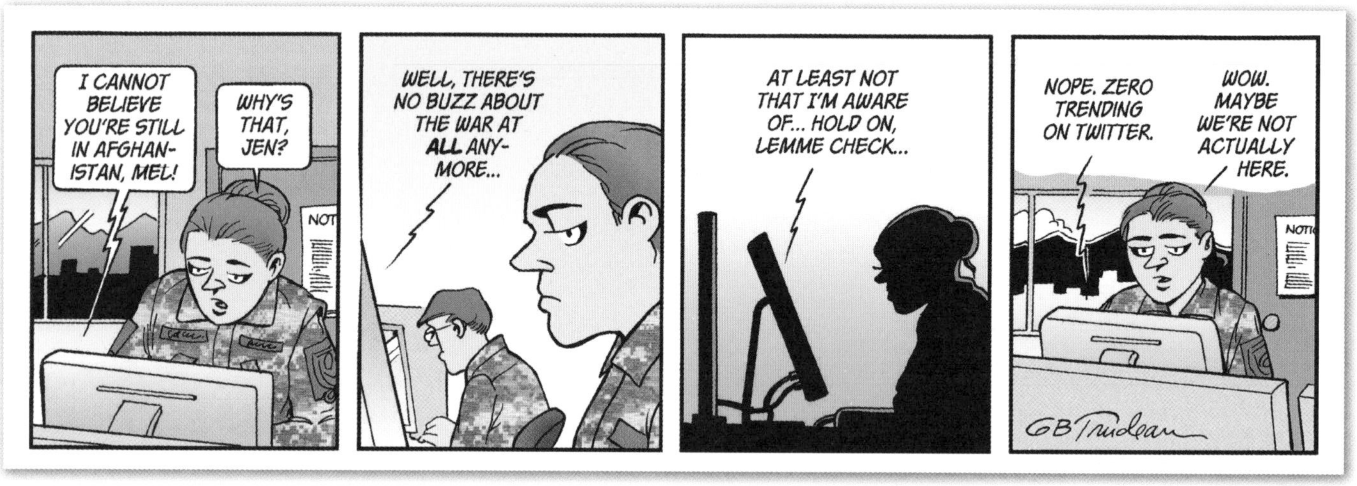
I CANNOT BELIEVE YOU'RE STILL IN AFGHANISTAN, MEL!
WHY'S THAT, JEN?
WELL, THERE'S NO BUZZ ABOUT THE WAR AT **ALL** ANYMORE...
AT LEAST NOT THAT I'M AWARE OF... HOLD ON, LEMME CHECK...
NOPE. ZERO TRENDING ON TWITTER.
WOW. MAYBE WE'RE NOT ACTUALLY HERE.
GB Trudeau

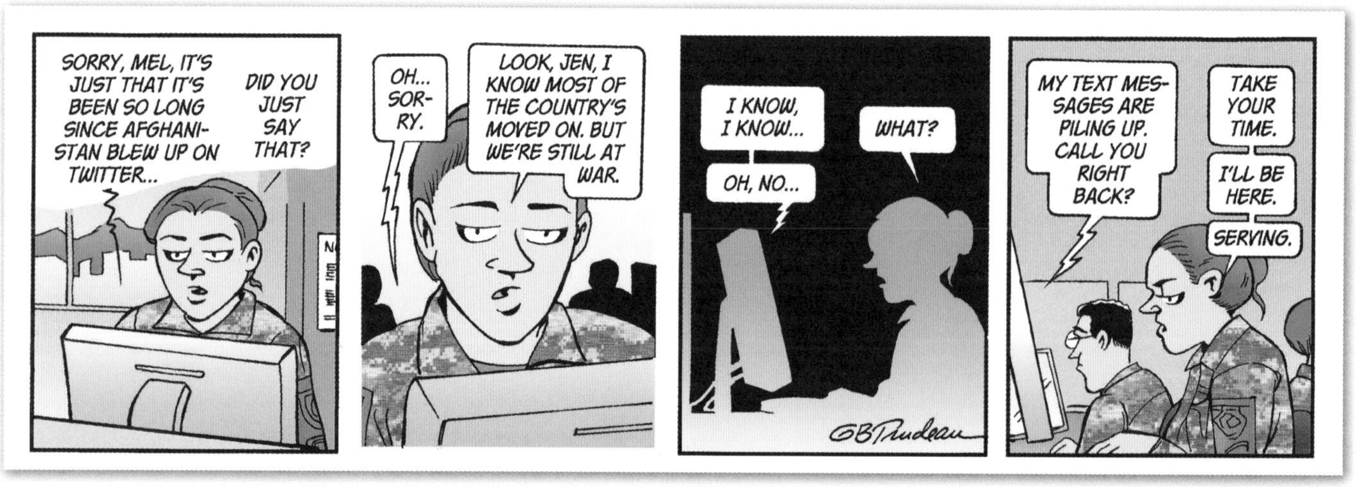
SORRY, MEL, IT'S JUST THAT IT'S BEEN SO LONG SINCE AFGHANISTAN BLEW UP ON TWITTER...
DID YOU JUST SAY THAT?
OH... SORRY.
LOOK, JEN, I KNOW MOST OF THE COUNTRY'S MOVED ON. BUT WE'RE STILL AT WAR.
I KNOW, I KNOW...
OH, NO...
WHAT?
MY TEXT MESSAGES ARE PILING UP. CALL YOU RIGHT BACK?
TAKE YOUR TIME.
I'LL BE HERE.
SERVING.
GB Trudeau

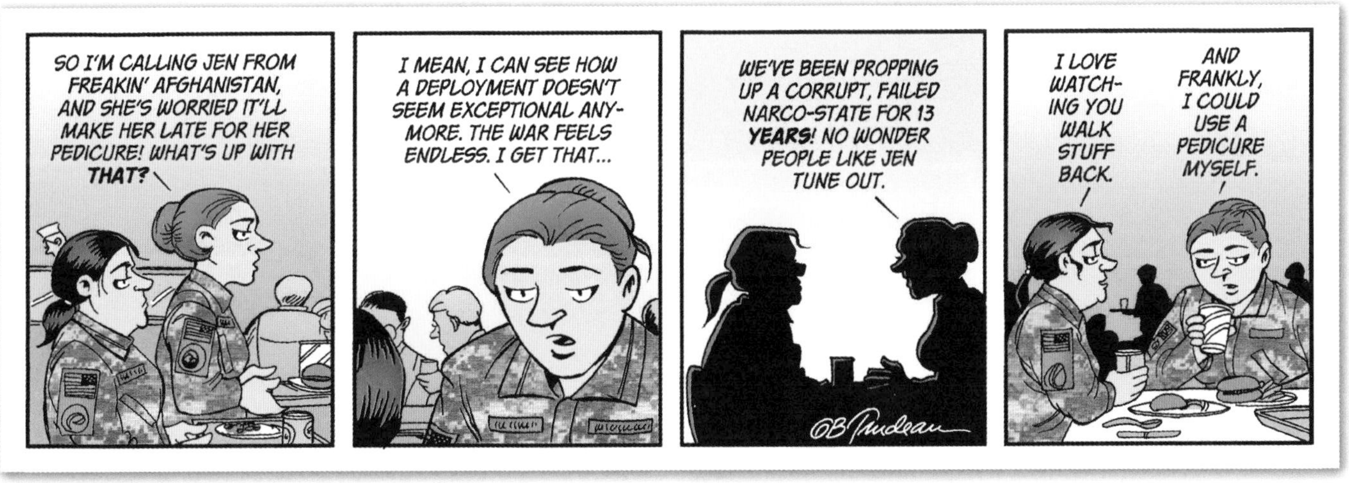
SO I'M CALLING JEN FROM FREAKIN' AFGHANISTAN, AND SHE'S WORRIED IT'LL MAKE HER LATE FOR HER PEDICURE! WHAT'S UP WITH **THAT?**
I MEAN, I CAN SEE HOW A DEPLOYMENT DOESN'T SEEM EXCEPTIONAL ANY-MORE. THE WAR FEELS ENDLESS. I GET THAT...
WE'VE BEEN PROPPING UP A CORRUPT, FAILED NARCO-STATE FOR 13 **YEARS!** NO WONDER PEOPLE LIKE JEN TUNE OUT.
I LOVE WATCH-ING YOU WALK STUFF BACK.
AND FRANKLY, I COULD USE A PEDICURE MYSELF.

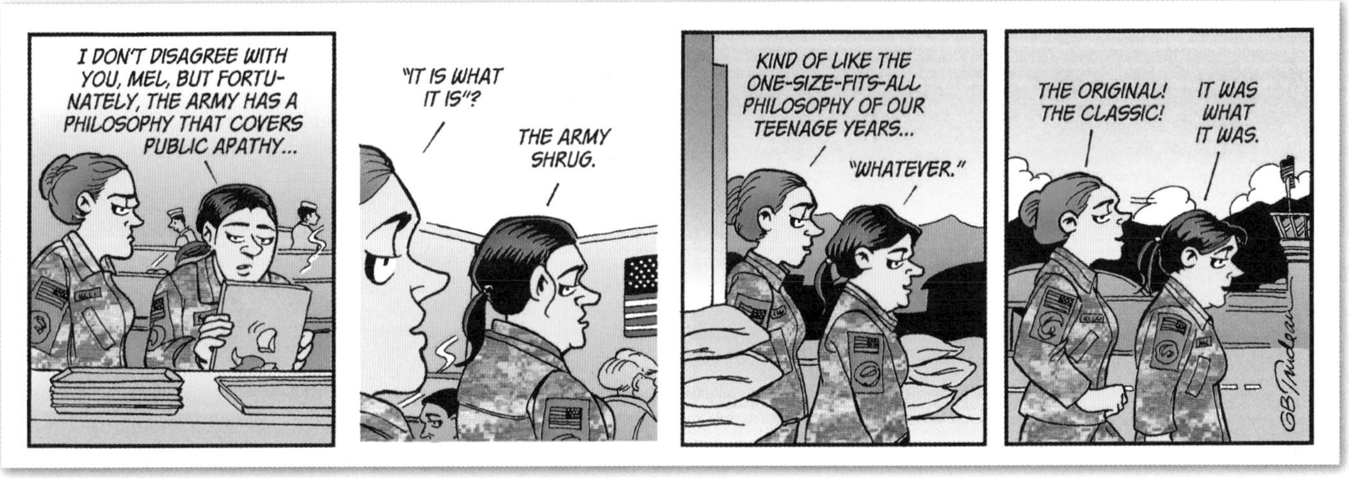
I DON'T DISAGREE WITH YOU, MEL, BUT FORTU-NATELY, THE ARMY HAS A PHILOSOPHY THAT COVERS PUBLIC APATHY...
"IT IS WHAT IT IS"?
THE ARMY SHRUG.
KIND OF LIKE THE ONE-SIZE-FITS-ALL PHILOSOPHY OF OUR TEENAGE YEARS...
"WHATEVER."
THE ORIGINAL! THE CLASSIC!
IT WAS WHAT IT WAS.

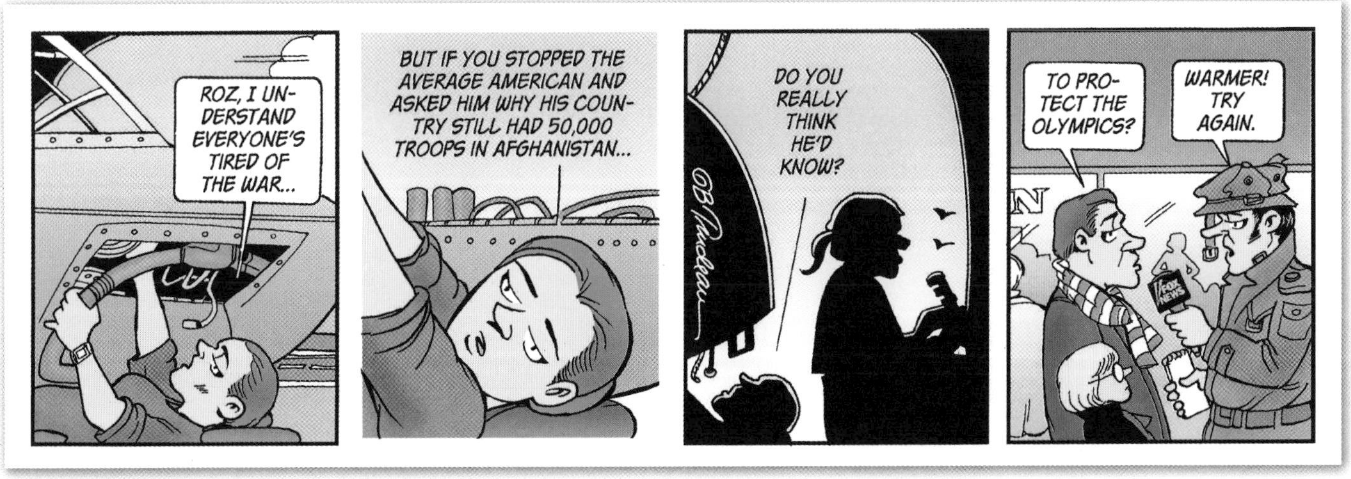
ROZ, I UN-DERSTAND EVERYONE'S TIRED OF THE WAR...
BUT IF YOU STOPPED THE AVERAGE AMERICAN AND ASKED HIM WHY HIS COUN-TRY STILL HAD 50,000 TROOPS IN AFGHANISTAN...
DO YOU REALLY THINK HE'D KNOW?
TO PRO-TECT THE OLYMPICS?
WARMER! TRY AGAIN.

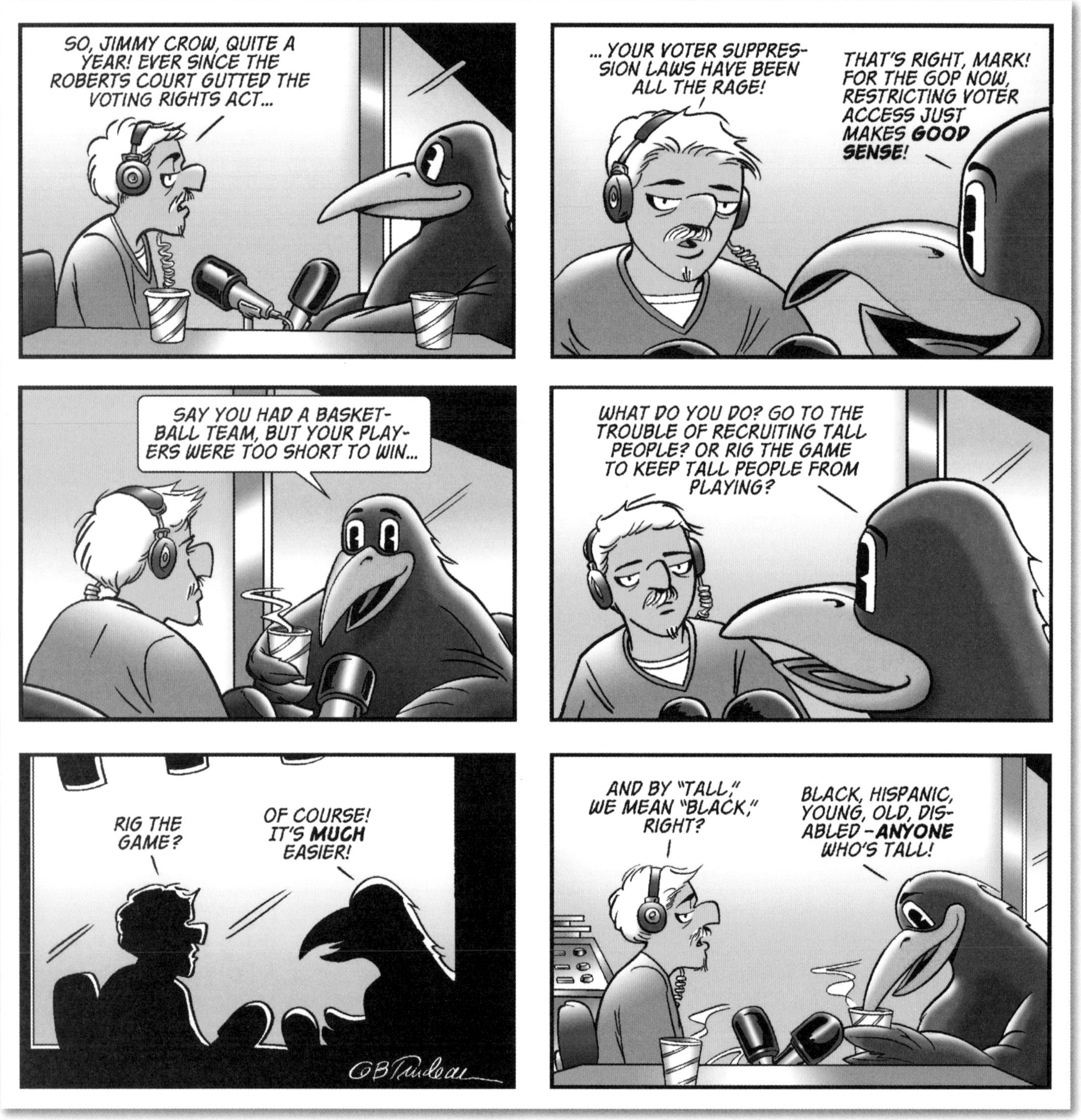
SO, JIMMY CROW, QUITE A YEAR! EVER SINCE THE ROBERTS COURT GUTTED THE VOTING RIGHTS ACT...
...YOUR VOTER SUPPRES-SION LAWS HAVE BEEN ALL THE RAGE!
THAT'S RIGHT, MARK! FOR THE GOP NOW, RESTRICTING VOTER ACCESS JUST MAKES GOOD SENSE!
SAY YOU HAD A BASKET-BALL TEAM, BUT YOUR PLAY-ERS WERE TOO SHORT TO WIN...
WHAT DO YOU DO? GO TO THE TROUBLE OF RECRUITING TALL PEOPLE? OR RIG THE GAME TO KEEP TALL PEOPLE FROM PLAYING?
RIG THE GAME?
OF COURSE! IT'S MUCH EASIER!
©BTrudeau
AND BY "TALL," WE MEAN "BLACK," RIGHT?
BLACK, HISPANIC, YOUNG, OLD, DIS-ABLED–ANYONE WHO'S TALL!

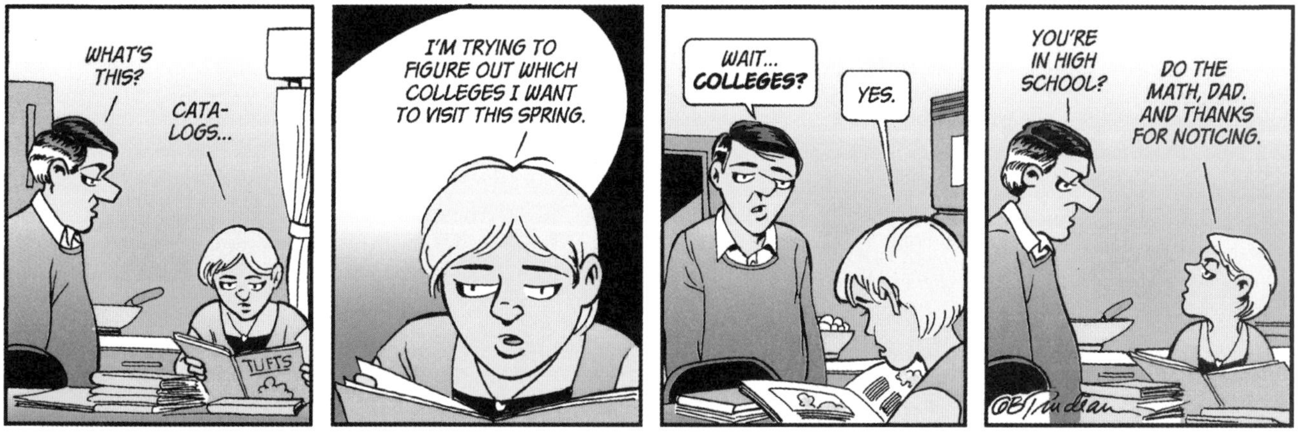
WHAT'S THIS?
CATA-LOGS...
I'M TRYING TO FIGURE OUT WHICH COLLEGES I WANT TO VISIT THIS SPRING.
WAIT... **COLLEGES?**
YES.
YOU'RE IN HIGH SCHOOL?
DO THE MATH, DAD. AND THANKS FOR NOTICING.

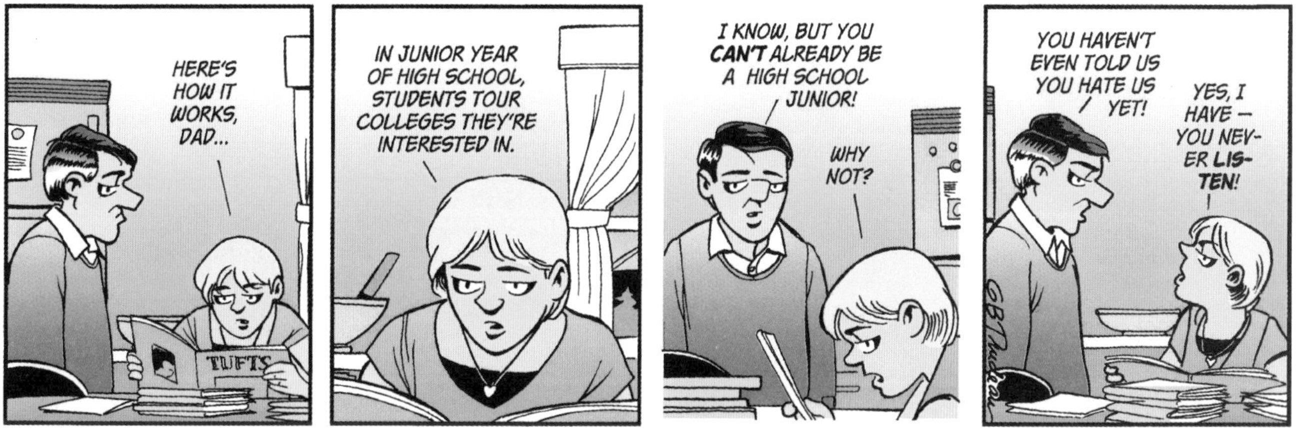
HERE'S HOW IT WORKS, DAD...
IN JUNIOR YEAR OF HIGH SCHOOL, STUDENTS TOUR COLLEGES THEY'RE INTERESTED IN.
I KNOW, BUT YOU **CAN'T** ALREADY BE A HIGH SCHOOL JUNIOR!
WHY NOT?
YOU HAVEN'T EVEN TOLD US YOU HATE US YET!
YES, I HAVE — YOU NEVER **LISTEN**!

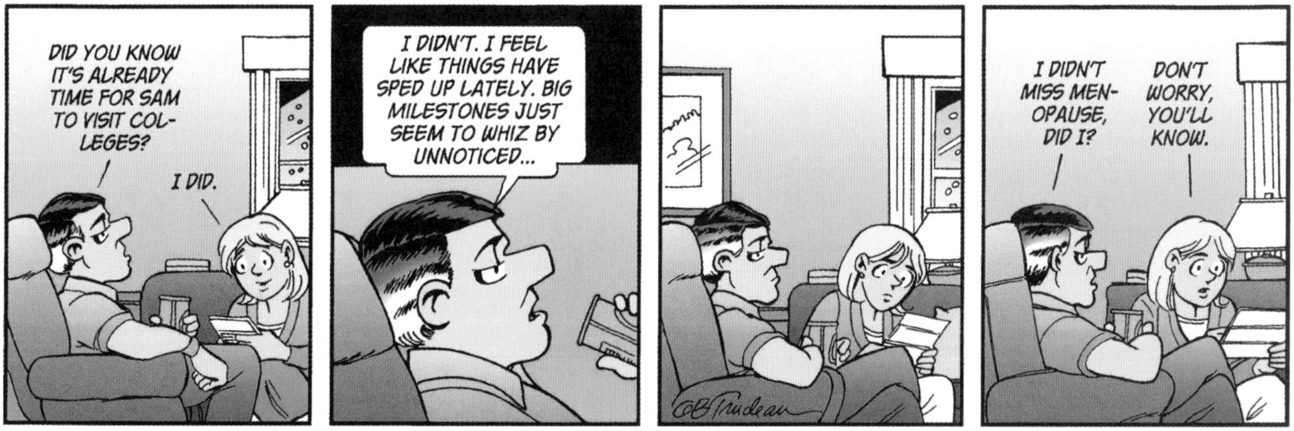
DID YOU KNOW IT'S ALREADY TIME FOR SAM TO VISIT COLLEGES?
I DID.
I DIDN'T. I FEEL LIKE THINGS HAVE SPED UP LATELY. BIG MILESTONES JUST SEEM TO WHIZ BY UNNOTICED...
I DIDN'T MISS MENOPAUSE, DID I?
DON'T WORRY, YOU'LL KNOW.

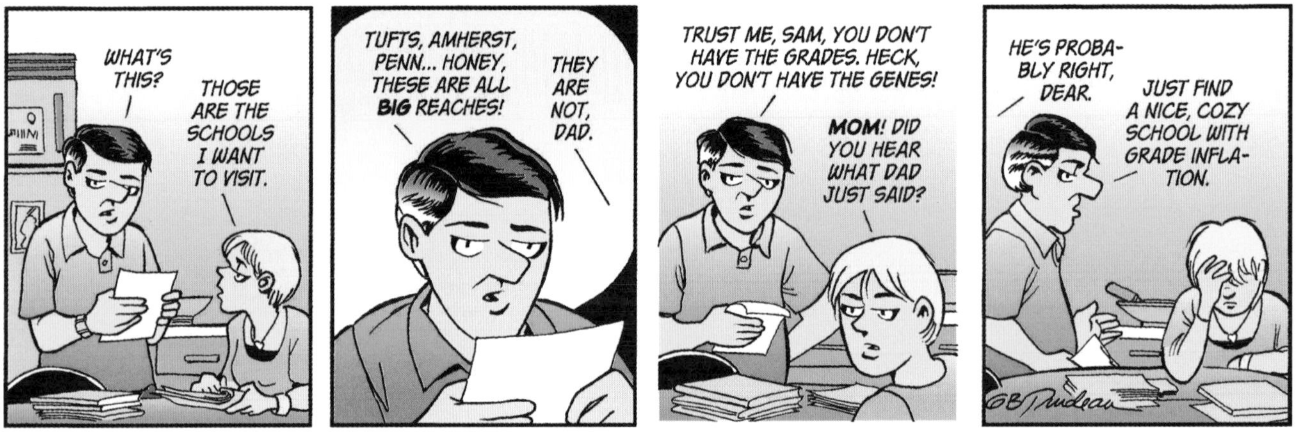
WHAT'S THIS?
THOSE ARE THE SCHOOLS I WANT TO VISIT.
TUFTS, AMHERST, PENN... HONEY, THESE ARE ALL **BIG** REACHES!
THEY ARE NOT, DAD.
TRUST ME, SAM, YOU DON'T HAVE THE GRADES. HECK, YOU DON'T HAVE THE GENES!
MOM! DID YOU HEAR WHAT DAD JUST SAID?
HE'S PROBA-BLY RIGHT, DEAR.
JUST FIND A NICE, COZY SCHOOL WITH GRADE INFLA-TION.
GB Trudeau

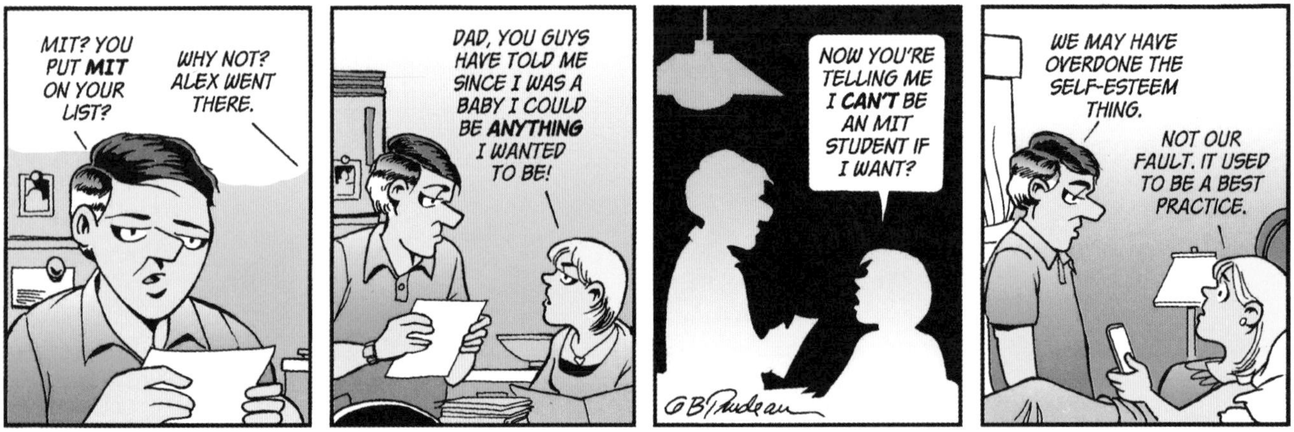
MIT? YOU PUT **MIT** ON YOUR LIST?
WHY NOT? ALEX WENT THERE.
DAD, YOU GUYS HAVE TOLD ME SINCE I WAS A BABY I COULD BE **ANYTHING** I WANTED TO BE!
NOW YOU'RE TELLING ME I **CAN'T** BE AN MIT STUDENT IF I WANT?
GB Trudeau
WE MAY HAVE OVERDONE THE SELF-ESTEEM THING.
NOT OUR FAULT. IT USED TO BE A BEST PRACTICE.

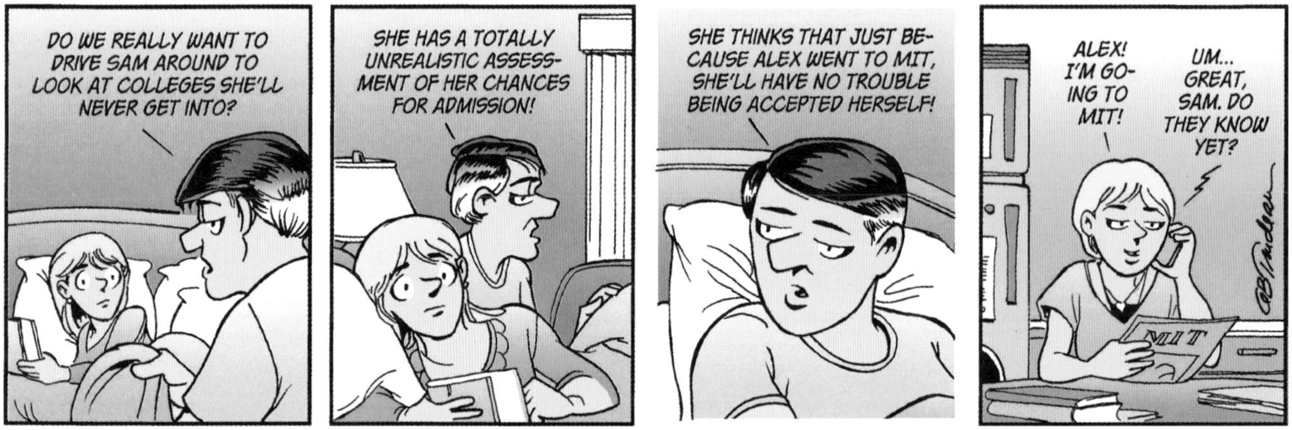
DO WE REALLY WANT TO DRIVE SAM AROUND TO LOOK AT COLLEGES SHE'LL NEVER GET INTO?
SHE HAS A TOTALLY UNREALISTIC ASSESS-MENT OF HER CHANCES FOR ADMISSION!
SHE THINKS THAT JUST BE-CAUSE ALEX WENT TO MIT, SHE'LL HAVE NO TROUBLE BEING ACCEPTED HERSELF!
ALEX! I'M GO-ING TO MIT!
UM... GREAT, SAM. DO THEY KNOW YET?
MIT
GB Trudeau

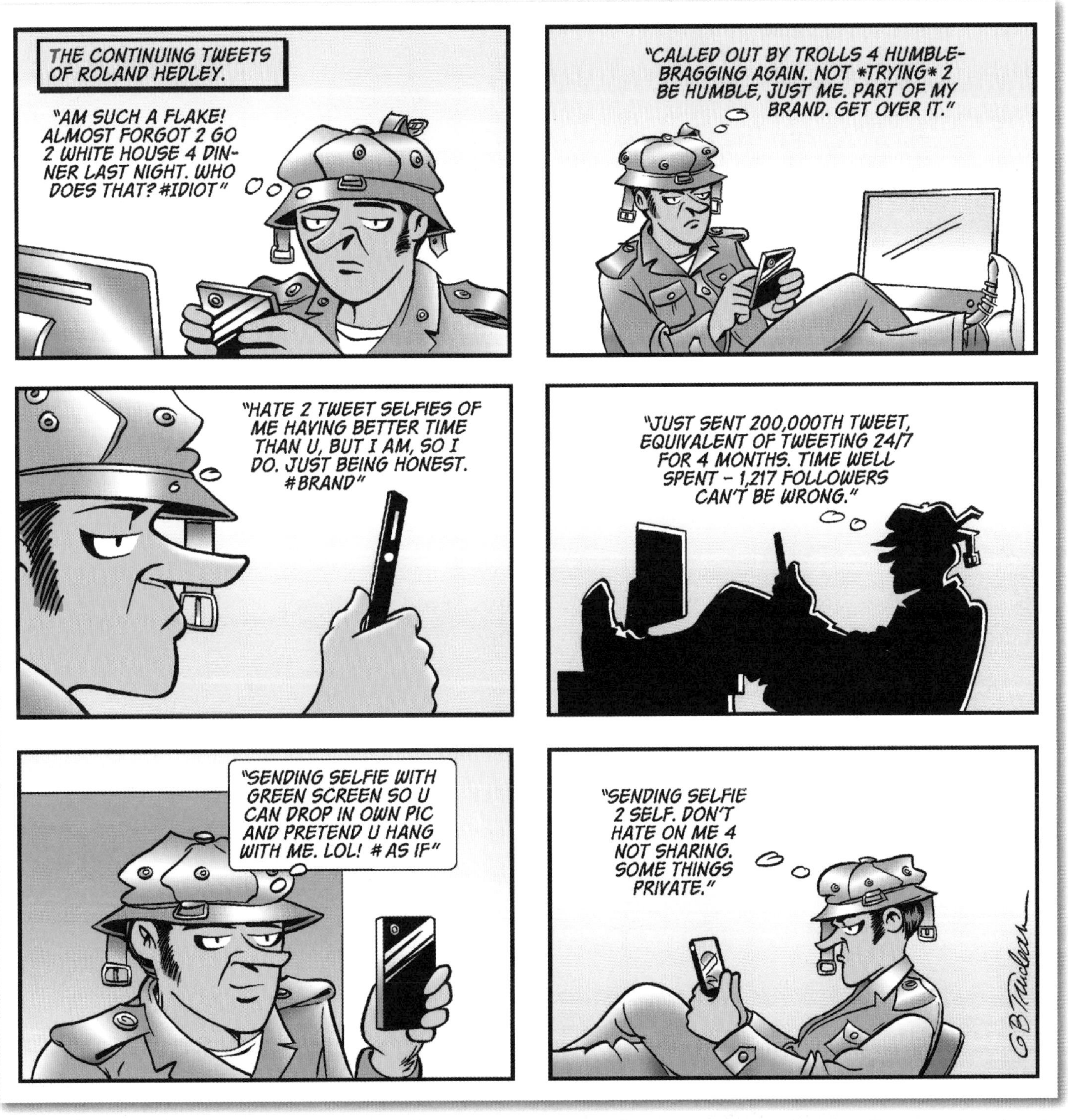
THE CONTINUING TWEETS OF ROLAND HEDLEY.
"AM SUCH A FLAKE! ALMOST FORGOT 2 GO 2 WHITE HOUSE 4 DINNER LAST NIGHT. WHO DOES THAT? #IDIOT"
"CALLED OUT BY TROLLS 4 HUMBLE-BRAGGING AGAIN. NOT *TRYING* 2 BE HUMBLE, JUST ME. PART OF MY BRAND. GET OVER IT."
"HATE 2 TWEET SELFIES OF ME HAVING BETTER TIME THAN U, BUT I AM, SO I DO. JUST BEING HONEST. #BRAND"
"JUST SENT 200,000TH TWEET, EQUIVALENT OF TWEETING 24/7 FOR 4 MONTHS. TIME WELL SPENT – 1,217 FOLLOWERS CAN'T BE WRONG."
"SENDING SELFIE WITH GREEN SCREEN SO U CAN DROP IN OWN PIC AND PRETEND U HANG WITH ME. LOL! #AS IF"
"SENDING SELFIE 2 SELF. DON'T HATE ON ME 4 NOT SHARING. SOME THINGS PRIVATE."
GBTrudeau

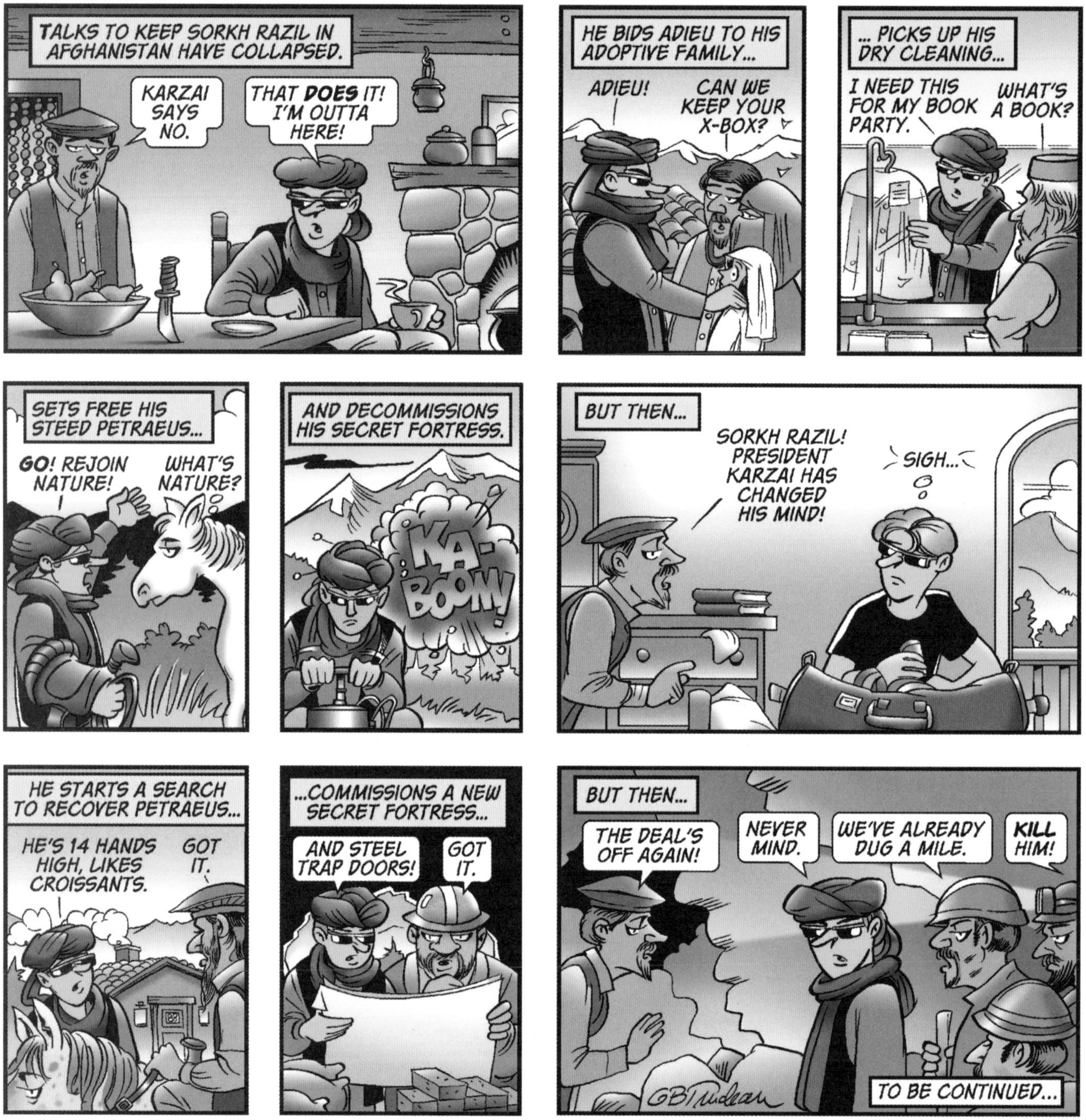

TALKS TO KEEP SORKH RAZIL IN AFGHANISTAN HAVE COLLAPSED.
KARZAI SAYS NO.
THAT DOES IT! I'M OUTTA HERE!
HE BIDS ADIEU TO HIS ADOPTIVE FAMILY...
ADIEU!
CAN WE KEEP YOUR X-BOX?
... PICKS UP HIS DRY CLEANING...
I NEED THIS FOR MY BOOK PARTY.
WHAT'S A BOOK?
SETS FREE HIS STEED PETRAEUS...
GO! REJOIN NATURE!
WHAT'S NATURE?
AND DECOMMISSIONS HIS SECRET FORTRESS.
KA-BOOM!
BUT THEN...
SORKH RAZIL! PRESIDENT KARZAI HAS CHANGED HIS MIND!
SIGH...
HE STARTS A SEARCH TO RECOVER PETRAEUS...
HE'S 14 HANDS HIGH, LIKES CROISSANTS.
GOT IT.
...COMMISSIONS A NEW SECRET FORTRESS...
AND STEEL TRAP DOORS!
GOT IT.
BUT THEN...
THE DEAL'S OFF AGAIN!
NEVER MIND.
WE'VE ALREADY DUG A MILE.
KILL HIM!
TO BE CONTINUED...
GBTrudeau

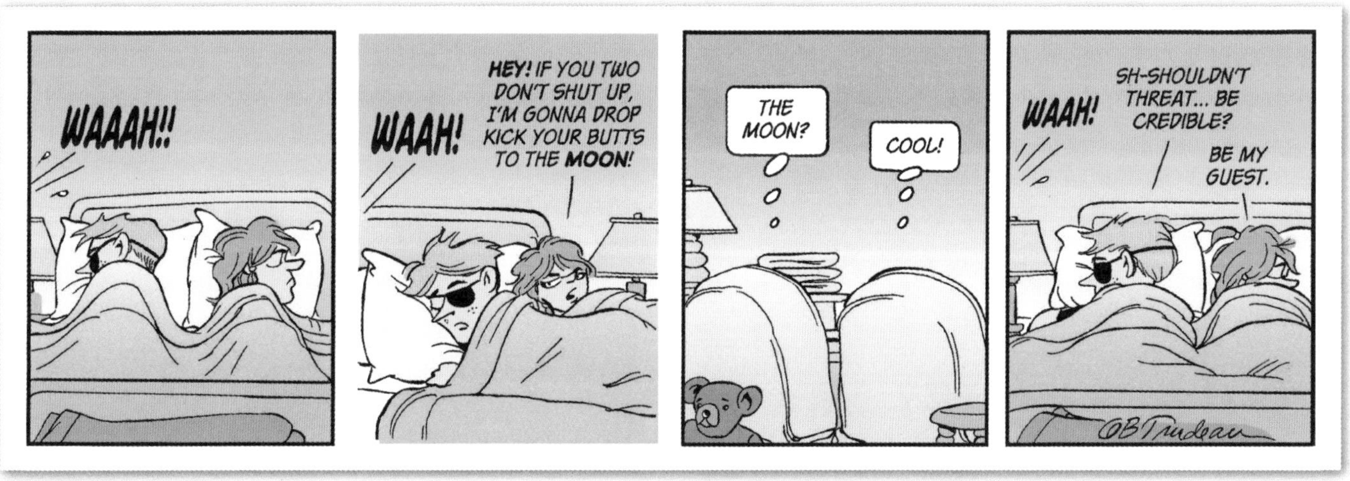
WAAAH!!
WAAH!
HEY! IF YOU TWO DON'T SHUT UP, I'M GONNA DROP KICK YOUR BUTTS TO THE MOON!
THE MOON?
COOL!
WAAH!
SH-SHOULDN'T THREAT... BE CREDIBLE?
BE MY GUEST.
GB Trudeau

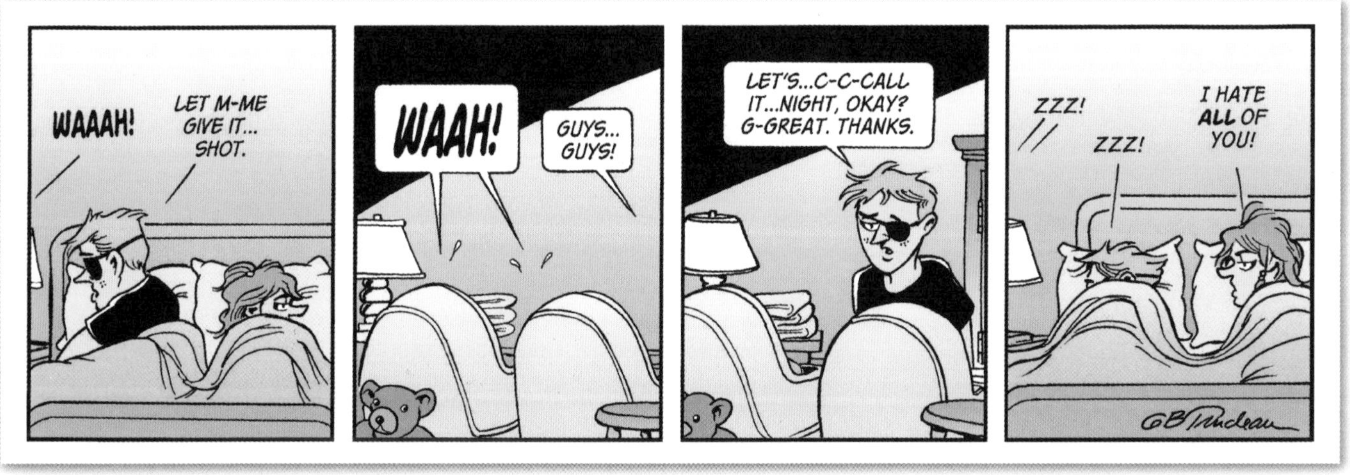
WAAAH!
LET M-ME GIVE IT... SHOT.
WAAH!
GUYS... GUYS!
LET'S...C-C-CALL IT...NIGHT, OKAY? G-GREAT. THANKS.
ZZZ!
ZZZ!
I HATE ALL OF YOU!
GB Trudeau

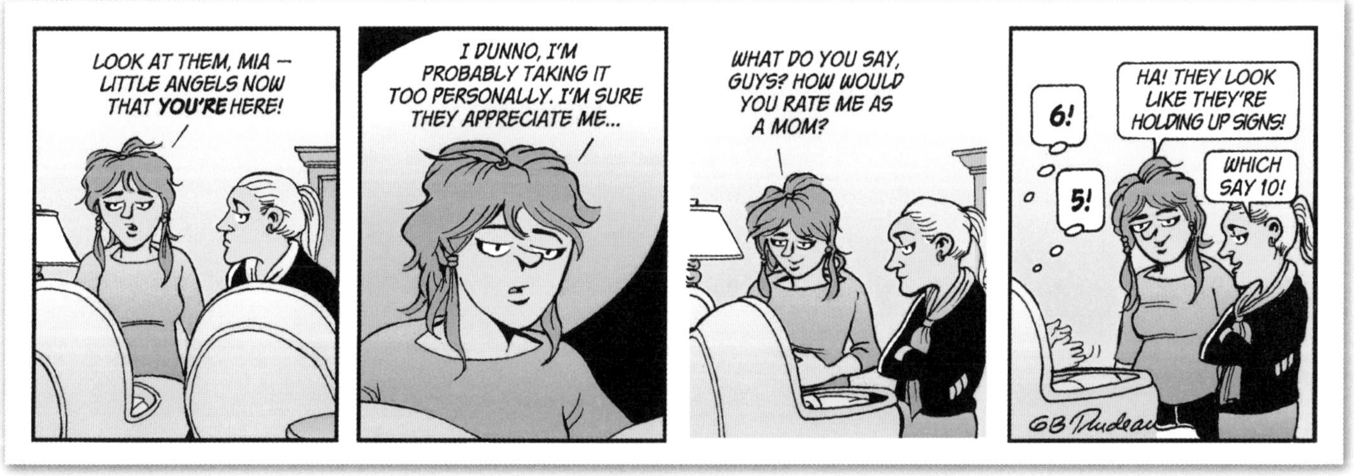
LOOK AT THEM, MIA — LITTLE ANGELS NOW THAT YOU'RE HERE!
I DUNNO, I'M PROBABLY TAKING IT TOO PERSONALLY. I'M SURE THEY APPRECIATE ME...
WHAT DO YOU SAY, GUYS? HOW WOULD YOU RATE ME AS A MOM?
6!
5!
HA! THEY LOOK LIKE THEY'RE HOLDING UP SIGNS!
WHICH SAY 10!
GB Trudeau

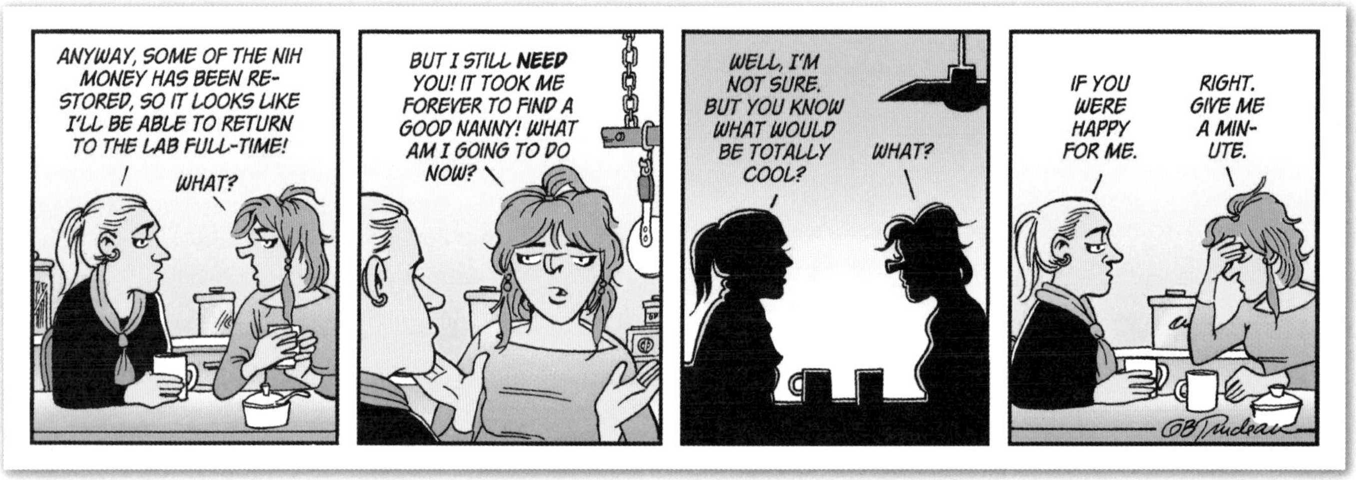
ANYWAY, SOME OF THE NIH MONEY HAS BEEN RE-STORED, SO IT LOOKS LIKE I'LL BE ABLE TO RETURN TO THE LAB FULL-TIME!
WHAT?
BUT I STILL **NEED** YOU! IT TOOK ME FOREVER TO FIND A GOOD NANNY! WHAT AM I GOING TO DO NOW?
WELL, I'M NOT SURE. BUT YOU KNOW WHAT WOULD BE TOTALLY COOL?
WHAT?
IF YOU WERE HAPPY FOR ME.
RIGHT. GIVE ME A MIN-UTE.
GB Trudeau

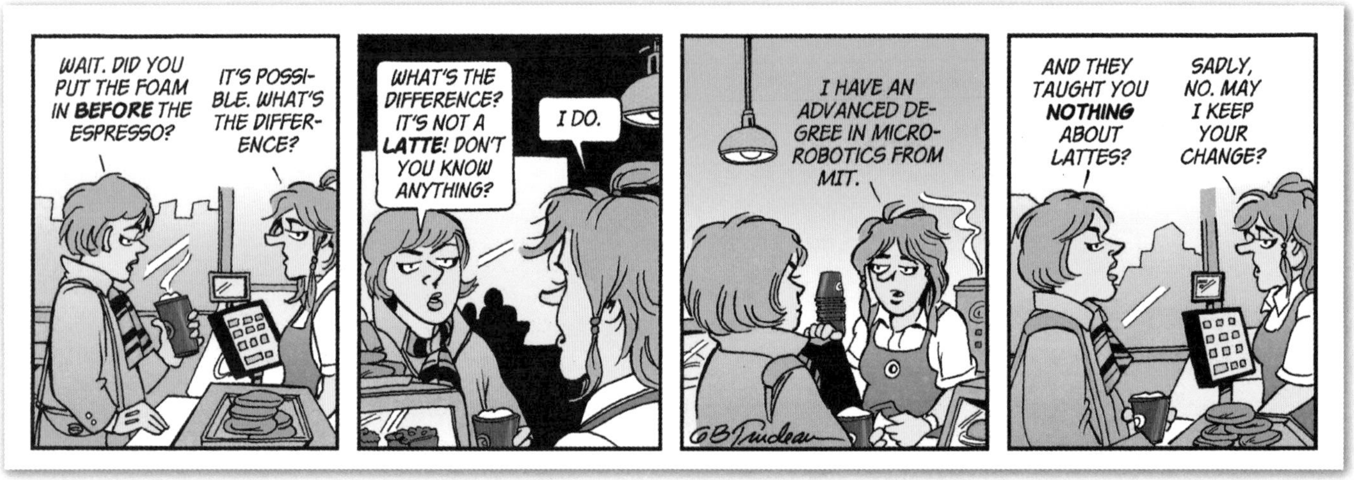
WAIT. DID YOU PUT THE FOAM IN **BEFORE** THE ESPRESSO?
IT'S POSSI-BLE. WHAT'S THE DIFFER-ENCE?
WHAT'S THE DIFFERENCE? IT'S NOT A **LATTE**! DON'T YOU KNOW ANYTHING?
I DO.
I HAVE AN ADVANCED DE-GREE IN MICRO-ROBOTICS FROM MIT.
GB Trudeau
AND THEY TAUGHT YOU **NOTHING** ABOUT LATTES?
SADLY, NO. MAY I KEEP YOUR CHANGE?

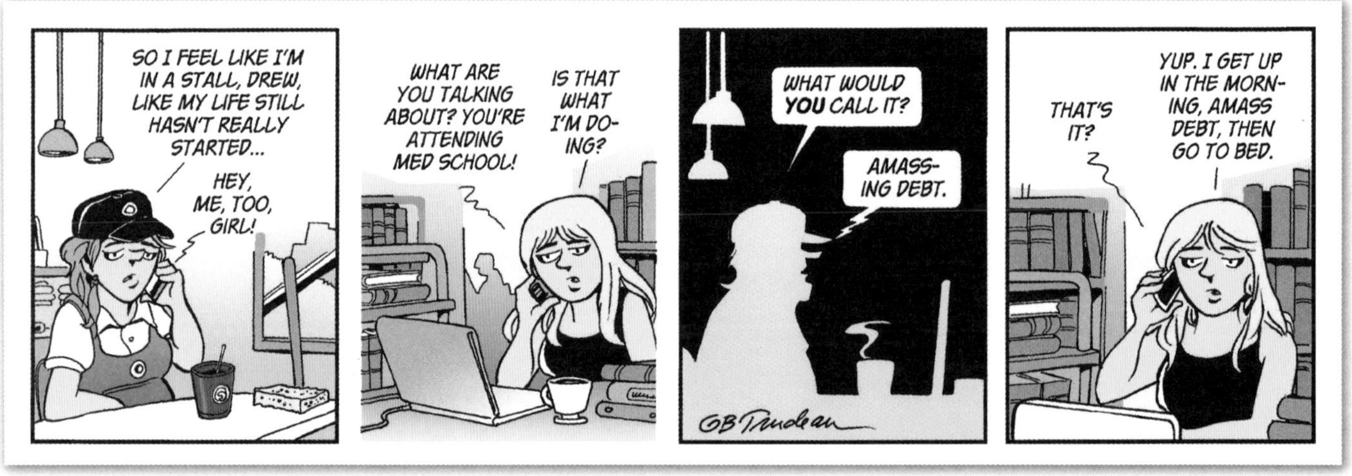
SO I FEEL LIKE I'M IN A STALL, DREW, LIKE MY LIFE STILL HASN'T REALLY STARTED...
HEY, ME, TOO, GIRL!
WHAT ARE YOU TALKING ABOUT? YOU'RE ATTENDING MED SCHOOL!
IS THAT WHAT I'M DO-ING?
WHAT WOULD **YOU** CALL IT?
AMASS-ING DEBT.
GB Trudeau
THAT'S IT?
YUP. I GET UP IN THE MORN-ING, AMASS DEBT, THEN GO TO BED.

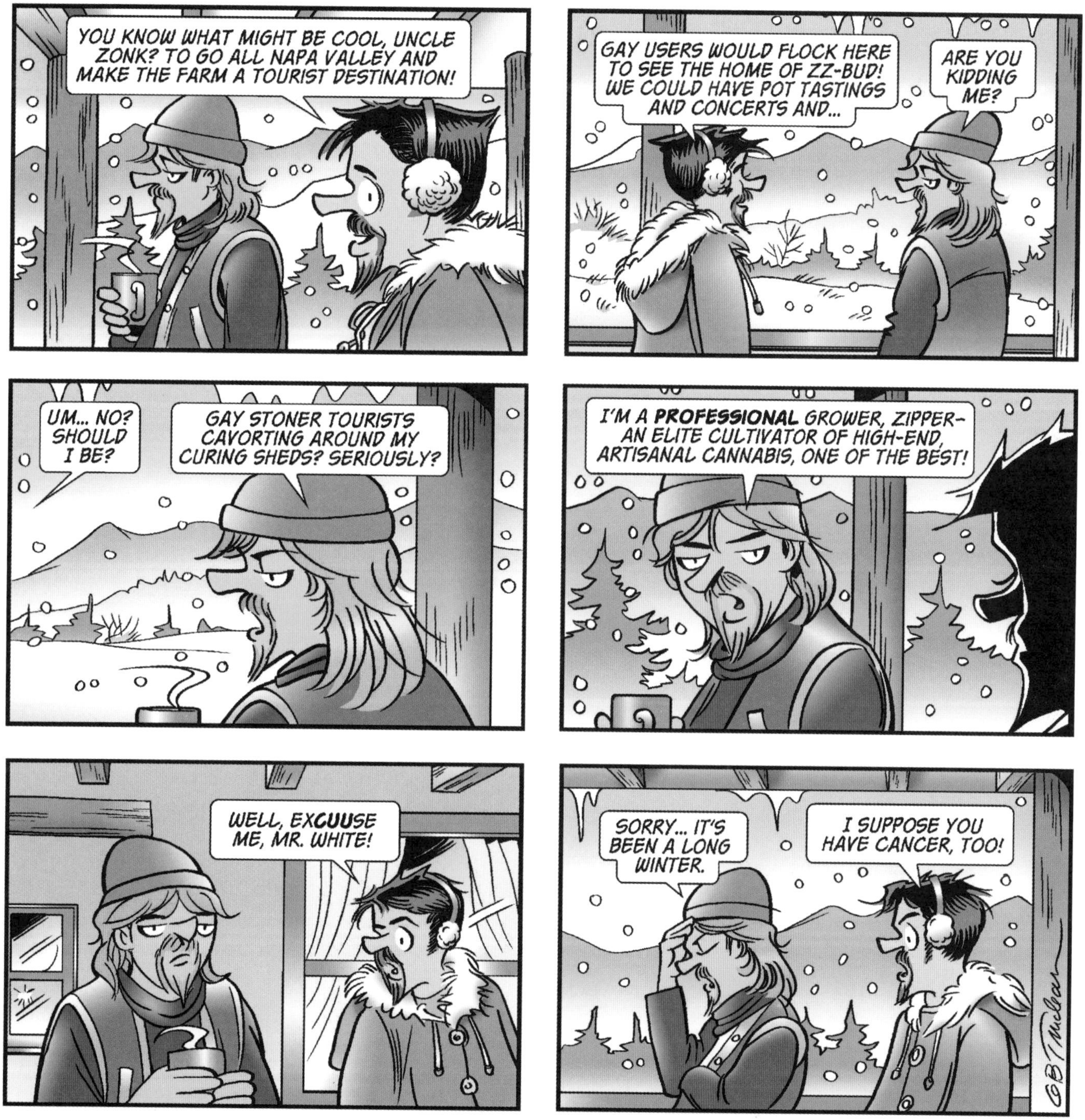
YOU KNOW WHAT MIGHT BE COOL, UNCLE ZONK? TO GO ALL NAPA VALLEY AND MAKE THE FARM A TOURIST DESTINATION!
GAY USERS WOULD FLOCK HERE TO SEE THE HOME OF ZZ-BUD! WE COULD HAVE POT TASTINGS AND CONCERTS AND...
ARE YOU KIDDING ME?
UM... NO? SHOULD I BE?
GAY STONER TOURISTS CAVORTING AROUND MY CURING SHEDS? SERIOUSLY?
I'M A PROFESSIONAL GROWER, ZIPPER-AN ELITE CULTIVATOR OF HIGH-END, ARTISANAL CANNABIS, ONE OF THE BEST!
WELL, EXCUUSE ME, MR. WHITE!
SORRY... IT'S BEEN A LONG WINTER.
I SUPPOSE YOU HAVE CANCER, TOO!
GBTrudeau

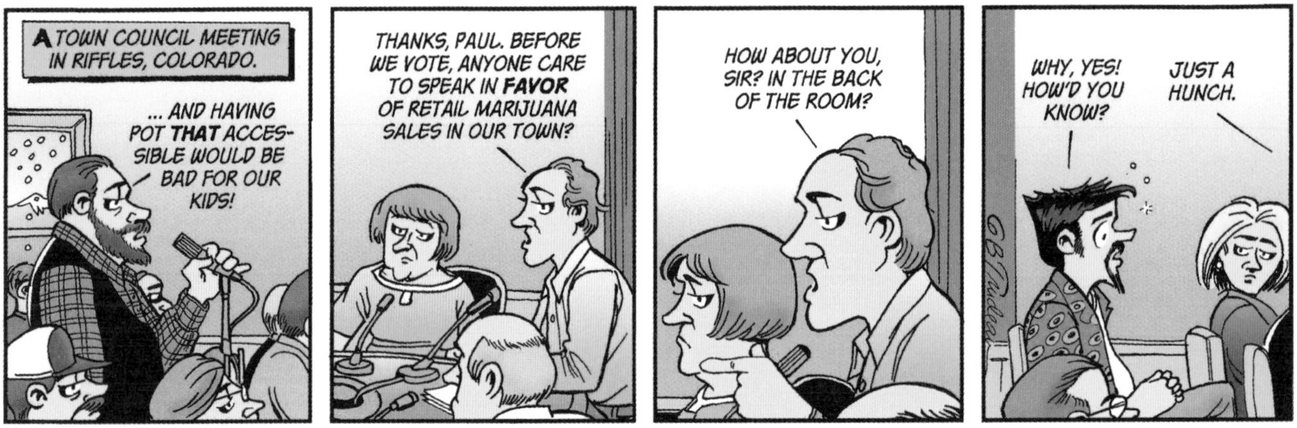
A TOWN COUNCIL MEETING IN RIFFLES, COLORADO.
... AND HAVING POT THAT ACCESSIBLE WOULD BE BAD FOR OUR KIDS!
THANKS, PAUL. BEFORE WE VOTE, ANYONE CARE TO SPEAK IN FAVOR OF RETAIL MARIJUANA SALES IN OUR TOWN?
HOW ABOUT YOU, SIR? IN THE BACK OF THE ROOM?
WHY, YES! HOW'D YOU KNOW?
JUST A HUNCH.

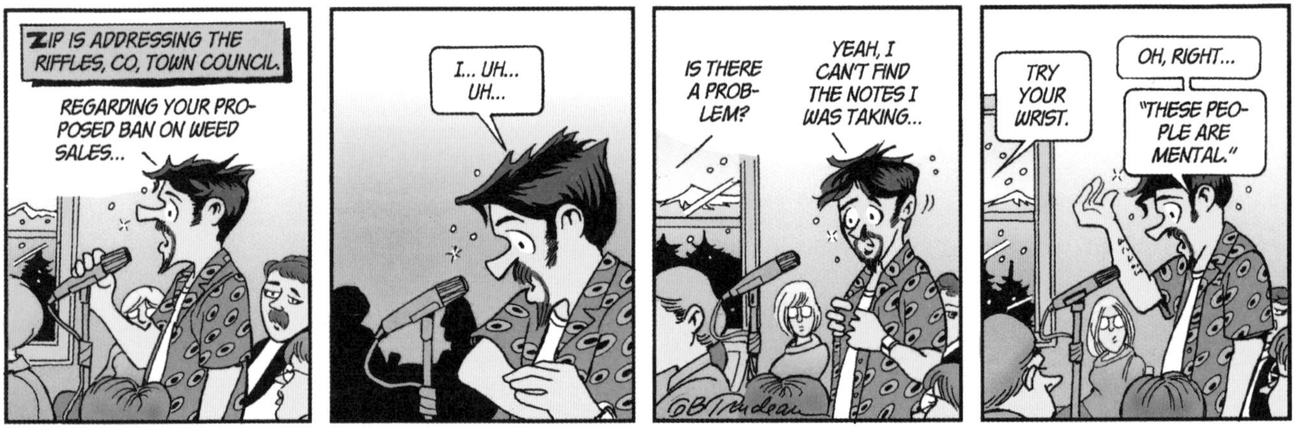
ZIP IS ADDRESSING THE RIFFLES, CO, TOWN COUNCIL.
REGARDING YOUR PROPOSED BAN ON WEED SALES...
I... UH... UH...
IS THERE A PROBLEM?
YEAH, I CAN'T FIND THE NOTES I WAS TAKING...
TRY YOUR WRIST.
OH, RIGHT...
"THESE PEOPLE ARE MENTAL."

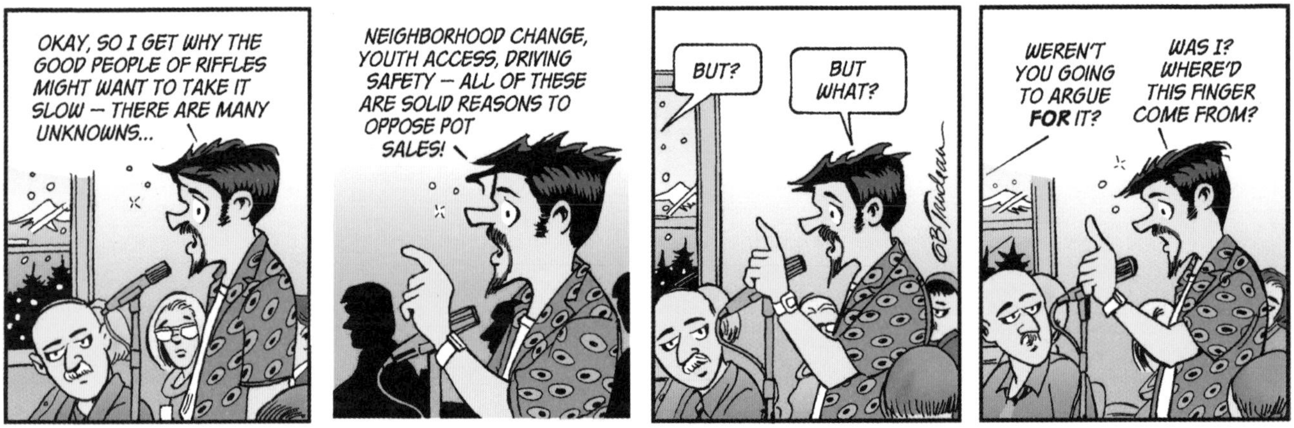
OKAY, SO I GET WHY THE GOOD PEOPLE OF RIFFLES MIGHT WANT TO TAKE IT SLOW — THERE ARE MANY UNKNOWNS...
NEIGHBORHOOD CHANGE, YOUTH ACCESS, DRIVING SAFETY — ALL OF THESE ARE SOLID REASONS TO OPPOSE POT SALES!
BUT?
BUT WHAT?
WEREN'T YOU GOING TO ARGUE FOR IT?
WAS I? WHERE'D THIS FINGER COME FROM?

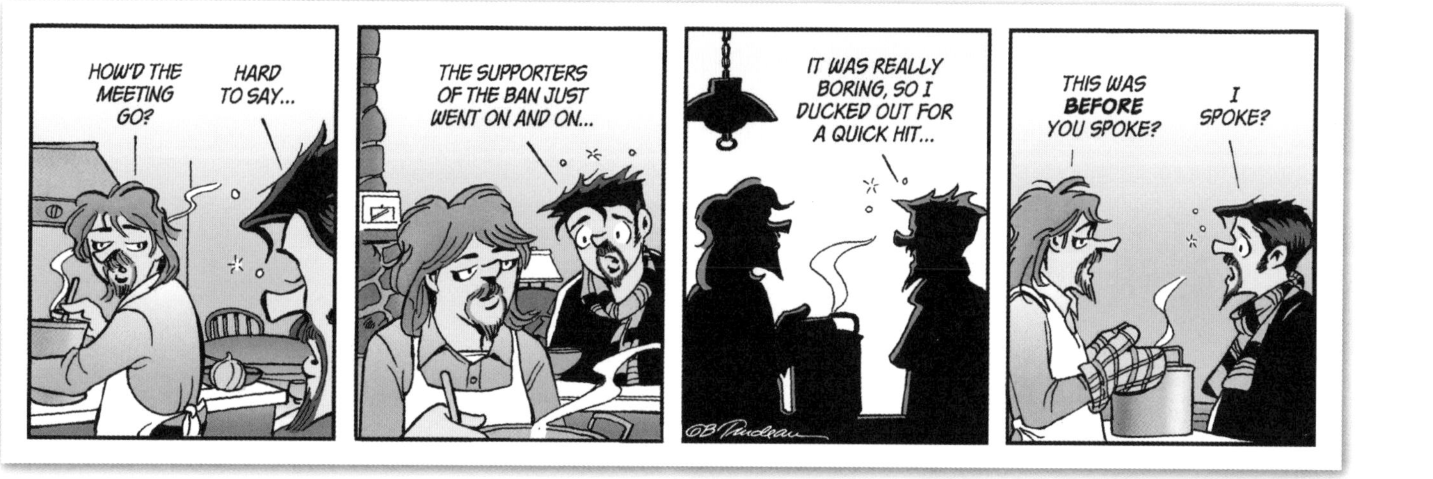
HOW'D THE MEETING GO?
HARD TO SAY...
THE SUPPORTERS OF THE BAN JUST WENT ON AND ON...
IT WAS REALLY BORING, SO I DUCKED OUT FOR A QUICK HIT...
GB Trudeau
THIS WAS **BEFORE** YOU SPOKE?
I SPOKE?

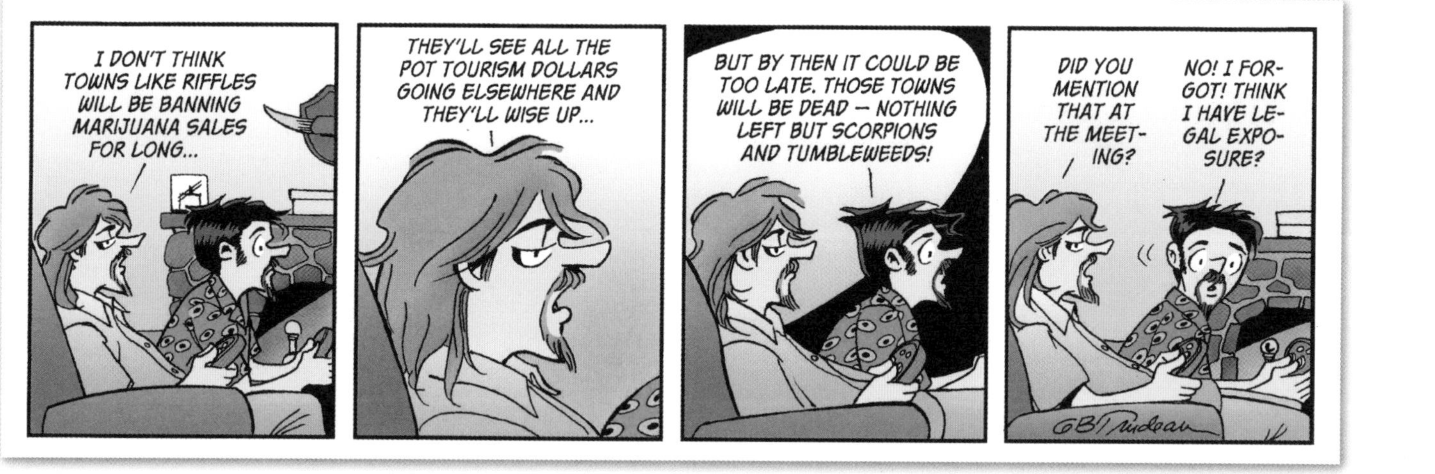
I DON'T THINK TOWNS LIKE RIFFLES WILL BE BANNING MARIJUANA SALES FOR LONG...
THEY'LL SEE ALL THE POT TOURISM DOLLARS GOING ELSEWHERE AND THEY'LL WISE UP...
BUT BY THEN IT COULD BE TOO LATE. THOSE TOWNS WILL BE DEAD — NOTHING LEFT BUT SCORPIONS AND TUMBLEWEEDS!
DID YOU MENTION THAT AT THE MEET-ING?
NO! I FOR-GOT! THINK I HAVE LE-GAL EXPO-SURE?
GB Trudeau

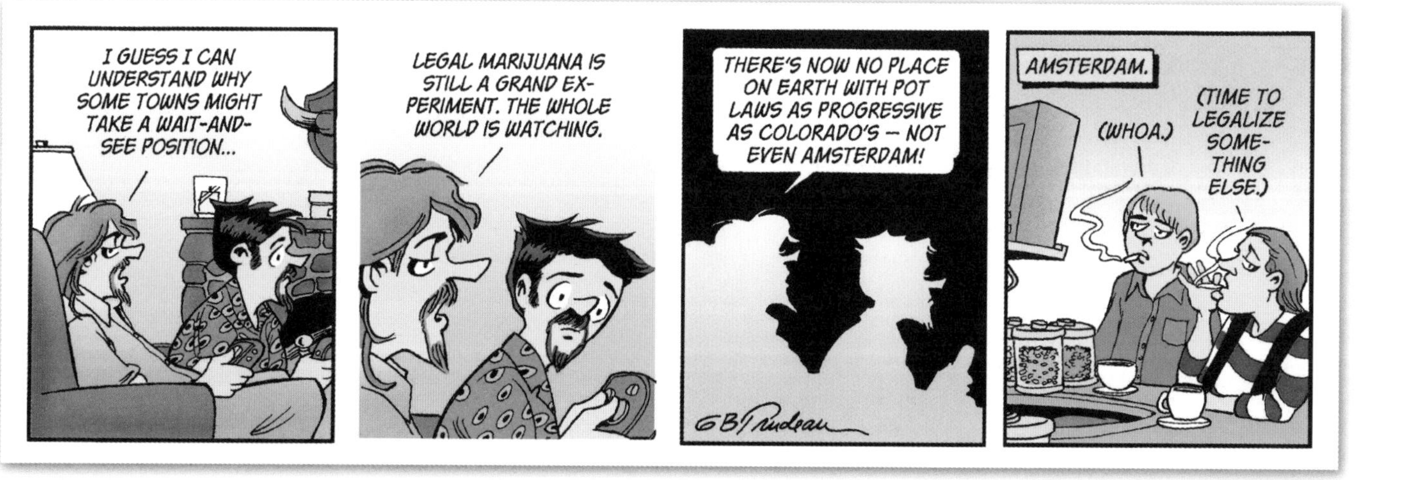
I GUESS I CAN UNDERSTAND WHY SOME TOWNS MIGHT TAKE A WAIT-AND-SEE POSITION...
LEGAL MARIJUANA IS STILL A GRAND EX-PERIMENT. THE WHOLE WORLD IS WATCHING.
THERE'S NOW NO PLACE ON EARTH WITH POT LAWS AS PROGRESSIVE AS COLORADO'S — NOT EVEN AMSTERDAM!
GB Trudeau
AMSTERDAM.
(WHOA.)
(TIME TO LEGALIZE SOME-THING ELSE.)

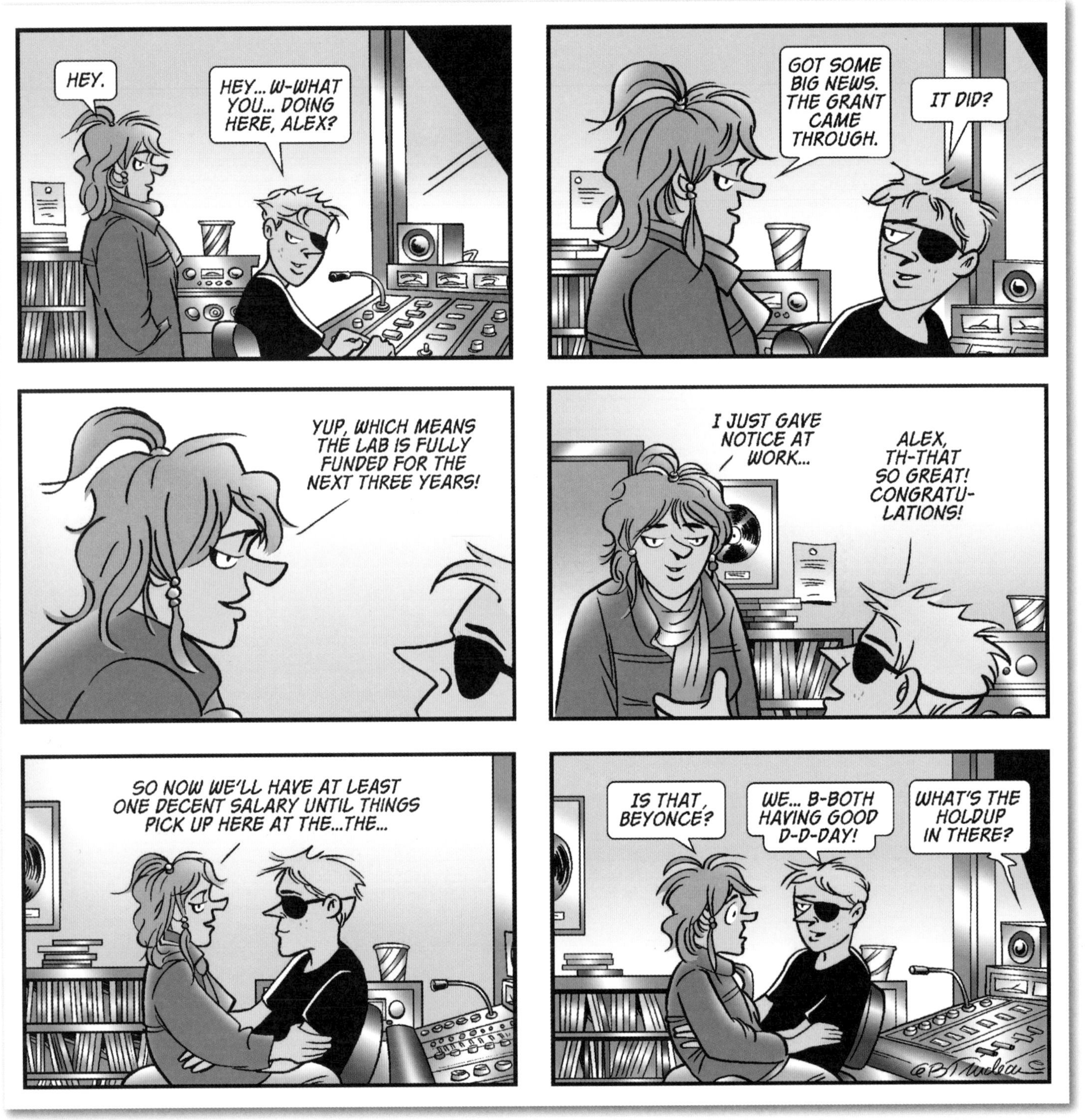
HEY.
HEY... W-WHAT YOU... DOING HERE, ALEX?
GOT SOME BIG NEWS. THE GRANT CAME THROUGH.
IT DID?
YUP, WHICH MEANS THE LAB IS FULLY FUNDED FOR THE NEXT THREE YEARS!
I JUST GAVE NOTICE AT WORK...
ALEX, TH-THAT SO GREAT! CONGRATU-LATIONS!
SO NOW WE'LL HAVE AT LEAST ONE DECENT SALARY UNTIL THINGS PICK UP HERE AT THE...THE...
IS THAT, BEYONCE?
WE... B-BOTH HAVING GOOD D-D-DAY!
WHAT'S THE HOLDUP IN THERE?

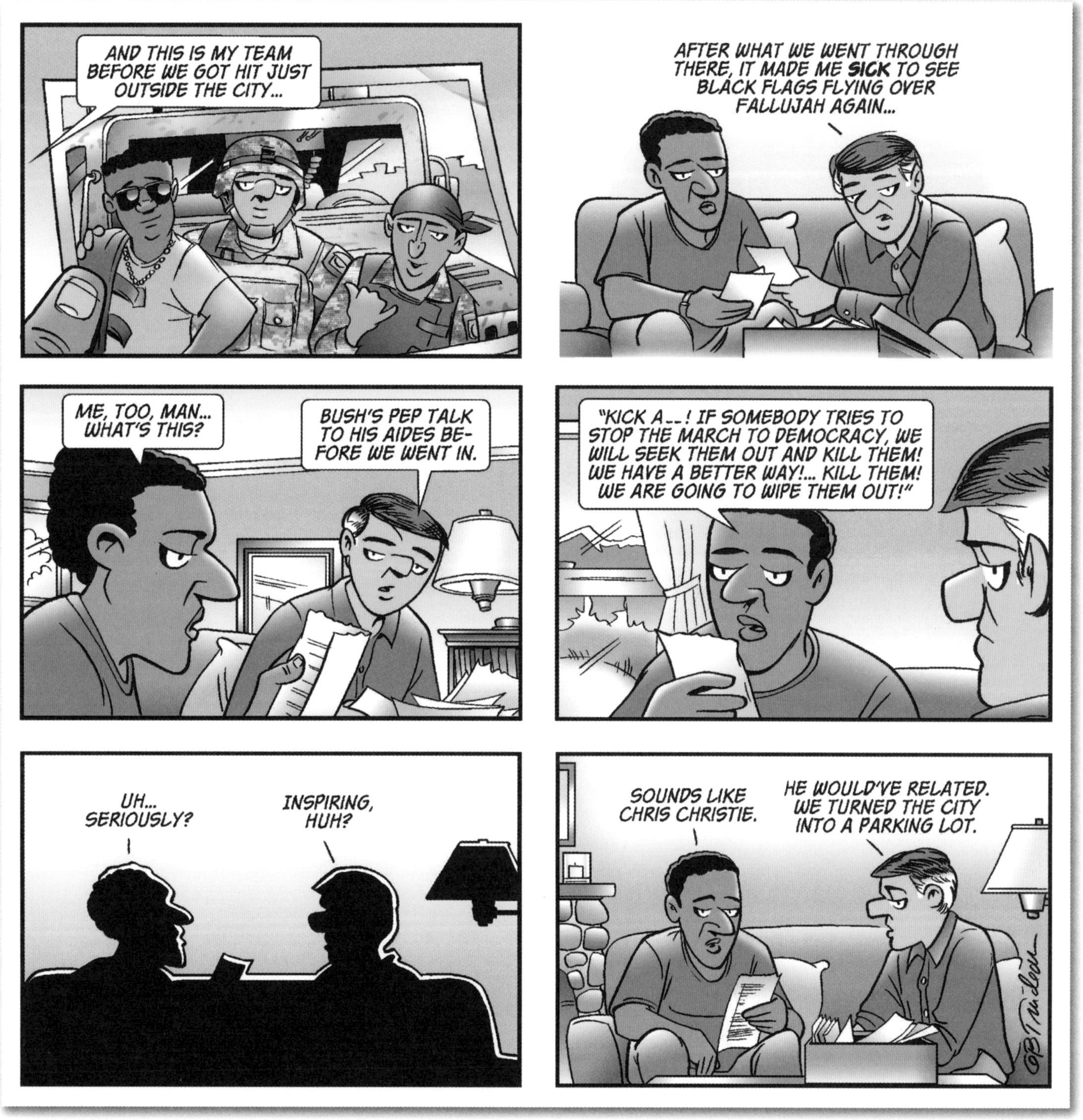
AND THIS IS MY TEAM BEFORE WE GOT HIT JUST OUTSIDE THE CITY...
AFTER WHAT WE WENT THROUGH THERE, IT MADE ME **SICK** TO SEE BLACK FLAGS FLYING OVER FALLUJAH AGAIN...
ME, TOO, MAN... WHAT'S THIS?
BUSH'S PEP TALK TO HIS AIDES BEFORE WE WENT IN.
"KICK A--! IF SOMEBODY TRIES TO STOP THE MARCH TO DEMOCRACY, WE WILL SEEK THEM OUT AND KILL THEM! WE HAVE A BETTER WAY!... KILL THEM! WE ARE GOING TO WIPE THEM OUT!"
UH... SERIOUSLY?
INSPIRING, HUH?
SOUNDS LIKE CHRIS CHRISTIE.
HE WOULD'VE RELATED. WE TURNED THE CITY INTO A PARKING LOT.
GBTrudeau

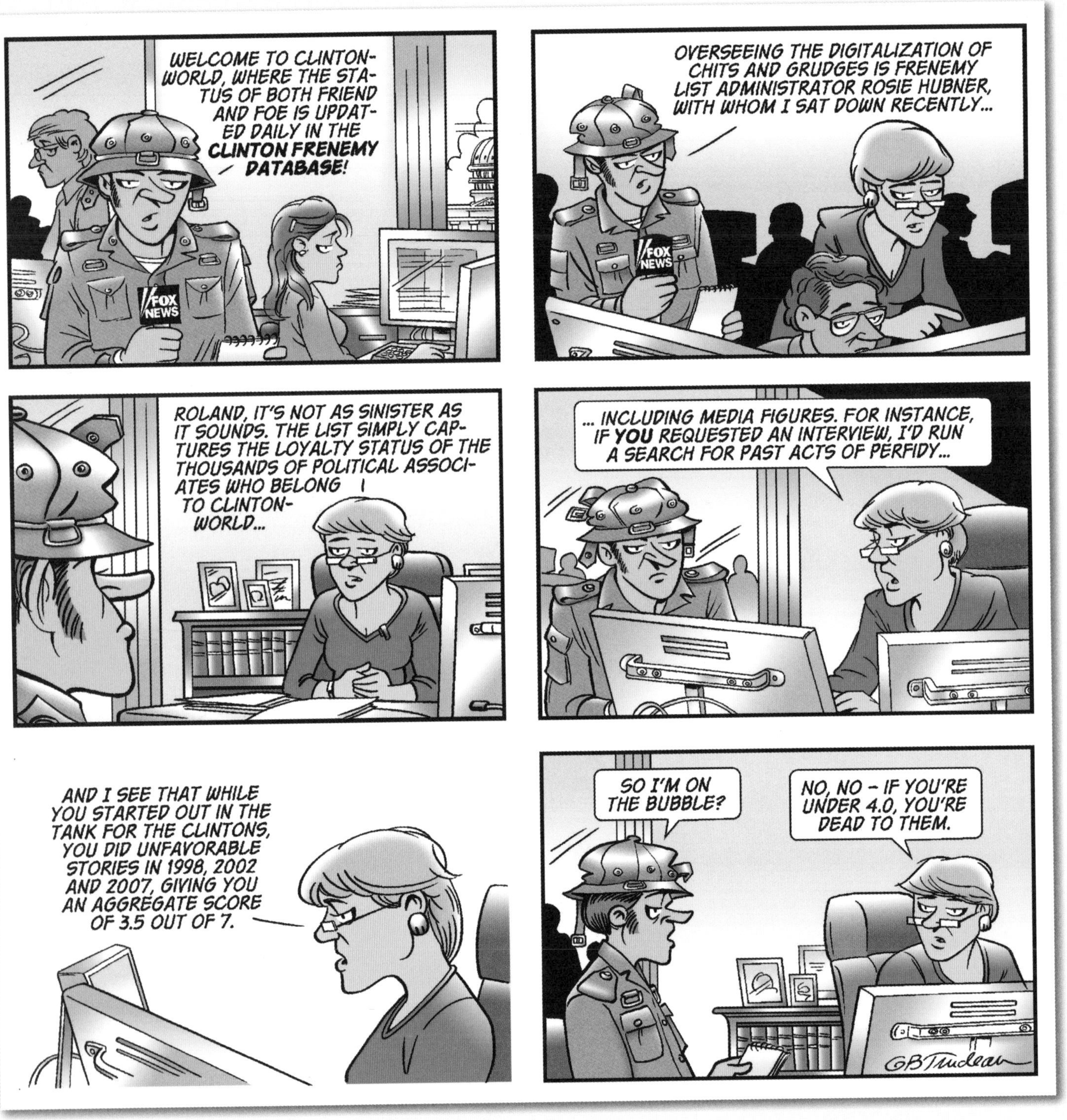
WELCOME TO CLINTON-WORLD, WHERE THE STATUS OF BOTH FRIEND AND FOE IS UPDATED DAILY IN THE **CLINTON FRENEMY DATABASE!**
OVERSEEING THE DIGITALIZATION OF CHITS AND GRUDGES IS FRENEMY LIST ADMINISTRATOR ROSIE HUBNER, WITH WHOM I SAT DOWN RECENTLY...
ROLAND, IT'S NOT AS SINISTER AS IT SOUNDS. THE LIST SIMPLY CAPTURES THE LOYALTY STATUS OF THE THOUSANDS OF POLITICAL ASSOCIATES WHO BELONG TO CLINTON-WORLD...
...INCLUDING MEDIA FIGURES. FOR INSTANCE, IF **YOU** REQUESTED AN INTERVIEW, I'D RUN A SEARCH FOR PAST ACTS OF PERFIDY...
AND I SEE THAT WHILE YOU STARTED OUT IN THE TANK FOR THE CLINTONS, YOU DID UNFAVORABLE STORIES IN 1998, 2002 AND 2007, GIVING YOU AN AGGREGATE SCORE OF 3.5 OUT OF 7.
SO I'M ON THE BUBBLE?
NO, NO – IF YOU'RE UNDER 4.0, YOU'RE DEAD TO THEM.
GBTrudeau

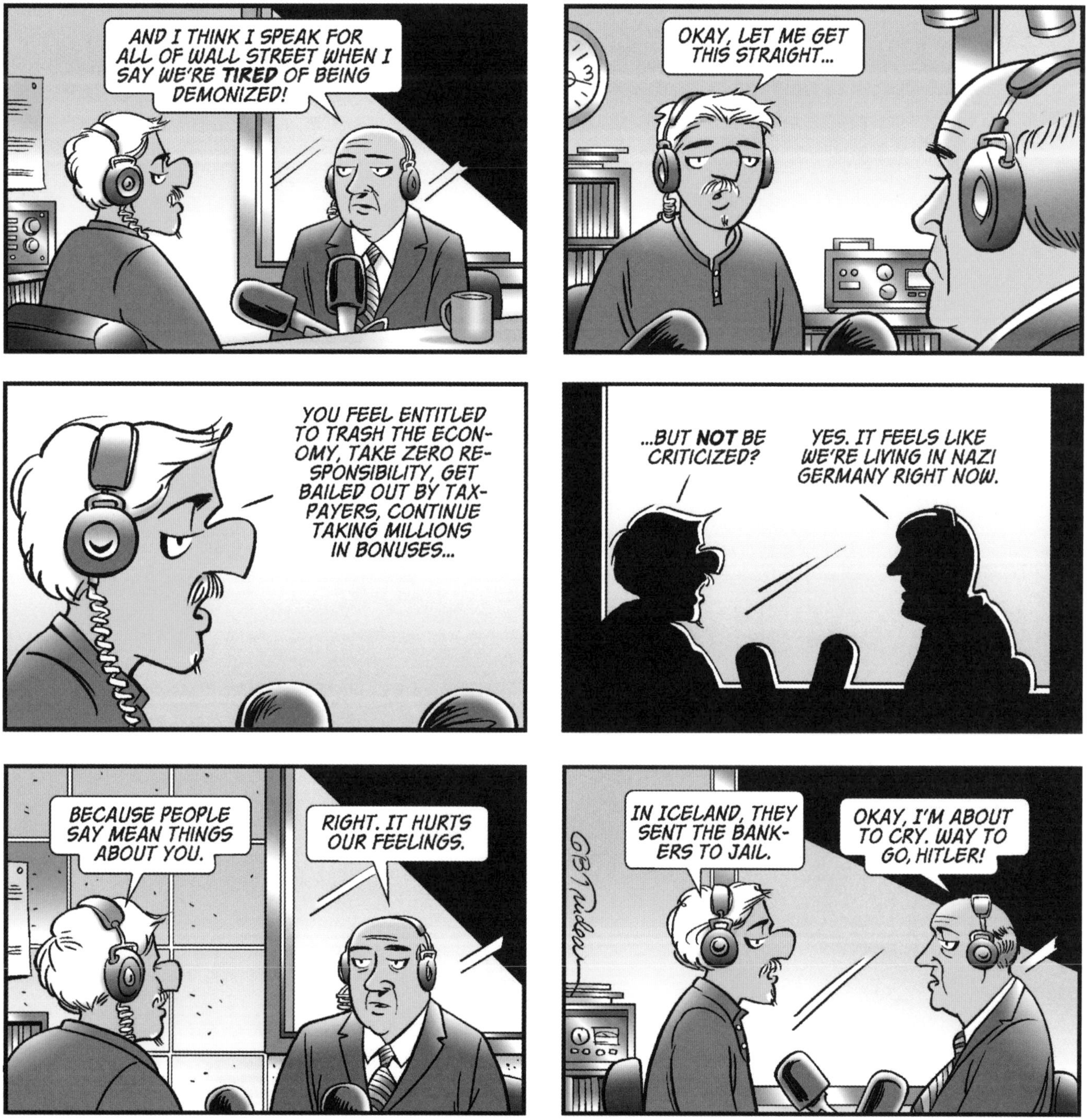
AND I THINK I SPEAK FOR ALL OF WALL STREET WHEN I SAY WE'RE **TIRED** OF BEING DEMONIZED!
OKAY, LET ME GET THIS STRAIGHT...
YOU FEEL ENTITLED TO TRASH THE ECONOMY, TAKE ZERO RESPONSIBILITY, GET BAILED OUT BY TAXPAYERS, CONTINUE TAKING MILLIONS IN BONUSES...
...BUT **NOT** BE CRITICIZED?
YES. IT FEELS LIKE WE'RE LIVING IN NAZI GERMANY RIGHT NOW.
BECAUSE PEOPLE SAY MEAN THINGS ABOUT YOU.
RIGHT. IT HURTS OUR FEELINGS.
IN ICELAND, THEY SENT THE BANKERS TO JAIL.
OKAY, I'M ABOUT TO CRY. WAY TO GO, HITLER!
GB Trudeau

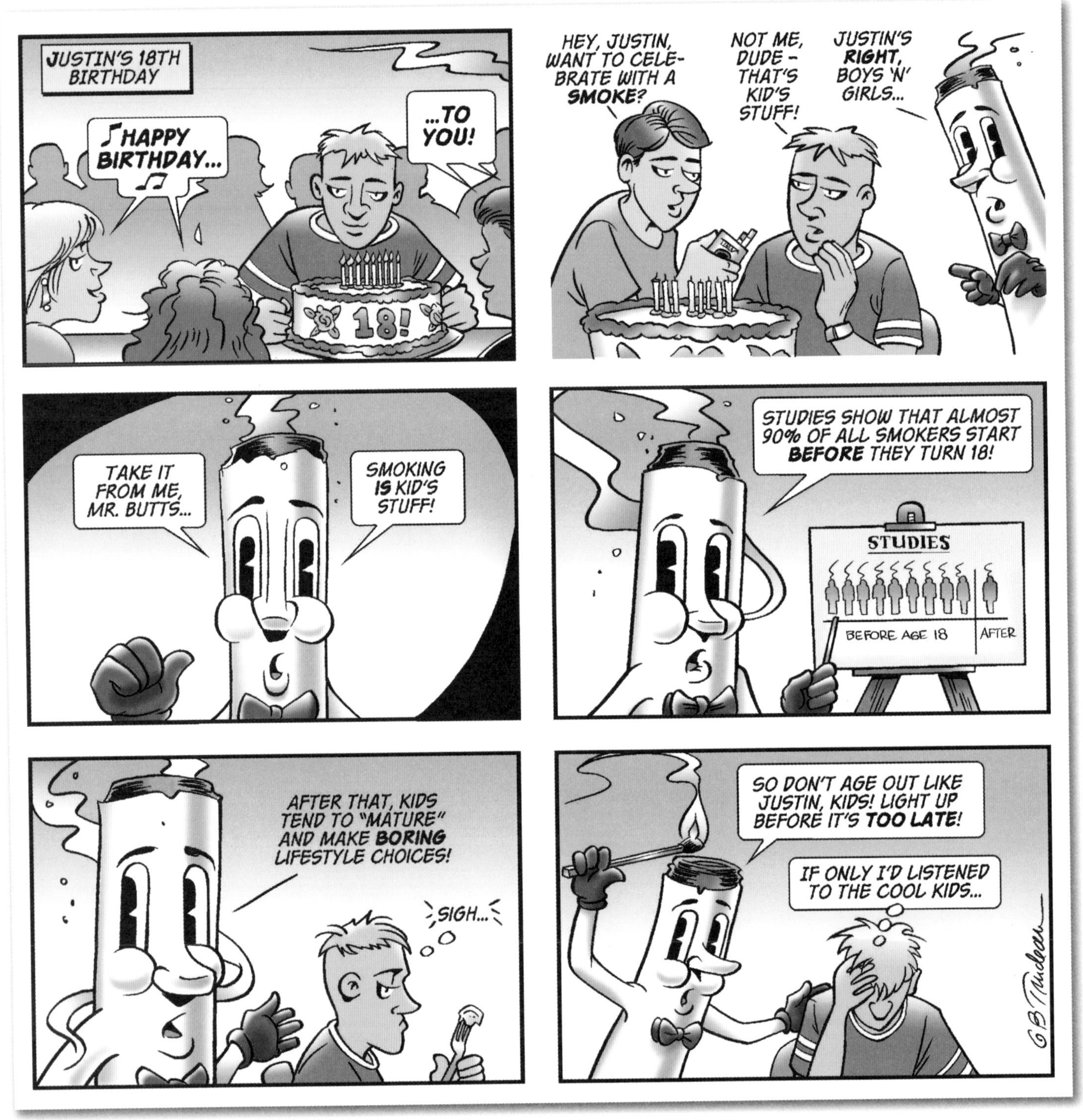
JUSTIN'S 18TH BIRTHDAY
♪HAPPY BIRTHDAY... ♫
...TO YOU!
18!
HEY, JUSTIN, WANT TO CELE-BRATE WITH A SMOKE?
NOT ME, DUDE – THAT'S KID'S STUFF!
JUSTIN'S RIGHT, BOYS 'N' GIRLS...
TAKE IT FROM ME, MR. BUTTS...
SMOKING IS KID'S STUFF!
STUDIES SHOW THAT ALMOST 90% OF ALL SMOKERS START BEFORE THEY TURN 18!
STUDIES
BEFORE AGE 18
AFTER
AFTER THAT, KIDS TEND TO "MATURE" AND MAKE BORING LIFESTYLE CHOICES!
SIGH...
SO DON'T AGE OUT LIKE JUSTIN, KIDS! LIGHT UP BEFORE IT'S TOO LATE!
IF ONLY I'D LISTENED TO THE COOL KIDS...
GB Trudeau

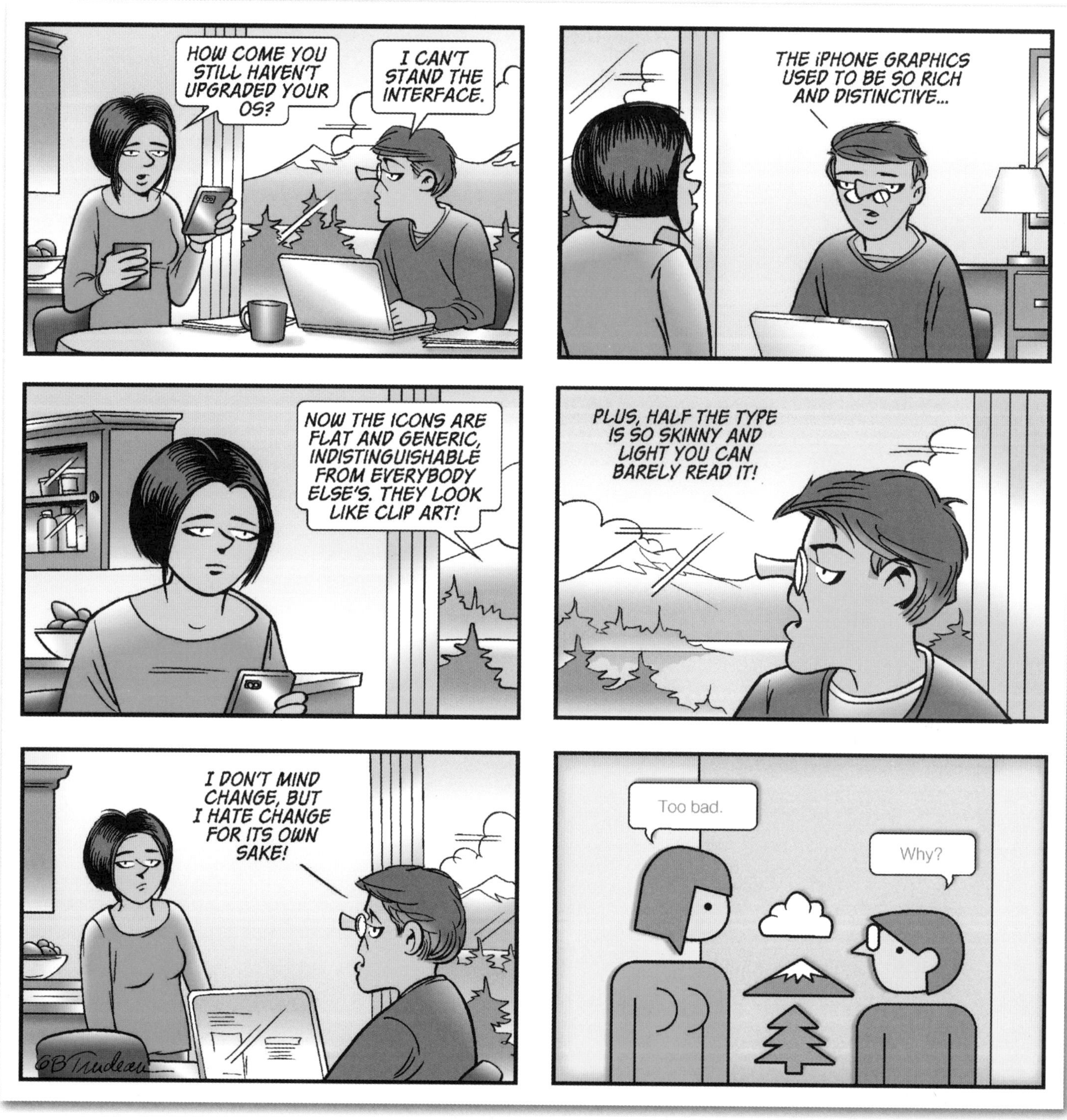
HOW COME YOU STILL HAVEN'T UPGRADED YOUR OS?
I CAN'T STAND THE INTERFACE.
THE iPHONE GRAPHICS USED TO BE SO RICH AND DISTINCTIVE...
NOW THE ICONS ARE FLAT AND GENERIC, INDISTINGUISHABLE FROM EVERYBODY ELSE'S. THEY LOOK LIKE CLIP ART!
PLUS, HALF THE TYPE IS SO SKINNY AND LIGHT YOU CAN BARELY READ IT!
I DON'T MIND CHANGE, BUT I HATE CHANGE FOR ITS OWN SAKE!
GBTrudeau
Too bad.
Why?

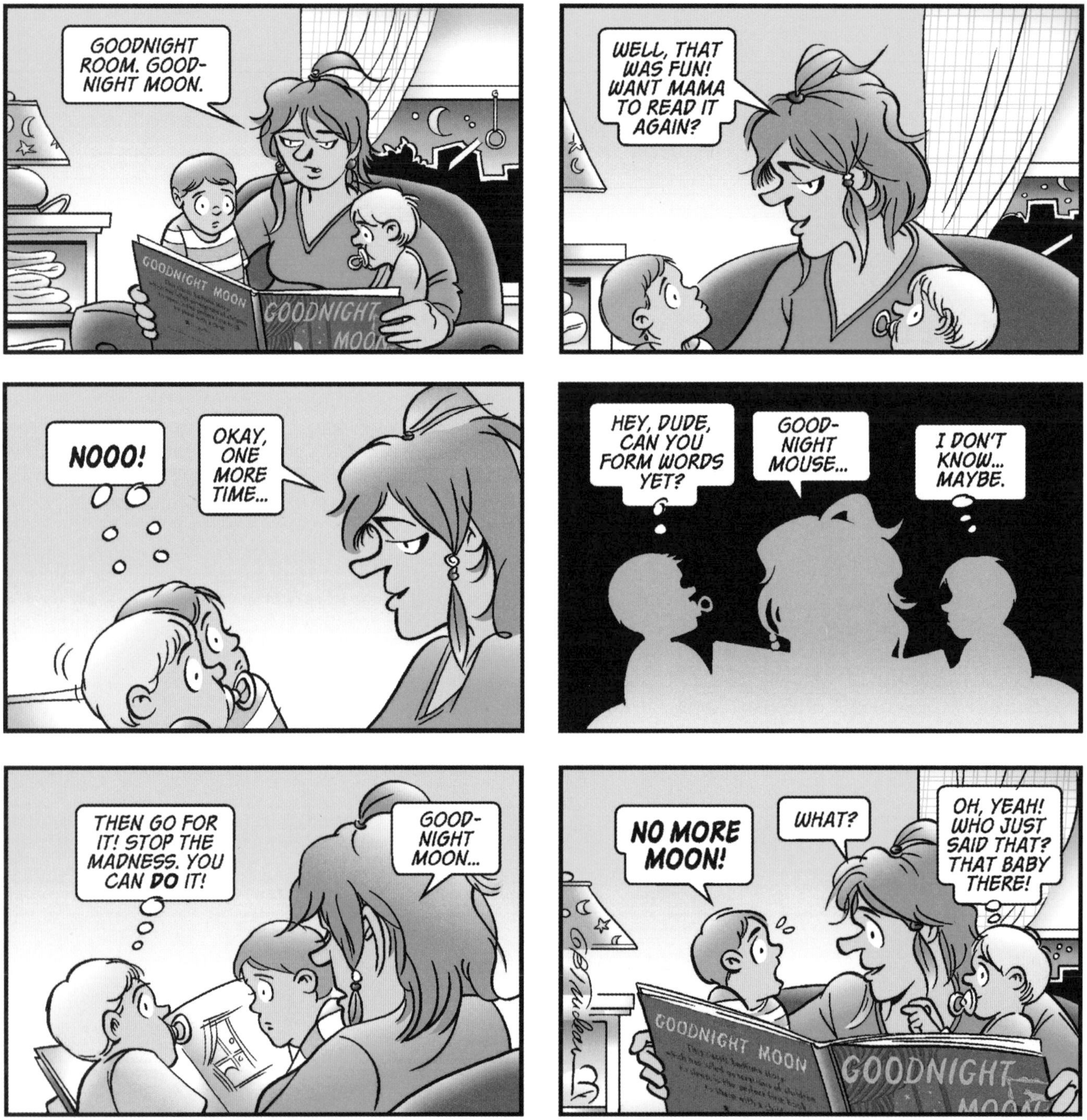
GOODNIGHT ROOM. GOOD-NIGHT MOON.
GOODNIGHT MOON
WELL, THAT WAS FUN! WANT MAMA TO READ IT AGAIN?
NOOO!
OKAY, ONE MORE TIME...
HEY, DUDE, CAN YOU FORM WORDS YET?
GOOD-NIGHT MOUSE...
I DON'T KNOW... MAYBE.
THEN GO FOR IT! STOP THE MADNESS. YOU CAN **DO** IT!
GOOD-NIGHT MOON...
NO MORE MOON!
WHAT?
OH, YEAH! WHO JUST SAID THAT? THAT BABY THERE!
GOODNIGHT MOON

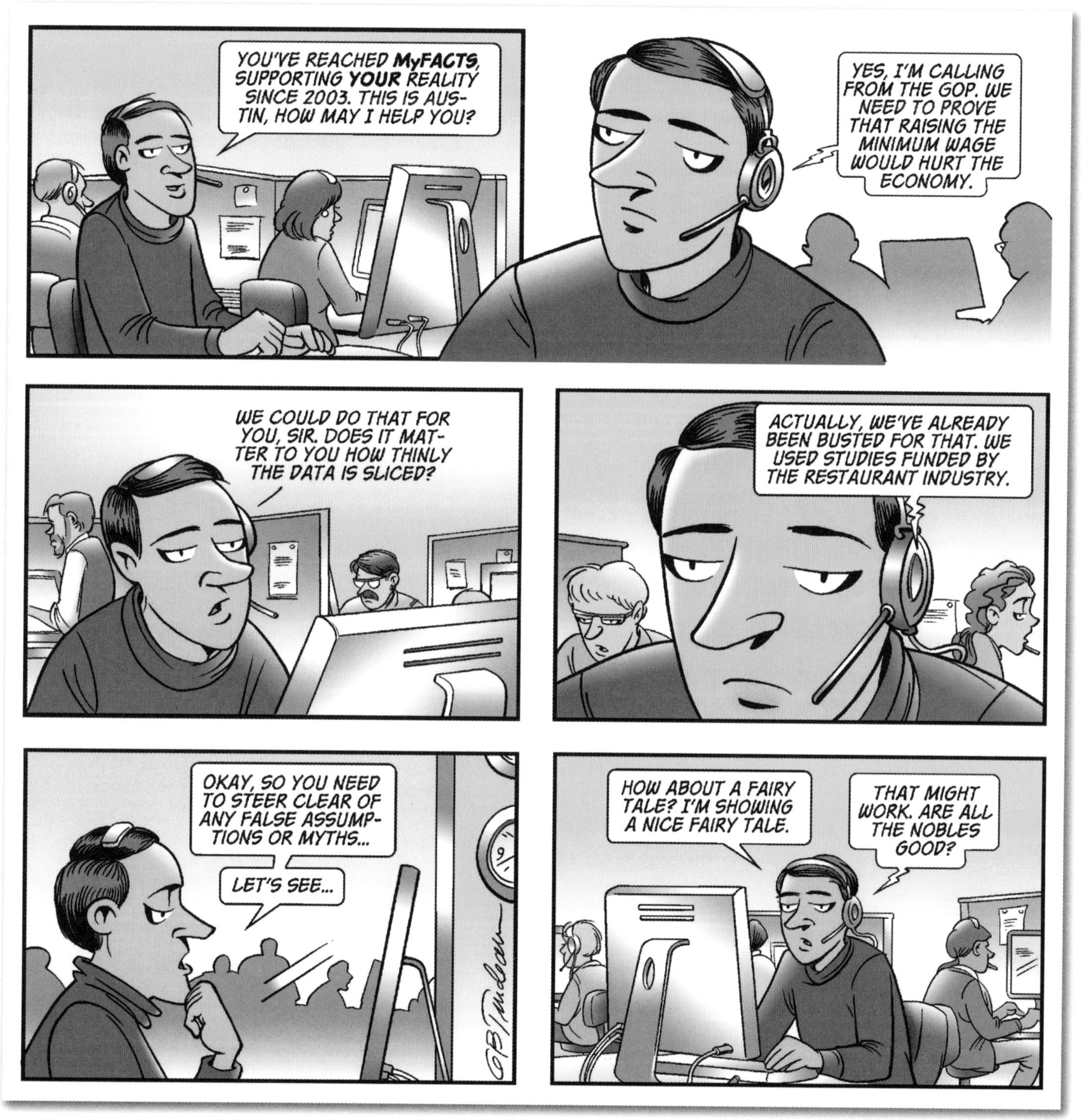
YOU'VE REACHED MyFACTS, SUPPORTING YOUR REALITY SINCE 2003. THIS IS AUSTIN, HOW MAY I HELP YOU?
YES, I'M CALLING FROM THE GOP. WE NEED TO PROVE THAT RAISING THE MINIMUM WAGE WOULD HURT THE ECONOMY.
WE COULD DO THAT FOR YOU, SIR. DOES IT MATTER TO YOU HOW THINLY THE DATA IS SLICED?
ACTUALLY, WE'VE ALREADY BEEN BUSTED FOR THAT. WE USED STUDIES FUNDED BY THE RESTAURANT INDUSTRY.
OKAY, SO YOU NEED TO STEER CLEAR OF ANY FALSE ASSUMPTIONS OR MYTHS...
LET'S SEE...
HOW ABOUT A FAIRY TALE? I'M SHOWING A NICE FAIRY TALE.
THAT MIGHT WORK. ARE ALL THE NOBLES GOOD?

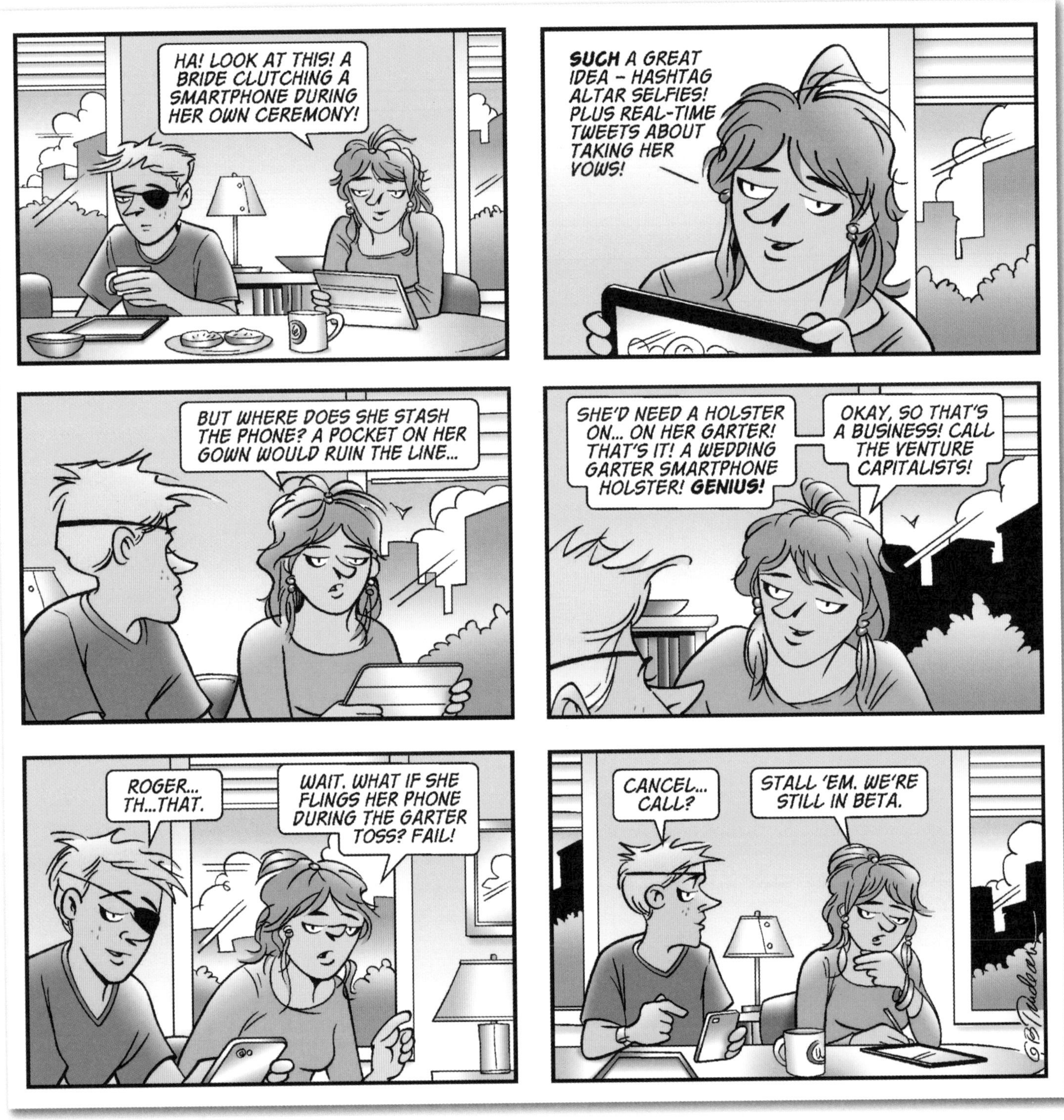
HA! LOOK AT THIS! A BRIDE CLUTCHING A SMARTPHONE DURING HER OWN CEREMONY!
SUCH A GREAT IDEA – HASHTAG ALTAR SELFIES! PLUS REAL-TIME TWEETS ABOUT TAKING HER VOWS!
BUT WHERE DOES SHE STASH THE PHONE? A POCKET ON HER GOWN WOULD RUIN THE LINE...
SHE'D NEED A HOLSTER ON... ON HER GARTER! THAT'S IT! A WEDDING GARTER SMARTPHONE HOLSTER! **GENIUS!**
OKAY, SO THAT'S A BUSINESS! CALL THE VENTURE CAPITALISTS!
ROGER... TH...THAT.
WAIT. WHAT IF SHE FLINGS HER PHONE DURING THE GARTER TOSS? FAIL!
CANCEL... CALL?
STALL 'EM. WE'RE STILL IN BETA.

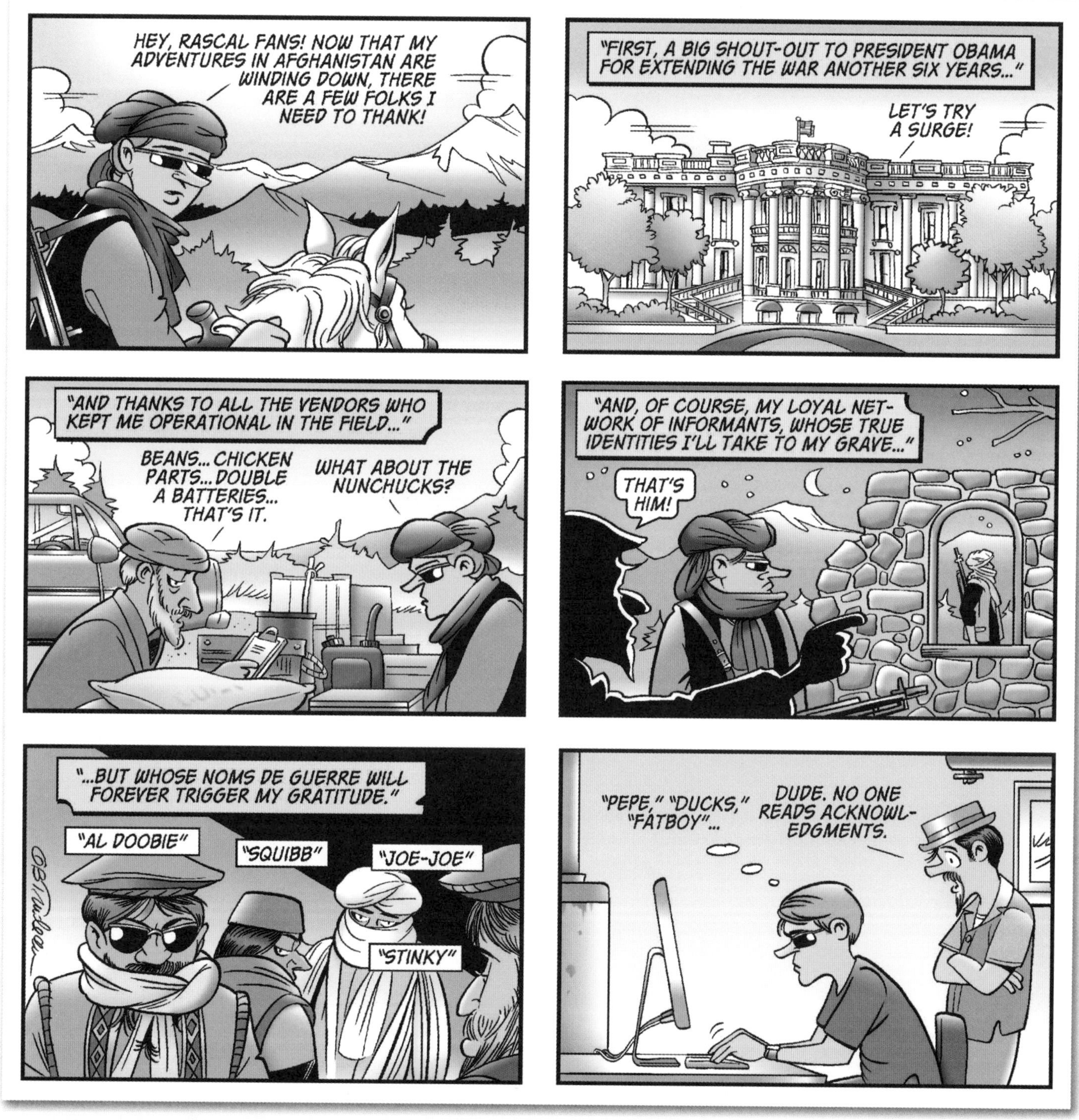
HEY, RASCAL FANS! NOW THAT MY ADVENTURES IN AFGHANISTAN ARE WINDING DOWN, THERE ARE A FEW FOLKS I NEED TO THANK!
"FIRST, A BIG SHOUT-OUT TO PRESIDENT OBAMA FOR EXTENDING THE WAR ANOTHER SIX YEARS..."
LET'S TRY A SURGE!
"AND THANKS TO ALL THE VENDORS WHO KEPT ME OPERATIONAL IN THE FIELD..."
BEANS... CHICKEN PARTS... DOUBLE A BATTERIES... THAT'S IT.
WHAT ABOUT THE NUNCHUCKS?
"AND, OF COURSE, MY LOYAL NETWORK OF INFORMANTS, WHOSE TRUE IDENTITIES I'LL TAKE TO MY GRAVE..."
THAT'S HIM!
"...BUT WHOSE NOMS DE GUERRE WILL FOREVER TRIGGER MY GRATITUDE."
"AL DOOBIE"
"SQUIBB"
"JOE-JOE"
"STINKY"
"PEPE," "DUCKS," "FATBOY"...
DUDE. NO ONE READS ACKNOWLEDGMENTS.

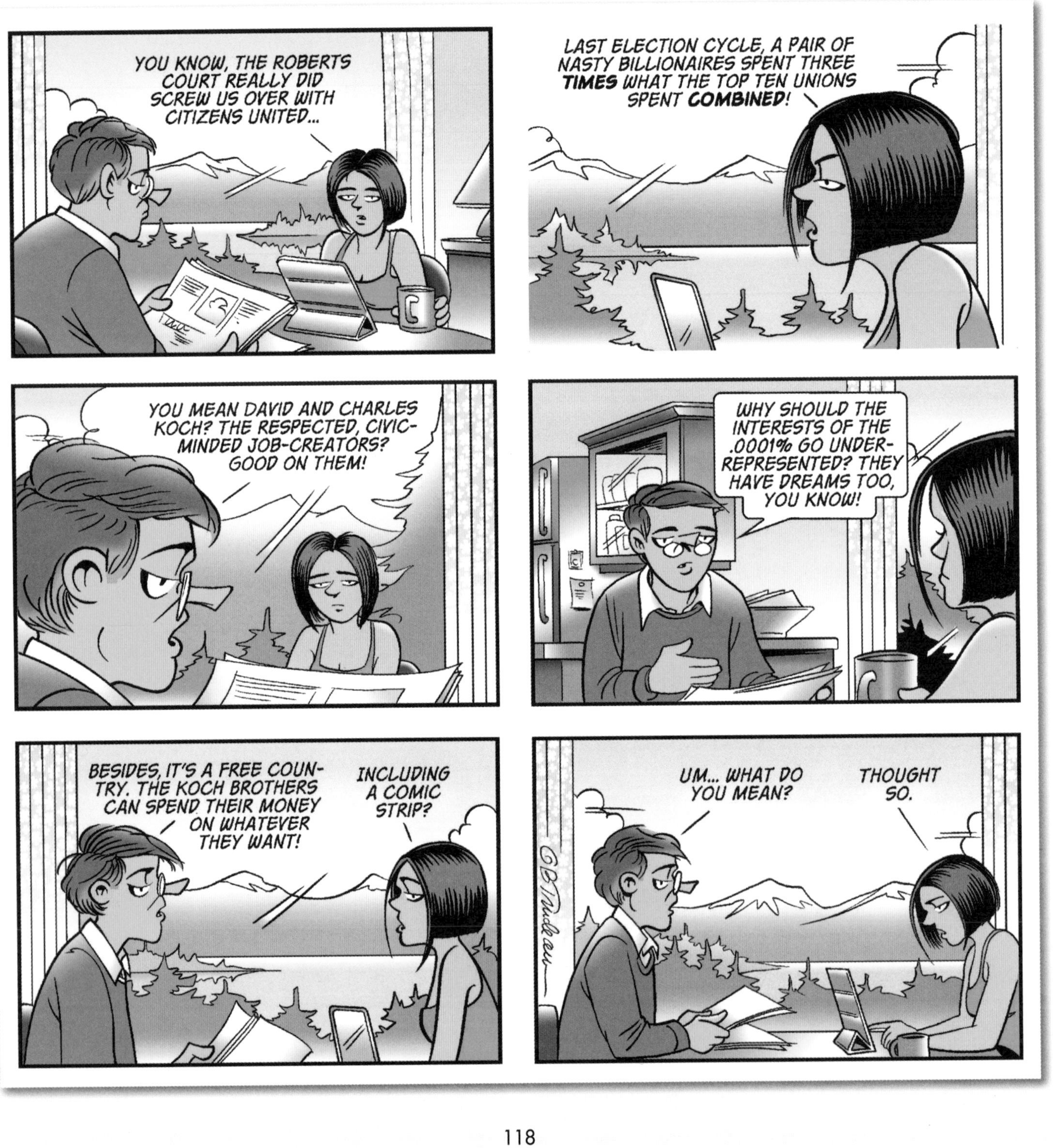
YOU KNOW, THE ROBERTS COURT REALLY DID SCREW US OVER WITH CITIZENS UNITED...
LAST ELECTION CYCLE, A PAIR OF NASTY BILLIONAIRES SPENT THREE **TIMES** WHAT THE TOP TEN UNIONS SPENT **COMBINED**!
YOU MEAN DAVID AND CHARLES KOCH? THE RESPECTED, CIVIC-MINDED JOB-CREATORS? GOOD ON THEM!
WHY SHOULD THE INTERESTS OF THE .0001% GO UNDER-REPRESENTED? THEY HAVE DREAMS TOO, YOU KNOW!
BESIDES, IT'S A FREE COUNTRY. THE KOCH BROTHERS CAN SPEND THEIR MONEY ON WHATEVER THEY WANT!
INCLUDING A COMIC STRIP?
UM... WHAT DO YOU MEAN?
THOUGHT SO.
©B Trudeau

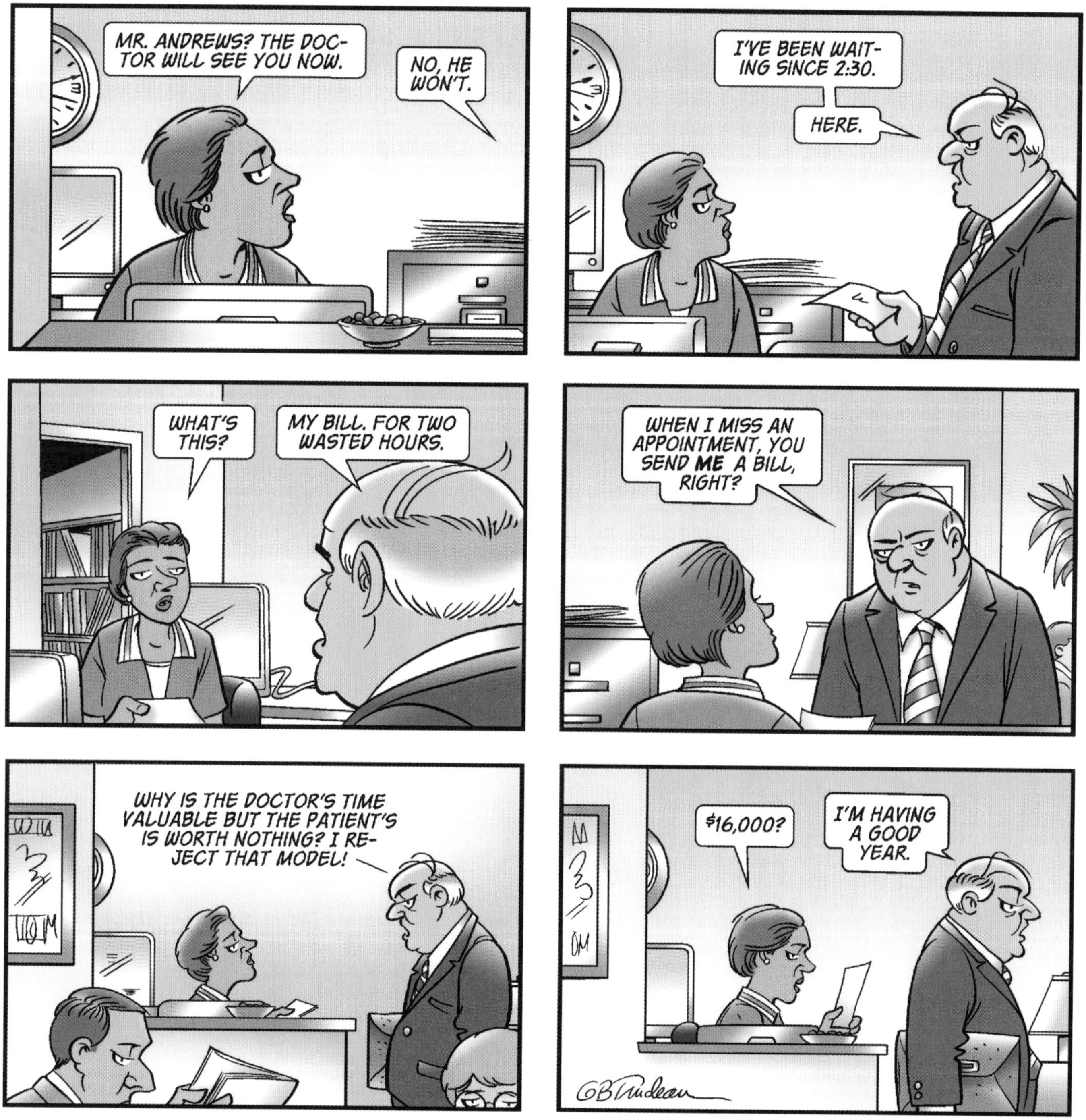
MR. ANDREWS? THE DOC-TOR WILL SEE YOU NOW.
NO, HE WON'T.
I'VE BEEN WAIT-ING SINCE 2:30.
HERE.
WHAT'S THIS?
MY BILL. FOR TWO WASTED HOURS.
WHEN I MISS AN APPOINTMENT, YOU SEND **ME** A BILL, RIGHT?
WHY IS THE DOCTOR'S TIME VALUABLE BUT THE PATIENT'S IS WORTH NOTHING? I RE-JECT THAT MODEL!
$16,000?
I'M HAVING A GOOD YEAR.
GBTrudeau

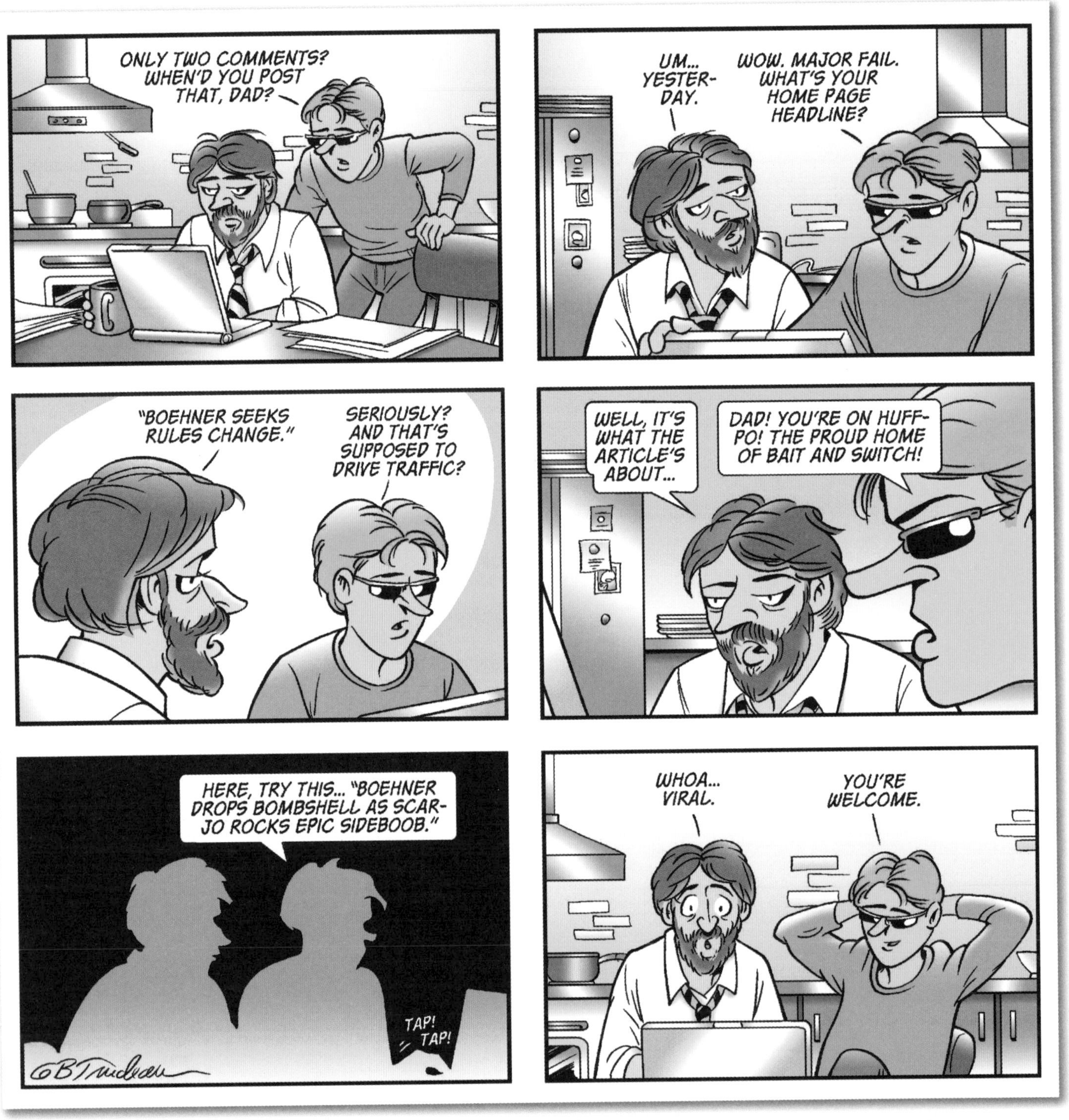
ONLY TWO COMMENTS? WHEN'D YOU POST THAT, DAD?
UM... YESTER-DAY.
WOW. MAJOR FAIL. WHAT'S YOUR HOME PAGE HEADLINE?
"BOEHNER SEEKS RULES CHANGE."
SERIOUSLY? AND THAT'S SUPPOSED TO DRIVE TRAFFIC?
WELL, IT'S WHAT THE ARTICLE'S ABOUT...
DAD! YOU'RE ON HUFF-PO! THE PROUD HOME OF BAIT AND SWITCH!
HERE, TRY THIS... "BOEHNER DROPS BOMBSHELL AS SCAR-JO ROCKS EPIC SIDEBOOB."
TAP! TAP!
GBTrudeau
WHOA... VIRAL.
YOU'RE WELCOME.

SORRY, SIR. WE'RE ABOUT TO CLOSE...

THE CROWDS HAVE THINNED OUT HERE AT THE BUSH PRESIDENTIAL LIBRARY...

...THE BETTER TO ADMIRE THIS AMAZING SUITE OF PORTRAITS OF WORLD LEADERS PAINTED BY FOLK ARTIST *GEORGE W. BUSH!*

HERE WE SEE AN INTIMATE RENDERING REDOLENT OF THE ARTIST'S BROMANCE WITH BRITAIN'S **TONY BLAIR**...

HERE, PUTIN, IN WHOSE EYES BUSH PEERED AND SENSED A "SOUL"...

...WHEN EVERYONE ELSE SAW ONLY THE DULL, BLANK STARE OF A STONE-COLD KILLER.

MOVING ON TO THE SELF-PORTRAITS...

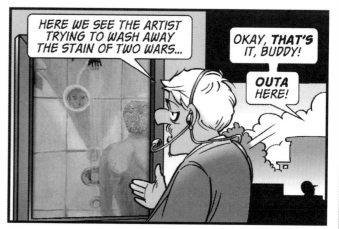

HERE WE SEE THE ARTIST TRYING TO WASH AWAY THE STAIN OF TWO WARS...

OKAY, **THAT'S** IT, BUDDY!

OUTA HERE!

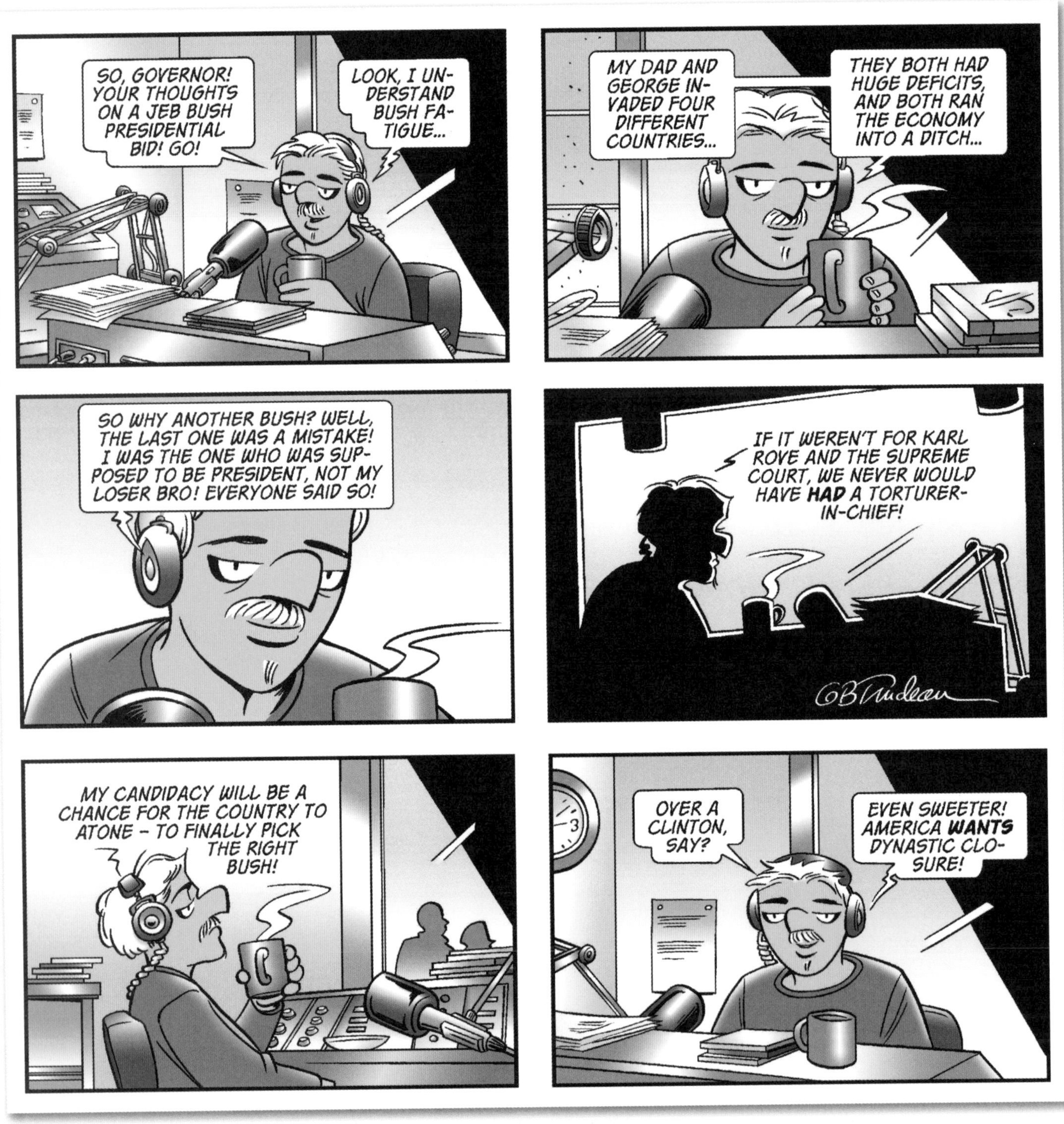
SO, GOVERNOR! YOUR THOUGHTS ON A JEB BUSH PRESIDENTIAL BID! GO!
LOOK, I UNDERSTAND BUSH FATIGUE...
MY DAD AND GEORGE INVADED FOUR DIFFERENT COUNTRIES...
THEY BOTH HAD HUGE DEFICITS, AND BOTH RAN THE ECONOMY INTO A DITCH...
SO WHY ANOTHER BUSH? WELL, THE LAST ONE WAS A MISTAKE! I WAS THE ONE WHO WAS SUPPOSED TO BE PRESIDENT, NOT MY LOSER BRO! EVERYONE SAID SO!
IF IT WEREN'T FOR KARL ROVE AND THE SUPREME COURT, WE NEVER WOULD HAVE **HAD** A TORTURER-IN-CHIEF!
GBTrudeau
MY CANDIDACY WILL BE A CHANCE FOR THE COUNTRY TO ATONE – TO FINALLY PICK THE RIGHT BUSH!
OVER A CLINTON, SAY?
EVEN SWEETER! AMERICA **WANTS** DYNASTIC CLOSURE!

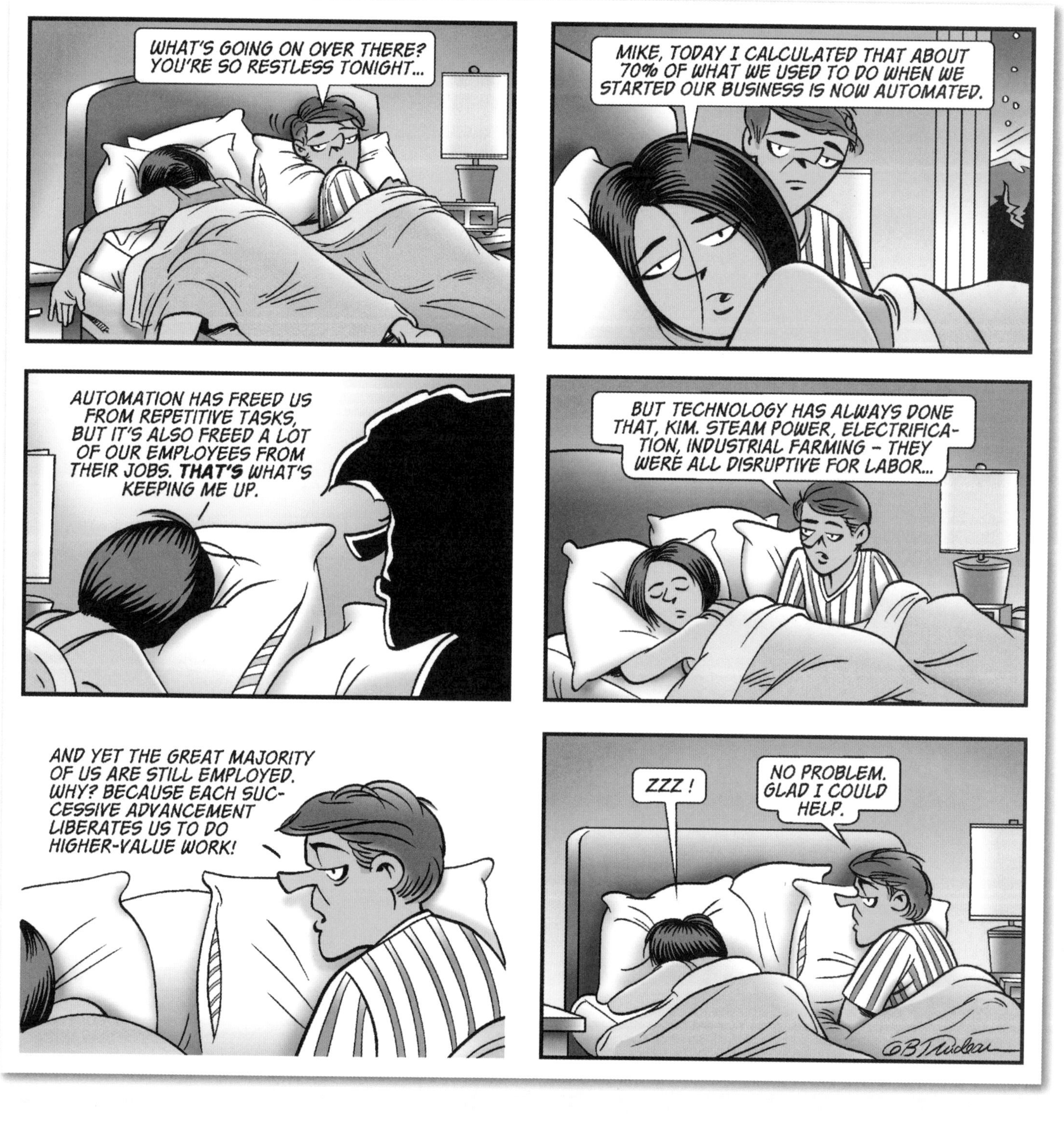
WHAT'S GOING ON OVER THERE? YOU'RE SO RESTLESS TONIGHT...
MIKE, TODAY I CALCULATED THAT ABOUT 70% OF WHAT WE USED TO DO WHEN WE STARTED OUR BUSINESS IS NOW AUTOMATED.
AUTOMATION HAS FREED US FROM REPETITIVE TASKS, BUT IT'S ALSO FREED A LOT OF OUR EMPLOYEES FROM THEIR JOBS. THAT'S WHAT'S KEEPING ME UP.
BUT TECHNOLOGY HAS ALWAYS DONE THAT, KIM. STEAM POWER, ELECTRIFICATION, INDUSTRIAL FARMING – THEY WERE ALL DISRUPTIVE FOR LABOR...
AND YET THE GREAT MAJORITY OF US ARE STILL EMPLOYED. WHY? BECAUSE EACH SUCCESSIVE ADVANCEMENT LIBERATES US TO DO HIGHER-VALUE WORK!
ZZZ !
NO PROBLEM. GLAD I COULD HELP.
GB Trudeau

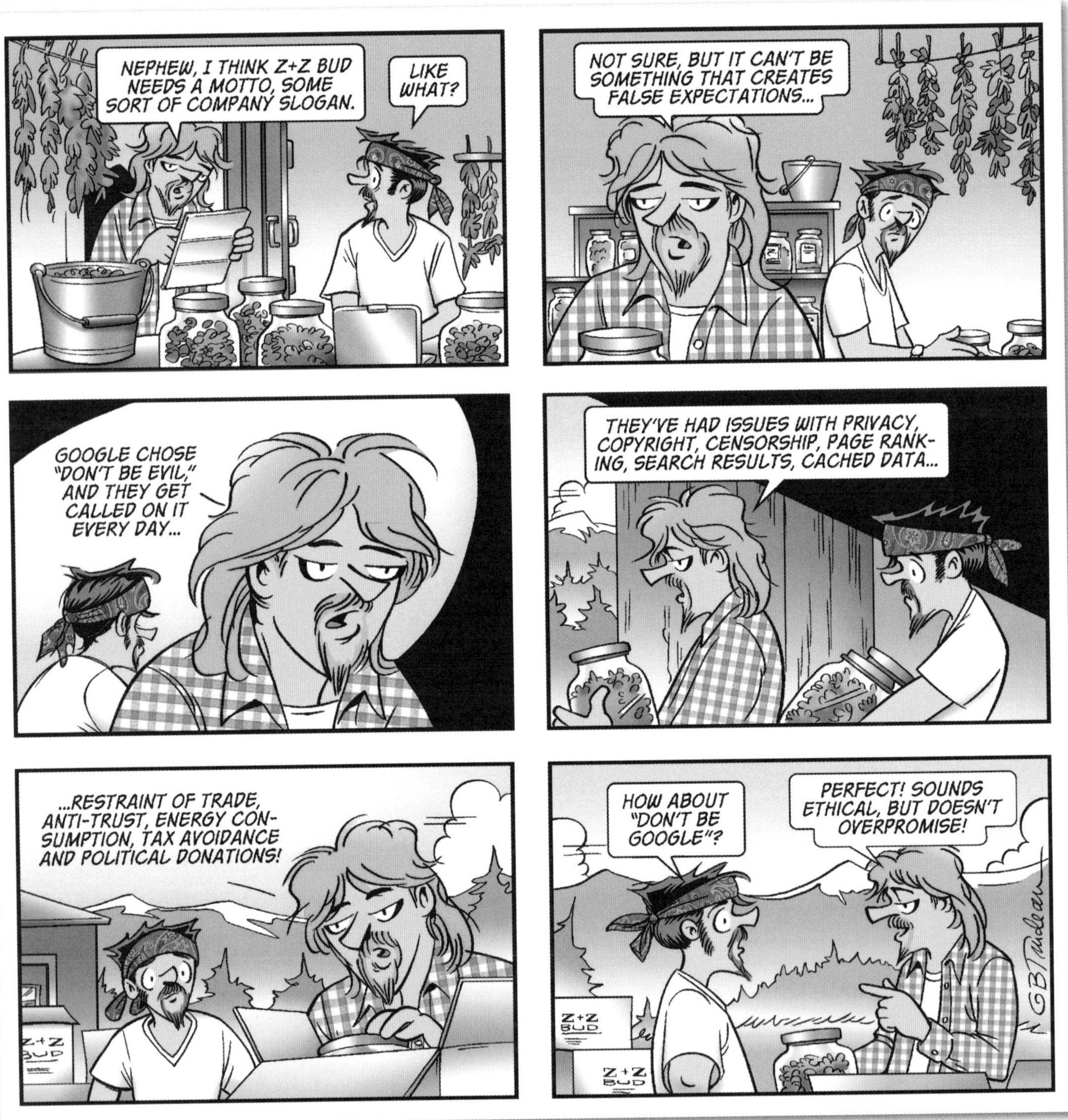
NEPHEW, I THINK Z+Z BUD NEEDS A MOTTO, SOME SORT OF COMPANY SLOGAN.
LIKE WHAT?
NOT SURE, BUT IT CAN'T BE SOMETHING THAT CREATES FALSE EXPECTATIONS...
GOOGLE CHOSE "DON'T BE EVIL," AND THEY GET CALLED ON IT EVERY DAY...
THEY'VE HAD ISSUES WITH PRIVACY, COPYRIGHT, CENSORSHIP, PAGE RANK-ING, SEARCH RESULTS, CACHED DATA...
...RESTRAINT OF TRADE, ANTI-TRUST, ENERGY CON-SUMPTION, TAX AVOIDANCE AND POLITICAL DONATIONS!
Z+Z BUD
HOW ABOUT "DON'T BE GOOGLE"?
PERFECT! SOUNDS ETHICAL, BUT DOESN'T OVERPROMISE!
Z+Z BUD
Z+Z BUD
GBTrudeau

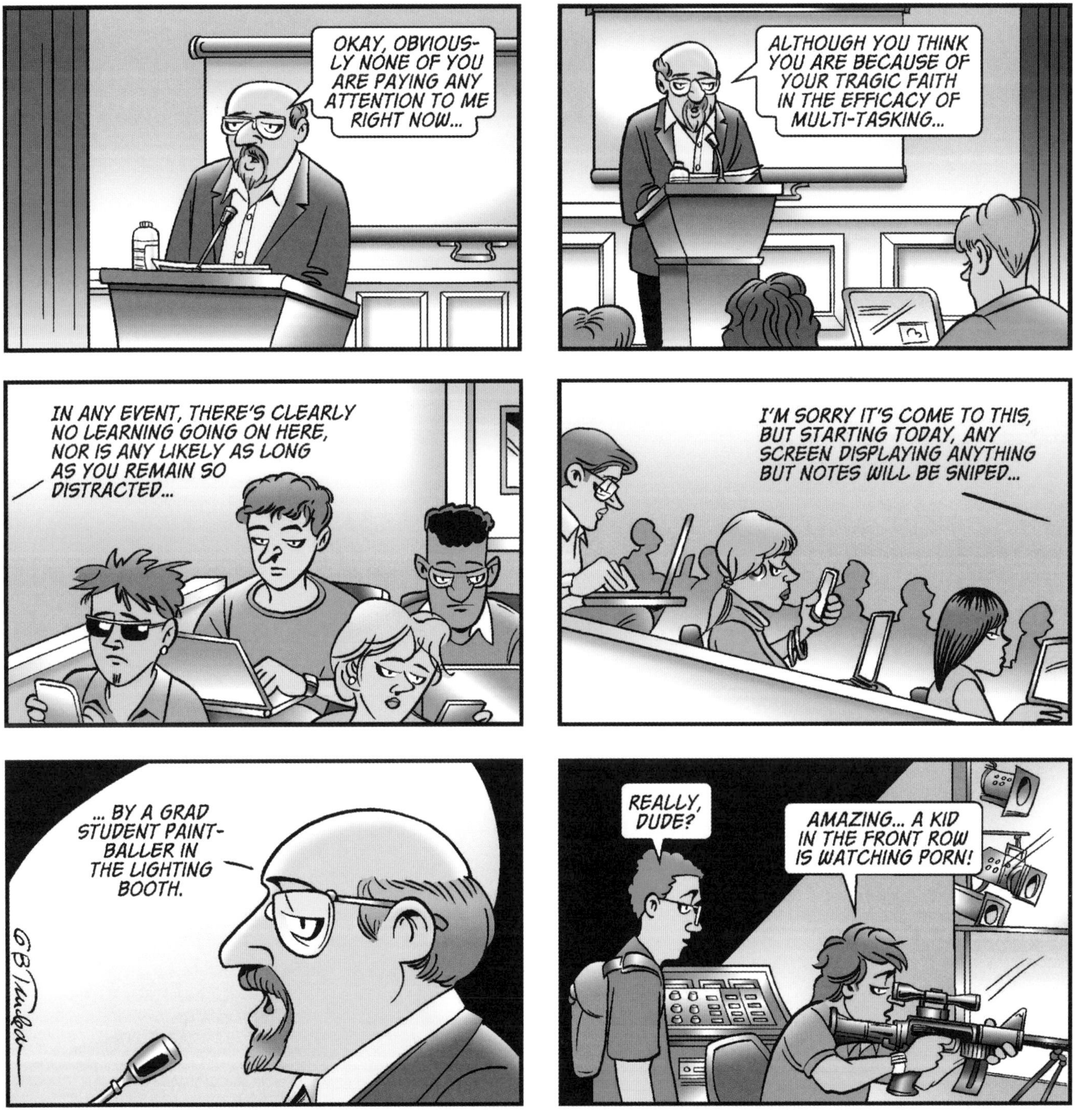
OKAY, OBVIOUSLY NONE OF YOU ARE PAYING ANY ATTENTION TO ME RIGHT NOW...
ALTHOUGH YOU THINK YOU ARE BECAUSE OF YOUR TRAGIC FAITH IN THE EFFICACY OF MULTI-TASKING...
IN ANY EVENT, THERE'S CLEARLY NO LEARNING GOING ON HERE, NOR IS ANY LIKELY AS LONG AS YOU REMAIN SO DISTRACTED...
I'M SORRY IT'S COME TO THIS, BUT STARTING TODAY, ANY SCREEN DISPLAYING ANYTHING BUT NOTES WILL BE SNIPED...
... BY A GRAD STUDENT PAINTBALLER IN THE LIGHTING BOOTH.
REALLY, DUDE?
AMAZING... A KID IN THE FRONT ROW IS WATCHING PORN!

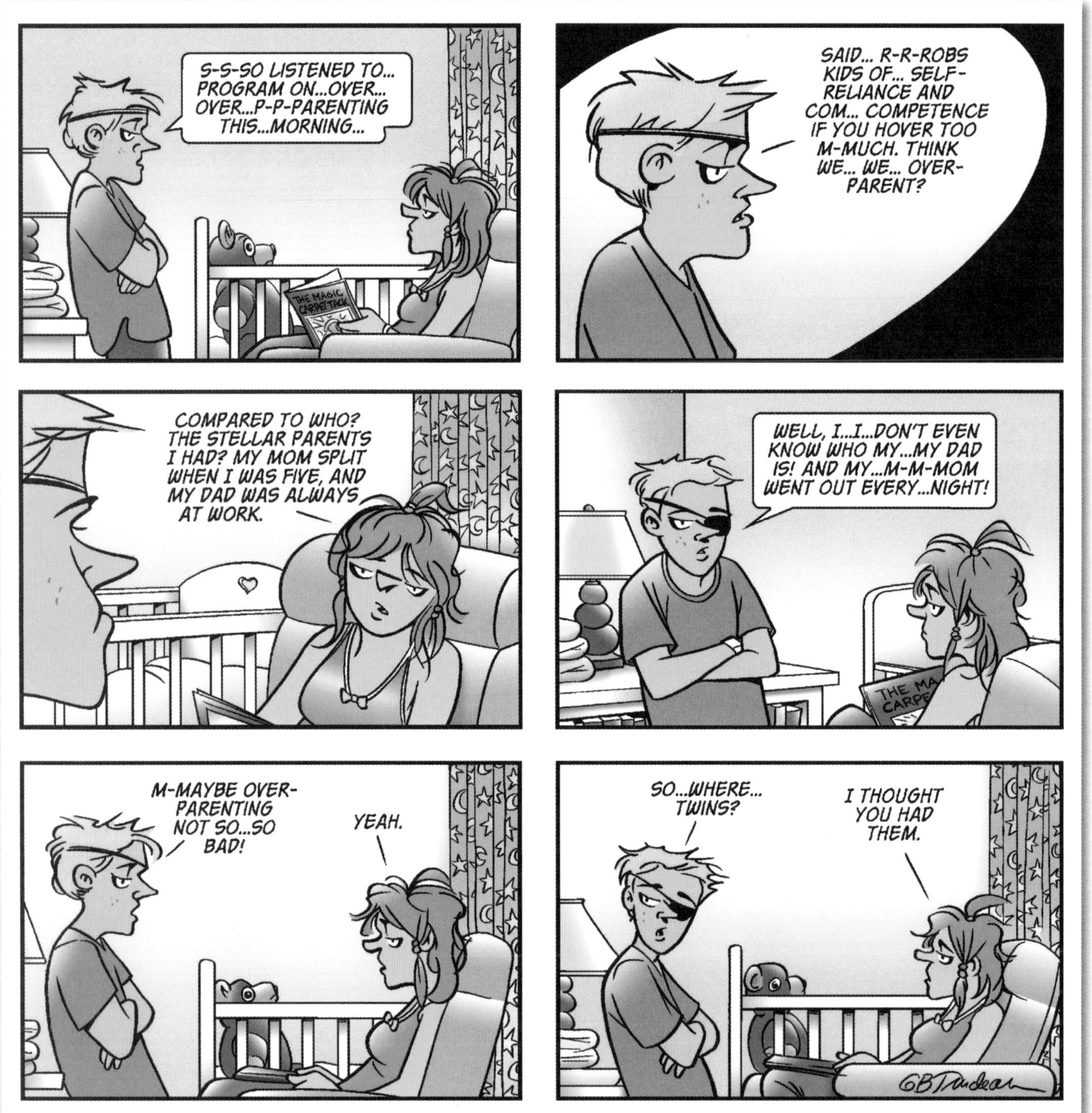
S-S-SO LISTENED TO... PROGRAM ON...OVER... OVER...P-P-PARENTING THIS...MORNING...
THE MAGIC CARPET TACK
SAID... R-R-ROBS KIDS OF... SELF-RELIANCE AND COM... COMPETENCE IF YOU HOVER TOO M-MUCH. THINK WE... WE... OVER-PARENT?
COMPARED TO WHO? THE STELLAR PARENTS I HAD? MY MOM SPLIT WHEN I WAS FIVE, AND MY DAD WAS ALWAYS AT WORK.
WELL, I...I...DON'T EVEN KNOW WHO MY...MY DAD IS! AND MY...M-M-MOM WENT OUT EVERY...NIGHT!
M-MAYBE OVER-PARENTING NOT SO...SO BAD!
YEAH.
SO...WHERE... TWINS?
I THOUGHT YOU HAD THEM.
GBTrudeau

DOC, DID YOU SEE THAT NEW CLIMATE CHANGE REPORT? **WHAT** A FAIRY TALE!

THE COLLECTIVISTS WILL SAY **ANYTHING** TO HARM OUR ENERGY INDUSTRY!

UH-HUH...

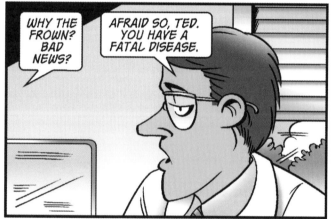

WHY THE FROWN? BAD NEWS?

AFRAID SO, TED. YOU HAVE A FATAL DISEASE.

WHAT?

THE GOOD NEWS IS IT'S TREATABLE WITH MEDICINE THAT 99 OUT OF 100 DOCTORS RECOMMEND.

WHAT WOULD THE 100TH DOCTOR RECOMMEND?

HE'D ADVISE YOU TO WAIT AND SEE.

@BTrudeau

THINK I COULD GET AN APPOINTMENT?

I'M SURE OF IT.

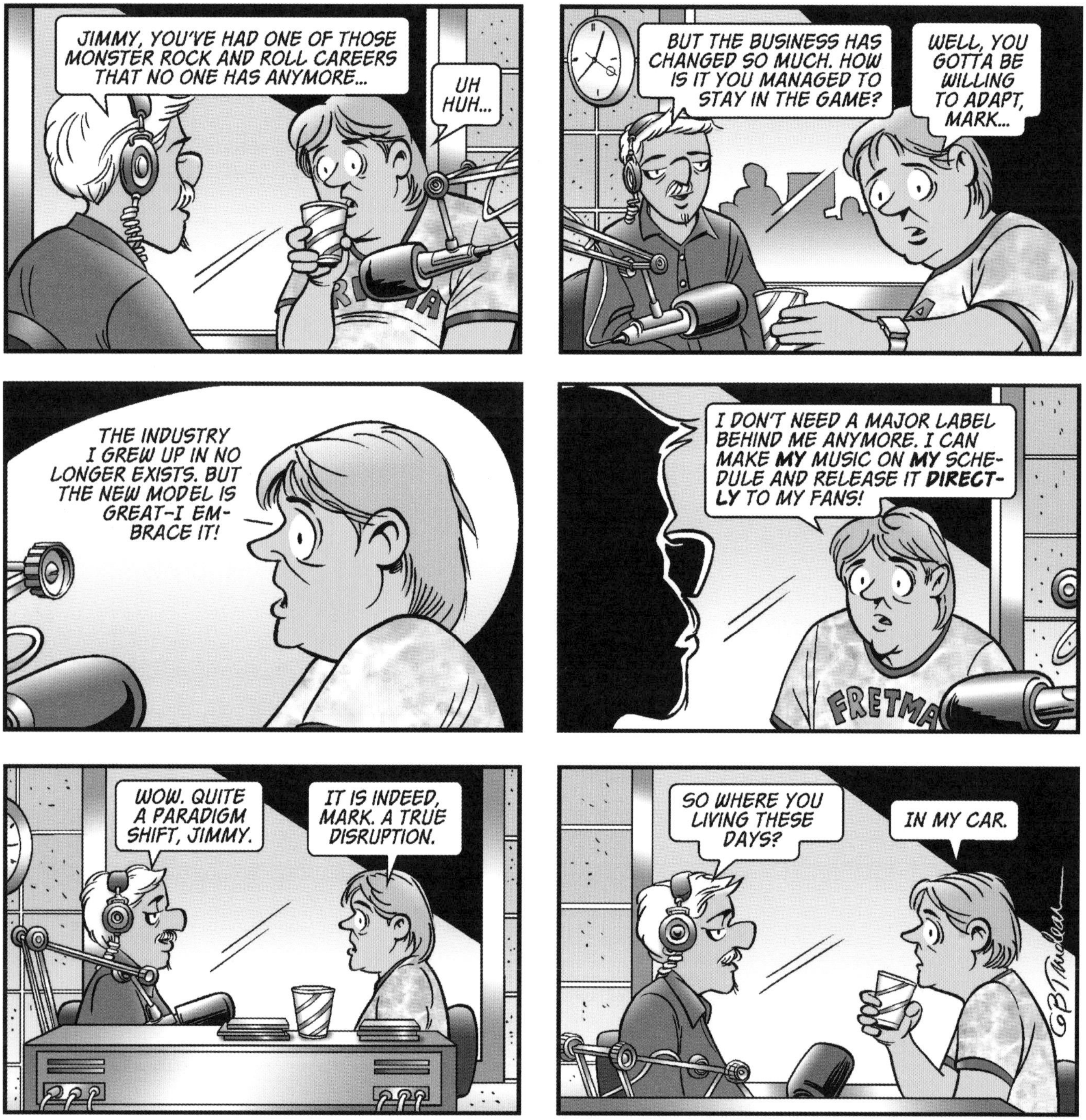
JIMMY, YOU'VE HAD ONE OF THOSE MONSTER ROCK AND ROLL CAREERS THAT NO ONE HAS ANYMORE...
UH HUH...
BUT THE BUSINESS HAS CHANGED SO MUCH. HOW IS IT YOU MANAGED TO STAY IN THE GAME?
WELL, YOU GOTTA BE WILLING TO ADAPT, MARK...
THE INDUSTRY I GREW UP IN NO LONGER EXISTS. BUT THE NEW MODEL IS GREAT–I EMBRACE IT!
I DON'T NEED A MAJOR LABEL BEHIND ME ANYMORE. I CAN MAKE **MY** MUSIC ON **MY** SCHEDULE AND RELEASE IT **DIRECTLY** TO MY FANS!
FRETMA
WOW. QUITE A PARADIGM SHIFT, JIMMY.
IT IS INDEED, MARK. A TRUE DISRUPTION.
SO WHERE YOU LIVING THESE DAYS?
IN MY CAR.
GBTrudeau

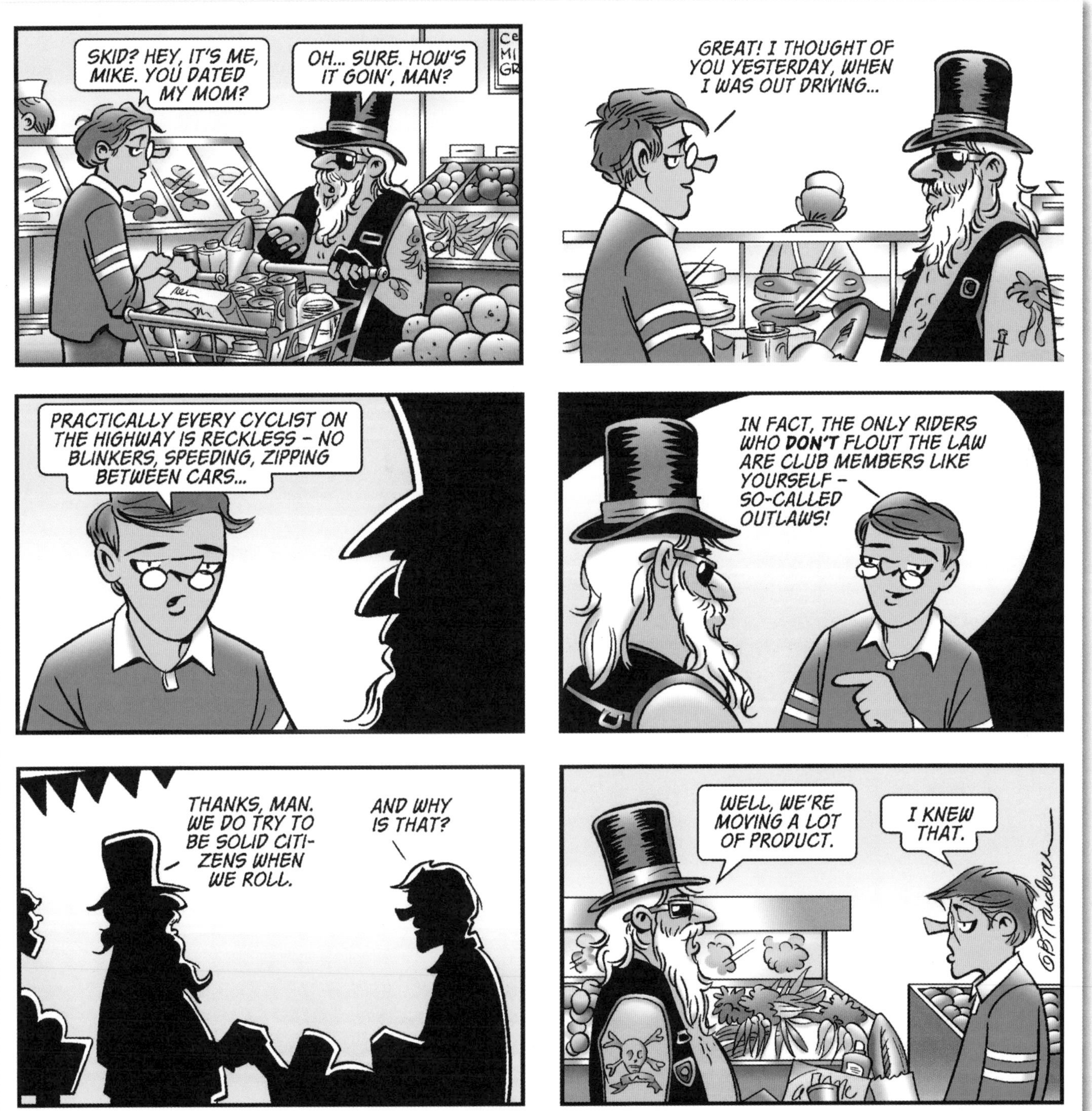
SKID? HEY, IT'S ME, MIKE. YOU DATED MY MOM?
OH... SURE. HOW'S IT GOIN', MAN?
GREAT! I THOUGHT OF YOU YESTERDAY, WHEN I WAS OUT DRIVING...
PRACTICALLY EVERY CYCLIST ON THE HIGHWAY IS RECKLESS – NO BLINKERS, SPEEDING, ZIPPING BETWEEN CARS...
IN FACT, THE ONLY RIDERS WHO **DON'T** FLOUT THE LAW ARE CLUB MEMBERS LIKE YOURSELF – SO-CALLED OUTLAWS!
THANKS, MAN. WE DO TRY TO BE SOLID CITIZENS WHEN WE ROLL.
AND WHY IS THAT?
WELL, WE'RE MOVING A LOT OF PRODUCT.
I KNEW THAT.

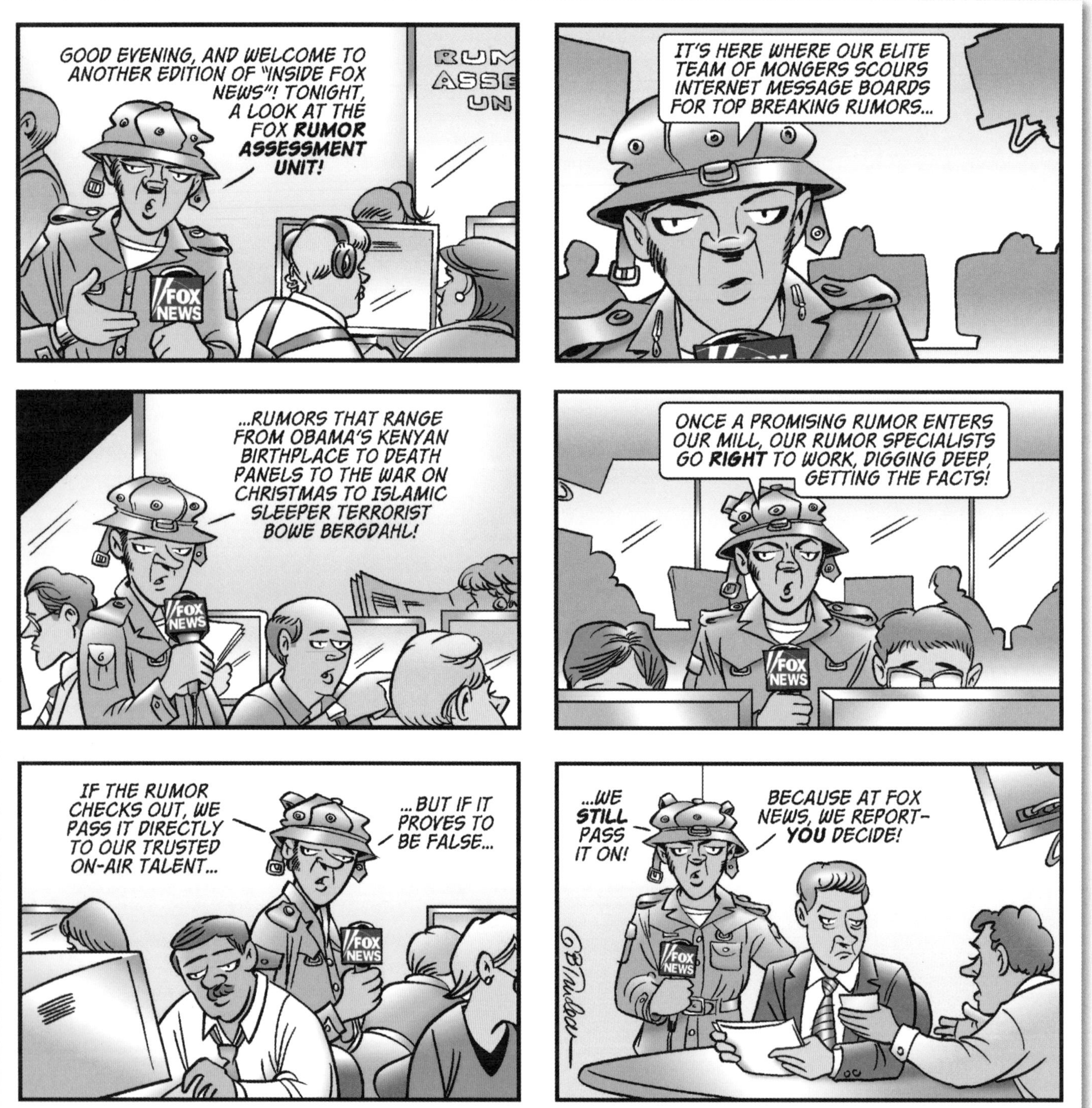
RUM
ASSE
UN
GOOD EVENING, AND WELCOME TO ANOTHER EDITION OF "INSIDE FOX NEWS"! TONIGHT, A LOOK AT THE FOX RUMOR ASSESSMENT UNIT!
FOX NEWS
IT'S HERE WHERE OUR ELITE TEAM OF MONGERS SCOURS INTERNET MESSAGE BOARDS FOR TOP BREAKING RUMORS...
...RUMORS THAT RANGE FROM OBAMA'S KENYAN BIRTHPLACE TO DEATH PANELS TO THE WAR ON CHRISTMAS TO ISLAMIC SLEEPER TERRORIST BOWE BERGDAHL!
FOX NEWS
ONCE A PROMISING RUMOR ENTERS OUR MILL, OUR RUMOR SPECIALISTS GO RIGHT TO WORK, DIGGING DEEP, GETTING THE FACTS!
FOX NEWS
IF THE RUMOR CHECKS OUT, WE PASS IT DIRECTLY TO OUR TRUSTED ON-AIR TALENT...
...BUT IF IT PROVES TO BE FALSE...
FOX NEWS
...WE STILL PASS IT ON!
BECAUSE AT FOX NEWS, WE REPORT– YOU DECIDE!
FOX NEWS
GBTrudeau

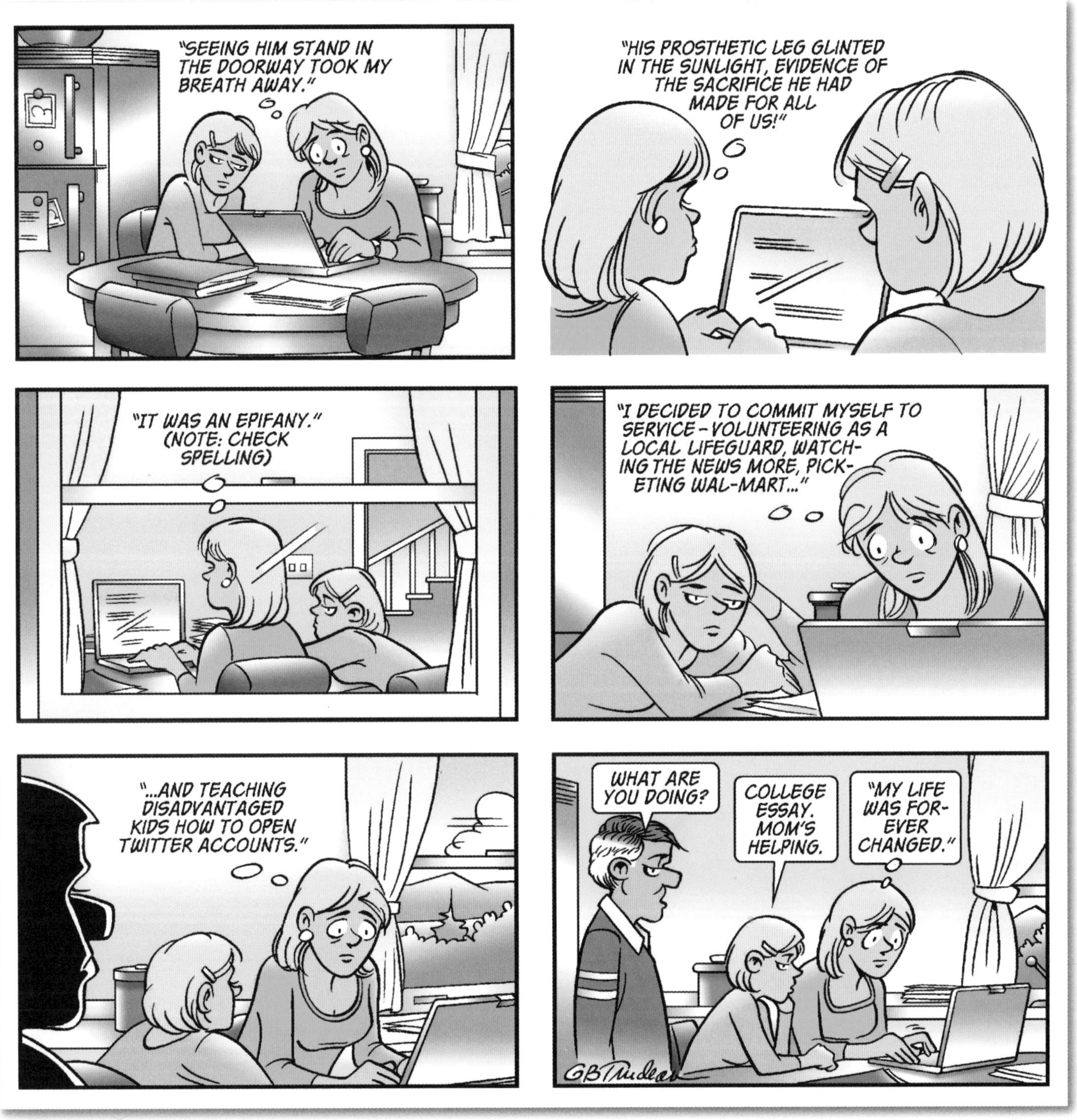
"SEEING HIM STAND IN THE DOORWAY TOOK MY BREATH AWAY."
"HIS PROSTHETIC LEG GLINTED IN THE SUNLIGHT, EVIDENCE OF THE SACRIFICE HE HAD MADE FOR ALL OF US!"
"IT WAS AN EPIFANY." (NOTE: CHECK SPELLING)
"I DECIDED TO COMMIT MYSELF TO SERVICE - VOLUNTEERING AS A LOCAL LIFEGUARD, WATCHING THE NEWS MORE, PICKETING WAL-MART..."
"...AND TEACHING DISADVANTAGED KIDS HOW TO OPEN TWITTER ACCOUNTS."
WHAT ARE YOU DOING?
COLLEGE ESSAY. MOM'S HELPING.
"MY LIFE WAS FOREVER CHANGED."
GBTrudeau

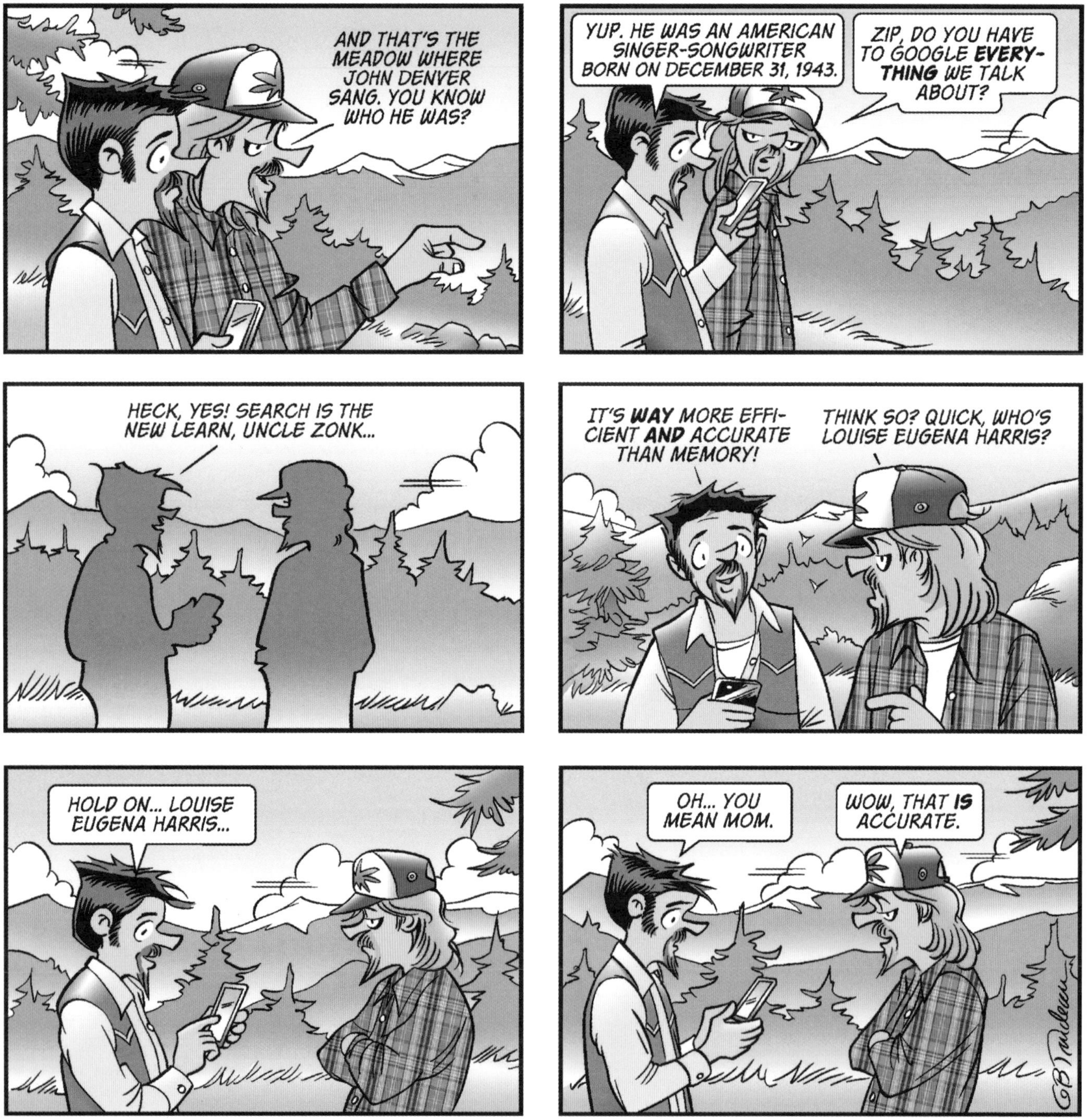
AND THAT'S THE MEADOW WHERE JOHN DENVER SANG. YOU KNOW WHO HE WAS?
YUP. HE WAS AN AMERICAN SINGER-SONGWRITER BORN ON DECEMBER 31, 1943.
ZIP, DO YOU HAVE TO GOOGLE **EVERY-THING** WE TALK ABOUT?
HECK, YES! SEARCH IS THE NEW LEARN, UNCLE ZONK...
IT'S **WAY** MORE EFFI-CIENT **AND** ACCURATE THAN MEMORY!
THINK SO? QUICK, WHO'S LOUISE EUGENA HARRIS?
HOLD ON... LOUISE EUGENA HARRIS...
OH... YOU MEAN MOM.
WOW, THAT **IS** ACCURATE.

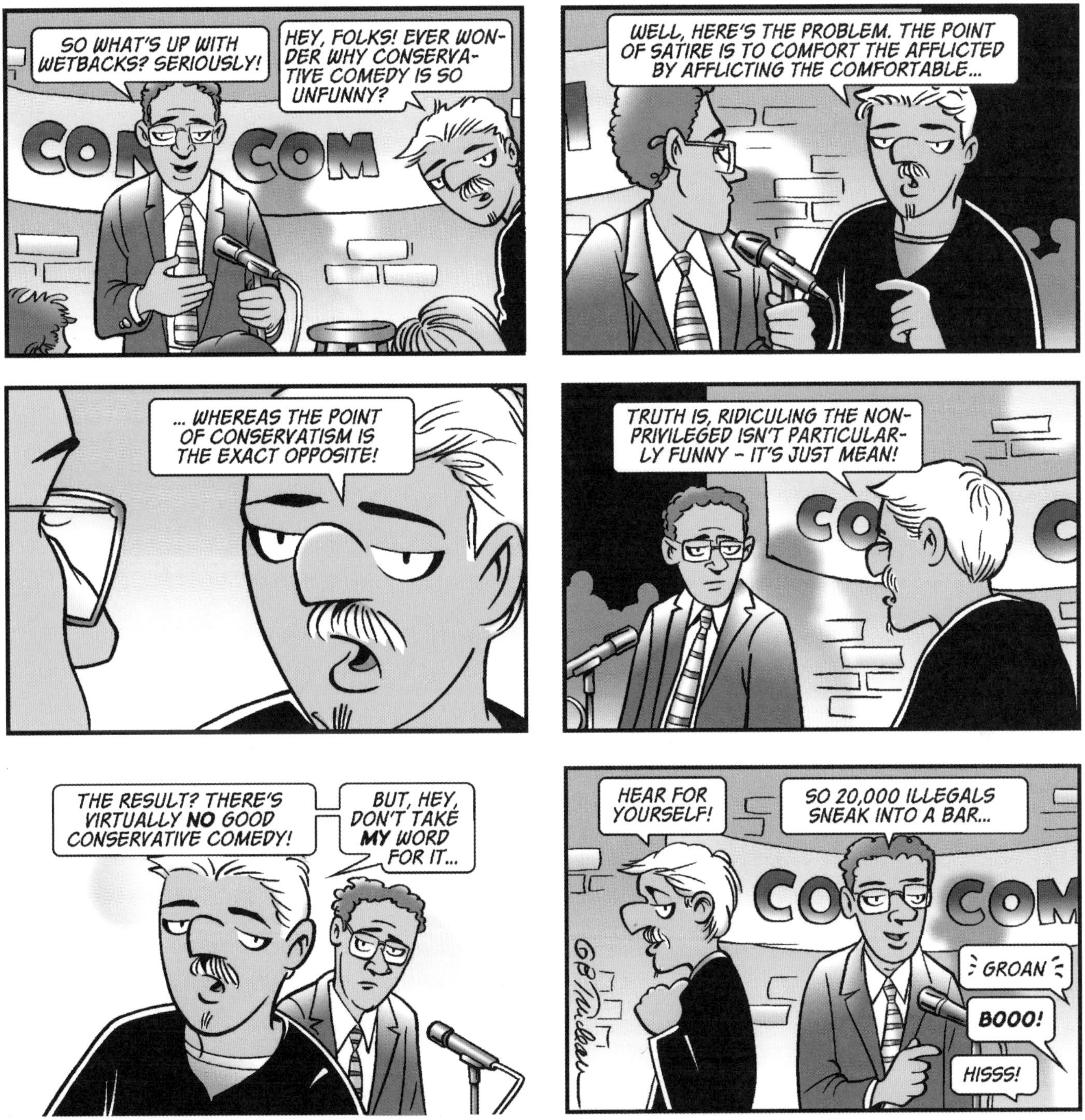
SO WHAT'S UP WITH WETBACKS? SERIOUSLY!
HEY, FOLKS! EVER WONDER WHY CONSERVATIVE COMEDY IS SO UNFUNNY?
CON COM
WELL, HERE'S THE PROBLEM. THE POINT OF SATIRE IS TO COMFORT THE AFFLICTED BY AFFLICTING THE COMFORTABLE...
... WHEREAS THE POINT OF CONSERVATISM IS THE EXACT OPPOSITE!
TRUTH IS, RIDICULING THE NON-PRIVILEGED ISN'T PARTICULARLY FUNNY – IT'S JUST MEAN!
THE RESULT? THERE'S VIRTUALLY **NO** GOOD CONSERVATIVE COMEDY!
BUT, HEY, DON'T TAKE **MY** WORD FOR IT...
HEAR FOR YOURSELF!
SO 20,000 ILLEGALS SNEAK INTO A BAR...
CON COM
GROAN
BOOO!
HISSS!

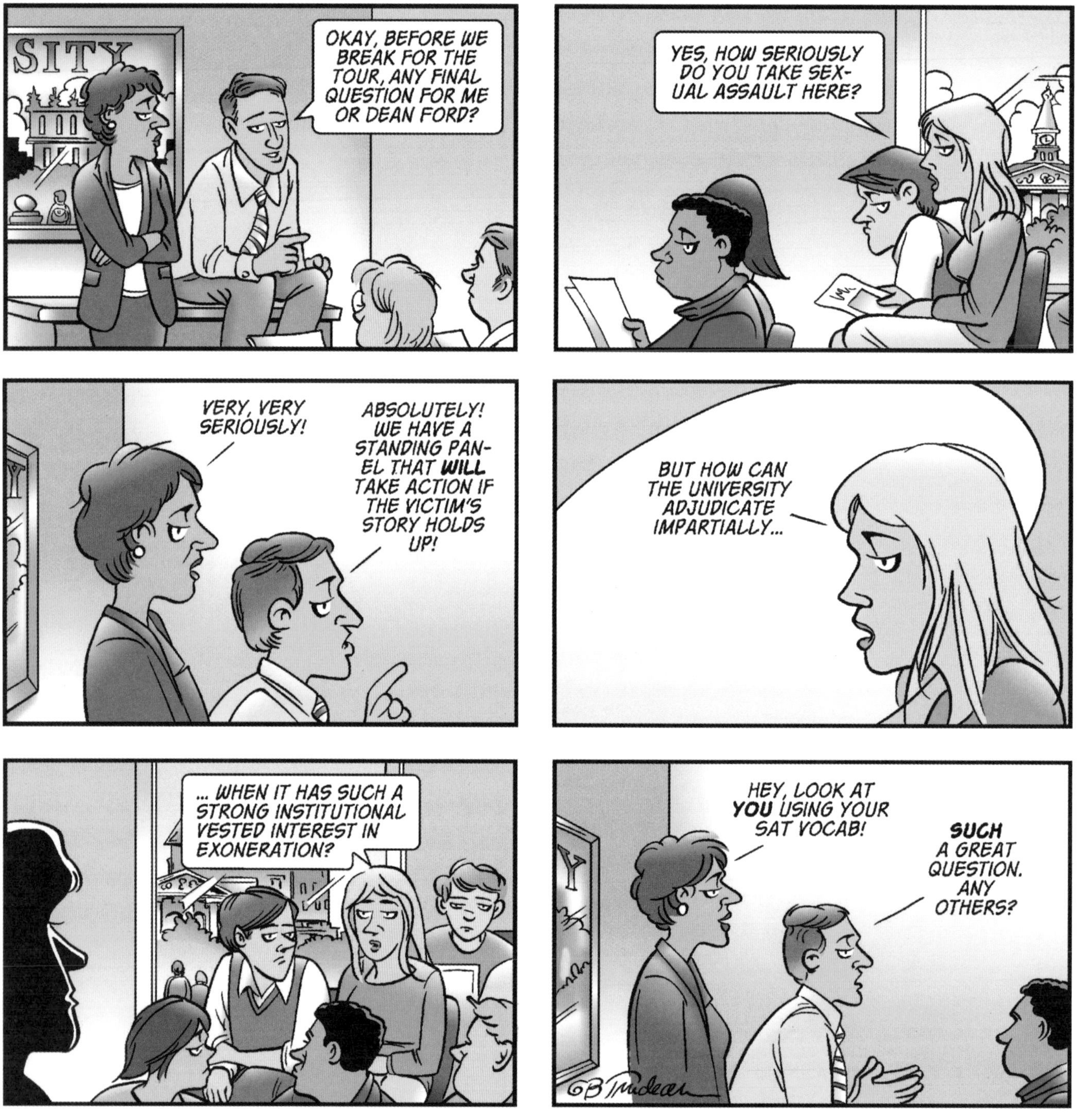
SITY
OKAY, BEFORE WE BREAK FOR THE TOUR, ANY FINAL QUESTION FOR ME OR DEAN FORD?
YES, HOW SERIOUSLY DO YOU TAKE SEX-UAL ASSAULT HERE?
VERY, VERY SERIOUSLY!
ABSOLUTELY! WE HAVE A STANDING PAN-EL THAT **WILL** TAKE ACTION IF THE VICTIM'S STORY HOLDS UP!
BUT HOW CAN THE UNIVERSITY ADJUDICATE IMPARTIALLY...
... WHEN IT HAS SUCH A STRONG INSTITUTIONAL VESTED INTEREST IN EXONERATION?
HEY, LOOK AT **YOU** USING YOUR SAT VOCAB!
SUCH A GREAT QUESTION. ANY OTHERS?
GB Trudeau

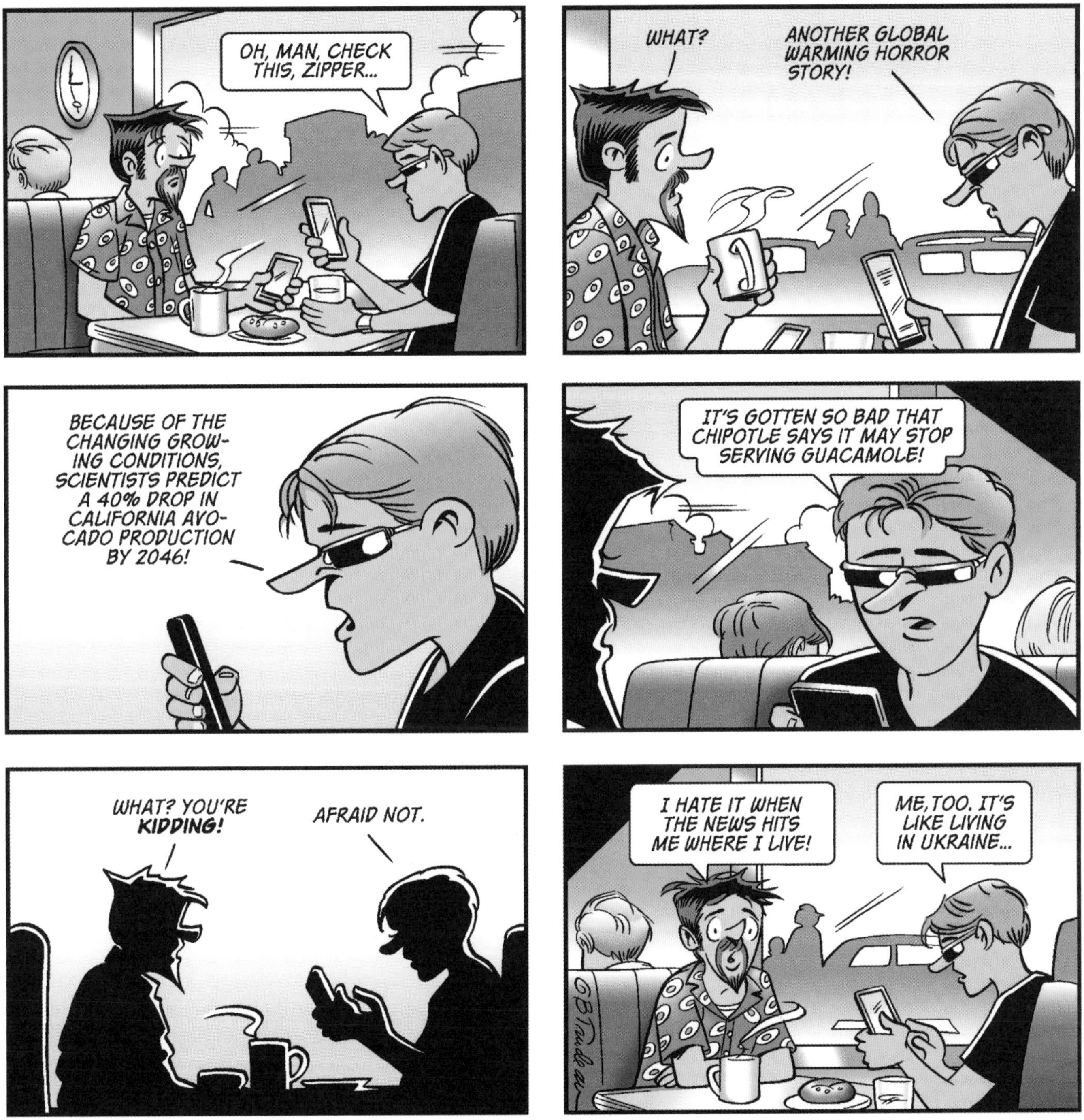
OH, MAN, CHECK THIS, ZIPPER...
WHAT?
ANOTHER GLOBAL WARMING HORROR STORY!
BECAUSE OF THE CHANGING GROWING CONDITIONS, SCIENTISTS PREDICT A 40% DROP IN CALIFORNIA AVOCADO PRODUCTION BY 2046!
IT'S GOTTEN SO BAD THAT CHIPOTLE SAYS IT MAY STOP SERVING GUACAMOLE!
WHAT? YOU'RE **KIDDING!**
AFRAID NOT.
I HATE IT WHEN THE NEWS HITS ME WHERE I LIVE!
ME, TOO. IT'S LIKE LIVING IN UKRAINE...
GBTrudeau

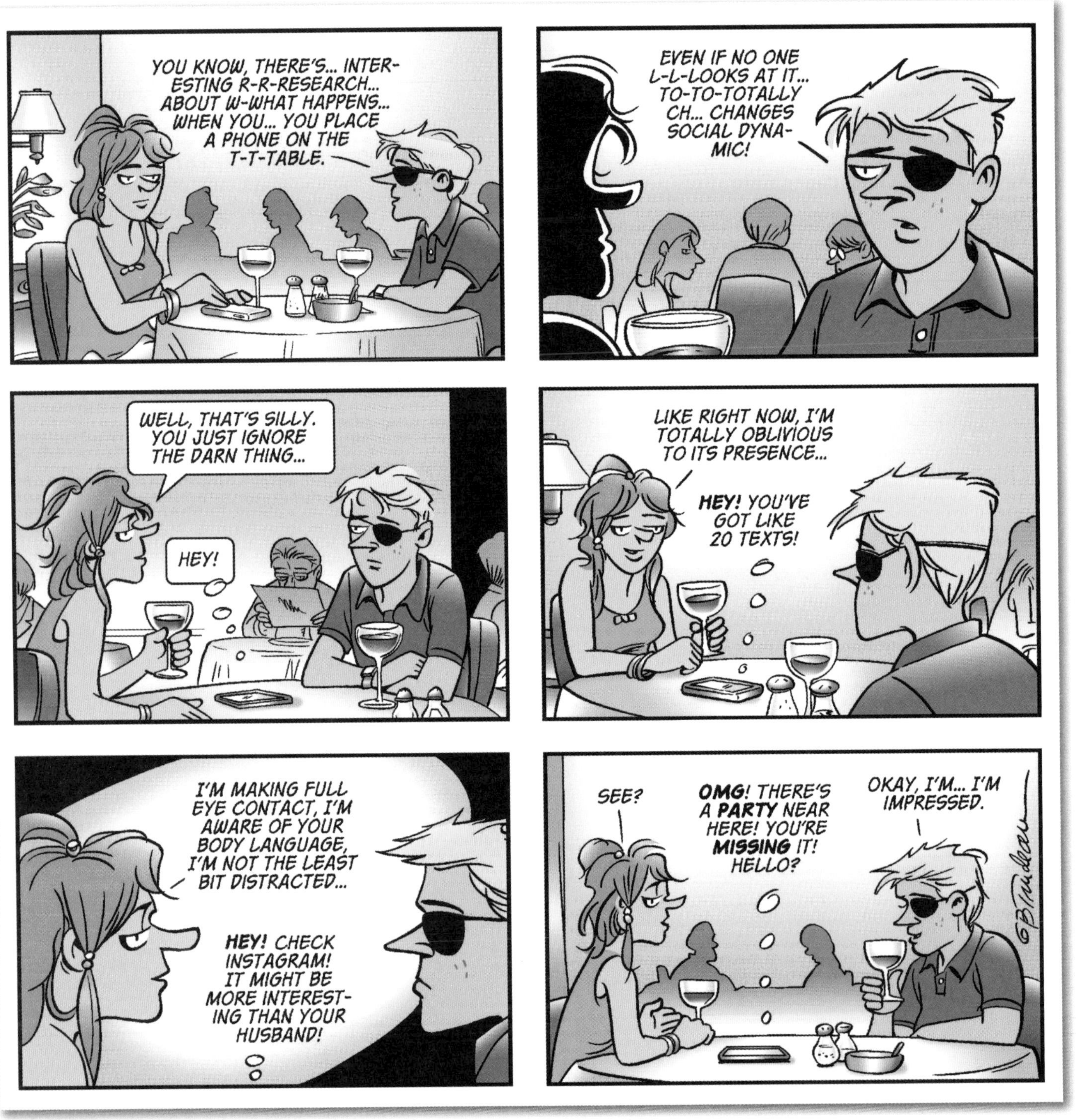

YOU KNOW, THERE'S... INTERESTING R-R-RESEARCH... ABOUT W-WHAT HAPPENS... WHEN YOU... YOU PLACE A PHONE ON THE T-T-TABLE.
EVEN IF NO ONE L-L-LOOKS AT IT... TO-TO-TOTALLY CH... CHANGES SOCIAL DYNAMIC!
WELL, THAT'S SILLY. YOU JUST IGNORE THE DARN THING...
HEY!
LIKE RIGHT NOW, I'M TOTALLY OBLIVIOUS TO ITS PRESENCE...
HEY! YOU'VE GOT LIKE 20 TEXTS!
I'M MAKING FULL EYE CONTACT, I'M AWARE OF YOUR BODY LANGUAGE, I'M NOT THE LEAST BIT DISTRACTED...
HEY! CHECK INSTAGRAM! IT MIGHT BE MORE INTERESTING THAN YOUR HUSBAND!
SEE?
OMG! THERE'S A **PARTY** NEAR HERE! YOU'RE **MISSING** IT! HELLO?
OKAY, I'M... I'M IMPRESSED.
©BTrudeau

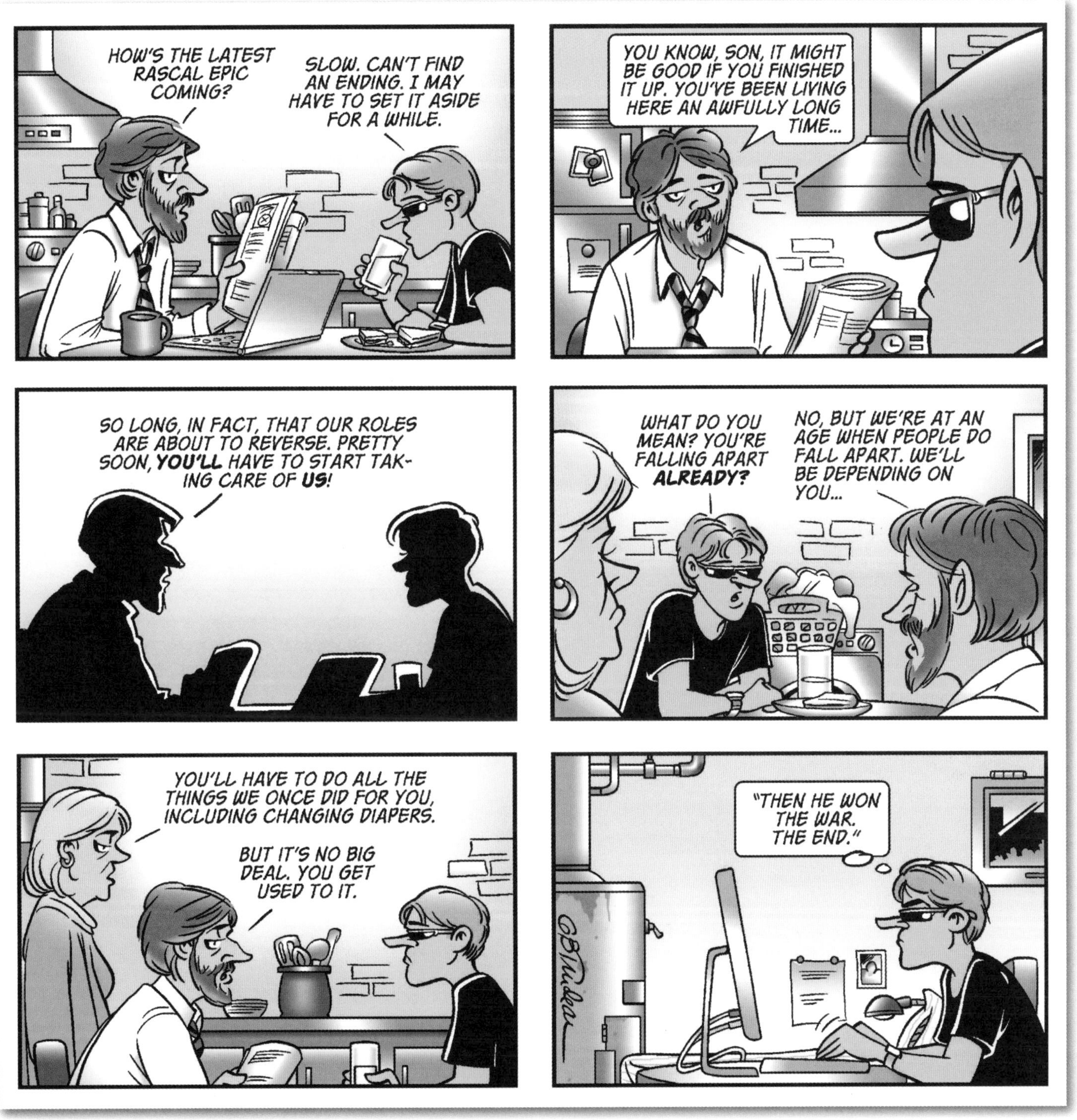
HOW'S THE LATEST RASCAL EPIC COMING?
SLOW. CAN'T FIND AN ENDING. I MAY HAVE TO SET IT ASIDE FOR A WHILE.
YOU KNOW, SON, IT MIGHT BE GOOD IF YOU FINISHED IT UP. YOU'VE BEEN LIVING HERE AN AWFULLY LONG TIME...
SO LONG, IN FACT, THAT OUR ROLES ARE ABOUT TO REVERSE. PRETTY SOON, **YOU'LL** HAVE TO START TAKING CARE OF **US**!
WHAT DO YOU MEAN? YOU'RE FALLING APART **ALREADY?**
NO, BUT WE'RE AT AN AGE WHEN PEOPLE DO FALL APART. WE'LL BE DEPENDING ON YOU...
YOU'LL HAVE TO DO ALL THE THINGS WE ONCE DID FOR YOU, INCLUDING CHANGING DIAPERS.
BUT IT'S NO BIG DEAL. YOU GET USED TO IT.
"THEN HE WON THE WAR. THE END."
GBTrudeau

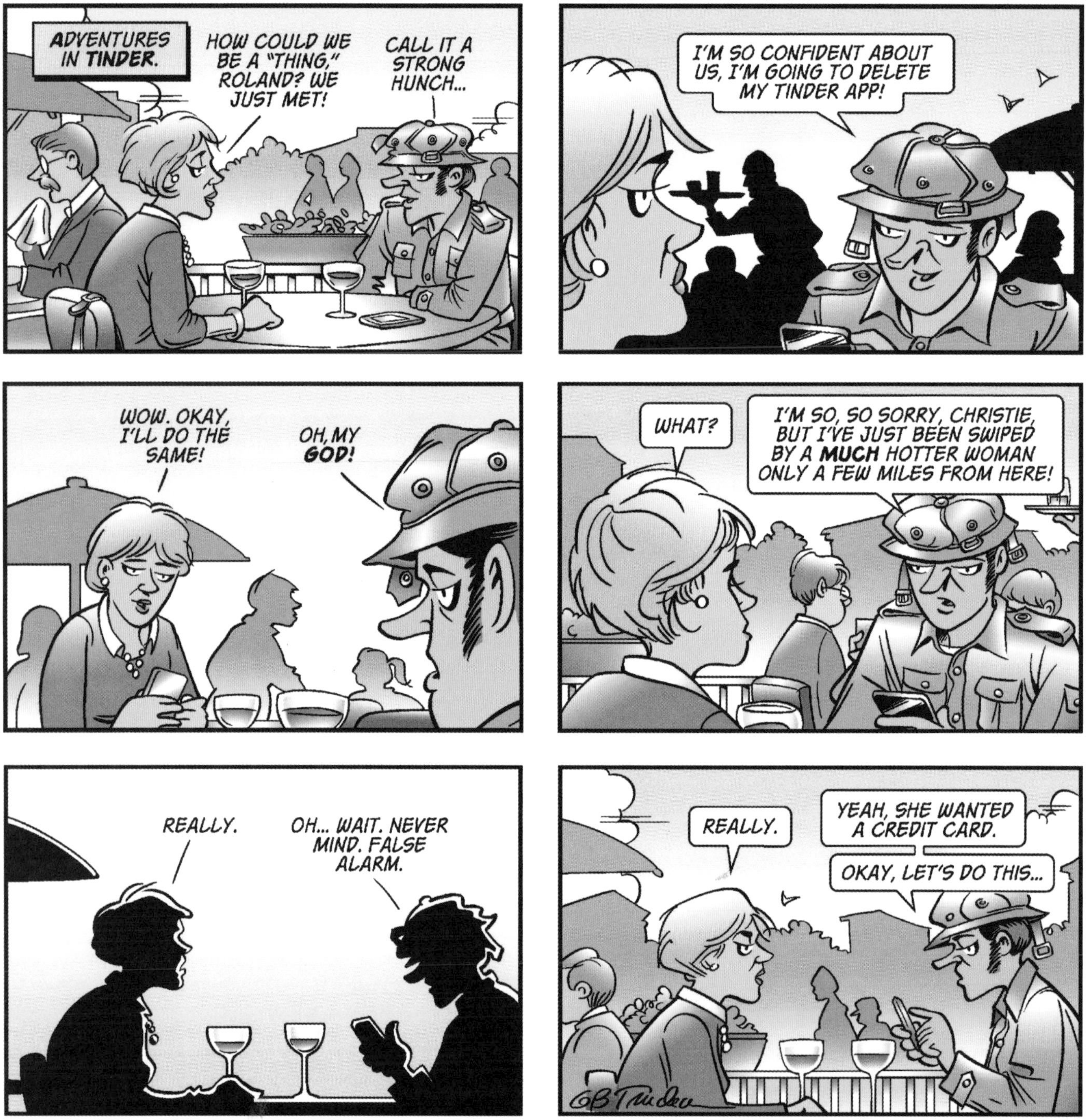
ADVENTURES IN TINDER.
HOW COULD WE BE A "THING," ROLAND? WE JUST MET!
CALL IT A STRONG HUNCH...
I'M SO CONFIDENT ABOUT US, I'M GOING TO DELETE MY TINDER APP!
WOW. OKAY, I'LL DO THE SAME!
OH, MY GOD!
WHAT?
I'M SO, SO SORRY, CHRISTIE, BUT I'VE JUST BEEN SWIPED BY A MUCH HOTTER WOMAN ONLY A FEW MILES FROM HERE!
REALLY.
OH... WAIT. NEVER MIND. FALSE ALARM.
REALLY.
YEAH, SHE WANTED A CREDIT CARD.
OKAY, LET'S DO THIS...
GB Trudeau

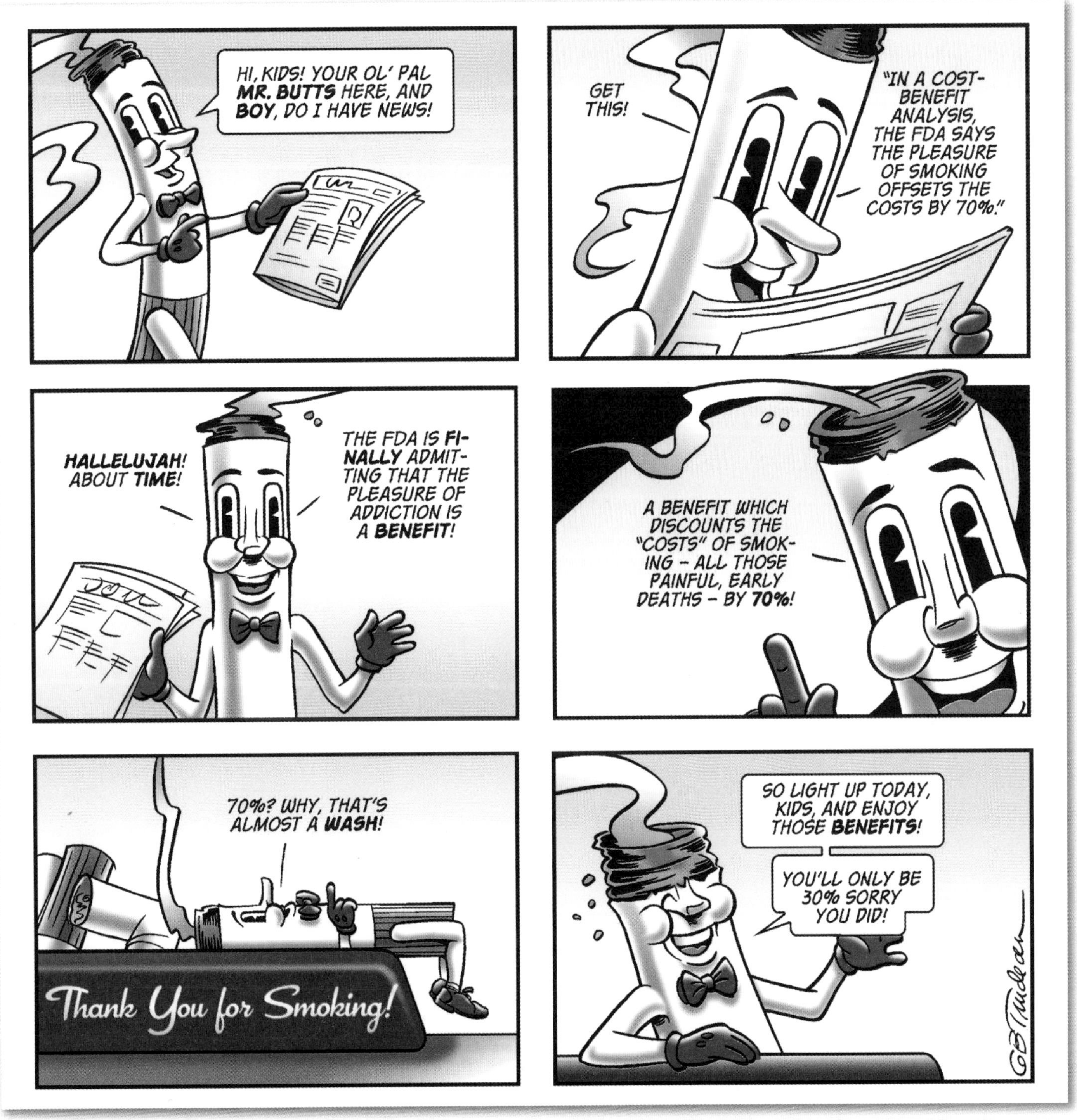
HI, KIDS! YOUR OL' PAL **MR. BUTTS** HERE, AND **BOY**, DO I HAVE NEWS!
GET THIS!
"IN A COST-BENEFIT ANALYSIS, THE FDA SAYS THE PLEASURE OF SMOKING OFFSETS THE COSTS BY 70%."
HALLELUJAH! ABOUT **TIME**!
THE FDA IS **FINALLY** ADMITTING THAT THE PLEASURE OF ADDICTION IS A **BENEFIT**!
A BENEFIT WHICH DISCOUNTS THE "COSTS" OF SMOKING – ALL THOSE PAINFUL, EARLY DEATHS – BY **70%**!
70%? WHY, THAT'S ALMOST A **WASH**!
Thank You for Smoking!
SO LIGHT UP TODAY, KIDS, AND ENJOY THOSE **BENEFITS**!
YOU'LL ONLY BE 30% SORRY YOU DID!
©BTrudeau

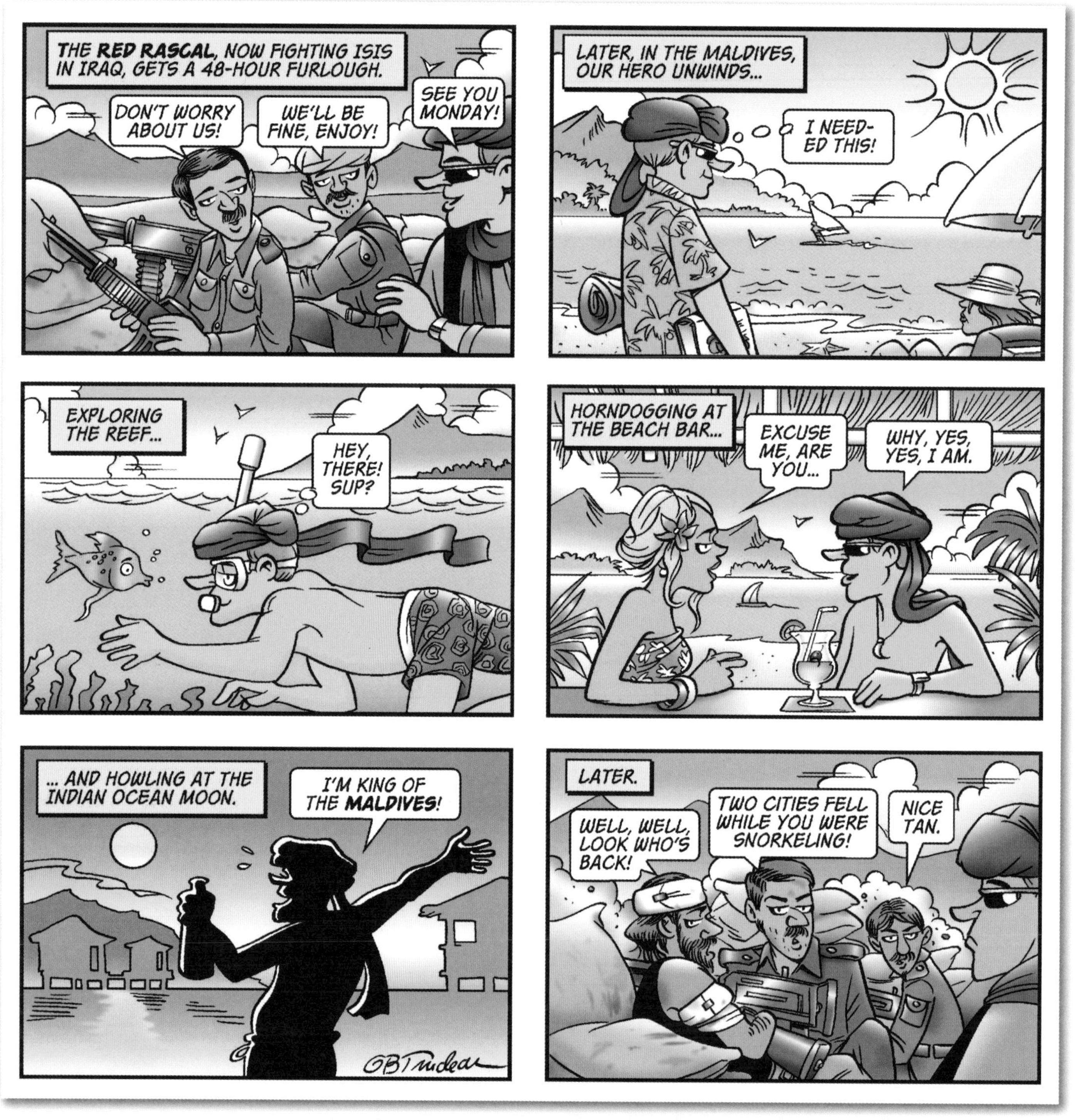
THE RED RASCAL, NOW FIGHTING ISIS IN IRAQ, GETS A 48-HOUR FURLOUGH.
DON'T WORRY ABOUT US!
WE'LL BE FINE, ENJOY!
SEE YOU MONDAY!
LATER, IN THE MALDIVES, OUR HERO UNWINDS...
I NEEDED THIS!
EXPLORING THE REEF...
HEY, THERE! SUP?
HORNDOGGING AT THE BEACH BAR...
EXCUSE ME, ARE YOU...
WHY, YES, YES, I AM.
... AND HOWLING AT THE INDIAN OCEAN MOON.
I'M KING OF THE MALDIVES!
GBTrudeau
LATER.
WELL, WELL, LOOK WHO'S BACK!
TWO CITIES FELL WHILE YOU WERE SNORKELING!
NICE TAN.

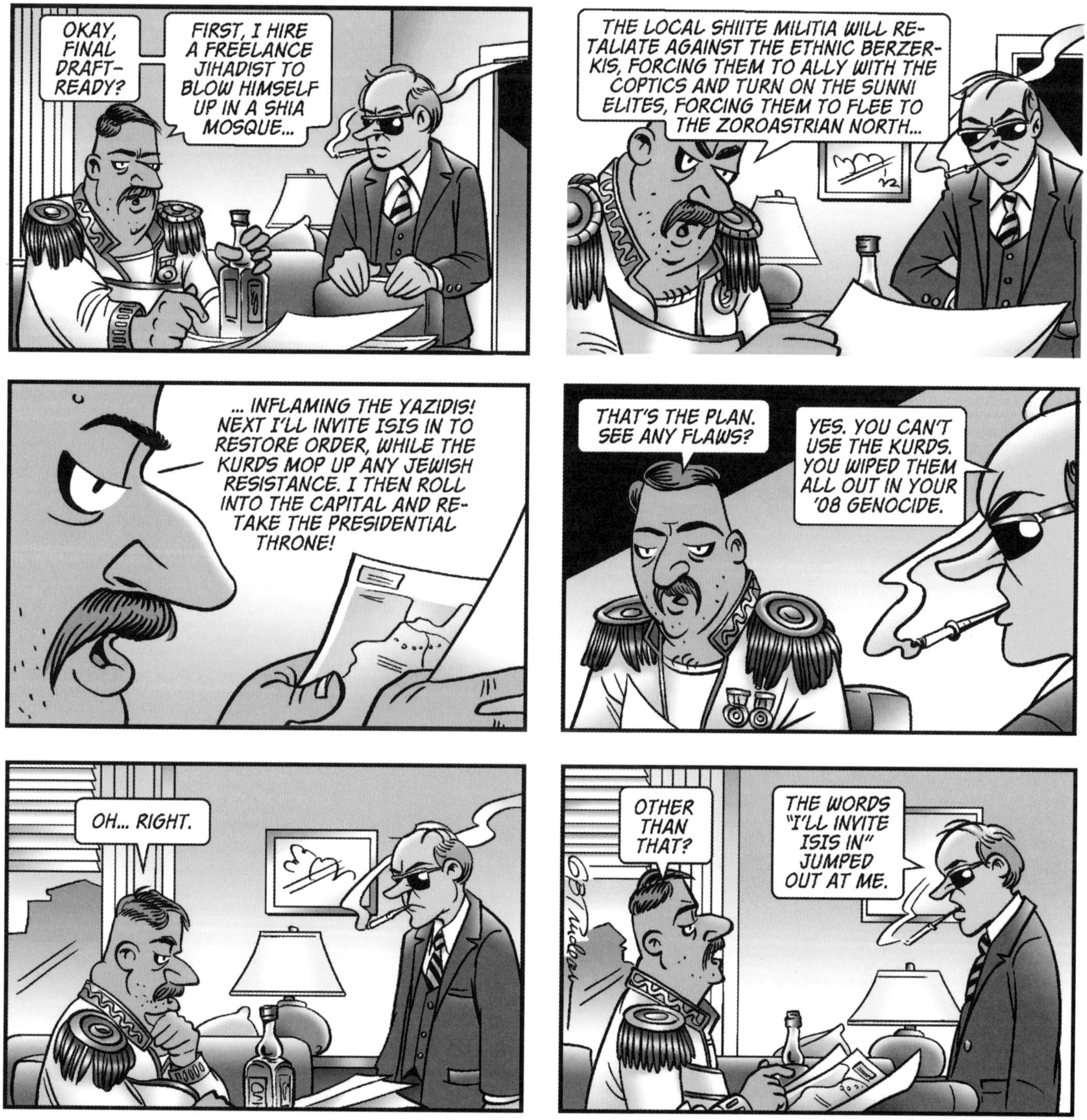
OKAY, FINAL DRAFT—READY?
FIRST, I HIRE A FREELANCE JIHADIST TO BLOW HIMSELF UP IN A SHIA MOSQUE...
THE LOCAL SHIITE MILITIA WILL RETALIATE AGAINST THE ETHNIC BERZERKIS, FORCING THEM TO ALLY WITH THE COPTICS AND TURN ON THE SUNNI ELITES, FORCING THEM TO FLEE TO THE ZOROASTRIAN NORTH...
... INFLAMING THE YAZIDIS! NEXT I'LL INVITE ISIS IN TO RESTORE ORDER, WHILE THE KURDS MOP UP ANY JEWISH RESISTANCE. I THEN ROLL INTO THE CAPITAL AND RETAKE THE PRESIDENTIAL THRONE!
THAT'S THE PLAN. SEE ANY FLAWS?
YES. YOU CAN'T USE THE KURDS. YOU WIPED THEM ALL OUT IN YOUR '08 GENOCIDE.
OH... RIGHT.
OTHER THAN THAT?
THE WORDS "I'LL INVITE ISIS IN" JUMPED OUT AT ME.

SIR, IS IT TRUE THE BOARD JUST RAISED YOUR SALARY TO $7 **MILLION**?
WELL, WE HAD A GREAT QUARTER, DEAN. THE BOARD WAS GRATEFUL.
YES, SIR, BUT THE TIMING'S A LITTLE AWKWARD. OUR GRADUATION RATE HAS PLUMMETED TO 22%.
WELL, THAT'S NOT THE WHOLE PICTURE, IS IT?
WALDEN IS MORE THAN A RAW NUMBER. IT'S ABOUT MAKING MEMORIES – OF FRIENDS AND FOOTBALL GAMES AND BINGES AND HOOKUPS AND CUTTING CLASSES!
NOTHING'S CHANGED. MY GOAL AS AN EDUCATOR IS THE SAME NOW AS IT'S ALWAYS BEEN – TO MAXIMIZE SHAREHOLDER VALUE!
OKAY, SO THERE MAY HAVE BEEN SOME MISSION CREEP.
I GUESS IT HAPPENS.

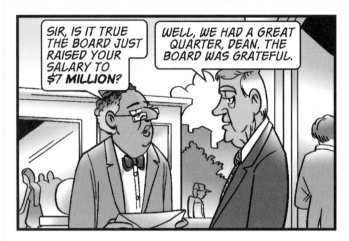

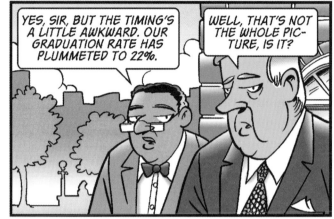

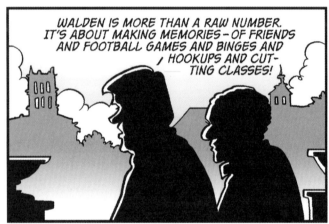

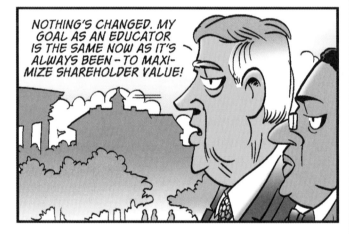

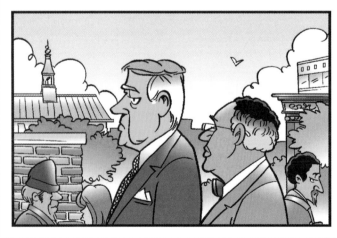

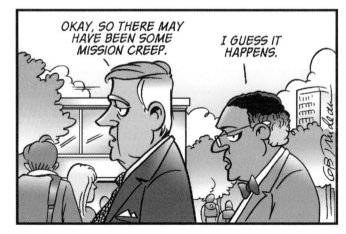

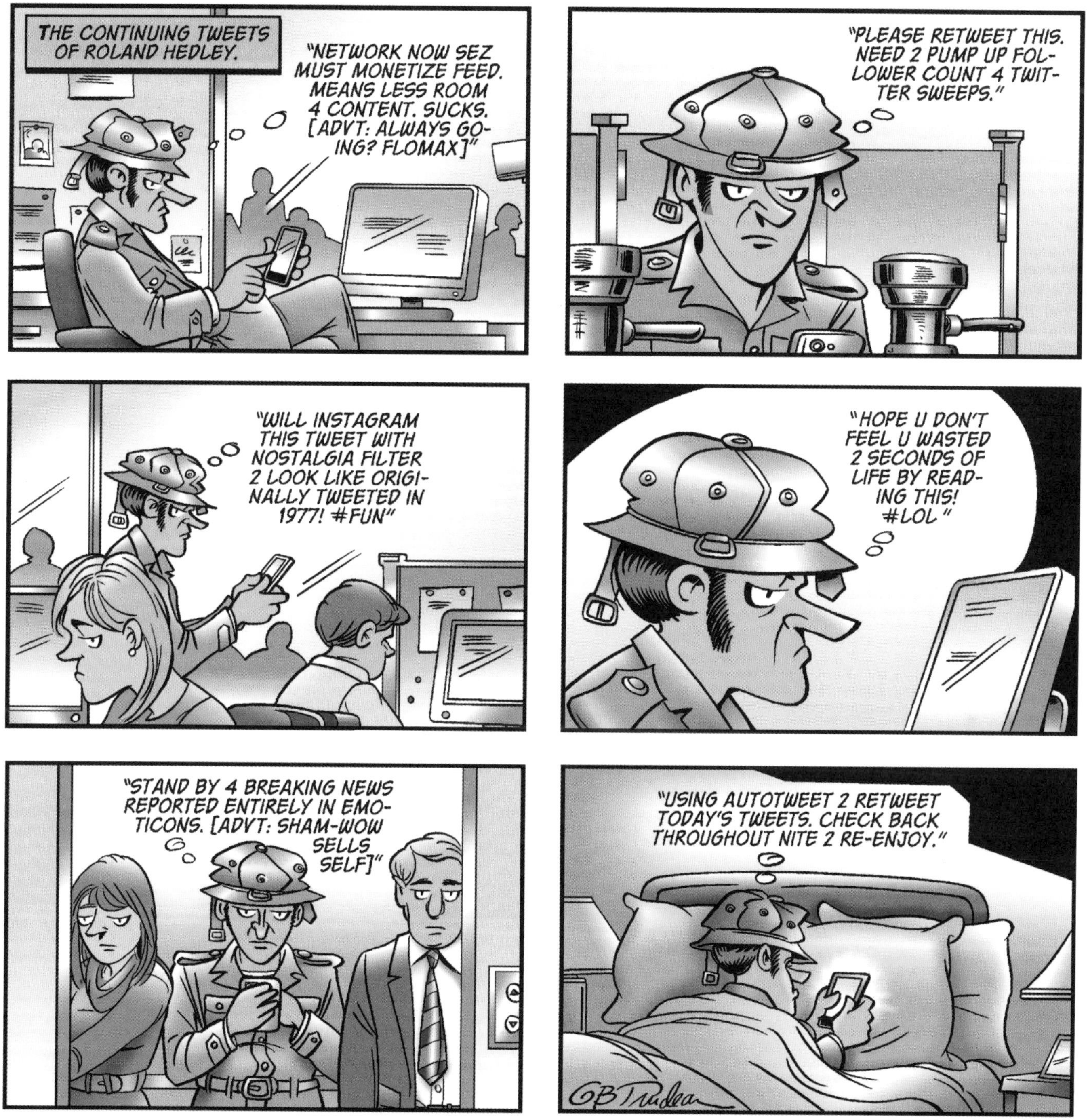
THE CONTINUING TWEETS OF ROLAND HEDLEY.
"NETWORK NOW SEZ MUST MONETIZE FEED. MEANS LESS ROOM 4 CONTENT. SUCKS. [ADVT: ALWAYS GOING? FLOMAX]"
"PLEASE RETWEET THIS. NEED 2 PUMP UP FOLLOWER COUNT 4 TWITTER SWEEPS."
"WILL INSTAGRAM THIS TWEET WITH NOSTALGIA FILTER 2 LOOK LIKE ORIGINALLY TWEETED IN 1977! #FUN"
"HOPE U DON'T FEEL U WASTED 2 SECONDS OF LIFE BY READING THIS! #LOL"
"STAND BY 4 BREAKING NEWS REPORTED ENTIRELY IN EMOTICONS. [ADVT: SHAM-WOW SELLS SELF]"
"USING AUTOTWEET 2 RETWEET TODAY'S TWEETS. CHECK BACK THROUGHOUT NITE 2 RE-ENJOY."
GBTrudeau

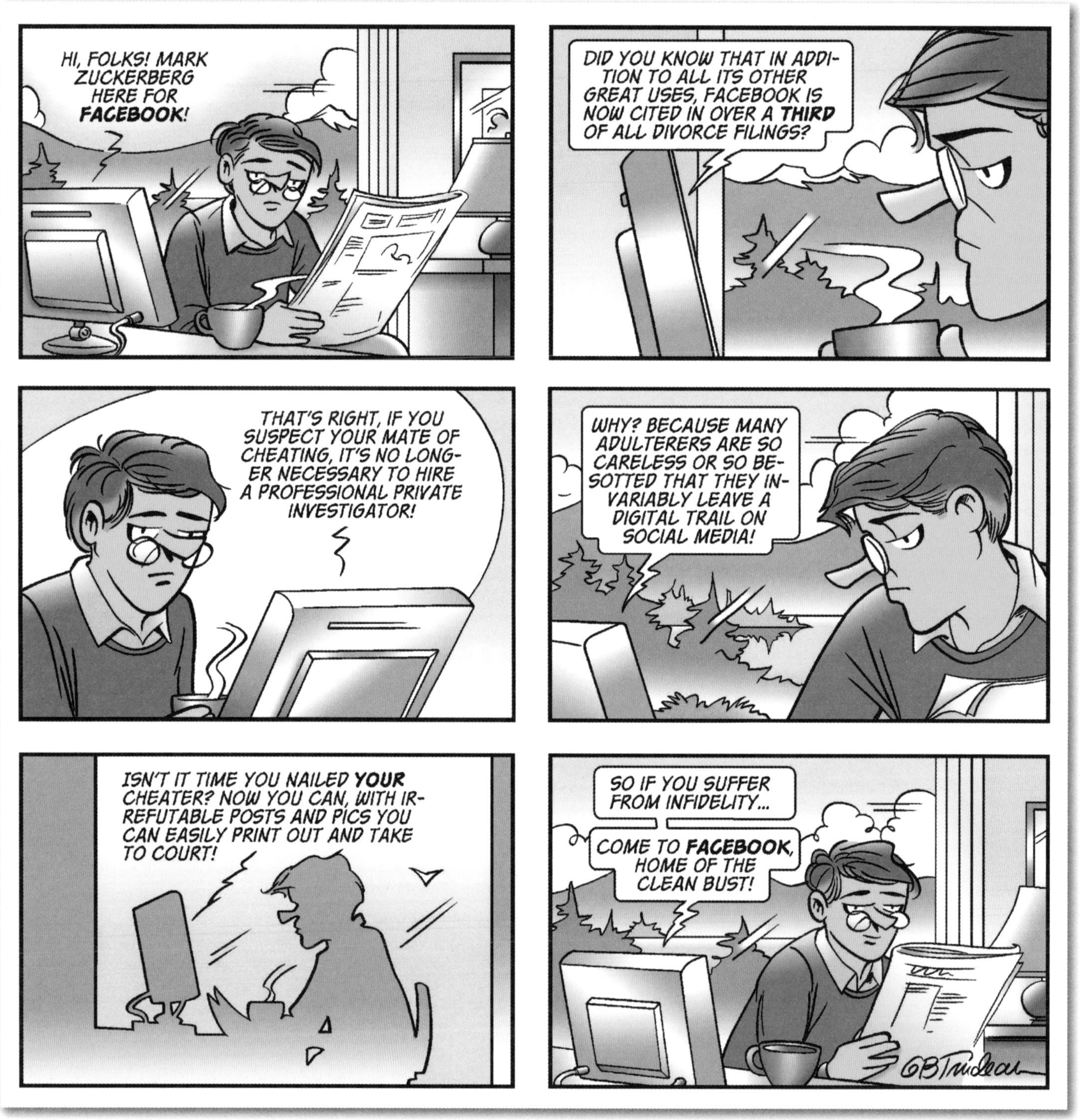
HI, FOLKS! MARK ZUCKERBERG HERE FOR **FACEBOOK**!
DID YOU KNOW THAT IN ADDITION TO ALL ITS OTHER GREAT USES, FACEBOOK IS NOW CITED IN OVER A **THIRD** OF ALL DIVORCE FILINGS?
THAT'S RIGHT, IF YOU SUSPECT YOUR MATE OF CHEATING, IT'S NO LONGER NECESSARY TO HIRE A PROFESSIONAL PRIVATE INVESTIGATOR!
WHY? BECAUSE MANY ADULTERERS ARE SO CARELESS OR SO BESOTTED THAT THEY INVARIABLY LEAVE A DIGITAL TRAIL ON SOCIAL MEDIA!
ISN'T IT TIME YOU NAILED **YOUR** CHEATER? NOW YOU CAN, WITH IRREFUTABLE POSTS AND PICS YOU CAN EASILY PRINT OUT AND TAKE TO COURT!
SO IF YOU SUFFER FROM INFIDELITY...
COME TO **FACEBOOK**, HOME OF THE CLEAN BUST!
GBTrudeau

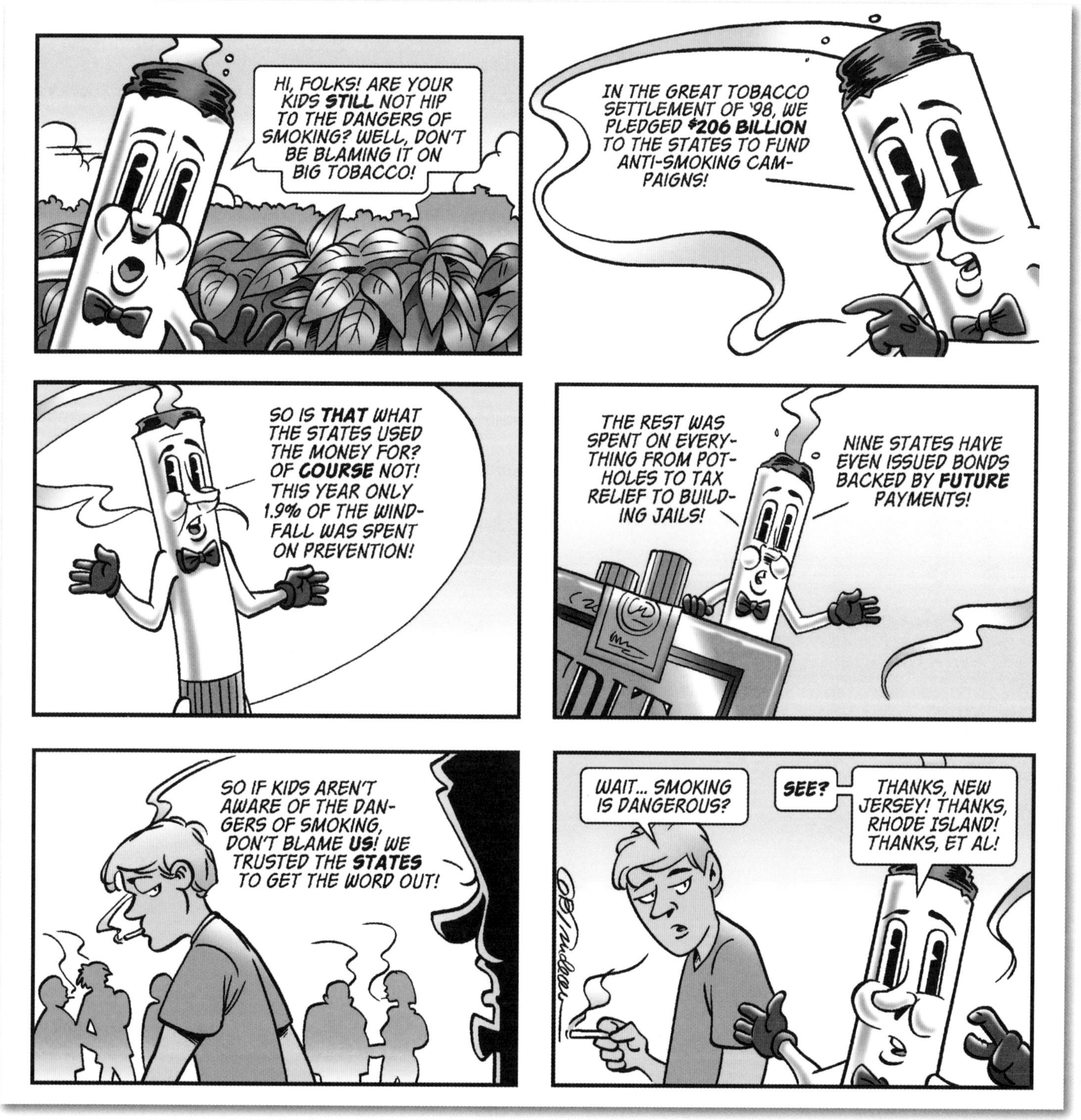
HI, FOLKS! ARE YOUR KIDS **STILL** NOT HIP TO THE DANGERS OF SMOKING? WELL, DON'T BE BLAMING IT ON BIG TOBACCO!
IN THE GREAT TOBACCO SETTLEMENT OF '98, WE PLEDGED **$206 BILLION** TO THE STATES TO FUND ANTI-SMOKING CAMPAIGNS!
SO IS **THAT** WHAT THE STATES USED THE MONEY FOR? OF **COURSE** NOT! THIS YEAR ONLY 1.9% OF THE WINDFALL WAS SPENT ON PREVENTION!
THE REST WAS SPENT ON EVERYTHING FROM POTHOLES TO TAX RELIEF TO BUILDING JAILS!
NINE STATES HAVE EVEN ISSUED BONDS BACKED BY **FUTURE** PAYMENTS!
SO IF KIDS AREN'T AWARE OF THE DANGERS OF SMOKING, DON'T BLAME **US**! WE TRUSTED THE **STATES** TO GET THE WORD OUT!
WAIT... SMOKING IS DANGEROUS?
SEE?
THANKS, NEW JERSEY! THANKS, RHODE ISLAND! THANKS, ET AL!

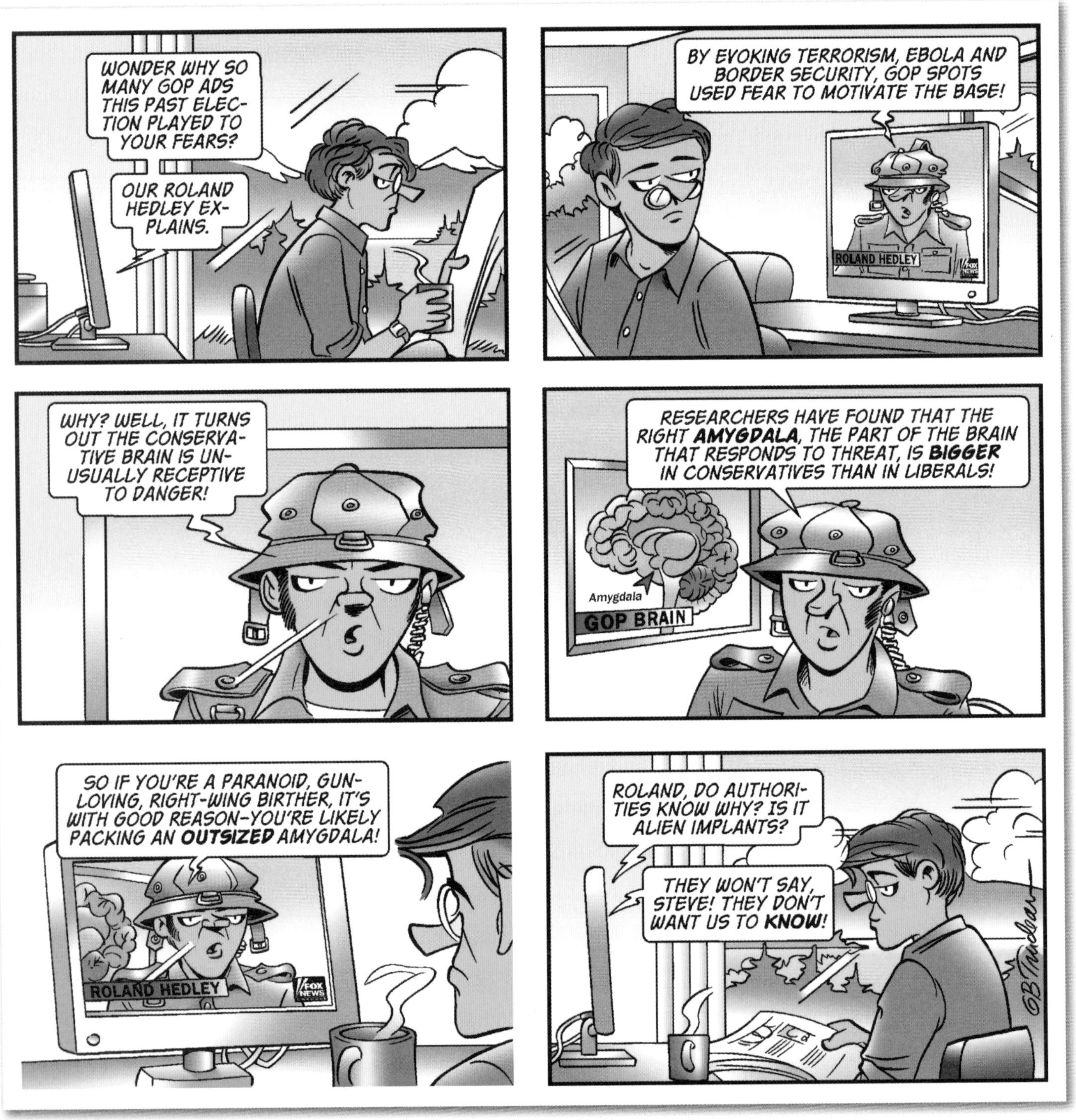
WONDER WHY SO MANY GOP ADS THIS PAST ELECTION PLAYED TO YOUR FEARS?
OUR ROLAND HEDLEY EXPLAINS.
BY EVOKING TERRORISM, EBOLA AND BORDER SECURITY, GOP SPOTS USED FEAR TO MOTIVATE THE BASE!
ROLAND HEDLEY
WHY? WELL, IT TURNS OUT THE CONSERVATIVE BRAIN IS UNUSUALLY RECEPTIVE TO DANGER!
RESEARCHERS HAVE FOUND THAT THE RIGHT AMYGDALA, THE PART OF THE BRAIN THAT RESPONDS TO THREAT, IS BIGGER IN CONSERVATIVES THAN IN LIBERALS!
Amygdala
GOP BRAIN
SO IF YOU'RE A PARANOID, GUN-LOVING, RIGHT-WING BIRTHER, IT'S WITH GOOD REASON—YOU'RE LIKELY PACKING AN OUTSIZED AMYGDALA!
ROLAND HEDLEY
ROLAND, DO AUTHORITIES KNOW WHY? IS IT ALIEN IMPLANTS?
THEY WON'T SAY, STEVE! THEY DON'T WANT US TO KNOW!
GBTrudeau

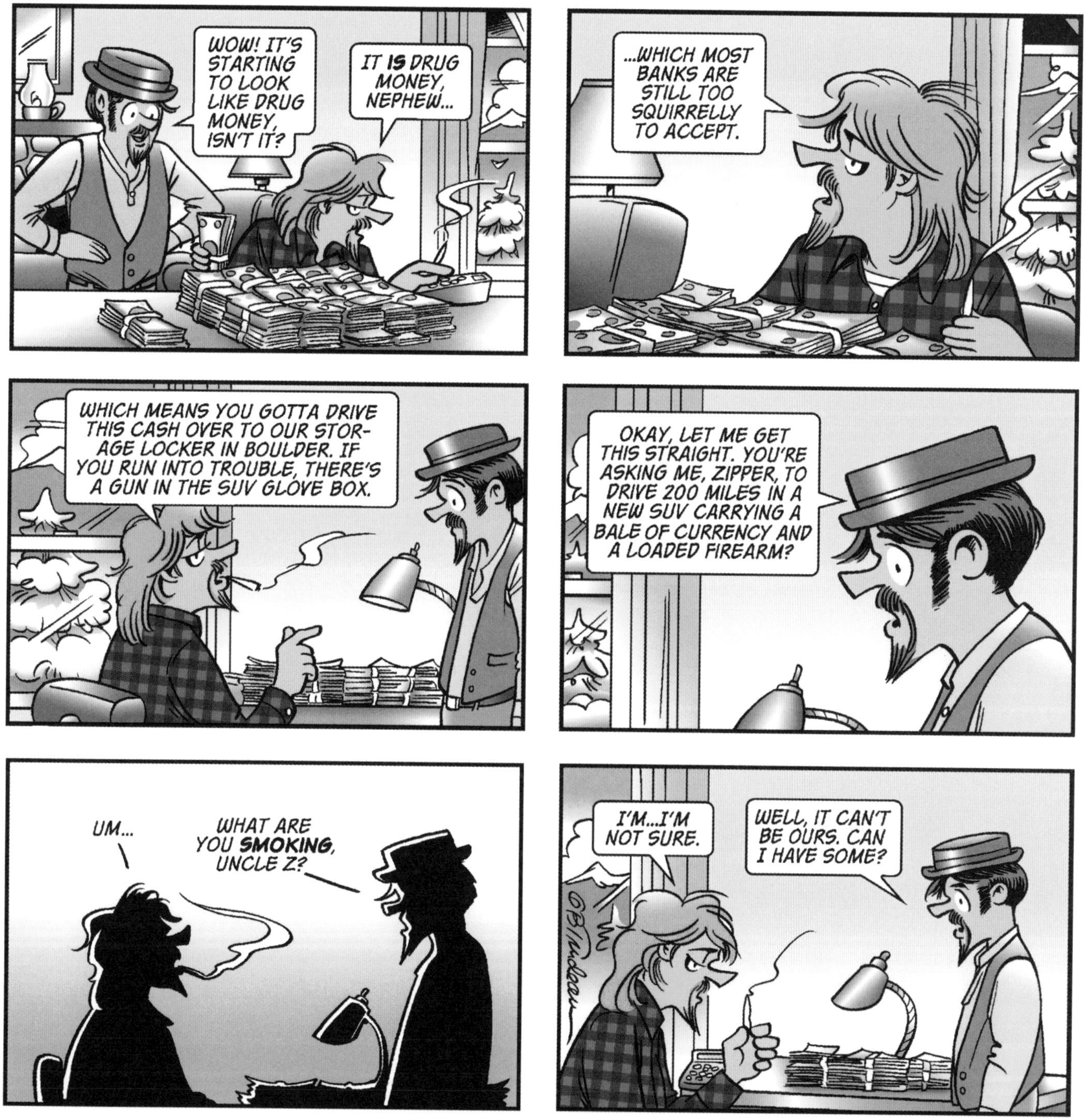
WOW! IT'S STARTING TO LOOK LIKE DRUG MONEY, ISN'T IT?
IT **IS** DRUG MONEY, NEPHEW...
...WHICH MOST BANKS ARE STILL TOO SQUIRRELLY TO ACCEPT.
WHICH MEANS YOU GOTTA DRIVE THIS CASH OVER TO OUR STORAGE LOCKER IN BOULDER. IF YOU RUN INTO TROUBLE, THERE'S A GUN IN THE SUV GLOVE BOX.
OKAY, LET ME GET THIS STRAIGHT. YOU'RE ASKING ME, ZIPPER, TO DRIVE 200 MILES IN A NEW SUV CARRYING A BALE OF CURRENCY AND A LOADED FIREARM?
UM...
WHAT ARE YOU **SMOKING**, UNCLE Z?
I'M...I'M NOT SURE.
WELL, IT CAN'T BE OURS. CAN I HAVE SOME?

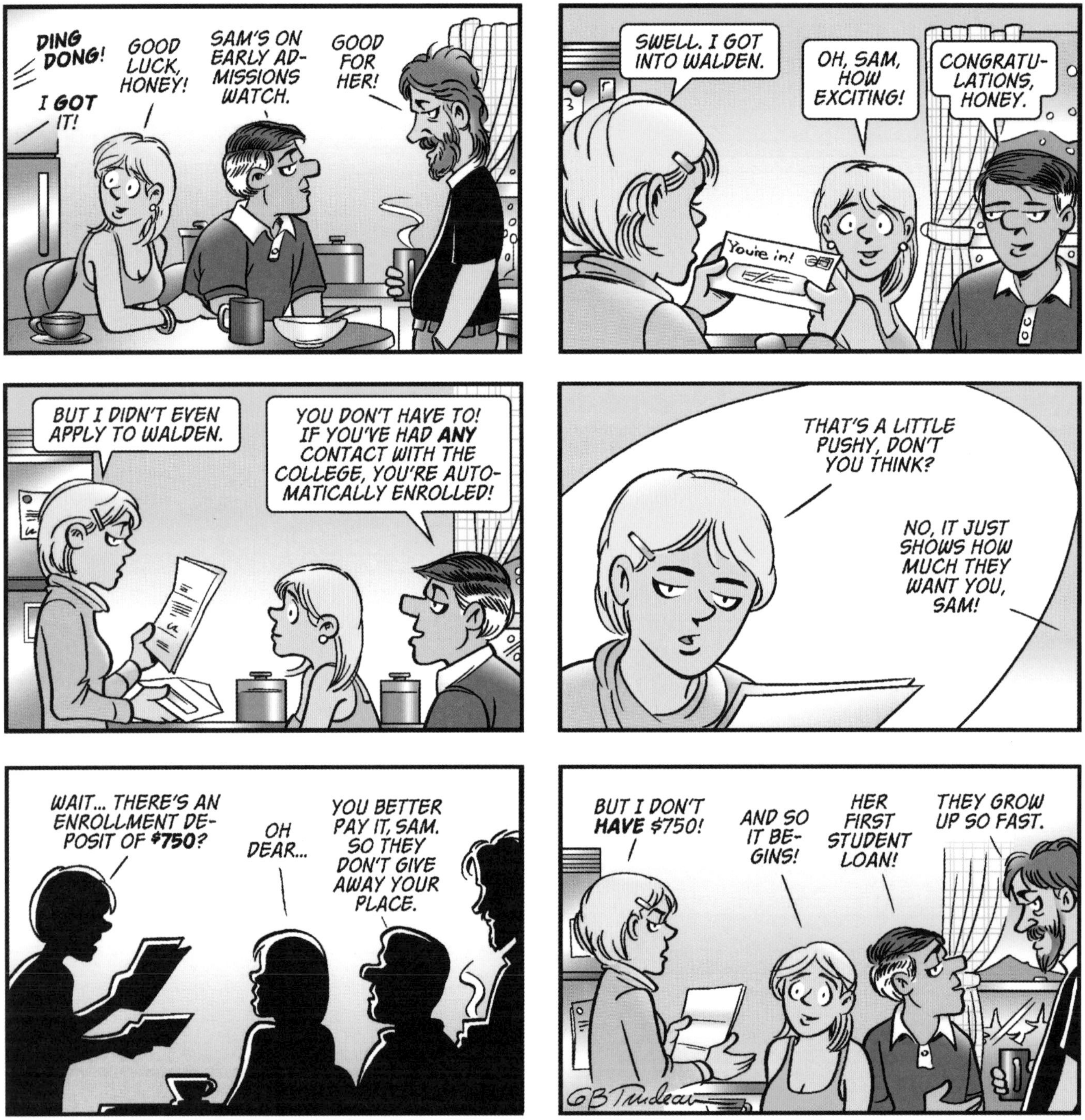
DING DONG!
I GOT IT!
GOOD LUCK, HONEY!
SAM'S ON EARLY ADMISSIONS WATCH.
GOOD FOR HER!
SWELL. I GOT INTO WALDEN.
You're in!
OH, SAM, HOW EXCITING!
CONGRATULATIONS, HONEY.
BUT I DIDN'T EVEN APPLY TO WALDEN.
YOU DON'T HAVE TO! IF YOU'VE HAD **ANY** CONTACT WITH THE COLLEGE, YOU'RE AUTOMATICALLY ENROLLED!
THAT'S A LITTLE PUSHY, DON'T YOU THINK?
NO, IT JUST SHOWS HOW MUCH THEY WANT YOU, SAM!
WAIT... THERE'S AN ENROLLMENT DEPOSIT OF **$750**?
OH DEAR...
YOU BETTER PAY IT, SAM. SO THEY DON'T GIVE AWAY YOUR PLACE.
BUT I DON'T **HAVE** $750!
AND SO IT BEGINS!
HER FIRST STUDENT LOAN!
THEY GROW UP SO FAST.
GBTrudeau

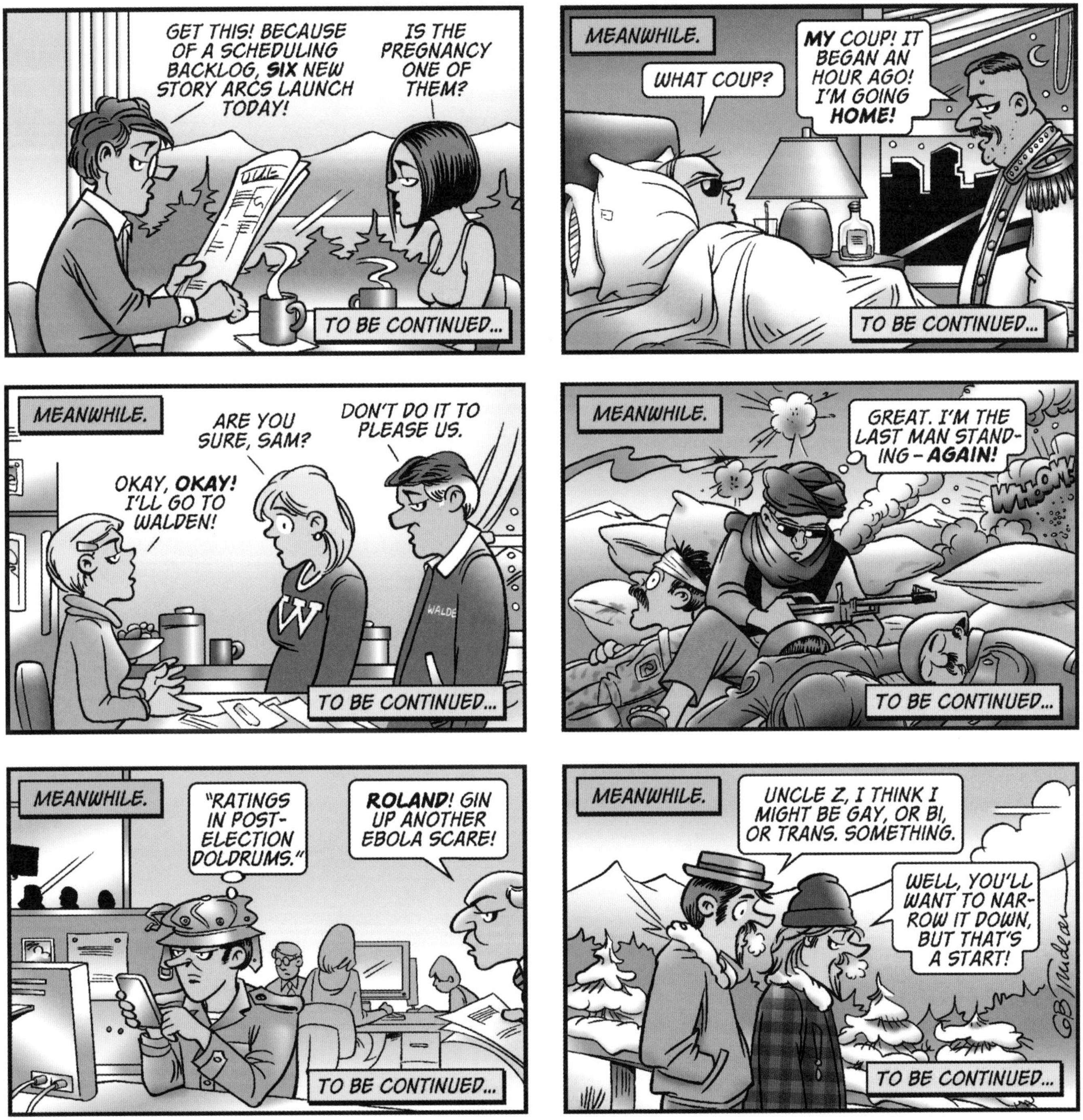
GET THIS! BECAUSE OF A SCHEDULING BACKLOG, SIX NEW STORY ARCS LAUNCH TODAY!
IS THE PREGNANCY ONE OF THEM?
TO BE CONTINUED...
MEANWHILE.
WHAT COUP?
MY COUP! IT BEGAN AN HOUR AGO! I'M GOING HOME!
TO BE CONTINUED...
MEANWHILE.
OKAY, OKAY! I'LL GO TO WALDEN!
ARE YOU SURE, SAM?
DON'T DO IT TO PLEASE US.
TO BE CONTINUED...
MEANWHILE.
GREAT. I'M THE LAST MAN STANDING–AGAIN!
TO BE CONTINUED...
MEANWHILE.
"RATINGS IN POST-ELECTION DOLDRUMS."
ROLAND! GIN UP ANOTHER EBOLA SCARE!
TO BE CONTINUED...
MEANWHILE.
UNCLE Z, I THINK I MIGHT BE GAY, OR BI, OR TRANS. SOMETHING.
WELL, YOU'LL WANT TO NARROW IT DOWN, BUT THAT'S A START!
TO BE CONTINUED...

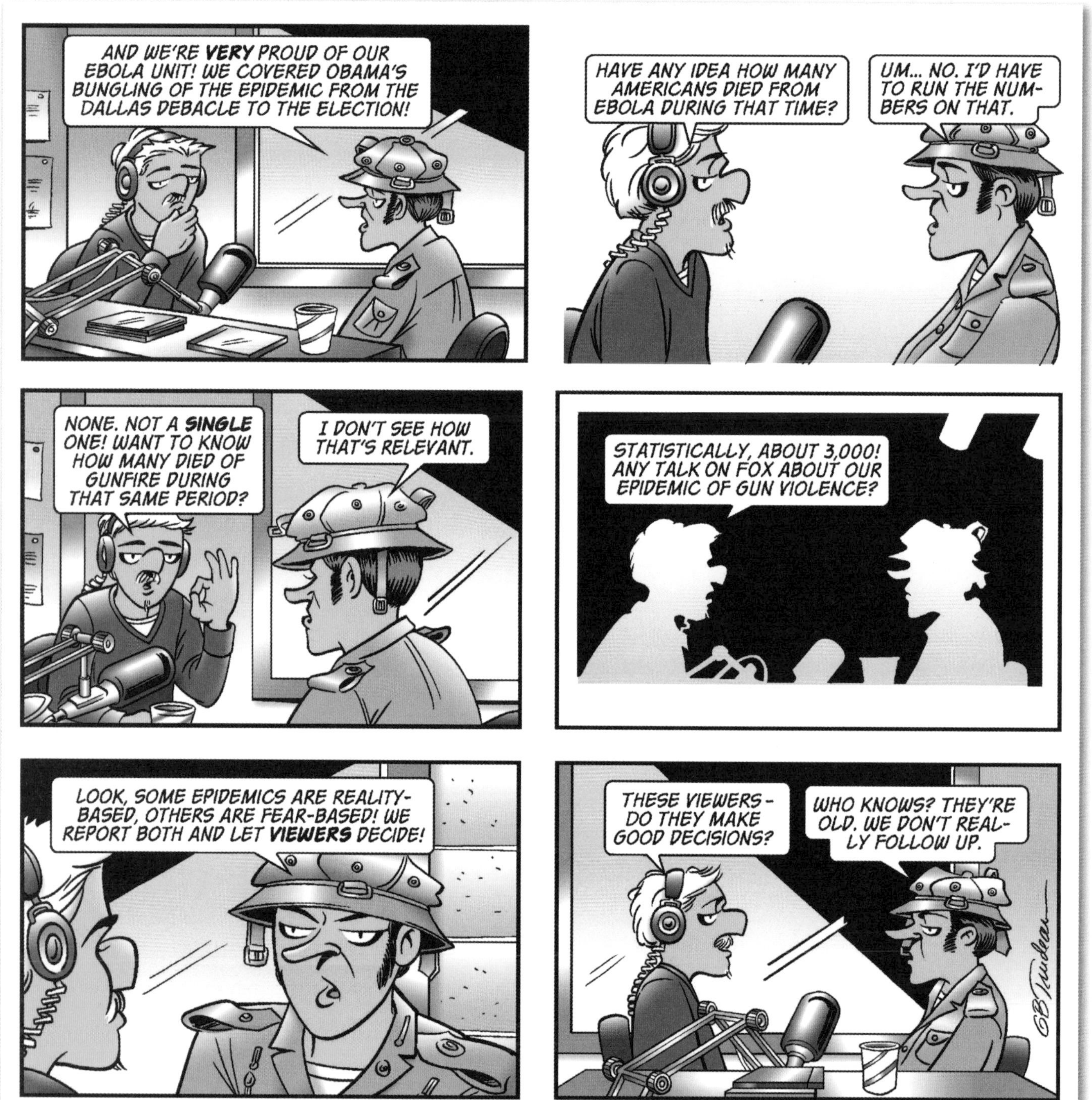
AND WE'RE **VERY** PROUD OF OUR EBOLA UNIT! WE COVERED OBAMA'S BUNGLING OF THE EPIDEMIC FROM THE DALLAS DEBACLE TO THE ELECTION!
HAVE ANY IDEA HOW MANY AMERICANS DIED FROM EBOLA DURING THAT TIME?
UM... NO. I'D HAVE TO RUN THE NUMBERS ON THAT.
NONE. NOT A **SINGLE** ONE! WANT TO KNOW HOW MANY DIED OF GUNFIRE DURING THAT SAME PERIOD?
I DON'T SEE HOW THAT'S RELEVANT.
STATISTICALLY, ABOUT 3,000! ANY TALK ON FOX ABOUT OUR EPIDEMIC OF GUN VIOLENCE?
LOOK, SOME EPIDEMICS ARE REALITY-BASED, OTHERS ARE FEAR-BASED! WE REPORT BOTH AND LET **VIEWERS** DECIDE!
THESE VIEWERS - DO THEY MAKE GOOD DECISIONS?
WHO KNOWS? THEY'RE OLD. WE DON'T REALLY FOLLOW UP.
GBTrudeau

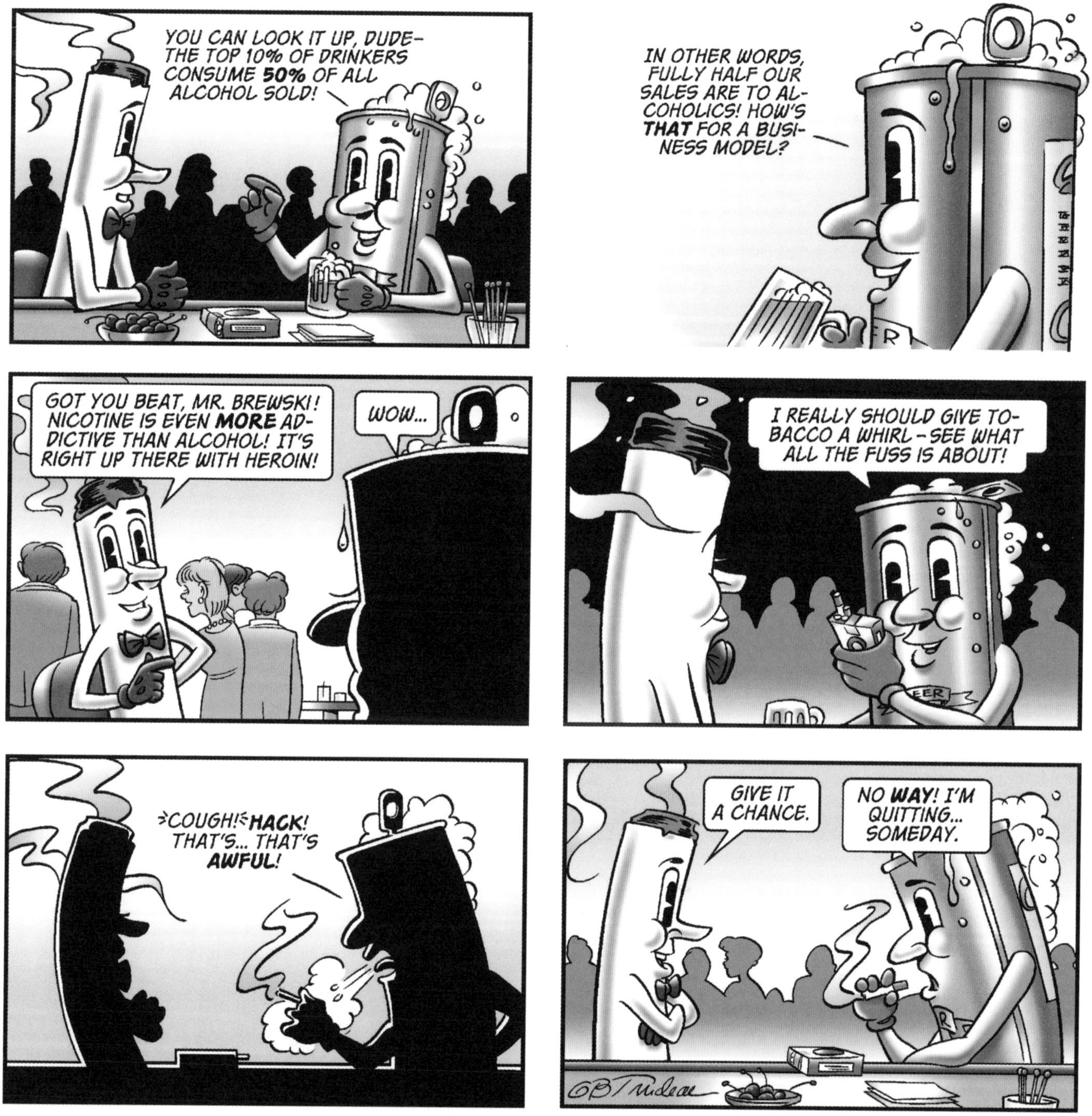
YOU CAN LOOK IT UP, DUDE— THE TOP 10% OF DRINKERS CONSUME 50% OF ALL ALCOHOL SOLD!
IN OTHER WORDS, FULLY HALF OUR SALES ARE TO ALCOHOLICS! HOW'S THAT FOR A BUSINESS MODEL?
GOT YOU BEAT, MR. BREWSKI! NICOTINE IS EVEN MORE ADDICTIVE THAN ALCOHOL! IT'S RIGHT UP THERE WITH HEROIN!
WOW...
I REALLY SHOULD GIVE TOBACCO A WHIRL – SEE WHAT ALL THE FUSS IS ABOUT!
COUGH! HACK! THAT'S... THAT'S AWFUL!
GIVE IT A CHANCE.
NO WAY! I'M QUITTING... SOMEDAY.
GB Trudeau

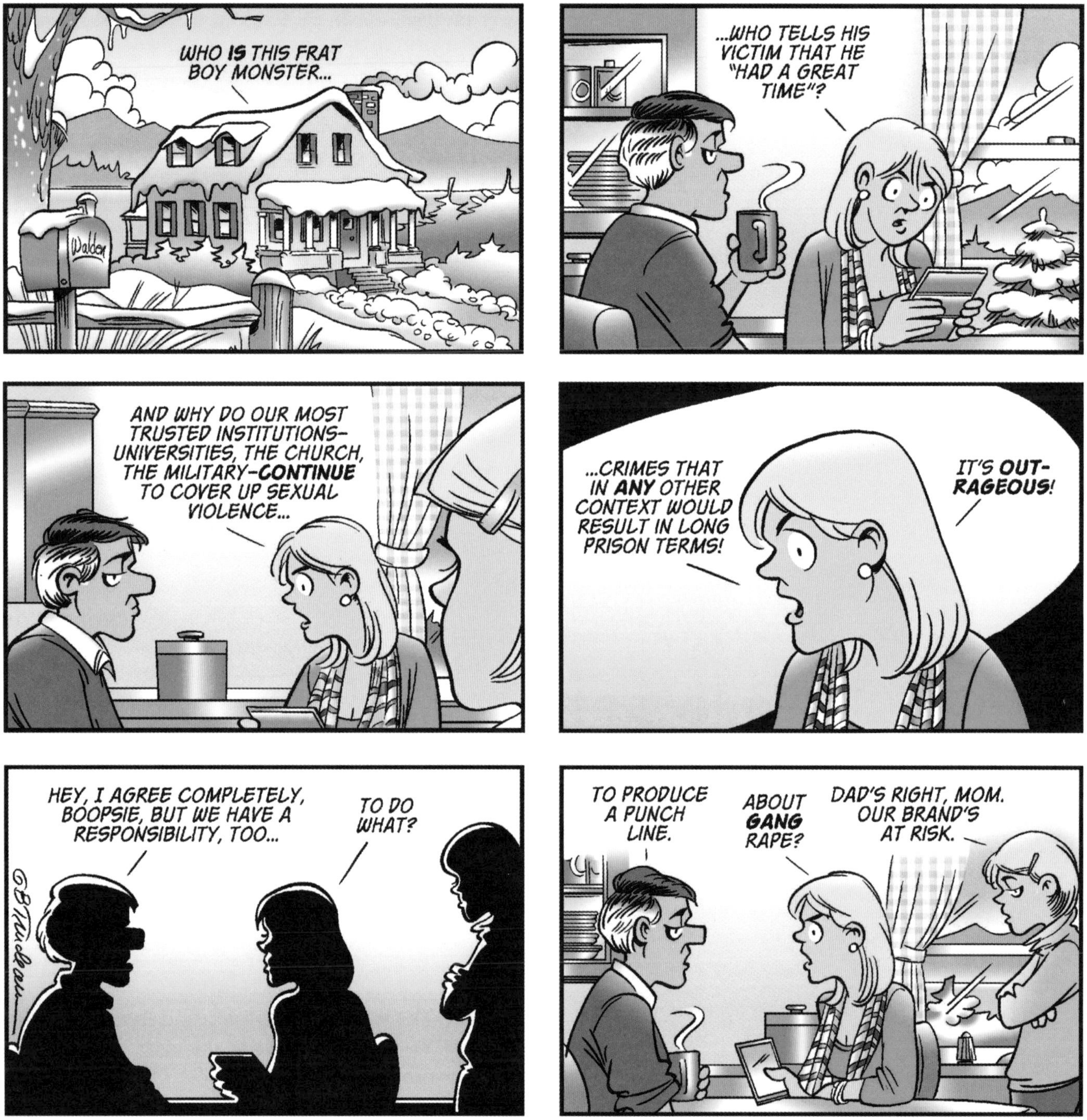
WHO IS THIS FRAT BOY MONSTER...
Walden
...WHO TELLS HIS VICTIM THAT HE "HAD A GREAT TIME"?
AND WHY DO OUR MOST TRUSTED INSTITUTIONS–UNIVERSITIES, THE CHURCH, THE MILITARY–CONTINUE TO COVER UP SEXUAL VIOLENCE...
...CRIMES THAT IN ANY OTHER CONTEXT WOULD RESULT IN LONG PRISON TERMS!
IT'S OUTRAGEOUS!
HEY, I AGREE COMPLETELY, BOOPSIE, BUT WE HAVE A RESPONSIBILITY, TOO...
TO DO WHAT?
TO PRODUCE A PUNCH LINE.
ABOUT GANG RAPE?
DAD'S RIGHT, MOM. OUR BRAND'S AT RISK.

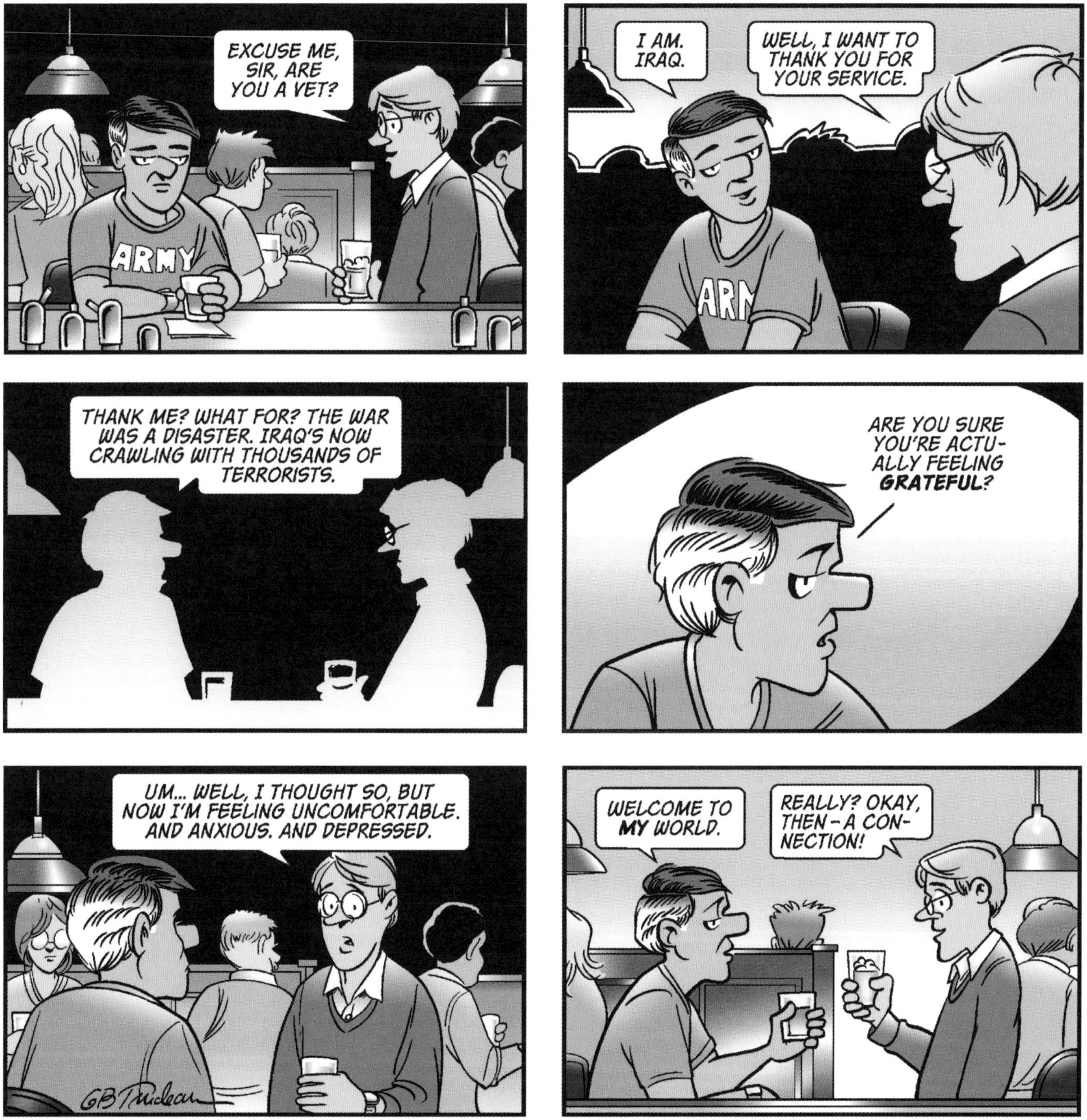
EXCUSE ME, SIR, ARE YOU A VET?
I AM. IRAQ.
WELL, I WANT TO THANK YOU FOR YOUR SERVICE.
THANK ME? WHAT FOR? THE WAR WAS A DISASTER. IRAQ'S NOW CRAWLING WITH THOUSANDS OF TERRORISTS.
ARE YOU SURE YOU'RE ACTU-ALLY FEELING GRATEFUL?
UM... WELL, I THOUGHT SO, BUT NOW I'M FEELING UNCOMFORTABLE. AND ANXIOUS. AND DEPRESSED.
WELCOME TO MY WORLD.
REALLY? OKAY, THEN – A CON-NECTION!
ARMY
GB Trudeau

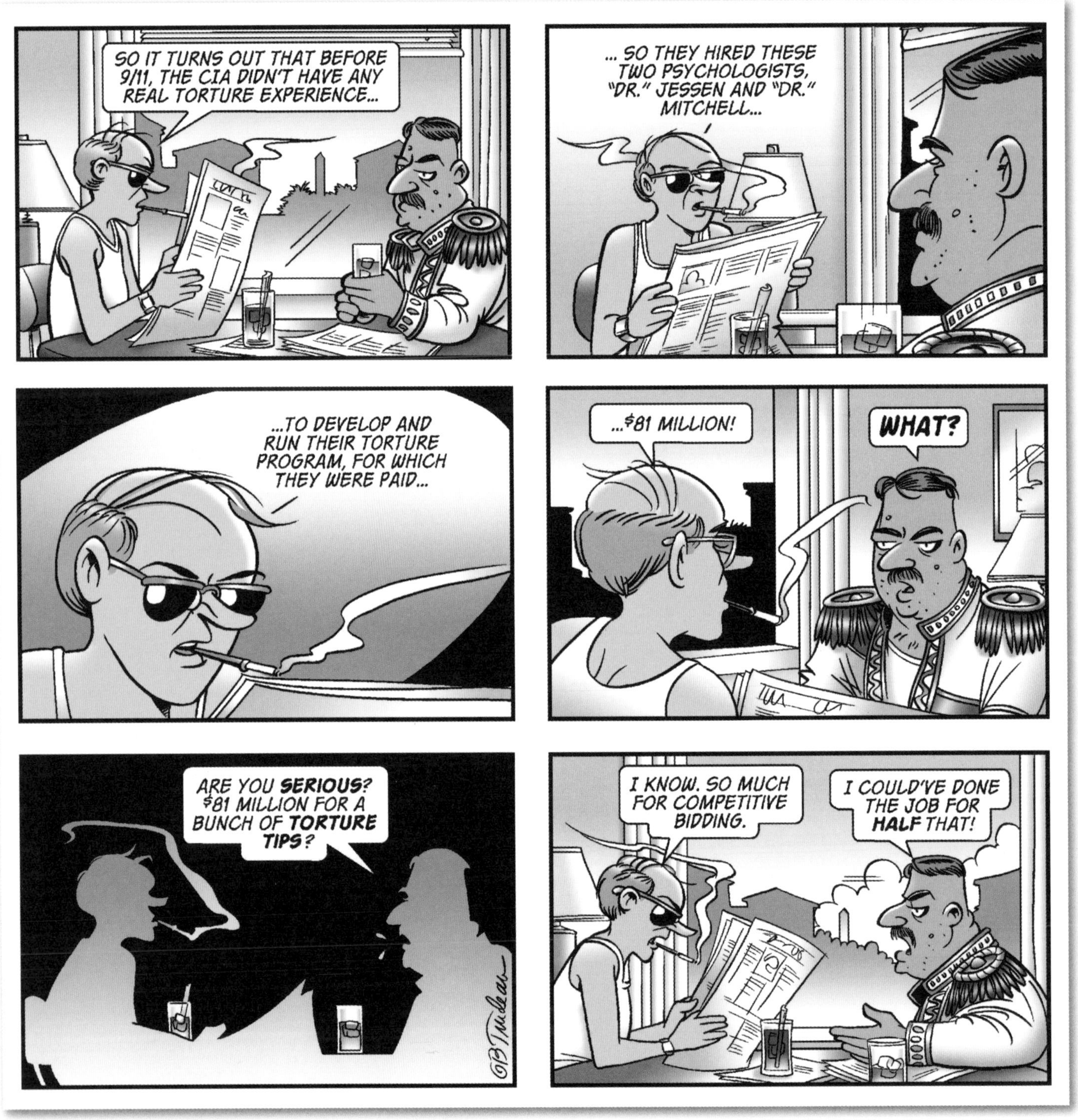
SO IT TURNS OUT THAT BEFORE 9/11, THE CIA DIDN'T HAVE ANY REAL TORTURE EXPERIENCE...
... SO THEY HIRED THESE TWO PSYCHOLOGISTS, "DR." JESSEN AND "DR." MITCHELL...
...TO DEVELOP AND RUN THEIR TORTURE PROGRAM, FOR WHICH THEY WERE PAID...
...$81 MILLION!
WHAT?
ARE YOU **SERIOUS**? $81 MILLION FOR A BUNCH OF **TORTURE TIPS**?
I KNOW. SO MUCH FOR COMPETITIVE BIDDING.
I COULD'VE DONE THE JOB FOR **HALF** THAT!
©B Trudeau

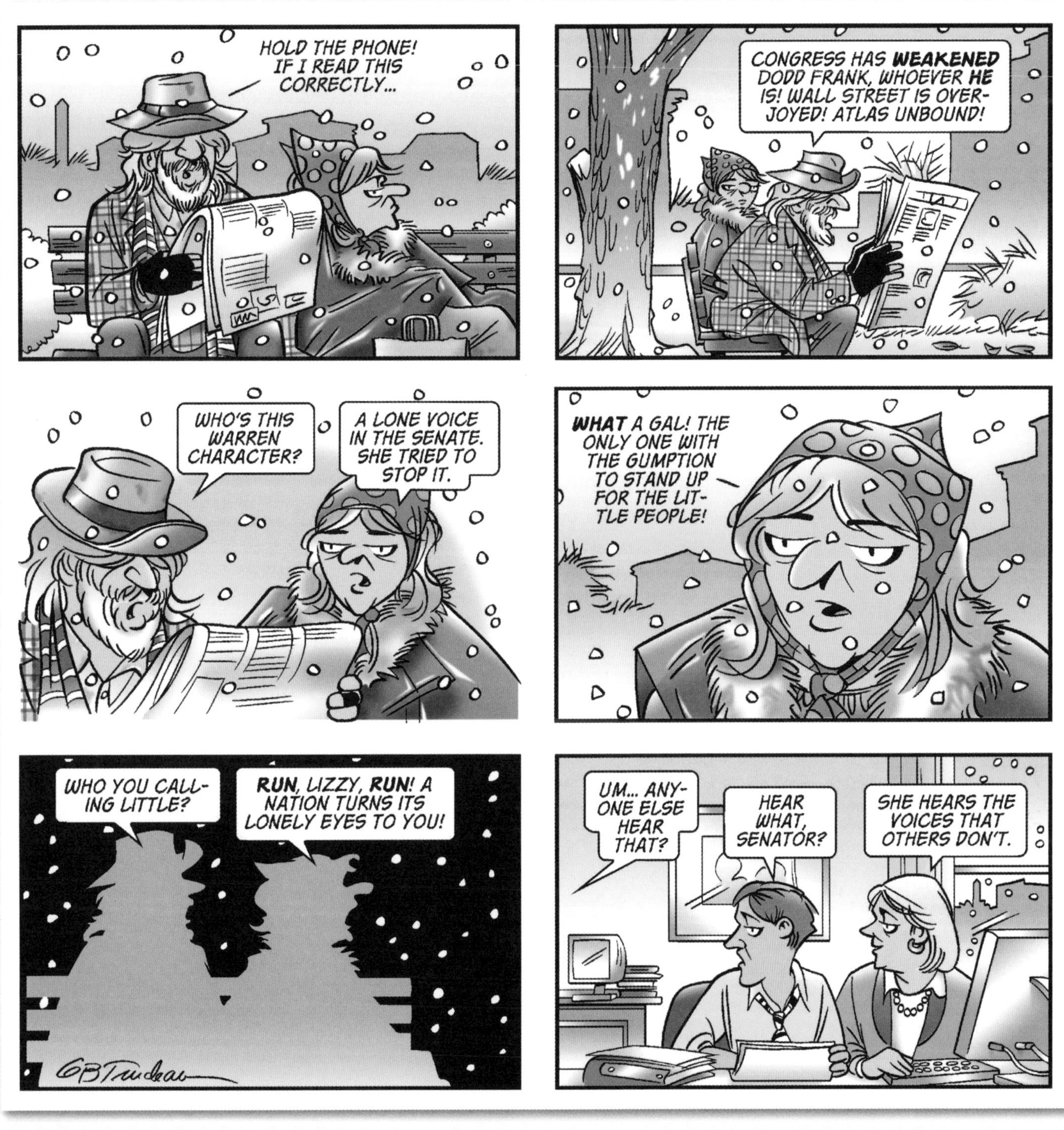
HOLD THE PHONE! IF I READ THIS CORRECTLY...
CONGRESS HAS **WEAKENED** DODD FRANK, WHOEVER **HE** IS! WALL STREET IS OVER-JOYED! ATLAS UNBOUND!
WHO'S THIS WARREN CHARACTER?
A LONE VOICE IN THE SENATE. SHE TRIED TO STOP IT.
WHAT A GAL! THE ONLY ONE WITH THE GUMPTION TO STAND UP FOR THE LIT-TLE PEOPLE!
WHO YOU CALL-ING LITTLE?
RUN, LIZZY, **RUN**! A NATION TURNS ITS LONELY EYES TO YOU!
GBTrudeau
UM... ANY-ONE ELSE HEAR THAT?
HEAR WHAT, SENATOR?
SHE HEARS THE VOICES THAT OTHERS DON'T.

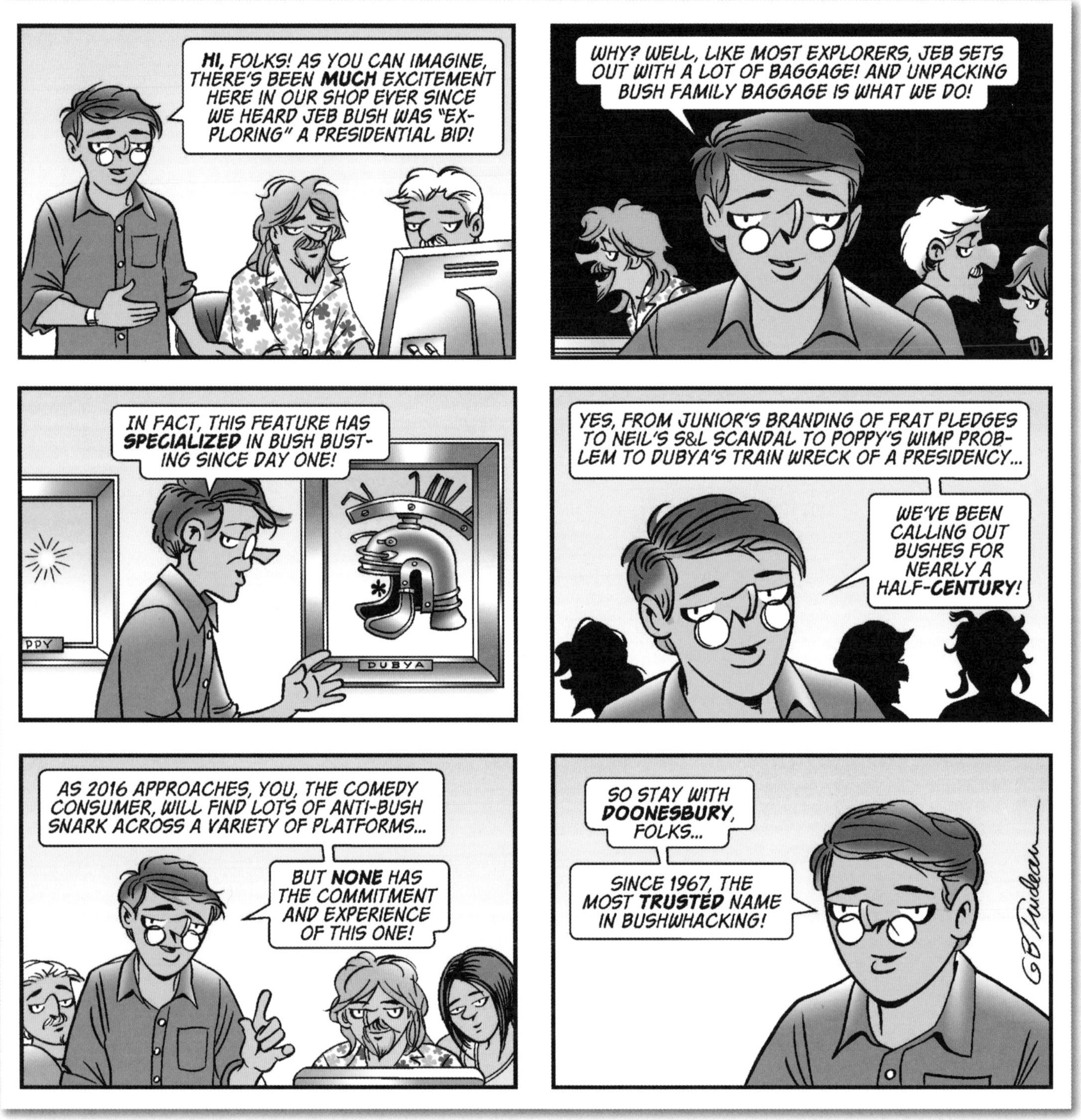
HI, FOLKS! AS YOU CAN IMAGINE, THERE'S BEEN MUCH EXCITEMENT HERE IN OUR SHOP EVER SINCE WE HEARD JEB BUSH WAS "EXPLORING" A PRESIDENTIAL BID!
WHY? WELL, LIKE MOST EXPLORERS, JEB SETS OUT WITH A LOT OF BAGGAGE! AND UNPACKING BUSH FAMILY BAGGAGE IS WHAT WE DO!
IN FACT, THIS FEATURE HAS SPECIALIZED IN BUSH BUSTING SINCE DAY ONE!
PPY
DUBYA
YES, FROM JUNIOR'S BRANDING OF FRAT PLEDGES TO NEIL'S S&L SCANDAL TO POPPY'S WIMP PROBLEM TO DUBYA'S TRAIN WRECK OF A PRESIDENCY...
WE'VE BEEN CALLING OUT BUSHES FOR NEARLY A HALF-CENTURY!
AS 2016 APPROACHES, YOU, THE COMEDY CONSUMER, WILL FIND LOTS OF ANTI-BUSH SNARK ACROSS A VARIETY OF PLATFORMS...
BUT NONE HAS THE COMMITMENT AND EXPERIENCE OF THIS ONE!
SO STAY WITH DOONESBURY, FOLKS...
SINCE 1967, THE MOST TRUSTED NAME IN BUSHWHACKING!
GBTrudeau

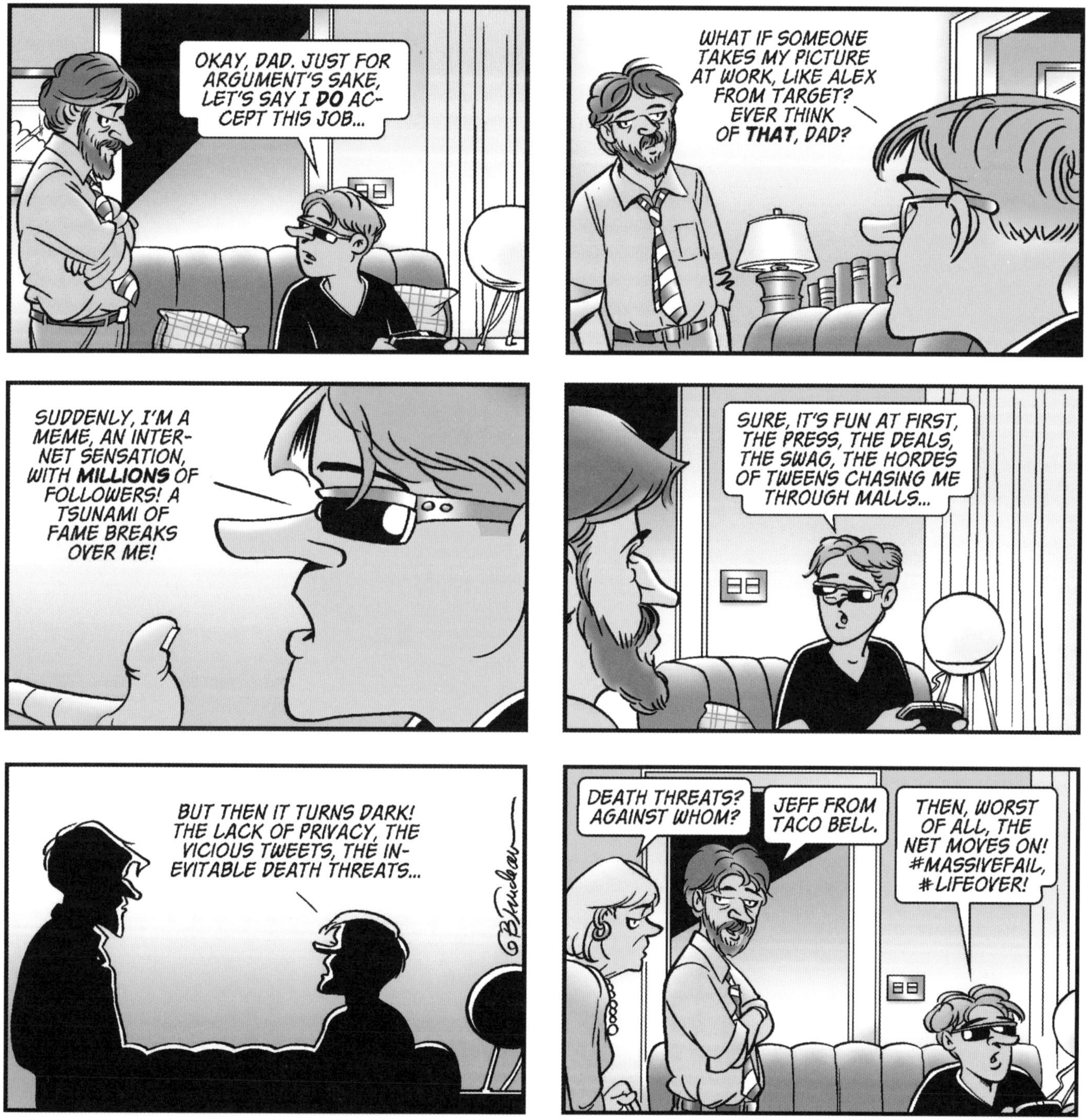
OKAY, DAD. JUST FOR ARGUMENT'S SAKE, LET'S SAY I DO ACCEPT THIS JOB...
WHAT IF SOMEONE TAKES MY PICTURE AT WORK, LIKE ALEX FROM TARGET? EVER THINK OF THAT, DAD?
SUDDENLY, I'M A MEME, AN INTERNET SENSATION, WITH MILLIONS OF FOLLOWERS! A TSUNAMI OF FAME BREAKS OVER ME!
SURE, IT'S FUN AT FIRST, THE PRESS, THE DEALS, THE SWAG, THE HORDES OF TWEENS CHASING ME THROUGH MALLS...
BUT THEN IT TURNS DARK! THE LACK OF PRIVACY, THE VICIOUS TWEETS, THE INEVITABLE DEATH THREATS...
©BTrudeau
DEATH THREATS? AGAINST WHOM?
JEFF FROM TACO BELL.
THEN, WORST OF ALL, THE NET MOVES ON! #MASSIVEFAIL, #LIFEOVER!

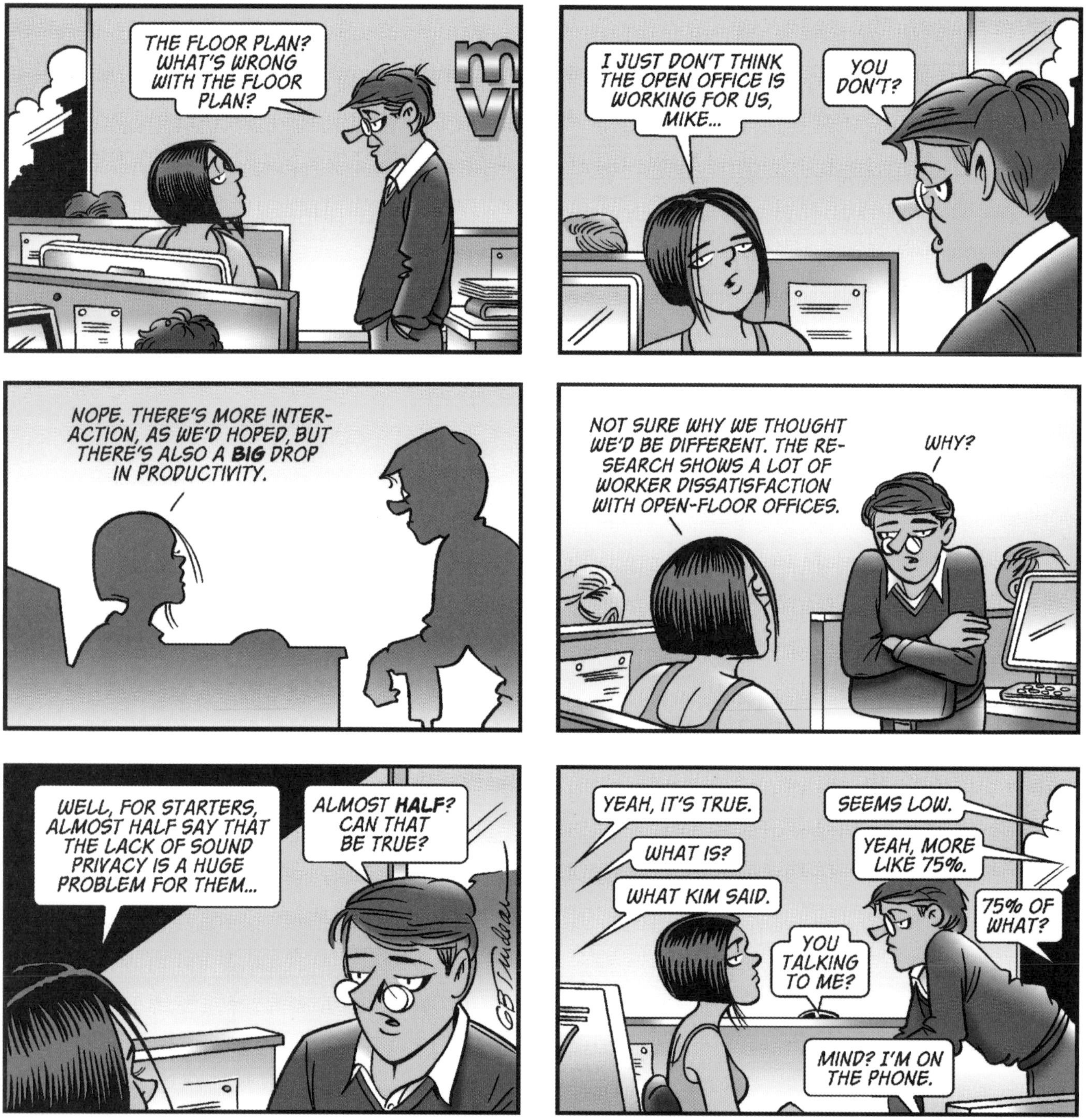
THE FLOOR PLAN? WHAT'S WRONG WITH THE FLOOR PLAN?
I JUST DON'T THINK THE OPEN OFFICE IS WORKING FOR US, MIKE...
YOU DON'T?
NOPE. THERE'S MORE INTERACTION, AS WE'D HOPED, BUT THERE'S ALSO A **BIG** DROP IN PRODUCTIVITY.
NOT SURE WHY WE THOUGHT WE'D BE DIFFERENT. THE RESEARCH SHOWS A LOT OF WORKER DISSATISFACTION WITH OPEN-FLOOR OFFICES.
WHY?
WELL, FOR STARTERS, ALMOST HALF SAY THAT THE LACK OF SOUND PRIVACY IS A HUGE PROBLEM FOR THEM...
ALMOST **HALF**? CAN THAT BE TRUE?
YEAH, IT'S TRUE.
SEEMS LOW.
WHAT IS?
YEAH, MORE LIKE 75%.
WHAT KIM SAID.
75% OF WHAT?
YOU TALKING TO ME?
MIND? I'M ON THE PHONE.

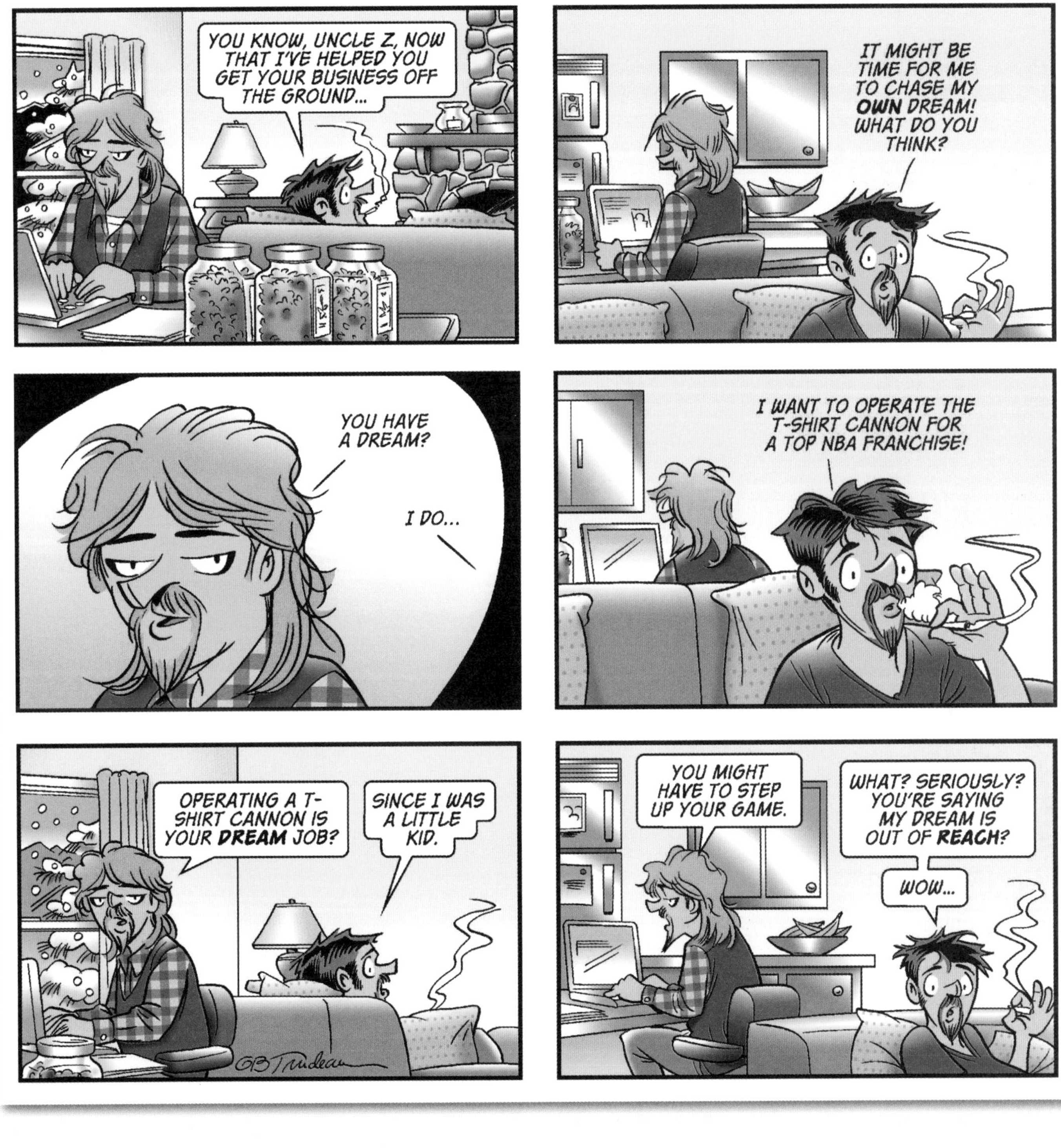
YOU KNOW, UNCLE Z, NOW THAT I'VE HELPED YOU GET YOUR BUSINESS OFF THE GROUND...
IT MIGHT BE TIME FOR ME TO CHASE MY **OWN** DREAM! WHAT DO YOU THINK?
YOU HAVE A DREAM?
I DO...
I WANT TO OPERATE THE T-SHIRT CANNON FOR A TOP NBA FRANCHISE!
OPERATING A T-SHIRT CANNON IS YOUR **DREAM** JOB?
SINCE I WAS A LITTLE KID.
GB Trudeau
YOU MIGHT HAVE TO STEP UP YOUR GAME.
WHAT? SERIOUSLY? YOU'RE SAYING MY DREAM IS OUT OF **REACH**?
WOW...

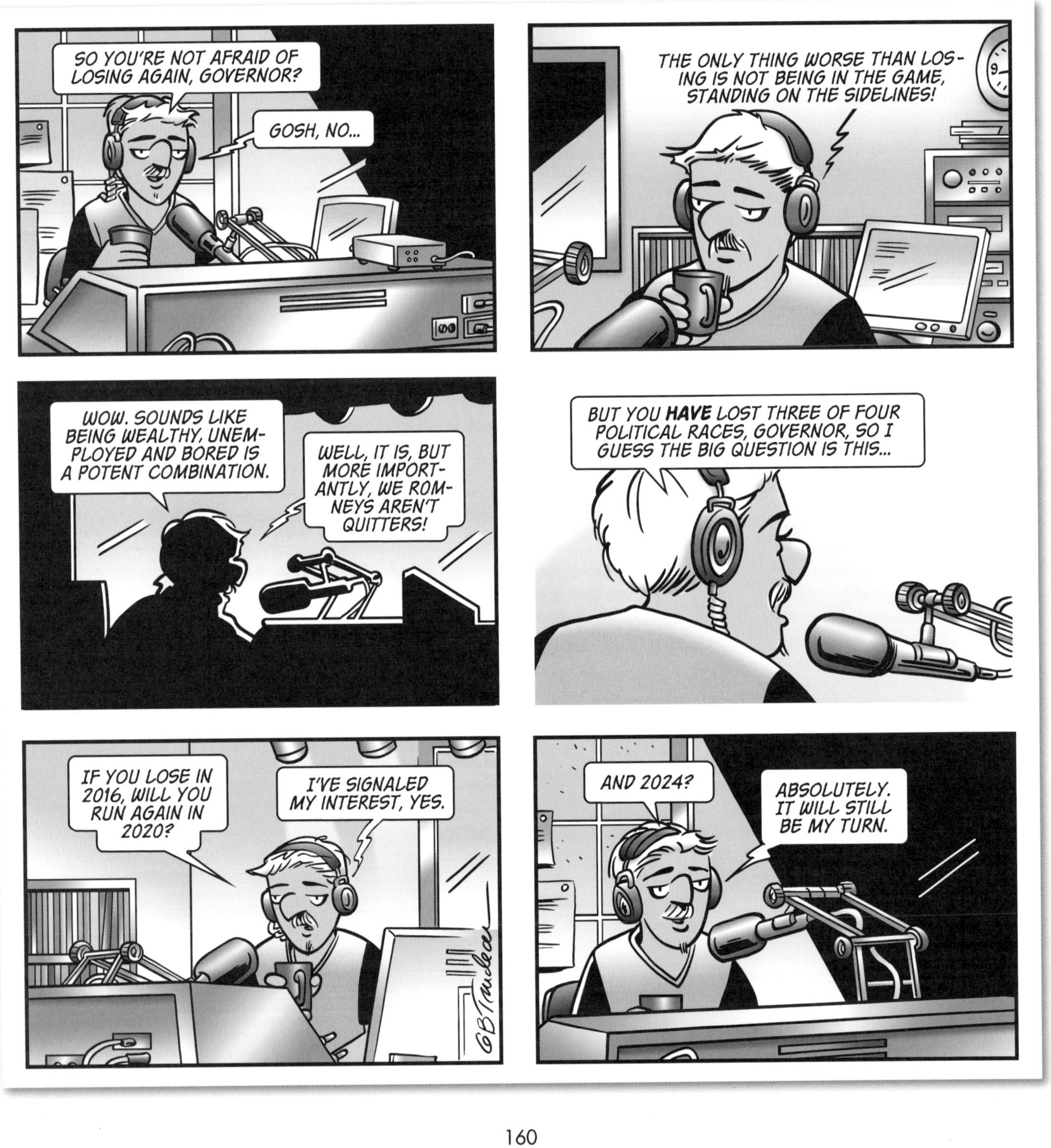
SO YOU'RE NOT AFRAID OF LOSING AGAIN, GOVERNOR?
GOSH, NO...
THE ONLY THING WORSE THAN LOSING IS NOT BEING IN THE GAME, STANDING ON THE SIDELINES!
WOW. SOUNDS LIKE BEING WEALTHY, UNEMPLOYED AND BORED IS A POTENT COMBINATION.
WELL, IT IS, BUT MORE IMPORTANTLY, WE ROMNEYS AREN'T QUITTERS!
BUT YOU **HAVE** LOST THREE OF FOUR POLITICAL RACES, GOVERNOR, SO I GUESS THE BIG QUESTION IS THIS...
IF YOU LOSE IN 2016, WILL YOU RUN AGAIN IN 2020?
I'VE SIGNALED MY INTEREST, YES.
AND 2024?
ABSOLUTELY. IT WILL STILL BE MY TURN.
GBTrudeau

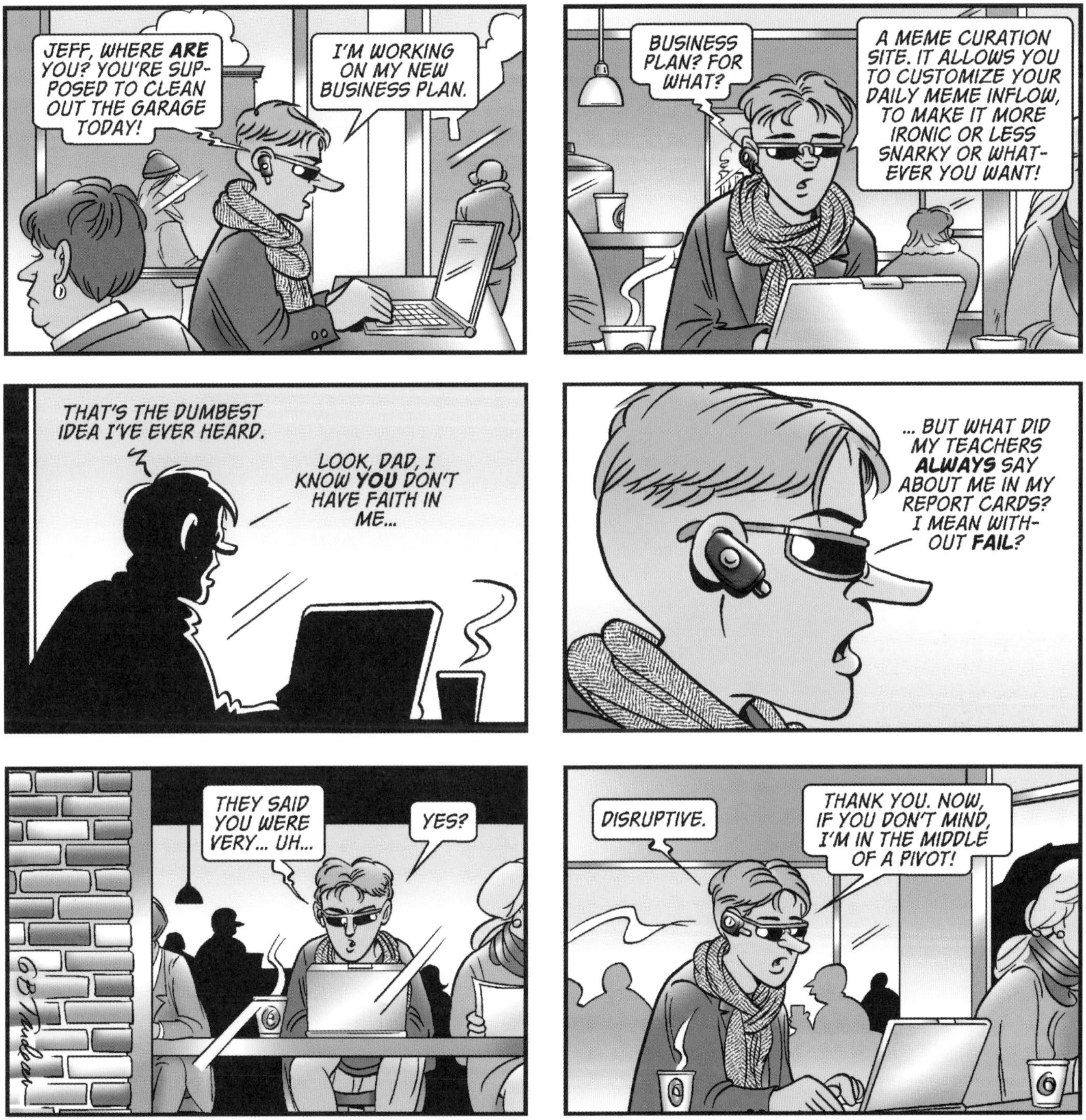
JEFF, WHERE **ARE** YOU? YOU'RE SUP-POSED TO CLEAN OUT THE GARAGE TODAY!
I'M WORKING ON MY NEW BUSINESS PLAN.
BUSINESS PLAN? FOR WHAT?
A MEME CURATION SITE. IT ALLOWS YOU TO CUSTOMIZE YOUR DAILY MEME INFLOW, TO MAKE IT MORE IRONIC OR LESS SNARKY OR WHAT-EVER YOU WANT!
THAT'S THE DUMBEST IDEA I'VE EVER HEARD.
LOOK, DAD, I KNOW **YOU** DON'T HAVE FAITH IN ME...
... BUT WHAT DID MY TEACHERS **ALWAYS** SAY ABOUT ME IN MY REPORT CARDS? I MEAN WITH-OUT **FAIL**?
THEY SAID YOU WERE VERY... UH...
YES?
DISRUPTIVE.
THANK YOU. NOW, IF YOU DON'T MIND, I'M IN THE MIDDLE OF A PIVOT!
© B Trudeau

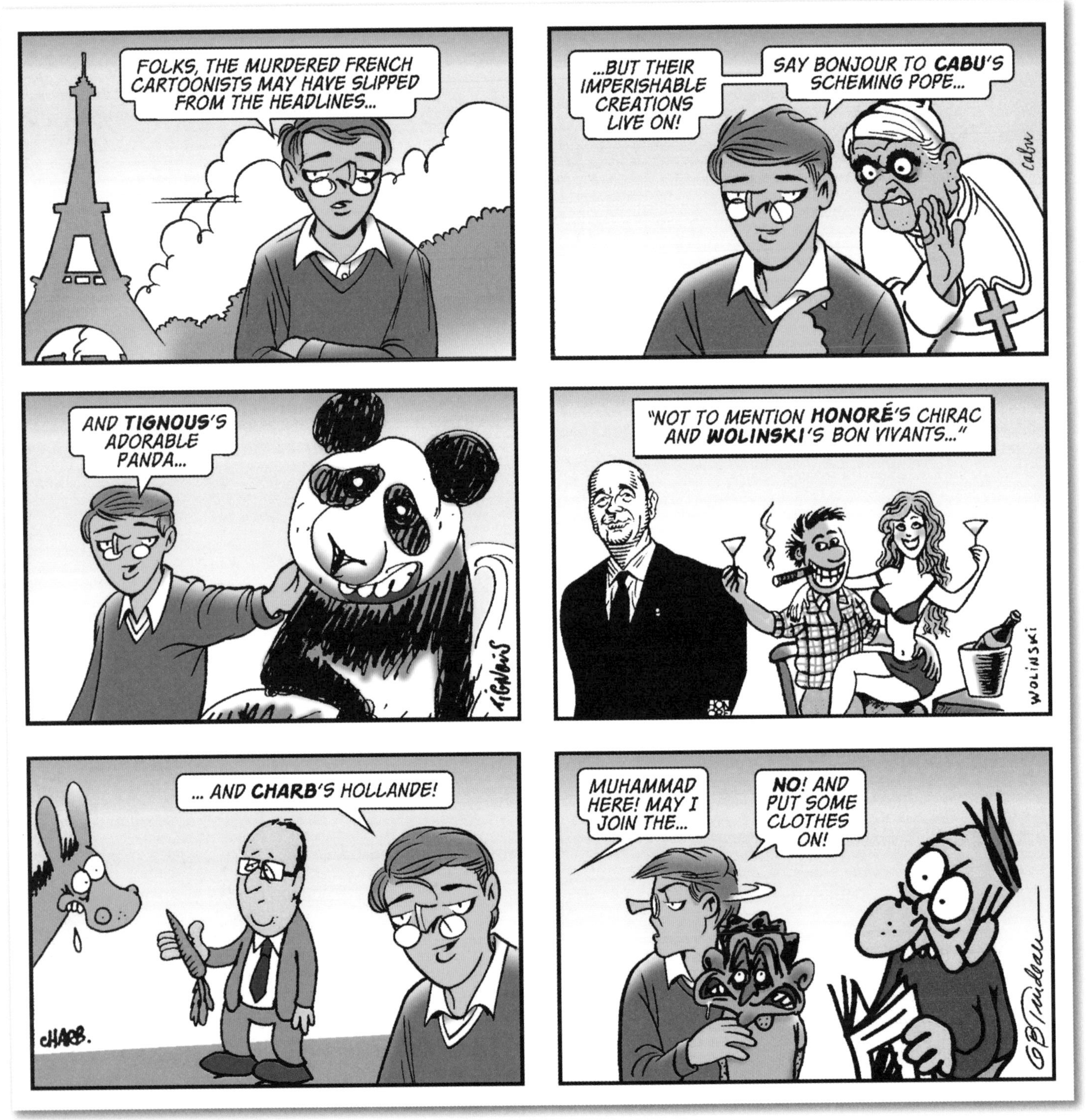
FOLKS, THE MURDERED FRENCH CARTOONISTS MAY HAVE SLIPPED FROM THE HEADLINES...
...BUT THEIR IMPERISHABLE CREATIONS LIVE ON!
SAY BONJOUR TO CABU'S SCHEMING POPE...
cabu
AND TIGNOUS'S ADORABLE PANDA...
TIGNOUS
"NOT TO MENTION HONORÉ'S CHIRAC AND WOLINSKI'S BON VIVANTS..."
WOLINSKI
... AND CHARB'S HOLLANDE!
CHARB.
MUHAMMAD HERE! MAY I JOIN THE...
NO! AND PUT SOME CLOTHES ON!
GBTrudeau

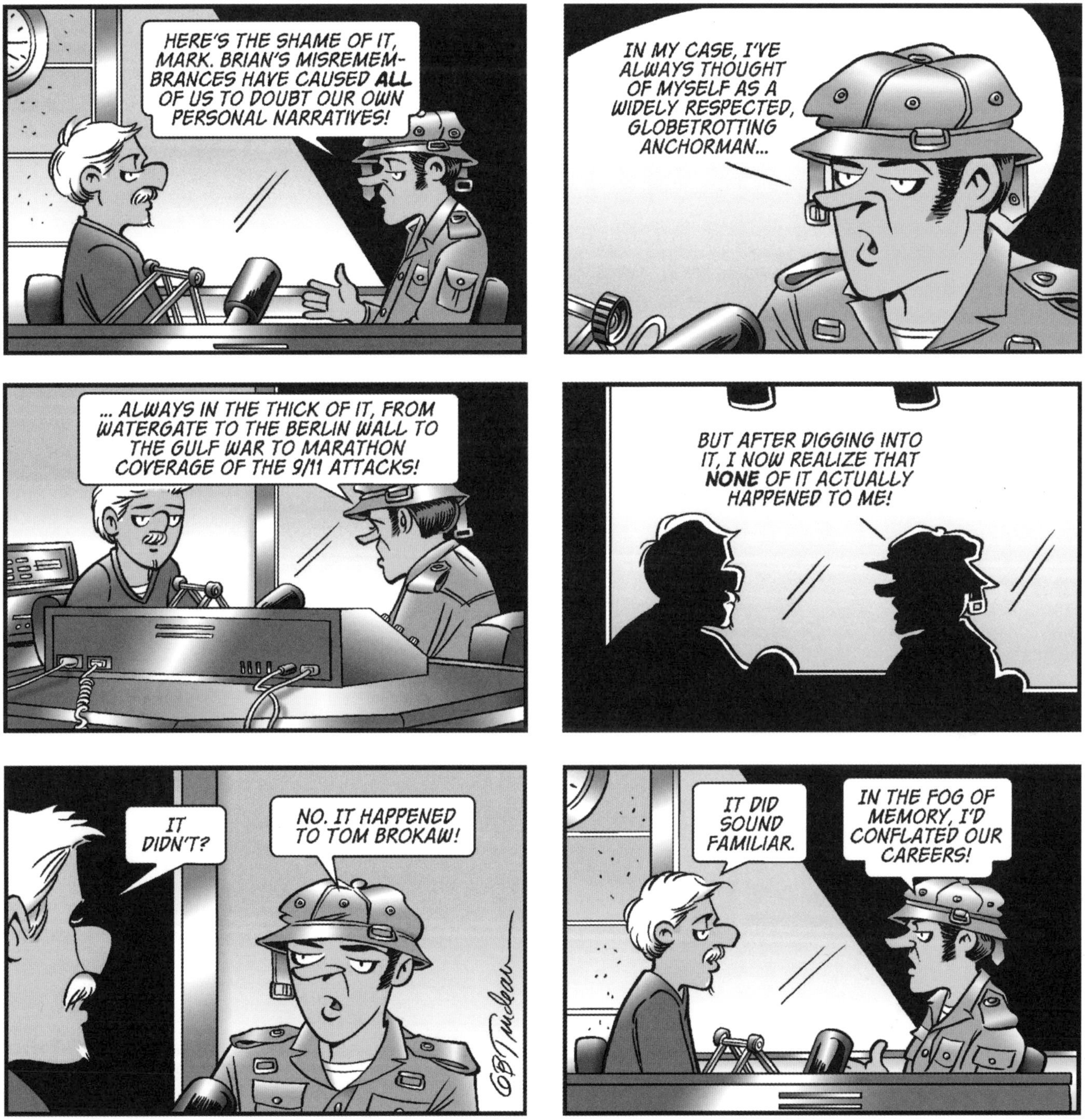
HERE'S THE SHAME OF IT, MARK. BRIAN'S MISREMEMBRANCES HAVE CAUSED **ALL** OF US TO DOUBT OUR OWN PERSONAL NARRATIVES!
IN MY CASE, I'VE ALWAYS THOUGHT OF MYSELF AS A WIDELY RESPECTED, GLOBETROTTING ANCHORMAN...
... ALWAYS IN THE THICK OF IT, FROM WATERGATE TO THE BERLIN WALL TO THE GULF WAR TO MARATHON COVERAGE OF THE 9/11 ATTACKS!
BUT AFTER DIGGING INTO IT, I NOW REALIZE THAT **NONE** OF IT ACTUALLY HAPPENED TO ME!
IT DIDN'T?
NO. IT HAPPENED TO TOM BROKAW!
IT DID SOUND FAMILIAR.
IN THE FOG OF MEMORY, I'D CONFLATED OUR CAREERS!

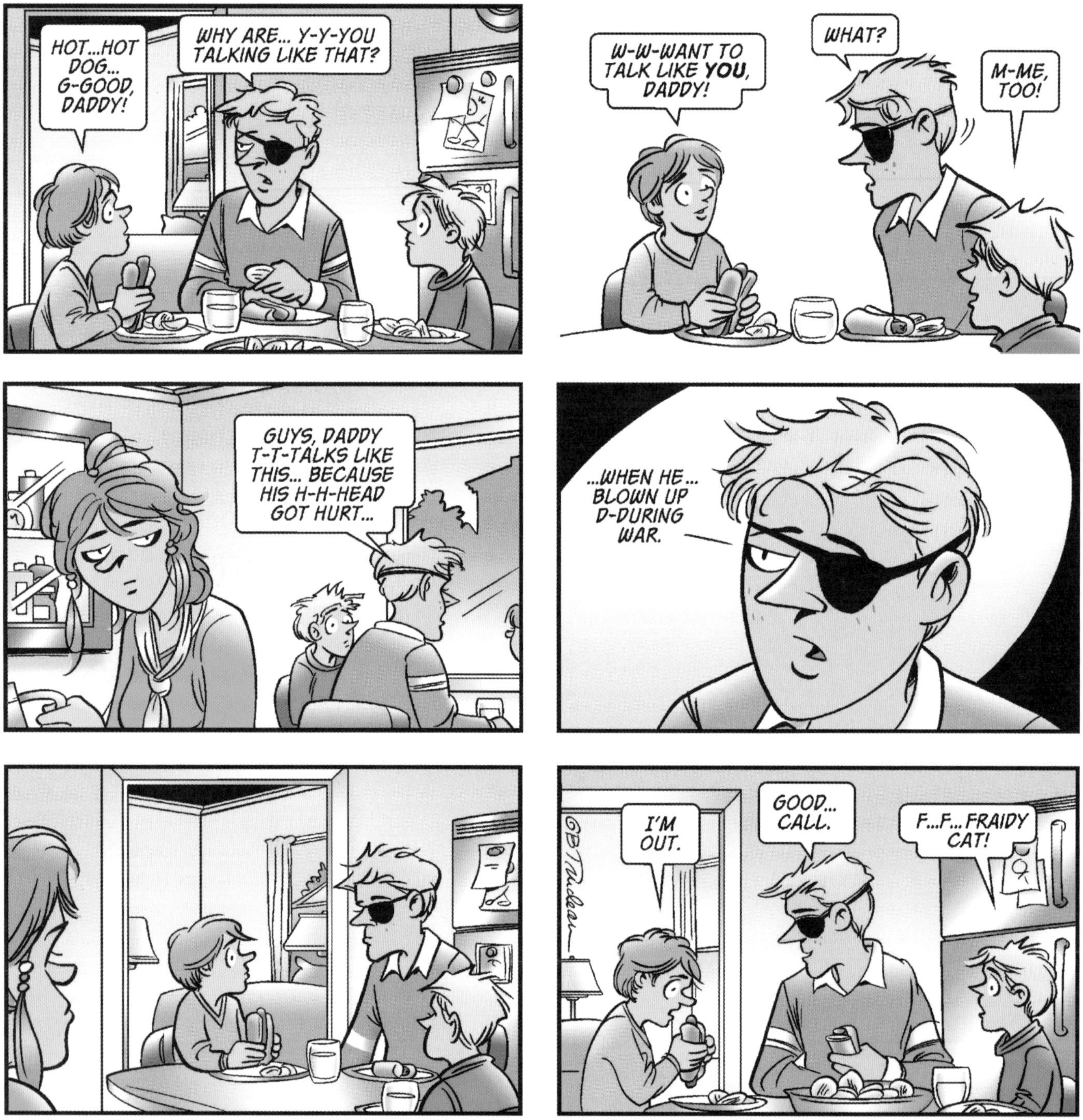
HOT...HOT DOG... G-GOOD, DADDY!
WHY ARE... Y-Y-YOU TALKING LIKE THAT?
W-W-WANT TO TALK LIKE **YOU**, DADDY!
WHAT?
M-ME, TOO!
GUYS, DADDY T-T-TALKS LIKE THIS... BECAUSE HIS H-H-HEAD GOT HURT...
...WHEN HE... BLOWN UP D-DURING WAR.
©B Trudeau
I'M OUT.
GOOD... CALL.
F...F... FRAIDY CAT!

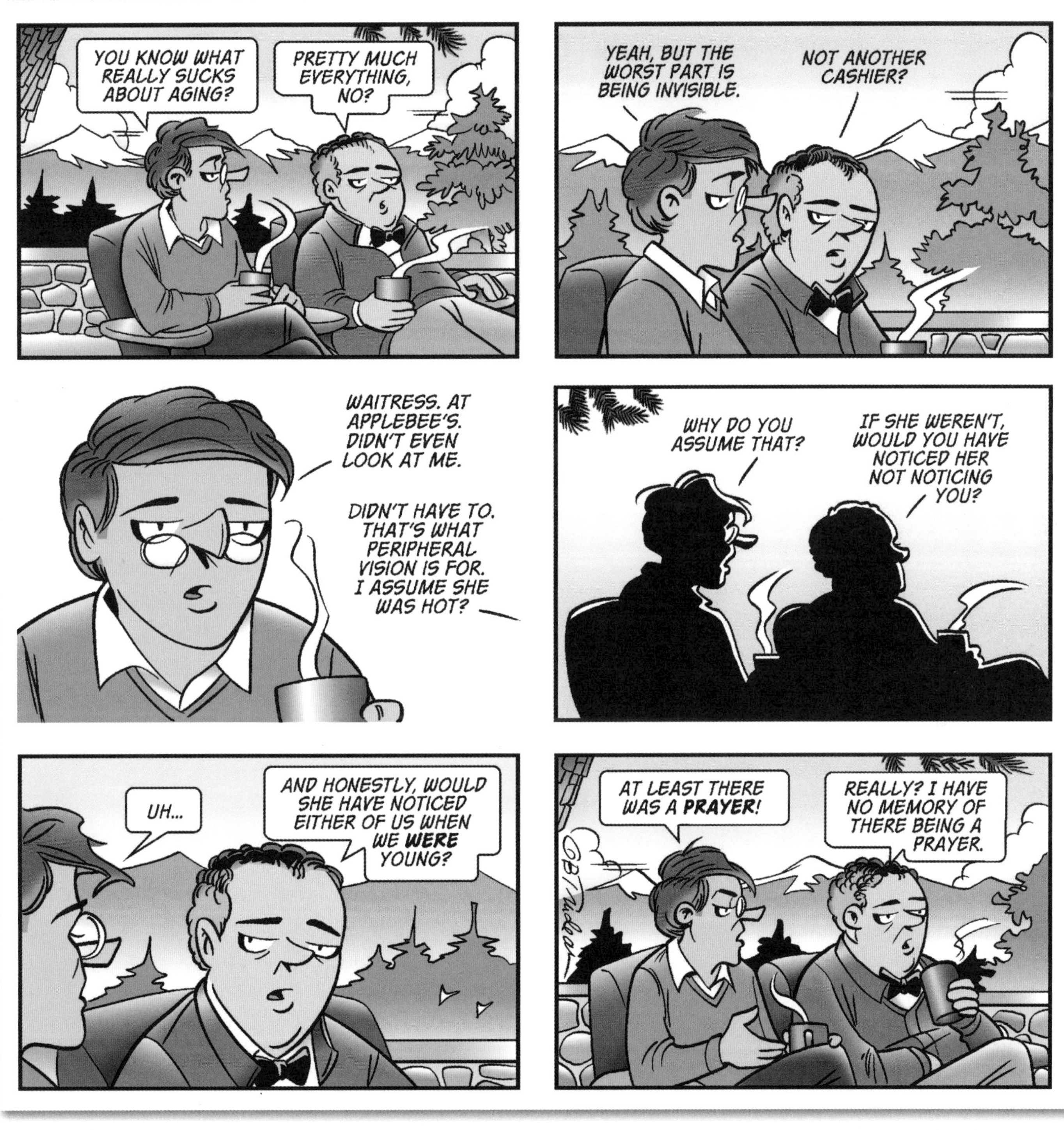
YOU KNOW WHAT REALLY SUCKS ABOUT AGING?
PRETTY MUCH EVERYTHING, NO?
YEAH, BUT THE WORST PART IS BEING INVISIBLE.
NOT ANOTHER CASHIER?
WAITRESS. AT APPLEBEE'S. DIDN'T EVEN LOOK AT ME.
DIDN'T HAVE TO. THAT'S WHAT PERIPHERAL VISION IS FOR. I ASSUME SHE WAS HOT?
WHY DO YOU ASSUME THAT?
IF SHE WEREN'T, WOULD YOU HAVE NOTICED HER NOT NOTICING YOU?
UH...
AND HONESTLY, WOULD SHE HAVE NOTICED EITHER OF US WHEN WE **WERE** YOUNG?
AT LEAST THERE WAS A **PRAYER**!
REALLY? I HAVE NO MEMORY OF THERE BEING A PRAYER.

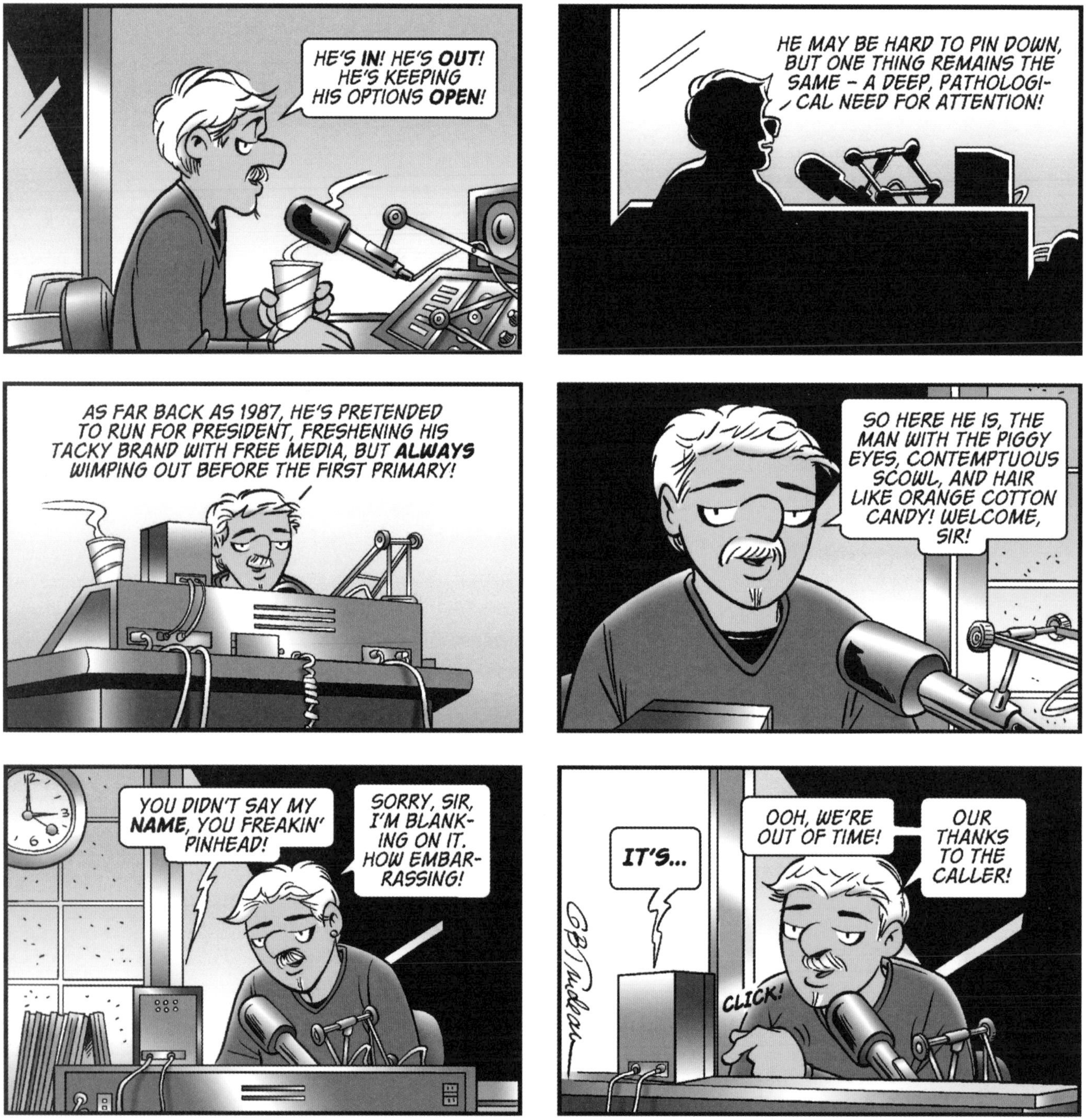
HE'S IN! HE'S OUT! HE'S KEEPING HIS OPTIONS OPEN!
HE MAY BE HARD TO PIN DOWN, BUT ONE THING REMAINS THE SAME – A DEEP, PATHOLOGICAL NEED FOR ATTENTION!
AS FAR BACK AS 1987, HE'S PRETENDED TO RUN FOR PRESIDENT, FRESHENING HIS TACKY BRAND WITH FREE MEDIA, BUT ALWAYS WIMPING OUT BEFORE THE FIRST PRIMARY!
SO HERE HE IS, THE MAN WITH THE PIGGY EYES, CONTEMPTUOUS SCOWL, AND HAIR LIKE ORANGE COTTON CANDY! WELCOME, SIR!
YOU DIDN'T SAY MY NAME, YOU FREAKIN' PINHEAD!
SORRY, SIR, I'M BLANKING ON IT. HOW EMBARRASSING!
IT'S...
CLICK!
OOH, WE'RE OUT OF TIME!
OUR THANKS TO THE CALLER!
GBTrudeau

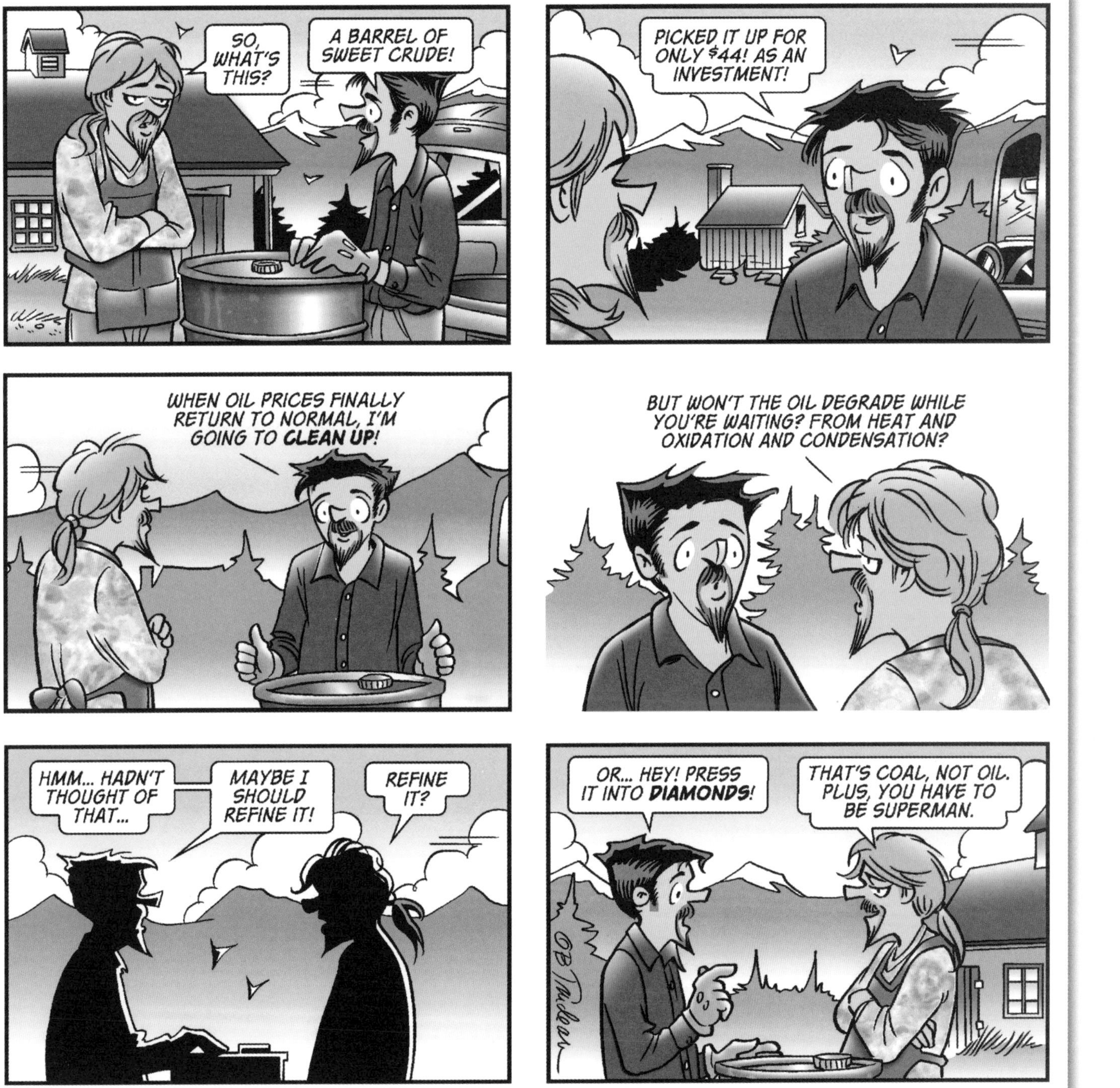
SO, WHAT'S THIS?
A BARREL OF SWEET CRUDE!
PICKED IT UP FOR ONLY $44! AS AN INVESTMENT!
WHEN OIL PRICES FINALLY RETURN TO NORMAL, I'M GOING TO **CLEAN UP**!
BUT WON'T THE OIL DEGRADE WHILE YOU'RE WAITING? FROM HEAT AND OXIDATION AND CONDENSATION?
HMM... HADN'T THOUGHT OF THAT...
MAYBE I SHOULD REFINE IT!
REFINE IT?
OR... HEY! PRESS IT INTO **DIAMONDS**!
THAT'S COAL, NOT OIL. PLUS, YOU HAVE TO BE SUPERMAN.
©B Tucker

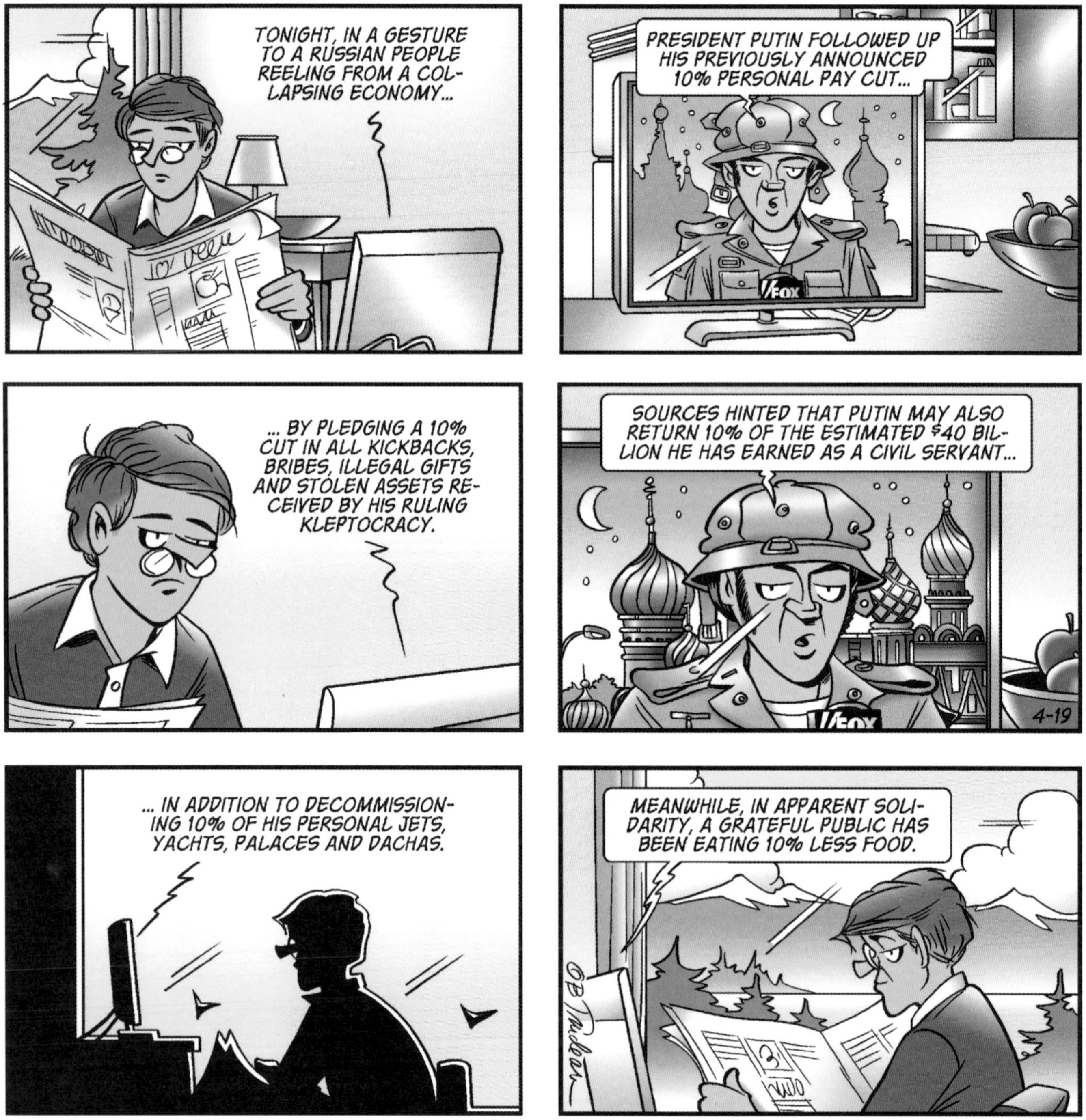
TONIGHT, IN A GESTURE TO A RUSSIAN PEOPLE REELING FROM A COLLAPSING ECONOMY...
PRESIDENT PUTIN FOLLOWED UP HIS PREVIOUSLY ANNOUNCED 10% PERSONAL PAY CUT...
... BY PLEDGING A 10% CUT IN ALL KICKBACKS, BRIBES, ILLEGAL GIFTS AND STOLEN ASSETS RECEIVED BY HIS RULING KLEPTOCRACY.
SOURCES HINTED THAT PUTIN MAY ALSO RETURN 10% OF THE ESTIMATED $40 BILLION HE HAS EARNED AS A CIVIL SERVANT...
FOX
4-19
... IN ADDITION TO DECOMMISSIONING 10% OF HIS PERSONAL JETS, YACHTS, PALACES AND DACHAS.
MEANWHILE, IN APPARENT SOLIDARITY, A GRATEFUL PUBLIC HAS BEEN EATING 10% LESS FOOD.
GB Trudeau

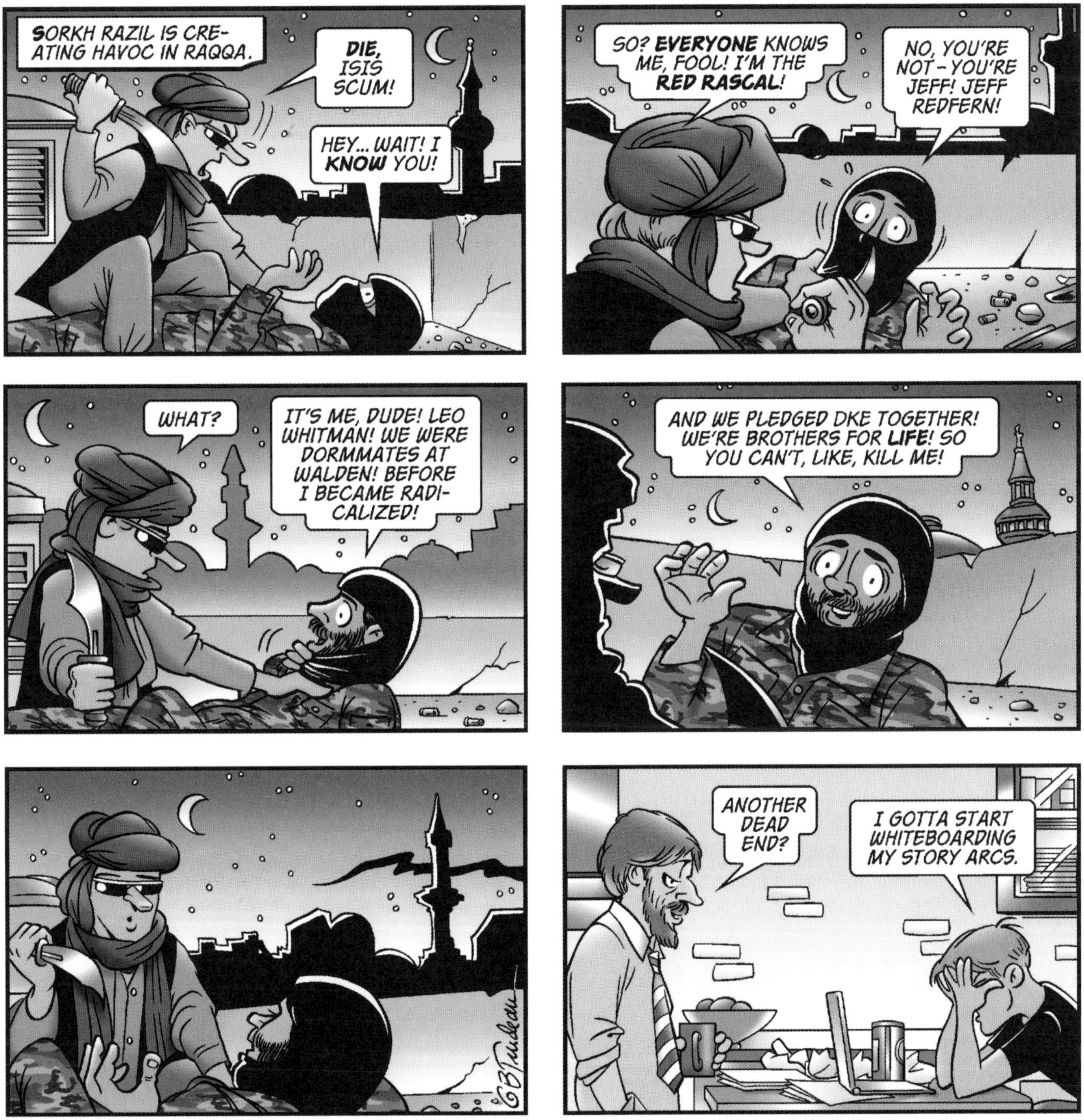
SORKH RAZIL IS CREATING HAVOC IN RAQQA.
DIE, ISIS SCUM!
HEY... WAIT! I KNOW YOU!
SO? EVERYONE KNOWS ME, FOOL! I'M THE RED RASCAL!
NO, YOU'RE NOT–YOU'RE JEFF! JEFF REDFERN!
WHAT?
IT'S ME, DUDE! LEO WHITMAN! WE WERE DORMMATES AT WALDEN! BEFORE I BECAME RADICALIZED!
AND WE PLEDGED DKE TOGETHER! WE'RE BROTHERS FOR LIFE! SO YOU CAN'T, LIKE, KILL ME!
GBTrudeau
ANOTHER DEAD END?
I GOTTA START WHITEBOARDING MY STORY ARCS.

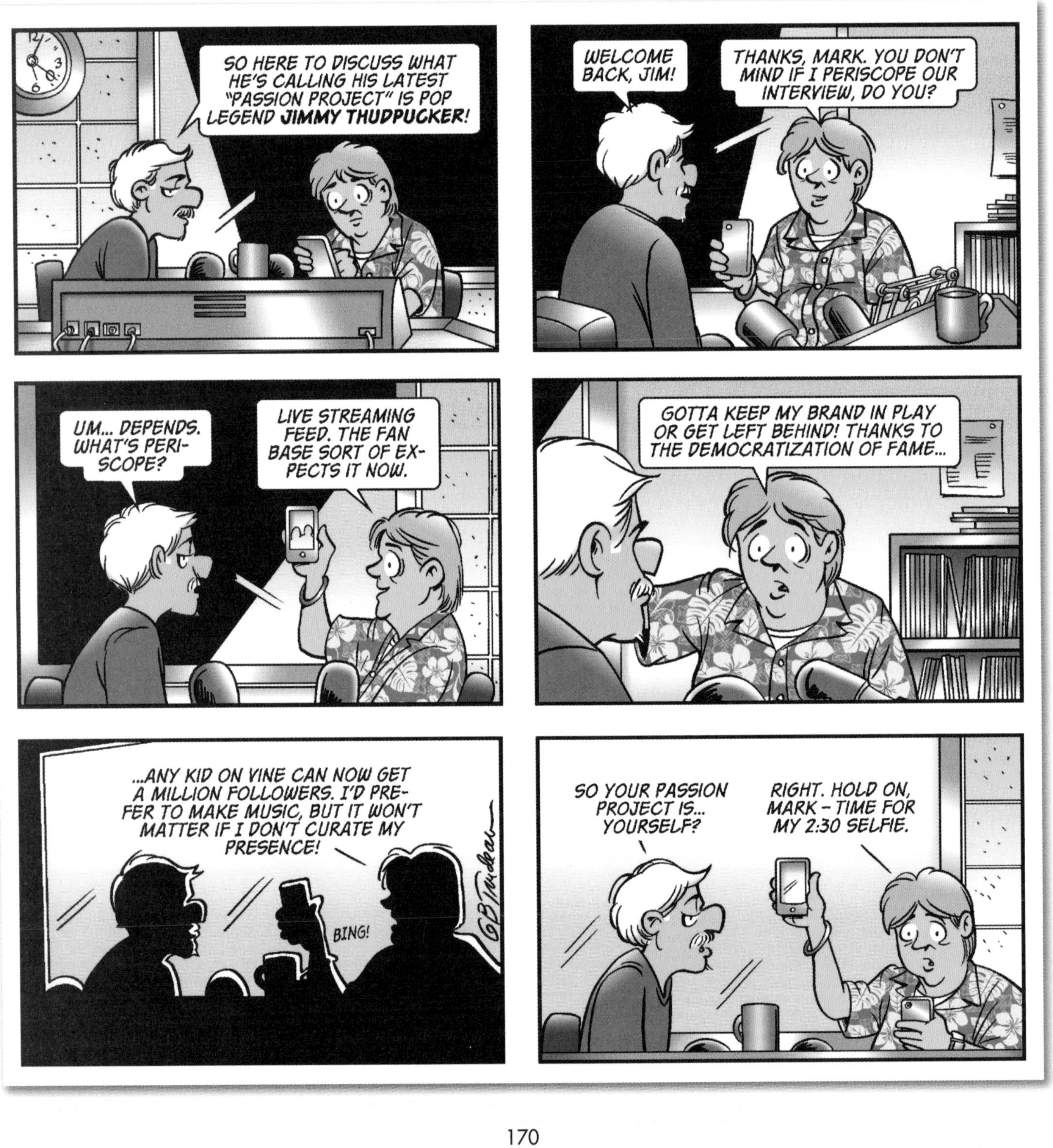
SO HERE TO DISCUSS WHAT HE'S CALLING HIS LATEST "PASSION PROJECT" IS POP LEGEND **JIMMY THUDPUCKER**!
WELCOME BACK, JIM!
THANKS, MARK. YOU DON'T MIND IF I PERISCOPE OUR INTERVIEW, DO YOU?
UM... DEPENDS. WHAT'S PERI-SCOPE?
LIVE STREAMING FEED. THE FAN BASE SORT OF EX-PECTS IT NOW.
GOTTA KEEP MY BRAND IN PLAY OR GET LEFT BEHIND! THANKS TO THE DEMOCRATIZATION OF FAME...
...ANY KID ON VINE CAN NOW GET A MILLION FOLLOWERS. I'D PRE-FER TO MAKE MUSIC, BUT IT WON'T MATTER IF I DON'T CURATE MY PRESENCE!
BING!
GB Trudeau
SO YOUR PASSION PROJECT IS... YOURSELF?
RIGHT. HOLD ON, MARK – TIME FOR MY 2:30 SELFIE.

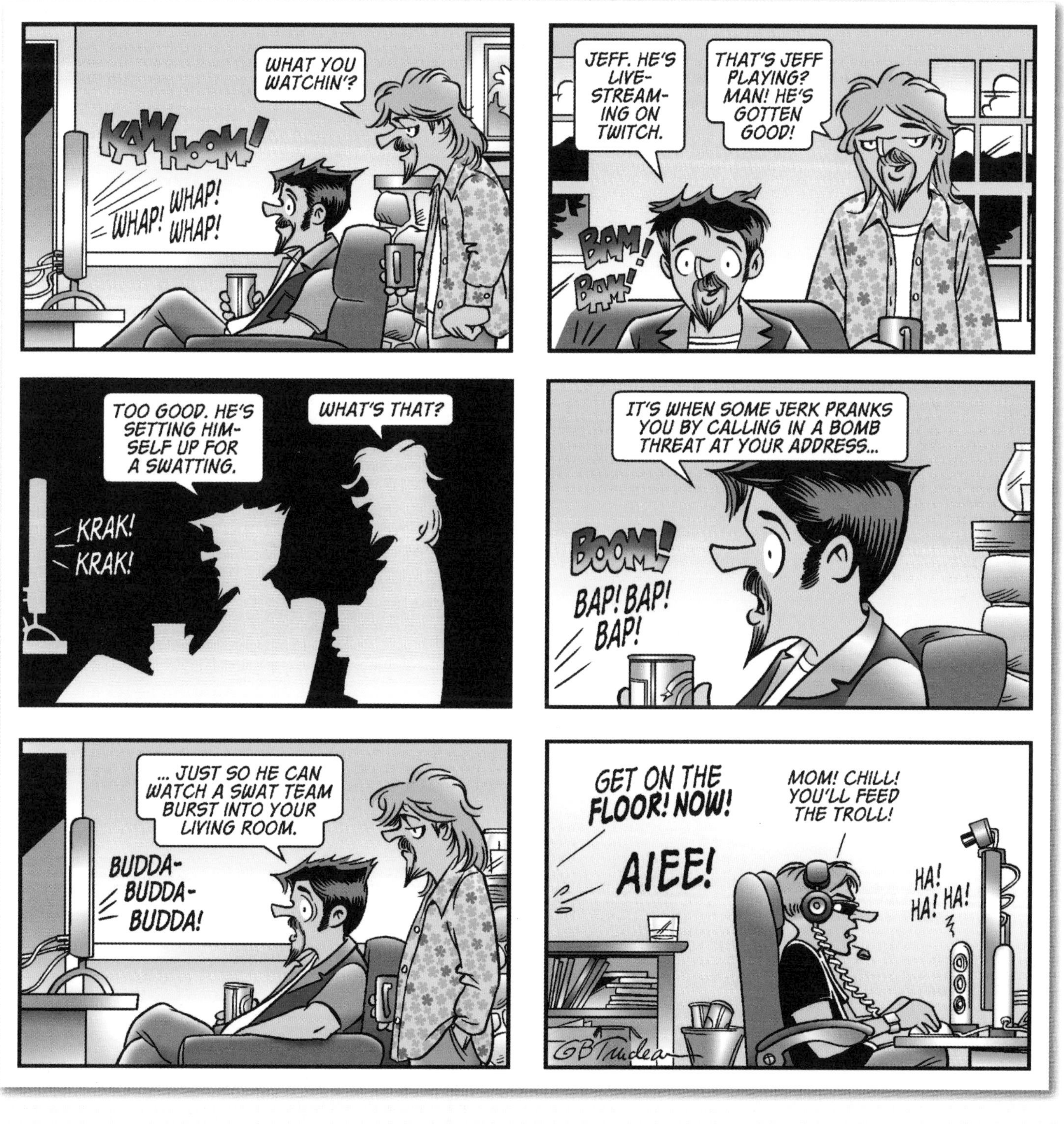
WHAT YOU WATCHIN'?
KAWHOOM!
WHAP! WHAP! WHAP! WHAP!
JEFF. HE'S LIVE-STREAMING ON TWITCH.
THAT'S JEFF PLAYING? MAN! HE'S GOTTEN GOOD!
BAM! BAM!
TOO GOOD. HE'S SETTING HIMSELF UP FOR A SWATTING.
WHAT'S THAT?
KRAK! KRAK!
IT'S WHEN SOME JERK PRANKS YOU BY CALLING IN A BOMB THREAT AT YOUR ADDRESS...
BOOM!
BAP! BAP! BAP!
... JUST SO HE CAN WATCH A SWAT TEAM BURST INTO YOUR LIVING ROOM.
BUDDA-BUDDA-BUDDA-BUDDA!
GET ON THE FLOOR! NOW!
AIEE!
MOM! CHILL! YOU'LL FEED THE TROLL!
HA! HA! HA!
GBTrudeau

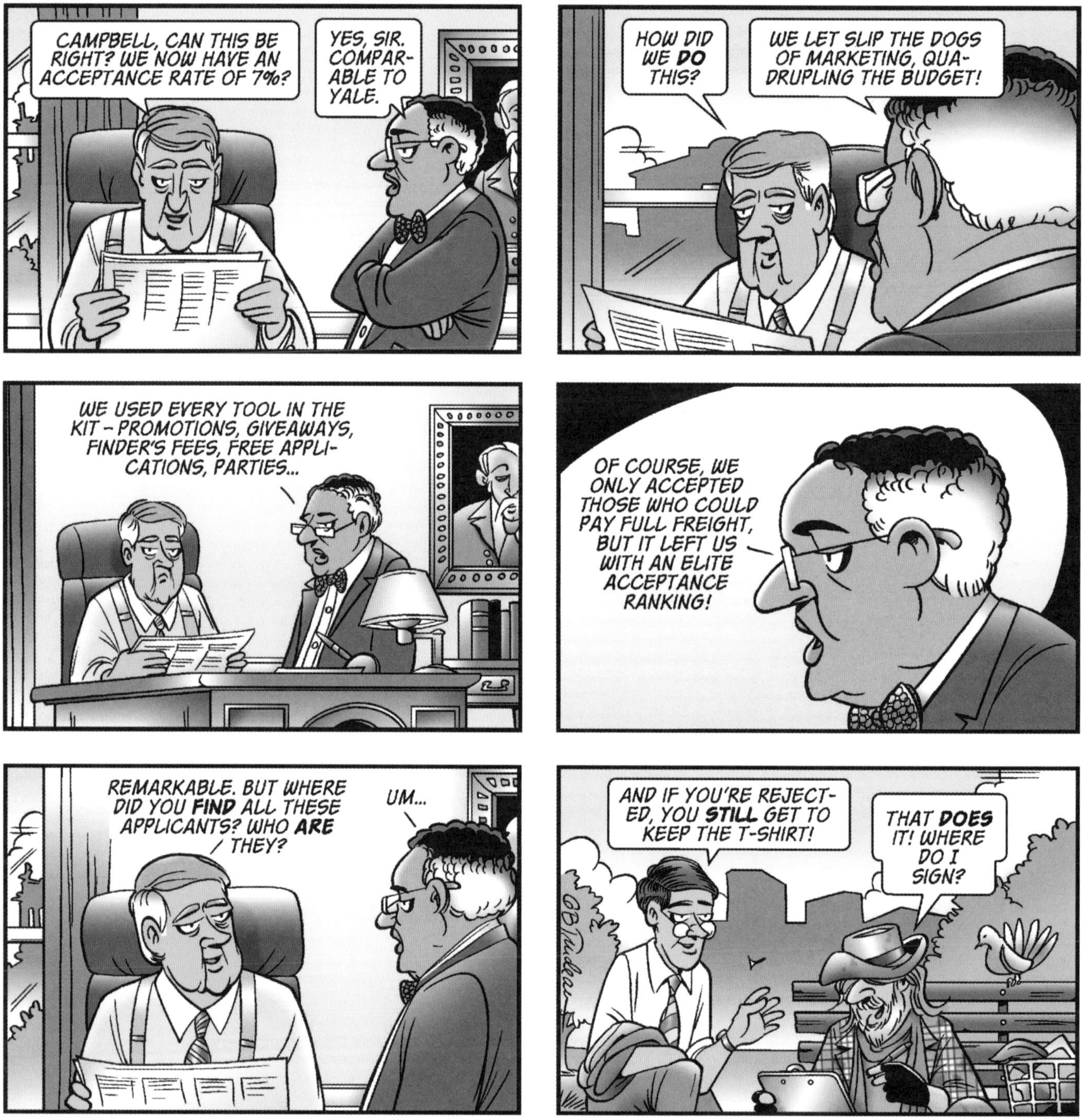
CAMPBELL, CAN THIS BE RIGHT? WE NOW HAVE AN ACCEPTANCE RATE OF 7%?
YES, SIR. COMPARABLE TO YALE.
HOW DID WE DO THIS?
WE LET SLIP THE DOGS OF MARKETING, QUADRUPLING THE BUDGET!
WE USED EVERY TOOL IN THE KIT – PROMOTIONS, GIVEAWAYS, FINDER'S FEES, FREE APPLICATIONS, PARTIES...
OF COURSE, WE ONLY ACCEPTED THOSE WHO COULD PAY FULL FREIGHT, BUT IT LEFT US WITH AN ELITE ACCEPTANCE RANKING!
REMARKABLE. BUT WHERE DID YOU FIND ALL THESE APPLICANTS? WHO ARE THEY?
UM...
AND IF YOU'RE REJECTED, YOU STILL GET TO KEEP THE T-SHIRT!
THAT DOES IT! WHERE DO I SIGN?

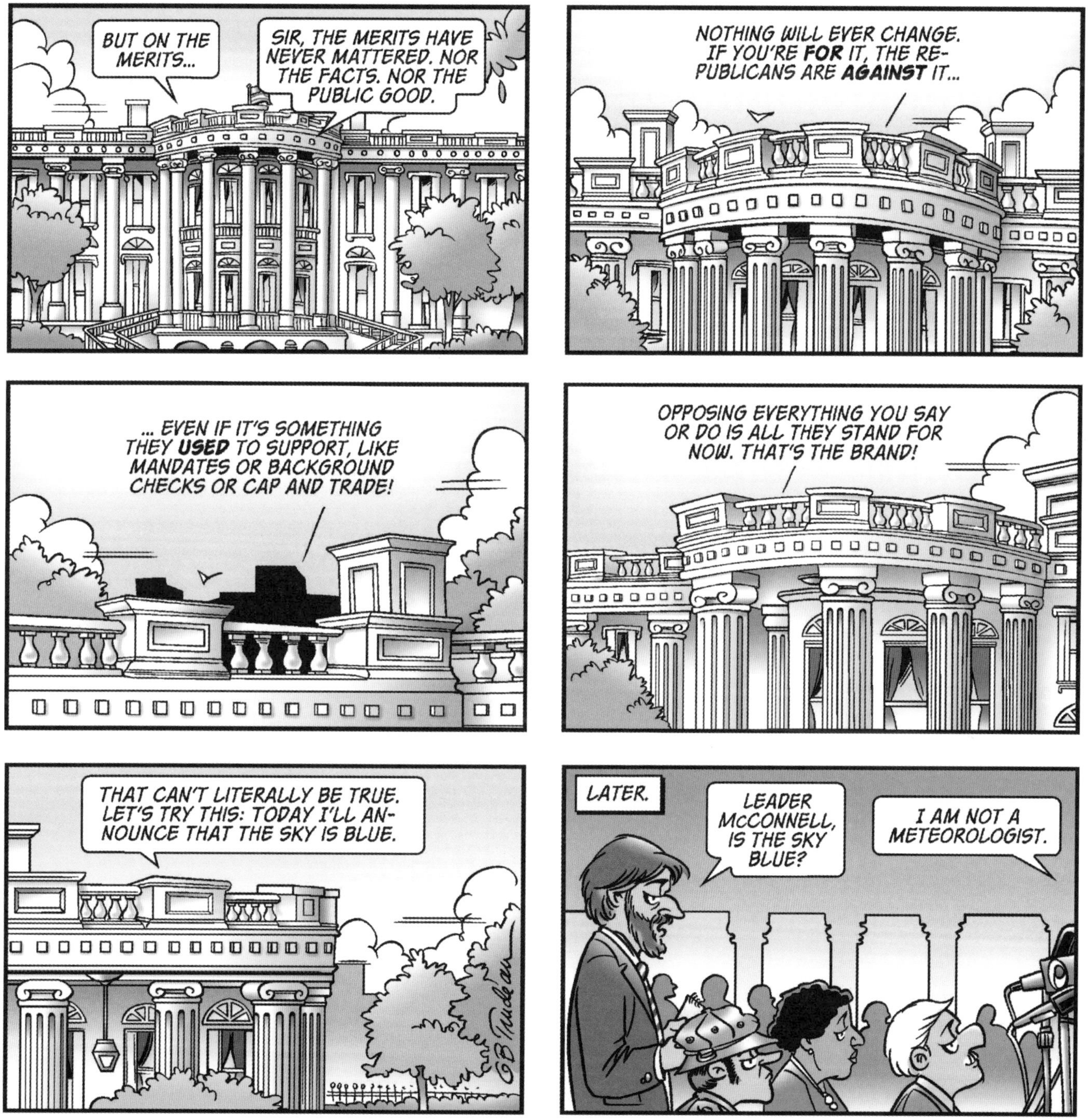
BUT ON THE MERITS...
SIR, THE MERITS HAVE NEVER MATTERED. NOR THE FACTS. NOR THE PUBLIC GOOD.
NOTHING WILL EVER CHANGE. IF YOU'RE **FOR** IT, THE RE-PUBLICANS ARE **AGAINST** IT...
... EVEN IF IT'S SOMETHING THEY **USED** TO SUPPORT, LIKE MANDATES OR BACKGROUND CHECKS OR CAP AND TRADE!
OPPOSING EVERYTHING YOU SAY OR DO IS ALL THEY STAND FOR NOW. THAT'S THE BRAND!
THAT CAN'T LITERALLY BE TRUE. LET'S TRY THIS: TODAY I'LL AN-NOUNCE THAT THE SKY IS BLUE.
GB Trudeau
LATER.
LEADER McCONNELL, IS THE SKY BLUE?
I AM NOT A METEOROLOGIST.

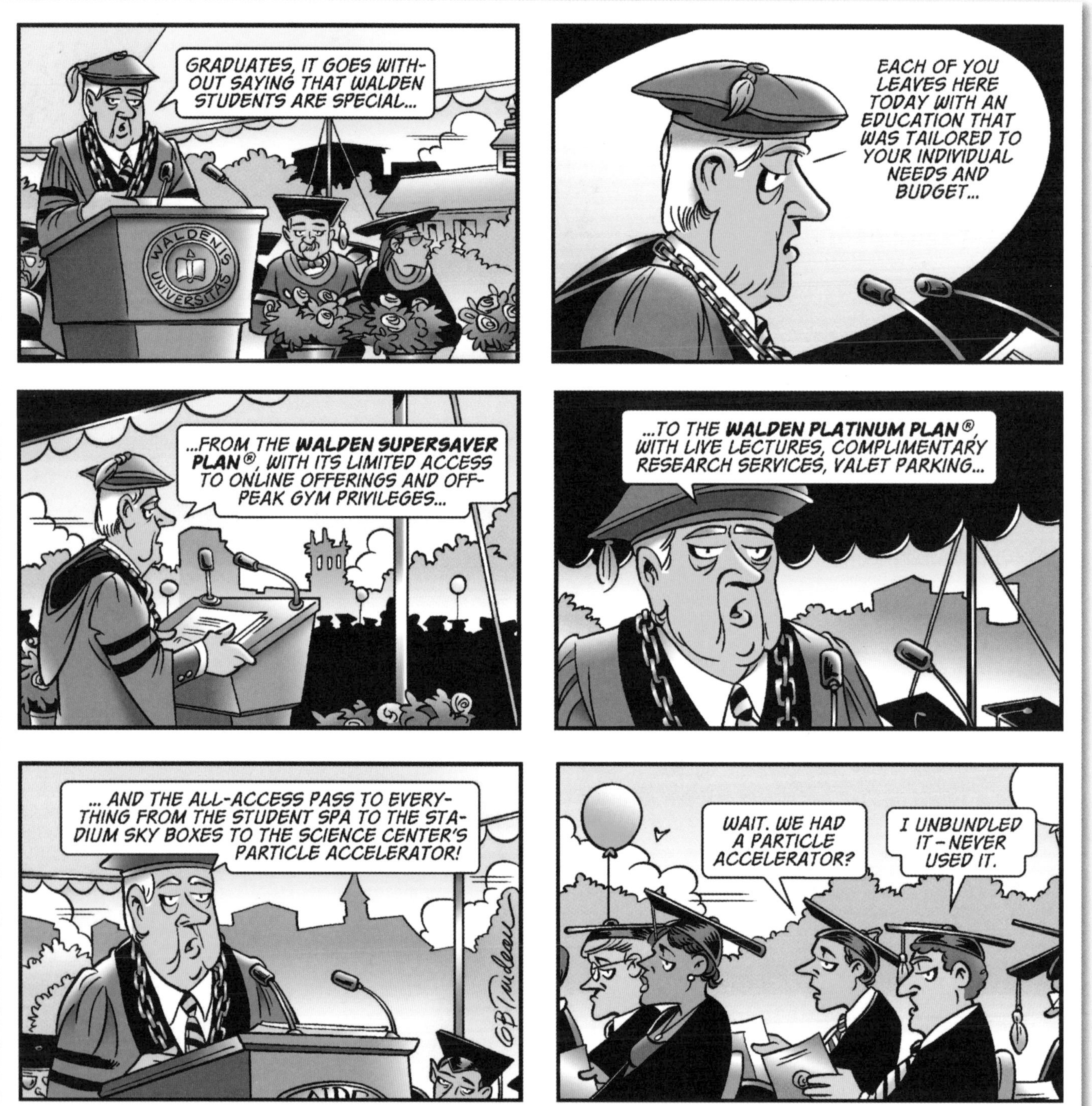
GRADUATES, IT GOES WITHOUT SAYING THAT WALDEN STUDENTS ARE SPECIAL...
WALDENIS UNIVERSITAS
EACH OF YOU LEAVES HERE TODAY WITH AN EDUCATION THAT WAS TAILORED TO YOUR INDIVIDUAL NEEDS AND BUDGET...
...FROM THE WALDEN SUPERSAVER PLAN®, WITH ITS LIMITED ACCESS TO ONLINE OFFERINGS AND OFF-PEAK GYM PRIVILEGES...
...TO THE WALDEN PLATINUM PLAN®, WITH LIVE LECTURES, COMPLIMENTARY RESEARCH SERVICES, VALET PARKING...
... AND THE ALL-ACCESS PASS TO EVERYTHING FROM THE STUDENT SPA TO THE STADIUM SKY BOXES TO THE SCIENCE CENTER'S PARTICLE ACCELERATOR!
GB Trudeau
WAIT. WE HAD A PARTICLE ACCELERATOR?
I UNBUNDLED IT – NEVER USED IT.

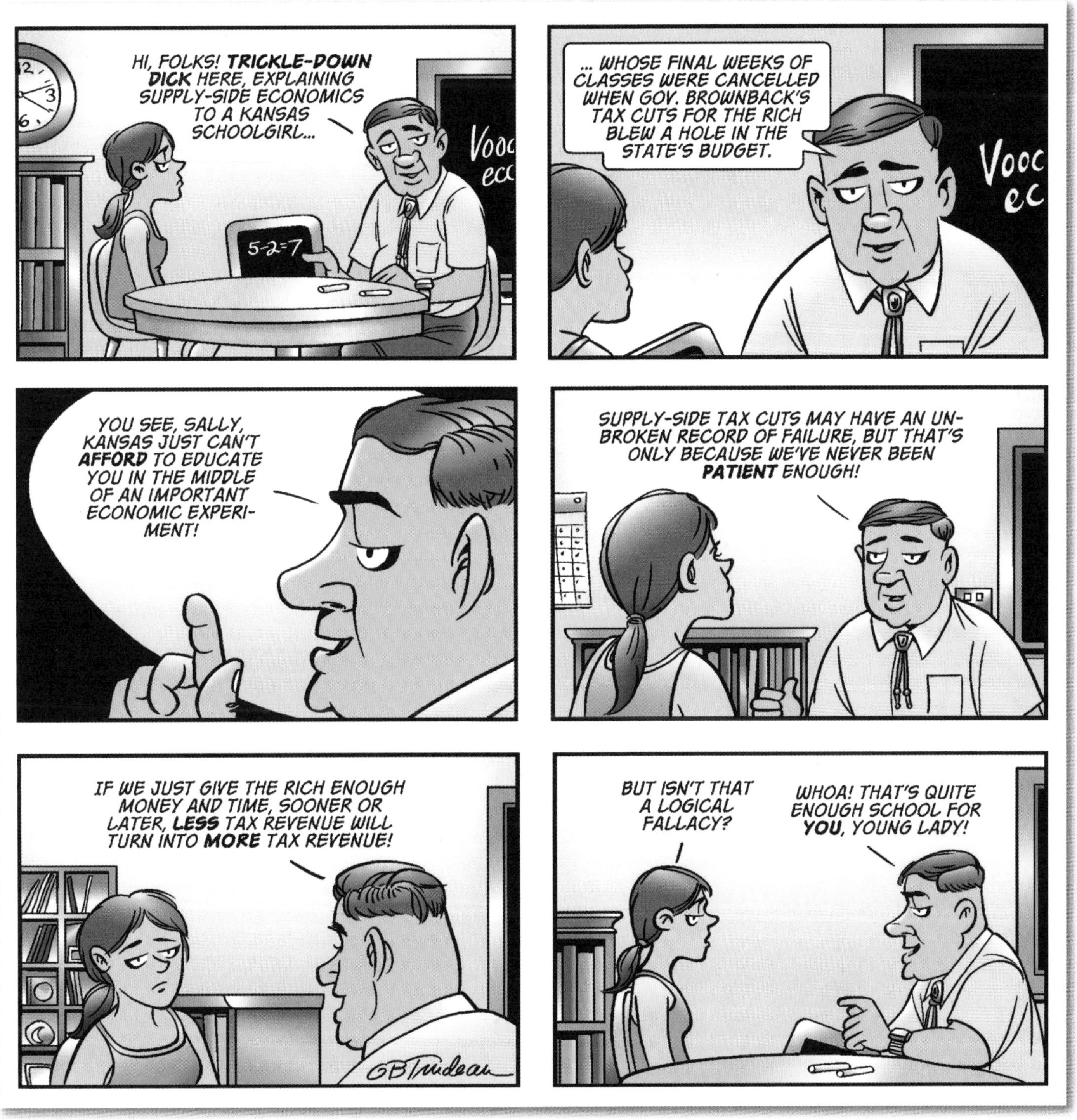
HI, FOLKS! TRICKLE-DOWN DICK HERE, EXPLAINING SUPPLY-SIDE ECONOMICS TO A KANSAS SCHOOLGIRL...
5-2=7
... WHOSE FINAL WEEKS OF CLASSES WERE CANCELLED WHEN GOV. BROWNBACK'S TAX CUTS FOR THE RICH BLEW A HOLE IN THE STATE'S BUDGET.
YOU SEE, SALLY, KANSAS JUST CAN'T AFFORD TO EDUCATE YOU IN THE MIDDLE OF AN IMPORTANT ECONOMIC EXPERIMENT!
SUPPLY-SIDE TAX CUTS MAY HAVE AN UNBROKEN RECORD OF FAILURE, BUT THAT'S ONLY BECAUSE WE'VE NEVER BEEN PATIENT ENOUGH!
IF WE JUST GIVE THE RICH ENOUGH MONEY AND TIME, SOONER OR LATER, LESS TAX REVENUE WILL TURN INTO MORE TAX REVENUE!
GBTrudeau
BUT ISN'T THAT A LOGICAL FALLACY?
WHOA! THAT'S QUITE ENOUGH SCHOOL FOR YOU, YOUNG LADY!

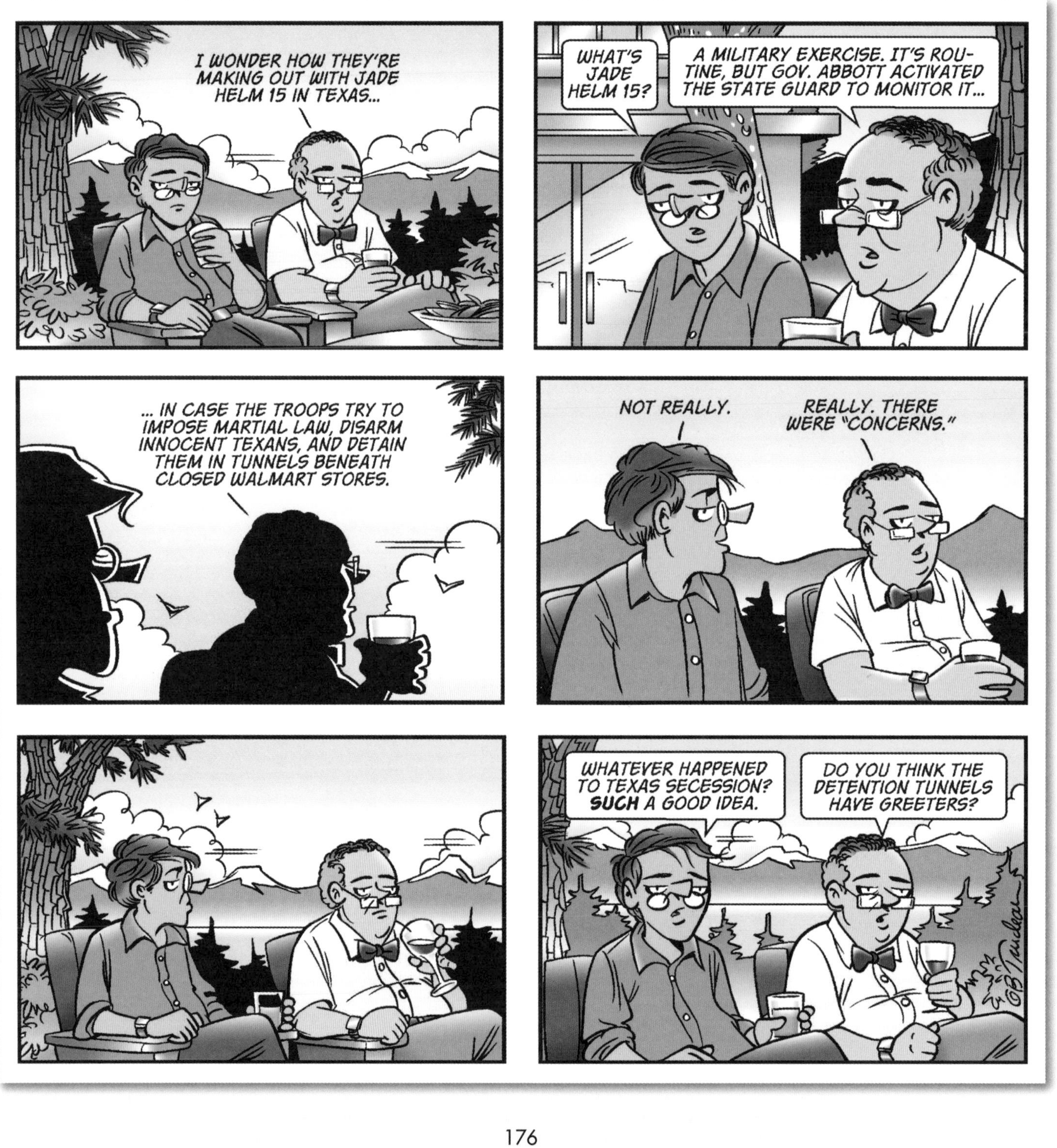
I WONDER HOW THEY'RE MAKING OUT WITH JADE HELM 15 IN TEXAS...
WHAT'S JADE HELM 15?
A MILITARY EXERCISE. IT'S ROU-TINE, BUT GOV. ABBOTT ACTIVATED THE STATE GUARD TO MONITOR IT...
... IN CASE THE TROOPS TRY TO IMPOSE MARTIAL LAW, DISARM INNOCENT TEXANS, AND DETAIN THEM IN TUNNELS BENEATH CLOSED WALMART STORES.
NOT REALLY.
REALLY. THERE WERE "CONCERNS."
WHATEVER HAPPENED TO TEXAS SECESSION? **SUCH** A GOOD IDEA.
DO YOU THINK THE DETENTION TUNNELS HAVE GREETERS?
©B Trudeau